RELATED KAPLAN BOOKS

College Admissions and Financial Aid
Access America's Guide to Studying in the U.S.A.
Guide to College Selection
Kaplan/Newsweek College Catalog
Parent's Guide to College Admissions
Scholarships
What to Study: 101 Fields in a Flash
You Can Afford College
The Yale Daily News Guide to Succeeding in College

Test Preparation
ACT Essential Review
SAT & PSAT
SAT & PSAT Essential Review
SAT Math Workbook
SAT or ACT? Test Your Best
SAT II: Biology
SAT II: Chemistry
SAT II: Mathematics
SAT II: Writing
SAT Verbal Workbook

ACT*

1999

BY THE STAFF OF
KAPLAN EDUCATIONAL CENTERS

SIMON & SCHUSTER

*ACT is a registered trademark of the ACT, which neither sponsors nor endorses this product.

Published by
Kaplan Educational Centers and Simon & Schuster
1230 Avenue of the Americas
New York, New York 10020

History of Western Civilization, A Handbook, Sixth Edition, Copyright © by William H. McNeill; The University of Chicago Press, Chicago.
Invitation to the Theatre, Copyright © 1967 by George Kernodle; Harcourt, Brace, & World Inc., publisher.
Remains of the Day, Copyright © 1989 by Kazuo Ishiguro; Alfred A. Knopf, Inc., publisher.
Light and Color in Nature and Art, Copyright © 1983 by Samuel J. Williamson; John Wiley & Sons, publisher.
Excerpt from *You Can't Go Home Again* by Thomas Wolfe, Copyright © 1934, 1937, 1938, 1939, 1940 by Maxwell Perkins as Executor of the Estate of Thomas Wolfe. Reprinted by permission of HarperCollins Publishers.
Excerpt from *The Western Intellectual Tradition: From Leonardo to Hegel* by J. Bronowski and Bruce Mazlish, Copyright © 1960. Reprinted by permission of HarperCollins Publishers.
A Short History of Western Civilization by John B. Harrison, Richard E. Sullivan, Dennis Sherman, © 1990 by McGraw-Hill, Inc. Reprinted by permission of McGraw-Hill, Inc.
Book #2942 *Violent Storms*, by Jon Erickson. © 1988 by TAB Books, a Division of McGraw-Hill, Inc., Blue Ridge Summit, PA.

All cartoons © 1997, 1996, and 1993 by Kaplan Educational Centers.

Chapter 21, "The Kaplan Advantage™ Stress Management System" by Dr. Ed Newman and Bob Verini, Copyright © 1996, Kaplan Educational Centers.

Project Editor: Amy Arner Sgarro
Cover Design: Cheung Tai
Production Editor: Maude Spekes
Desktop Publishing Manager: Michael Shevlin
Managing Editor: Brent Gallenberger
Executive Editor: Del Franz
Executive Director, Pre-College Programs: Seppy Basili

Special thanks to: Alyssa Ayres, Jeff Barton, Doreen Beauregard, Don Bless, Rosa Buzzetta, David Cameron, Mike Cantwell, Gerard Capistrano, Fred Danzig, Gordon Drummond, Jessica Dworkin, Lee Fitzgerald, Kate Foster, Amparo Graf, Paul Glovinsky, Robert Greenberg, Matthew Hart, Kate Holum, Eric Horowitz, Eirik Johnson, Jay Johnson, Jennifer Katz, Andrew Klein, Dianne Lake, Holly Lapp, Rich Lowenthal, Annaliza Martinez, Kiernan McGuire, Kate Mahoney, Jasper Milvain, Aileen Murphy, John Polstein, Donna Ratajczak, Robert Reiss, David Rodman, Jobim Rose, Bob Stanton, Ian Streicher, David Stuart, Linda Volpano, Karla Westphal, Chris Woods, and Elizabeth Wojtusik

Manufactured in the United States of America
Published Simultaneously in Canada

July 1998

10 9 8 7 6 5 4 3 2 1

ISBN 0-684-84974-7
ISSN 1093-3387

CONTENTS

PREFACE

Scientists work to discover how smart whales really *are.*

The ACT is an opportunity, not a barrier. In fact, you should be grateful that you have to take it. Really. Because a strong ACT score is one credential that doesn't depend on things you can't control. It doesn't depend on how good or bad your high school is. It doesn't depend on how many academic luminaries you know, or how rich and famous your family is, or whether any of your teachers are gullible enough to swear in a letter of recommendation that you're the greatest scientific mind since Isaac Newton. No, your ACT score depends only on you.

Granted, the ACT is a tough exam. It's probably one of the toughest exams you'll ever take. But you should be grateful for that too. Really. If the ACT were easy, everyone would do well. A good score wouldn't mean much. But because it's such a bear of a test, the ACT can be your single best opportunity to show what you can do, to prove to colleges that you are the candidate of choice—for admission, for advanced placement, for scholarships.

It's important, though, that you take the test in the right spirit. Don't be timid in the face of the ACT. Don't let it bully you. You've got to take control of the test. Our mission in this book is to show you exactly how to do that.

It helps to think of the ACT challenge as a contest—not only between you and the test, but also between you and that other person trying to get your spot in college. The ACT, after all, is meant to provide a way for all college applicants to compete on an even playing field. How do you compete successfully in a fair academic fight? You train—harder and smarter than the next guy. First, you learn whatever knowledge and skills you need to know. But then, just as important, you learn how to show what you know, in ways that the test is designed to reward. You learn how to be a savvy test taker.

And that's where Kaplan comes in. We've been helping students prepare for college entrance exams for decades, and one thing we've learned is that great standardized test takers are made, not born. We believe that anybody, given the right kind of training, can earn a strong ACT score. Why? Because ACT test taking is a learnable art. True, the ACT is designed to measure a complex set of skills, knowledge, habits, and intellectual powers that add up to a good college prep background. But it can't help measuring something else at the same time—namely, how well you take the ACT. That's why you need more than the typical academic training you get in high school. You need focused, test-smart preparation, designed specifically for success on the ACT.

This book represents just that kind of preparation. By using it conscientiously, you'll learn everything you need to know to earn your "personal best" ACT score. You'll gain the familiarity with the test necessary for optimum performance, but you'll also develop the kind of test mastery that gives you confidence, self-assurance, and that certain special way of handling your No. 2 pencils.

At Kaplan, we've been helping students take control of the test-taking experience—and raising their scores—for over fifty years. Our founder, Stanley Kaplan himself, was the inventor of test prep. We know what it takes. So start putting aside some choice study time in your schedule, and let us help you boost your score.

HOW TO USE THIS BOOK

THE CLASSIC PLAN

Ideally, you should take a couple of months to work through this book, though it's certainly possible to read it in far less time. Here's how you should go about training with it:

1. Read the section entitled *The Kaplan Advantage™ Stress Management System* to set the stage for your training and testing success.

2. Read the section entitled **ACT Basics** to get a handle on the test, its format, and the basic Kaplan strategies for approaching the test.

3. Go on to the **Skill-Building Workouts**. These will prepare you in a more focused way for each type of ACT question, and teach you all sorts of test-taking strategies and techniques that will amaze your friends and family. If you find that you're weak in one of the knowledge-based areas (if, for instance, your geometry principles are a little rusty) refer to the **Appendices** at the back of the book.

4. When you've finished the Workouts, review what you've learned by going over the **Strategic Summaries**.

5. Take the **Practice Test** *under strictly timed conditions*.

6. Go over the **Explanations for the Practice Test**. Find out where you need help and then review the appropriate Workouts.

7. Read the **Last-Minute Tips** and review the **Strategic Summaries** once more before taking your actual ACT.

8. Give yourself a day of rest right before the real exam.

If you have time, do just two or three Workouts a week, and let it sink in slowly. Don't hesitate to take some time off from the ACT when you need to. Nobody can take this stuff day in and day out for weeks at a time without a break.

HOW TO USE THIS BOOK

THE PANIC PLAN

Of course, many of you don't have a couple of months. Maybe you have only two or three weeks. Or even less. Don't freak! This book has been designed to work for students in your situation, too. If you go through a Workout or two every day, you can finish this book in a couple of weeks. If you have *very* limited time to prepare for the ACT (less than two weeks), we suggest you do the following:

1. Take a slow, deep breath. Read the section entitled *The Kaplan Advantage™ Stress Management System* to maximize your study and testing time.

2. Read the section entitled **ACT Basics**.

3. Skip to the **Strategic Summaries** and go over them thoroughly.

4. Take the **Practice Test** *under timed conditions*.

5. Review your results, with special attention to the questions you missed. Then read the **Last-Minute Tips**.

6. Give yourself the day before the test off.

If you have more time, read as many of the Workouts as you can, especially in areas you know will give you trouble. The English and Math subtests require specific knowledge (of the rules of grammar and mathematics) to a far greater extent than do the Reading and Science Reasoning subject tests. If you have trouble with English or Math because you just don't know the material being tested, we suggest you use the Appendices.

Scattered throughout the text you'll find what we call "spotlights"—special points that we feel deserve emphasis and amplificaton. Pay special attention to these points, which spotlight some very important test-prep information. Sidebars also highlight key points, fun facts, and real-world stories.

PRACTICE

This book contains a complete practice test written by our staff of Kaplan ACT gurus to provide you with real testlike practice. We have included explanations for this test, so you can better understand your mistakes (and your successes) and use that information to shore up your weak points before test day.

For additional practice, you should consider using the published "retired ACTs." They are called "Form 8939B" and "Form 9139C." If you want to use these real past exams for additional practice, obtain these tests as quickly as possible. One of the tests is included in the ACT registration materials. To order any official ACT materials, including copies of the booklets called *Registering for the ACT Assessment* and *Preparing for the ACT Assessment*, you should write or call: ACT Registration Department, P.O. Box 414, Iowa City, IA 52243-0414; (319) 337-1270. This is also the place to register for the ACT if you can't do it through your high school.

A SPECIAL NOTE FOR
INTERNATIONAL STUDENTS

Approximately 500,000 international students pursued academic degrees at the undergraduate, graduate, or professional school level at U.S. universities during the 1997–1998 academic year, according to the Institute of International Education's Open Doors report. Almost 50 percent of these students were studying for a bachelor's or first university degree. This trend of pursuing higher education in the United States is expected to continue well into the next century. Business, management, engineering, and the physical and life sciences are particularly popular majors for students coming to the United States from other countries.

If you are not from the United States, but are considering attending a U.S. college or university, here's what you'll need to get started:

- If English is not your first language, start there. You'll probably need to take the computerized or paper-and-pencil version of the Test of English as a Foreign Language (TOEFL), or show some other evidence that you are fully proficient in English in order to complete an academic degree program. Colleges and universities in the United States will differ on what they consider to be an acceptable TOEFL score. A minimum TOEFL score of 550 or better is often expected by the more prestigious and competitive institutions. Because American undergraduate programs require all students to take a certain number of general education courses, all students, even math and computer science students, need to be able to communicate well in spoken and written English.

- You may also need to take the Scholastic Assessment Test (SAT) or the American College Test (ACT). Many undergraduate institutions in the United States require both the SAT and TOEFL of international students.

- There are over 2,700 accredited colleges and universities in the United States, so selecting the correct undergraduate school can be a confusing task for anyone. You will need to get help from a good advisor or at least a good college guide that explains the different types of programs and gives you some information on how to choose wisely. Since admission to many undergraduate programs is quite competitive, you may also want to select three or four colleges and complete applications for each school.

A SPECIAL NOTE TO INTERNATIONAL STUDENTS

- You should begin the application process at least a year in advance. An increasing number of schools accept applications year round. In any case, find out the application deadlines and plan accordingly. Although September (the fall semester) is the traditional time to begin university study in the United States, at most schools you can also enter in January (the spring semester).

- Finally, you will need to obtain an I-20 Certificate of Eligibility in order to obtain an F-1 Student Visa to study in the United States. This you will request from the university. The school will send you the I-20 document once you have been accepted.

For details about the admissions requirements, curriculum, and other vital information on top colleges and universities, see Kaplan's *Guide to College Selection*.

ACCESS AMERICA ENGLISH LANGUAGE PROGRAMS

If you need more help with the complex process of undergraduate school admissions and information about the variety of programs available, you may be interested in Kaplan's Access America® program.

Kaplan created Access America to assist students and professionals from outside the United States who want to enter the U.S. university system. The program was designed for students who have received the bulk of their primary and secondary education outside the United States in a language other than English. Access America also has programs for obtaining professional certification in the United States. Here's a brief description of some of the help available through Access America.

The Access English Course

At the heart of the Access America program is the intensive Access English program. This comprehensive academic English course prepares students to achieve a high level of proficiency in English in order to successfully complete an academic degree. The course covers all areas necessary to gain admission to and succeed in a university program—reading, writing, listening, conversation, grammar, and TOEFL test-taking strategies. The Access English course combines personalized instruction with guided self-study to help students gain this proficiency in a short time. Certificates of Achievement in English are awarded to certify each student's level of proficiency.

Undergraduate School/ACT Preparation

If your goal is to complete a bachelor of arts (B.A.) or bachelor of science (B.S.) degree in the United States, Kaplan will help you prepare for the SAT or ACT, while helping you understand the American system of education.

Applying to Access America

To get more information, or to apply for admission to any of Kaplan's programs for international students or professionals, you can write to us at:

> Kaplan Educational Centers
> International Admissions Department
> 888 Seventh Avenue, New York, NY 10106

Or call us at 1-800-527-8378 from within the United States, or 01-212-262-4980 outside the United States. Our fax number is 01-212-957-1654. Our E-mail address is world@kaplan.com. You can also get more information or even apply through the Internet at http:/www.kaplan.com/intl.

SECTION I

ACT BASICS

INTRODUCTION TO THE ACT

There are three basic commandments for achieving ACT success. Following any of these by itself will improve your score. Following all three together will make you nothing less than awesome.

1. THOU SHALT LEARN THE TEST

The ACT is very predictable. You'd think the test makers would get bored after a while, but they don't. The same kinds of questions, testing the same skills and concepts, appear every time the ACT is given.

Because the test specifications rarely change, you should know in advance what to expect on every section. Just a little familiarity can make an enormous difference on the ACT. Here are a few ways in which learning the test will boost your score:

- **You'll learn the directions.** Why waste valuable time reading directions when you can have them down pat beforehand? You need every second during the test to answer questions and get points.

- **You'll learn the difficulty range of questions.** It's a fact that a typical ACT test taker gets only about half the questions right. Knowing this will stop you from panicking when you hit an impossible science passage or trigonometry question. Relax! You can skip many tough questions on the ACT and still get a great score! And once you know that the questions aren't arranged in order of difficulty, you'll know that just beyond that awful question will be one, two, or even three easy questions that you can score on with no sweat at all.

- **You'll learn how to get extra points by guessing.** Unlike some other standardized tests, the ACT has no wrong-answer penalty. Knowing that simple fact can boost your score significantly. If you can't answer a question, guess.

We'll help you get a better understanding of the ACT in the chapter following this one, entitled "The Four Subject Tests: A Preview."

2. THOU SHALT LEARN THE STRATEGIES

The ACT isn't a normal exam. Most normal exams test your memory. The ACT isn't like that. The ACT tests problem-solving skills rather than memory, and it does so in a standardized-test format. That makes the test highly vulnerable to test-smart strategies and techniques.

Most students miss a lot of ACT questions for no good reason. They see a tough-looking question, say to themselves, "Uh-oh, I don't remember how to do that," and then they start to gnaw on their No. 2 pencils.

But many ACT questions can be answered without perfect knowledge of the material being tested. Often, all you need to do to succeed on the ACT is to think strategically and creatively. We call this kind of strategic, creative frame of mind "The ACT Mindset."

How do you put yourself into the ACT Mindset? You continually ask yourself questions like: "What does this mean? How can I put this into a form I can understand and use? How can I do this faster?" Once you develop some savvy test-taking skills, you'll find yourself capable of working out problems that at first reading might have scared you half to death! In fact, we'll show you how you can sometimes get right answers when you don't even understand the question or the passage it's attached to!

There are many, many specific strategies you can use to boost your score. For instance, here are just a couple of things you'll learn:

- **You'll learn the peculiarities of the ACT format.** The ACT is a multiple-choice test. The correct answer is always right there in front of you. We'll show you how to develop specific tactics for each question type to maximize the chances of selecting the correct answer. The wrong answers are often predictable. For example, in English the shortest answer is the correct answer with surprising frequency. Strange, but true. Knowing statistical information like this can give you an important edge.

- **You'll learn a plan of attack for each subject test.** We'll show you some really useful ways of attacking each subject test. You'll learn how to do "question triage"— deciding which questions to do now and which to save for later. You'll learn a 3-step strategic approach to each subject test designed to get you points quickly and systematically. You'll learn gridding techniques to avoid any answer-sheet disasters.

- **You'll learn "unofficial" ways of getting right answers *fast*.** On the ACT, nobody cares how you decide which choice to select. The only thing that matters is picking the right answer. That's different from the way it works on most high school tests, where you get credit for showing that you've done the questions the "right" way (that is, the way you were taught to do them by Mrs. Crabapple in high school). We'll show you how to find creative shortcuts to the correct answers—"unofficial" methods that will save you precious time and net you extra points.

The basic test-smart techniques and strategies for the whole test are covered in the chapter called "Taking Control: The Top Ten Strategies." General strategies for each subject test, plus specific hints, techniques, and strategies for individual question types, are found in the Skill-Building Workouts. These are then summarized in the Strategic Summaries.

3. THOU SHALT LEARN THE MATERIAL TESTED

The ACT is designed to test skills and concepts learned in high school and needed for college. Familiarity with the test, coupled with smart test-taking strategies, will take you only so far. For your best score you need to sharpen up the skills and knowledge that the ACT rewards. Sometimes, in other words, you've just got to eat your spinach.

The good news is that most of the content of the ACT is pretty basic. You've probably already learned most of what the ACT expects you to know. But you may need help remembering. That's partly what this book is for—to remind you of the knowledge you already have and to build and refine the specific skills you've developed in high school. Here's just a few of the things we'll "remind" you of:

- **You'll learn how to read graphs and tables.** Many Science Reasoning questions rely on your ability to use data presented in the form of graphs and tables. Yes, you learned how to do that stuff in school. But let us remind you. (We'll teach you how to read graphs and tables in Science Reasoning Workout 1.)

- **You'll learn how to do trigonometry problems.** Do you remember exactly what a cotangent is? A cosine? We didn't think so. But there are four trig problems on every ACT. We'll remind you how to do them. (You can learn about trigonometry problems in the Appendix B, #96–100.)

- **You'll learn the difference between "lie" and "lay."** Is it "I lay down on the couch" or "I lie down on the couch"? You may want to lie down yourself if you encounter such issues on the ACT. But don't fret. We'll remind you of the common grammar traps the test lays for you (or is it *lies* for you???). (For a discussion of this conundrum, see Classic Grammar Error #9 in English Workout 3.)

Specifics like those mentioned above comprise what we call the ACT "knowledge base." The components of this knowledge base are reviewed along the way throughout this book. The two appendices then summarize this information for the two sections of the ACT that explicitly test knowledge—English and Math.

In sum, then, follow these three commandments:

- Thou shalt learn the test.

- Thou shalt learn the strategies.

- Thou shalt learn the material tested.

If you do, you'll find yourself just where you should be on test day: in full command of your ACT test-taking experience. Count on it.

WHAT IS THE ACT?

It was Atilla the Hun who first coined this epigram: Knowing the enemy is the first step in conquering the enemy. Atilla, of course, was talking about waging wars on the steppes of Central Asia, but his advice also works for taking standardized tests in central Illinois. In fact, that's probably why Atilla got a Composite Score of 30 on the ACT.

Well, to be honest, we haven't fact-checked Atilla the Hun's ACT score, but the point remains valid. To succeed on the ACT, you've got to *know* the ACT.

But is the ACT really your enemy? Only in a manner of speaking. The test is more like an adversary in a game of chess. If you know your adversary's entire repertoire of moves and clever stratagems, you're going to find it that much easier to beat him or her. Myths about the ACT are common. Even high school teachers and guidance counselors sometimes give out inaccurate information (we know you're shocked to hear this). To earn your best score, you need to know how the ACT is *really* put together.

So, before anything, take some time and get to know this so-called adversary—the American College Test. Let's start with the basics. The ACT is a three-hour exam (two hours and fifty-five minutes, to be precise) taken by high school juniors and seniors for admission to college. Contrary to the myths you may have heard, the ACT is *not* an IQ test. It's a test of problem-solving skills—which means that you *can* improve your performance by preparing for it.

Speaking of myths, you may have heard that the ACT is really the only thing colleges look at when deciding whether to admit you. Untrue. Most admissions officers say the ACT is only one of *several* factors they take into consideration.

But let's be realistic about ACT scores. Here's this neat and easy way of comparing all students numerically, no matter what their academic backgrounds and no matter how much grade inflation exists at their high schools. You *know* the admissions people are going to take a serious look at your test scores.

The ACT consists of four subject tests: English, Math, Reading, and Science Reasoning. All four subject tests are primarily designed to test skills rather than knowledge, though some knowledge is required—particularly in English, for which a familiarity with grammar and writing mechanics is important, and in Math, for which you need to know the basic math concepts taught in a regular high school curriculum.

THE ACT . . .

- Is about three hours long

- Includes a short break (between the second and third subtests)

- Consists of a total of 215 scored questions

- Is comprised of four subject tests:

English	(45 minutes, 75 questions)
Math	(60 minutes, 60 questions)
Reading	(35 minutes, 40 questions)
Science Reasoning	(35 minutes, 40 questions)

- Was not invented as a way of torturing high school students

HOW IS THE ACT SCORED?

No, your ACT score is not merely the sum total of questions you got correct. That would be too simple. Instead, what the test makers do is add up all of your correct answers to get what they call a "raw score." Then they put that raw score into a very large computer, which proceeds to shake, rattle, smoke, and wheeze before spitting out an official score at the other end. That score—which has been put through what they call a scoring formula—is your "scaled score."

 ## WHAT'S A GOOD ACT SCORE?

Most ACT test takers score between 17 and 23. A score below 17 will seriously limit your choice of colleges. But any ACT score above 23 will become an asset in your quest for admission to a competitive college.

ACT scaled scores range from 1 to 36. Nearly half of all test takers score within a much narrower range: 17–23. Tests at different dates vary slightly, but the following data is typical.

ACT Approximate Percentile Rank*	Composite Score	Percentage of Questions Correct
99%	31	90%
90%	26	75%
76%	23	63%
54%	20	53%
28%	17	43%

* Percentage of ACT takers scoring at or below given score

Notice that to earn a score of 20 (the national average), you need to answer only about 53 percent of the questions correctly. On most tests, getting only a bit more than half the questions right would be terrible. Not so on the ACT. Getting about half of the ACT questions correct and earning a score of 20 won't earn you a lifetime membership in the Academy of Arts and Sciences, maybe, but it's nothing to be ashamed of. But on the ACT, answering just 75 percent of the questions correctly earns you a score of about 26, putting you in the top ten percent of ACT takers.

If you earn a score of 23, you'll be in about the 76th percentile. That means that 76 percent of the test takers did as well as, or worse than, you did—in other words, that only 24 percent did better than you. It means you're in the "top quarter" of the people who take the ACT. That's a good score. But notice that to earn this score, you need only about 63 percent of the questions correct. On most tests, a score of 63 is probably a D or an F. But on the ACT, it's about a B+.

A LITTLE GOES A LONG WAY

Just a few questions right or wrong on the ACT can make a big difference. Answering only five extra questions correctly on each subject test can move you from the bottom of the applicant pool into the middle, or from the middle up to the top.

Take another look at the score data. They include two very strong scores: 26 and 31. Either score would impress almost any college admissions officer. A 26 would put you in the top 10 percent of the students who take the exam, and a 31 would put you in the top 1 percent. Notice that even a 31 requires only that you get about 90 percent of the questions correct. Nobody expects you to get all of the questions right. The best student in your high school will probably get at least a dozen questions wrong. There are questions that even your smartest teachers would get wrong.

HOW MANY ACT SCORES WILL YOU GET?

The "ACT scaled score" we've talked about so far is technically called the "Composite Score." It's the really important one. But when you take the ACT, you actually receive twelve (count 'em, twelve) different scores: the Composite Score, four subject scores, and seven subscores.

We'll show you a breakdown of the subject scores and subscores. Though the subject scores *can* play a role in decisions at some schools, the seven subscores usually aren't important for most people, so feel free to ignore the spotlight if you don't feel like looking at it.

Here's the full battery of ACT scores (1–36) you'll receive. Few people (except your parents, maybe) will care about anything except your Composite Score for college admissions, though some schools use subscores for course placement:

English Score (1–36) Usage/Mechanics subscore (1–18); Rhetorical Skills subscore (1–18)
Math Score (1–36) Prealgebra/Elementary Algebra subscore (1–18); Algebra/Coordinate Geometry subscore (1–18); Plane Geometry/Trigonometry subscore (1–18)
Reading Score (1–36) Social Sciences/Sciences subscore (1–18); Arts/Literature subscore (1–18)
Science Score (1–36) There are no subscores in Science.

HOW DO COLLEGES USE YOUR ACT SCORE?

The most important score for most test takers is the Composite Score (which is an average of the four subject scores). This is the score used by most colleges and universities in the admissions process, and the one that you'll want to mention casually at parties during your freshman year of college. The four subject scores and seven subscores may be used for advanced placement or occasionally for scholarships, but are primarily used by college advisors to help students select majors and first-year courses.

Although many schools deny that they use benchmark scores as cutoffs, we're not sure we really believe them. Big Ten universities and colleges with similarly competitive admissions generally decline to accept students with Composite Scores below 22 or 23. For less competitive schools, the benchmark score may be lower than that; for some very selective schools, the cutoff may be higher.

To be fair, no school uses the ACT as an absolute bar to admission, no matter how low it is. But for most applicants, a low ACT score is decisive. As a rule, only students whose backgrounds are extremely unusual or who have overcome enormous disadvantages are accepted if their ACT scores are below the benchmark. It also sometimes helps if you can convince your parents to donate a gymnasium to the school you're aiming for.

SHOULD YOU GUESS ON THE ACT?

The short answer? Yes! The long answer? Yes, of course!

As we saw, ACT scores are based on the number of *correct* answers only. This means that questions left blank and questions answered incorrectly simply don't count. Unlike some other standardized tests, the ACT has no "wrong-answer penalty." That's why you should always take a guess on every ACT question you can't answer, even if you don't have time to read it. Though the questions vary enormously in difficulty, harder questions are worth exactly the same as easier ones, so it pays to guess on the really hard questions and spend your time breezing through the really easy ones. We'll show you just how to do this in the chapter called "Taking Control: The Top Ten Strategies."

IMPORTANT STRATEGY

By the end of each subject test, you should have answered every question, even if you had to take a random guess on some. A lucky guess will raise your score, and an unlucky guess will leave you no worse off. There's no penalty for a wrong answer. None. Zippo.

CAN YOU RETAKE THE TEST?

You can take the ACT as many times as you like. You can then select whichever test score you prefer to be sent to colleges when you apply. However, you *cannot* take advantage of this option if, at the time you register for the test, you designate certain colleges to receive your scores. Thus it's *crucial* that you *not* designate any colleges at the time you register for the test. You can (for a small additional fee) have ACT scores sent to colleges at any time you desire *after* the scores are reported.

Unless you don't have enough money for that small extra fee or if you're taking the ACT under the wire and you need your scores to reach the schools your applying to ASAP, give yourself the freedom to retake the test. What this means, of course, is that even if you blow the ACT once, you can give yourself another chance without the schools of your choice knowing about it. The ACT is one of the few areas of your academic life in which you get a second chance.

CRUCIALLY IMPORTANT POINT

When you sign up for the ACT, you have the option of designating colleges to receive your score. Unless time is of the essence, don't do it, even though the first three score reports are sent free of charge. Wait until you receive your score, then send it along (for a small additional fee) if you're happy. If you hate your score, you can take the test again and send only the new, improved score.

THE FOUR SUBJECT TESTS
A PREVIEW

Okay, you've seen how the ACT is set up. But to really know your adversary, you've got to know something about the four ACT subject tests (which, by the way, always appear in the following order):

- English
- Mathematics
- Reading
- Science Reasoning

As we'll see, the questions in every subject test vary widely in difficulty. Some are so easy that most elementary school students could answer them. Others would give even Einstein a little trouble. But, again: The questions are not arranged in order of difficulty. That's different from some other tests, in which easier questions come first. **Skipping past hard questions is very important, since otherwise you may never reach easy ones toward the end of the exam.**

 ## DON'T GET BOGGED DOWN

ACT questions are not arranged in order of ascending difficulty. Theoretically, the first question you see could be the hardest on the test. Who needs that kind of aggravation? Not you. Skip past the tough questions and spend your first minutes on the test piling up some easy points.

Here's a preview of the types of questions you'll encounter on the four subject tests. We'll keep them toward the easy end of the difficulty scale here, as you're just becoming familiar with the test. Later, in the Skill-Building Workouts, we'll be less kind.

ENGLISH

> *Reality Check: The English test is 45 minutes long and includes 75 questions. That works out to about 30 seconds per question, but in practice you should spend less time on easier questions and more on harder questions. The test is divided into five passages, each with about 15 questions.*

Students nearly always get more questions correct in English than in any other section. That tends to make students think that English is a lot easier than the rest of the ACT. But, alas, it's not that simple. Because most students do well, the test makers have much higher expectations for English than for other parts of the test. They *know* that it's generally easier to get English questions right than, say, Science Reasoning questions. They've got a whole department of little statistician elves who keep track of things like this. That's why, to earn an average English subscore (a 20, say), you have to get almost two-thirds of the questions right, while on the rest of the test you need to get only about half right.

The Directions

The English directions are a good illustration of why you have a big advantage if you know the directions beforehand. The English directions are long and complicated. Here's what they'll look like, but take our advice. Don't even bother reading them. We'll show you exactly how to do what you need to do:

> **Directions:** In the following five passages, certain words and phrases have been underlined and numbered. You will find alternatives for each underlined portion in the right-hand column. Select the one that best expresses the idea, that makes the statement acceptable in standard written English, or that is phrased most consistently with the style and tone of the entire passage. If you feel that the original version is best, select "NO CHANGE." You will also find questions asking about a section of the passage or about the entire passage. For these questions, decide which choice gives the most appropriate response to the given question. For each question in the test, select the best choice and fill in the corresponding space on the answer folder. You may wish to read each passage through before you begin to answer the questions associated with it. Most answers cannot be determined without reading several sentences around the phrases in question. Make sure to read far enough ahead each time you choose an alternative.

The Format

To put the directions more concisely, let's say that almost all of the English questions follow a standard format. A word, phrase, or sentence in a passage is underlined. You're given four options: to leave the underlined portion alone ("NO CHANGE," which is always the first choice), or to replace it with one of three alternatives (the ones proposed in the other three choices). For example:

...Pike's Peak in Southwest Colorado is

named <u>before Zebulon Pike, an early</u>
             37
<u>explorer.</u> He traveled through the
   37
area, exploring...

37. A. NO CHANGE
    B. before Zebulon Pike
        became an explorer,
    C. after Zebulon Pike,
        when,
    D. after Zebulon Pike.

The best answer for number 37 above is D. The other choices all have various problems—grammatical, stylistic, logical. They make the passage look and sound like it was written by your baby brother. Only D makes the sentence sensible and correct. That's why it's the answer.

Notice that a single question can test several different kinds of writing errors. We find that about a third of the questions on the English section test your ability to write concisely (we call them Economy Questions), about another third test for logic and sense (Sense Questions) and that only the remaining third test hard-and-fast rules of grammar (Technicality Questions). There's a lot of overlap between these question types, so don't worry too much about categories. We provide them mostly to give you an idea of the kind of errors you'll be expected to correct.

To Omit or Not to Omit

Some standard-format English questions offer, as one of the alternatives, the chance to completely omit the underlined portion, usually as the last of the four choices. For example:

Later, Pike fell while valiantly defending

America in the War of 1812.

<u>It goes without saying that this took</u>
          40
<u>place after he discovered Pike's Peak.</u>
          40
He actually died near York (now called

Toronto)...

40. F. NO CHANGE
    G. Clearly, this must have occurred
        subsequent to his discovering
        Pike's Peak.
    H. This was after he found Pike's
        Peak.
    J. OMIT the underlined portion.

In this case, J is correct. The idea really does "go without saying." For that reason, it shouldn't be said. On recent ACTs, when OMIT has occurred as an answer choice, it's been correct more than half of the time (As you can see, the ACT makers aren't the only ones with a department of little statistician elves . . .). This doesn't mean you should always select "OMIT," however, since it's also been wrong almost half of the time.

Nonstandard Format Questions

Some ACT English questions—usually about ten per exam—don't follow this standard format.

These items pose a question and offer four possible responses. In many cases, the responses are either "yes" or "no," with an explanation. Pay attention to the reasoning. Question 40 could have appeared in a nonstandard format as follows:

...Later, Pike fell while valiantly

defending America in the War of 1812. 40

He actually died near York (now called

Toronto)...

40. Suppose the author considered adding the following sentence at this point: "It goes without saying that this occurred after he discovered Pikes Peak."
Given the overall purpose of the passage, would this sentence be appropriate?
   F. No, because the sentence adds nothing to the meaning of the passage.
   G. No, because the passage is not concerned with Pike's achievements.
   H. Yes, because otherwise the sequence of events would be unclear.
   J. Yes; though the sentence is not needed, the author recognizes this fact by using the phrase *it goes without saying.*

The correct answer for this question is F. Though G correctly indicates that the sentence doesn't belong in the passage, it offers a pretty inappropriate reason. The passage *is* concerned with Pike's achievements. Choices H and J are wrong because they recommend including a sentence that's clearly redundant.

Many of the nonstandard questions occur at the end of a passage. Some ask about the meaning, purpose, or tone of individual paragraphs or of the passage as a whole. Others ask you to evaluate the passage. And still others ask you to determine the proper order of words, sentences, or paragraphs that have been scrambled in the passage.

We think you'll like the English subject test. It can actually be fun, which is probably why the test makers put it first. We'll cover strategies for all of the English question types in the English Workouts.

MATHEMATICS

> **Reality Check:** *The Math test is 60 minutes long and includes 60 questions. That works out to a minute a question, but you'll want to spend less time on easy questions and more on the tough ones.*

14

The Format

All of the math questions have the same, basic multiple-choice format. They ask a question and offer five possible choices (unlike questions on the other three subject tests, which have only four choices each). Why the math test has five choices while the other test have only four is one of those mysteries that only the ACT makers understand.

The questions cover a full range of math topics, from prealgebra and elementary algebra through intermediate algebra, coordinate geometry, plane geometry, and even trigonometry. We'll tell you the exact number of questions in each area later, in Math Workout 1. If you have specific weaknesses in any of these areas, the Math Appendix at the end of this book will help.

Although the math questions, like those in other sections, aren't ordered in terms of difficulty, questions drawn from elementary school or junior high tend to come earlier in the section, while those from high school math curricula tend to come later. But this doesn't mean that the easy questions come first and the hardest ones come later. We've found that high school subjects tend to be fresher in most student's minds than things they were taught years ago, so you may actually find the later questions *easier*. (Do *you* remember the math you learned in seventh grade?)

The Directions

Here's what the Math directions will look like:

> **Directions:** Solve each of the following problems, select the correct answer, and then fill in the corresponding space on your answer sheet.
>
> Don't linger over problems that are too time-consuming. Do as many as you can, then come back to the others in the time you have remaining.
>
> **Note:** Unless otherwise noted, all of the following should be assumed:
> 1. Illustrative figures are *not* necessarily drawn to scale.
> 2. All geometric figures lie in a plane.
> 3. The term *line* indicates a straight line.
> 4. The term *average* indicates arithmetic mean.

Again, when it comes to directions on the ACT, the golden rule is: *Don't read them on Test Day!* You'll already know what they say by the time you take the test.

The math directions don't really tell you much anyway. Of the four special notes at the end of the math directions, #2, #3, and #4 almost go without saying. Note #1—that figures are *not* necessarily drawn to scale—seems pretty scary, but in fact the vast majority of ACT figures *are* drawn to scale, a fact that, as we'll see, has significant implications for how to guess on geometry questions.

Reading and Drawing Diagrams

We find that about a third of the Math questions either give you a diagram or describe a situation that should be diagrammed. For these questions, the diagrams are crucial. For example:

1. The figure below contains five congruent triangles. The longest side of each triangle is 4 meters long. What is the area of the whole figure?

- **A.** 12.5 square meters
- **B.** 15 square meters
- **C.** 20 square meters
- **D.** 30 square meters
- **E.** Cannot be determined from the given information

The key to this question is to let the diagram tell you what you need to know—that each triangle represents one-quarter of the area of the square, and that the sides of the *square* are 4 meters (you can figure this out because the top side of the square is the hypotenuse—or longest side—of the triangle that makes the "roof"). Since the area of a square can be found by squaring the side, the area of the square is 16 square meters. Thus, each triangle has an area one-fourth as much—4 square meters. Since the whole figure consists of *five* triangles, each with area 4, the total area is $5 \times 4 = 20$. The answer is C.

> **HINT:** *In ACT math questions, the answer choice "cannot be determined" is rare. When it does appear, it's usually wrong. "Cannot be determined" is almost always wrong in a question that comes with a diagram or for which you can draw one.*

How to Get that Story
We find that about another third of the math questions are story problems like the following:

2. Evan drove halfway home at 20 miles per hour, then speeded up and drove the rest of the way at 30 miles per hour. What was his average speed for the entire trip?
- **F.** 20 miles per hour
- **G.** 22 miles per hour
- **H.** 24 miles per hour
- **J.** 25 miles per hour
- **K.** 28 miles per hour

A good way to comprehend—and resolve—a story problem like this is to think of a real situation just like the one in the story. For example, what if Evan had 120 miles to drive? (You should pick a distance that's easily divisible by both rates). He would go 60 miles at 30 mph, then 60 miles at 20 mph. How long would it take? Well, 60 miles at 30 mph is 2 hours; 60 miles at 20 mph is 3 hours. That's a total of 120 miles in 5 hours; 120 divided by 5 gives an average speed of 24 mph. The correct answer is thus H. (Note: We'll show you alternative ways to answer questions like this later on.)

KAPLAN

Getting the Concept

Finally, we find that about a third of the questions directly ask you to demonstrate your knowledge of specific math concepts. For example:

3. If angles *A* and *B* are supplementary, and the measure of angle *A* is
57°, what is the measure, in degrees, of angle *B* ?

   A.   33

   B.   43

   C.   47

   D.   123

   E.   147

This question simply requires that you know the concept of "supplementary angles." Two angles are *supplementary* when they form a straight line—in other words, when they add up to 180°. Thus, question 3 boils down to this: What number, added to 57, makes 180? The answer is D.

These three types of math questions, of course, will be discussed more fully in the Math Workouts.

READING

> **Reality Check:** *The Reading test is 35 minutes long and includes 40 questions. The test contains four passages, each of which is followed by 10 questions. When you factor in the amount of time you'll initially spend on the passages, this works out to about 30 seconds per question—again, more for the tough ones,*
> *less for the easy ones.*

The Format

There are four categories of reading passages: Social Studies, Natural Sciences, Humanities, and Prose Fiction. You'll get one passage in each category. The passages are about 1,000 words long and are written at about the same difficulty level as college textbooks and readings.

The Social Studies, Natural Sciences, and Humanities passages are usually well-organized essays. Each has a very specific theme. Questions expect you to recognize this theme, to comprehend specific facts contained in the passage, and to understand the structure of the essay. Prose Fiction passages require you to understand the thoughts, feelings, and motivations of fictional characters, even when these are not explicitly stated in the passage (we'll have a special section on Prose Fiction passages in Reading Workout 3).

After each passage, you'll find ten questions. There are really only three different categories of Reading question:

- Specific Detail Questions

- Inference Questions

- Big Picture Questions

The Directions

Here's what the Reading directions will look like:

> **Directions:** This test contains four passages, each followed by several questions. After reading a passage, select the best answer to each question and fill in the corresponding oval on your answer sheet. You are allowed to refer to the passages while answering the questions.

Nothing stupefying here. But nothing very substantive either. We'll be a little more specific and strategic than the test makers when we suggest a plan of attack in the three Reading Workouts.

Nailing Down the Details

Specific Detail Questions ask about things stated explicitly in the passage. The challenge with these questions is, first, finding the proper place in the passage where the answer can be found (sometimes you'll be given a line reference, sometimes not), and second, being able to match up what you see in the passage with the correct answer, which will probably be worded differently. Many wrong choices will be designed to trip you up by including details from other parts of the passage, or by using the same wording as the passage while distorting the meaning:

When we say "Bach" we almost always refer to Johann Sebastian Bach (1685–1750), but in fact the name "Bach" belongs to a whole family of Baroque German musicians...

(7 paragraphs and 950 words omitted)

The works of Johann Christian Bach, J. S. Bach's son, clearly prefigure the rich musical developments that followed the Baroque period. Thus, it is both surprising and unfortunate that the rest of J. S. Bach's family isn't more well known.

6. According to the author, J. S. Bach is the best-known:
   F. German Baroque musician.
   G. member of a musical family.
   H. organist in German history.
   J. composer of Lutheran hymns.

7. Johann Christian Bach was:
   A. born earlier than Johann Sebastian Bach.
   B. a composer of the "Romantic" school of music.
   C. a composer whose works are transitional in style.
   D. well known during his own lifetime.

The correct answer for question 6 is G. Both the first and last sentences in the passage refer to J. S. Bach as the most famous member of a whole family of musicians. *You* might think J. S. Bach is the best-known "German Baroque musician" (choice F), but that's not what the passage says, so it's wrong.

The correct answer for question 7 is C. At the end of the passage the author says that Johann Christian's work "prefigure[d]" the music that followed the Baroque. Thus, it must have had some Baroque characteristics and some new aspects. In other words, it was transitional.

Making an Inference

We find that most Reading passages also include a large number of Inference Questions, which require you to make an inference from the passage (to "read between the lines"). They differ somewhat from Specific Detail Questions. For one thing, students usually consider them harder. Here's an example of each:

...though schizophrenia and multiple personality disorder (M.P.D.) may be related, and are often confused by laymen, the two terms have radically different meanings...

32. Which of the following best expresses the relationship between schizophrenia and multiple personality disorder?

    F. They are two terms that describe essentially the same phenomenon.

    G. The two disorders have nothing in common.

    H. Though the two have some similarities, they are fundamentally different.

    J. The two are not exactly alike, but are very close.

33. Suppose that a patient has been diagnosed with schizophrenia. Based on the passage, which of the following is least likely?

    A. The patient's doctors immediately assume that the patient also suffers from M.P.D.

    B. The patient is a layman.

    C. The patient denies that he has M.P.D.

    D. The patient has several separate personalities.

Note the differences between Specific Detail and Inference Questions: Question 32, a Specific Detail Question, requires that you understand the explicitly stated idea that schizophrenia and M.P.D. have some connection, but are not the same. That's what choice H says. Question 33, on the other hand, requires you to *apply* the idea that the two disorders are different. If they are, it's highly unlikely that doctors would simply assume that a patient suffering from one disorder must suffer from the other. Therefore, choice A is least likely—and therefore correct. The other choices may or may not be true, and nothing in the passage leads us to think one way or the other about them. Question 33 is what we'd call a garden-variety Inference Question.

Getting the Big Picture

Although the majority of Reading questions are Specific Detail and Inference Questions, the Reading subtest also includes another type of question that we call Big Picture Questions. Some Big Picture Questions ask about the passage as a whole, requiring you to find the theme, tone, or structure of the passage. Others ask you to evaluate the writing. Here's a typical Big Picture Question that might have appeared with the Bach family passage we talked about earlier:

9. The author's main point in the passage is to:

   A. show that many of the lesser-known members of the Bach family also influenced music history.

   B. argue that J. C. Bach was actually a greater composer than his father, J. S. Bach.

   C. demonstrate that musical talent always runs in families.

   D. dispute the claim that the Bach family was the best-known family of German Baroque musicians.

In order to answer this kind of question, you've got to have a good sense of the Big Picture—of the shape and flow of the whole passage. Of course, we printed only a few selected lines from the passage, but that should have been enough to lead you to A as the answer. The first line definitely indicates that the subject of the passage is going to be the entire Bach family, with a focus on the ones who aren't as well known as the big cheese, J. S. himself.

We'll discuss strategies for all passage- and question-types in the Reading Workouts.

SCIENCE REASONING

> *Reality Check: The Science Reasoning test is 35 minutes long and includes 40 questions. The test contains seven passages, each with 5 to 7 questions. Factoring in the amount of time you'll initially spend on the passage, that will give you something over 30 seconds for each question.*

No, you don't have to be a scientist to succeed on the ACT Science Reasoning test. You don't have to know the atomic number of cadmium or the preferred mating habits of the monarch butterfly. All that's required is common sense (though a knowledge of standard scientific processes and procedures sure does help). You'll be given passages containing various kinds of scientific information—drawn from the fields of biology, chemistry, physics, geology, astronomy, and meteorology—which you'll have to understand and use as a basis for inferences.

The Format

On most Science Reasoning subtests, there are six passages that present scientific data, often based on specific experiments. Also, there's usually one passage in which two scientists state opposing views on the same issue. Each passage will generate between five and seven questions. A warning: Some passages will be very difficult to understand, but they'll usually make up for that fact by having many easy questions attached to them. The test makers do show some mercy once in a while.

The Directions

Here's what the Science Reasoning directions will look like:

> **Directions:** Each of the following seven passages is followed by several questions. After reading each passage, decide on the best answer to each question and fill in the corre-

sponding oval on your answer sheet. You are allowed to refer to the passages while answering the questions.

Sounds a lot like the set of directions for Reading, doesn't it? Not much substance here, either. But don't worry. We'll show you the best *strategic* way to attack the Science Reasoning subject test in the three Science Workouts.

Analyzing Data

About a third of the questions in the Science subtest require you to read data from graphs or tables. In easier questions, you need only report the information. In harder questions, you may need to draw inferences or note patterns in the data. For example:

1. A test taker who scores in approximately the 40th percentile has correctly answered about what fraction of the questions?

   A. $\frac{9}{10}$

   B. $\frac{2}{3}$

   C. $\frac{1}{2}$

   D. $\frac{1}{5}$

2. Which of the following best describes the relationship between percentile rank and percent of questions correct?

   F. As percentile rank increases, percent of correct questions also increases.

   G. Percentile rank is inversely proportional to the percent of correct questions.

   H. As percentile rank increases, the percent of correct questions decreases.

   J. As percentile rank decreases, percent of correct questions usually, but not always, also decreases.

The correct answer to question 1 is C. The point for the 40th percentile is slightly above the fifty percent point on the horizontal axis (percent correct). Fifty percent is the same as $\frac{1}{2}$. Note that this question involves a little simple arithmetic (translating a percent into a fraction)—not uncommon for Science Reasoning questions.

In question 2, the correct answer is F. The points that are higher on the graph (higher percentile) are always farther to the right (higher percentage of correct questions). Note that answers G and H say essentially the same thing (we'll discuss direct and inverse proportionality in Science Workout 1), and thus are wrong for the same reason: they get the relationship backwards. J is wrong because it says that the percent of correct questions does not *always* decrease as percentile rank decreases.

Conducting Experiments

Other Science questions require that you understand the way experiments are designed and what they prove. For example, part of a passage might describe an experiment as follows:

Experiment 1

A scientist adds one drop of nitric acid to Beakers A, B, and C. Each Beaker contains water from a different stream. The water in Beaker A came from Stream A, that in Beaker B came from Stream B, and that in Beaker C came from Stream C. Precipitates form in Beakers B and C, but not in Beaker A.

12. Which of the following could properly be inferred on the basis of Experiment 1?
- **F.** Stream A is more polluted than Streams B and C.
- **G.** Streams B and C are more polluted than A.
- **H.** Stream A contains material that neutralizes nitric acid.
- **J.** Streams B and C contain some substance that reacts in the presence of nitric acid.

The correct answer for question 12 is J. Since a precipitate forms when nitric acid is added to Beakers B and C, which contain water from Streams B and C, something in these streams must be involved. However, we don't know that it is pollution, so answers F and G are unwarranted. We also don't know exactly *why* no precipitate formed in Beaker A, so H is also an unwarranted conclusion. Scientists *hate* unwarranted conclusions.

The Principle of the Thing

The remaining Science questions require you either to logically apply a principle, or to identify ways of defending or attacking a principle. Often, the question will involve two scientists stating opposing views on the same subject. But this is not always the case. For example, a passage might describe a theory of the process whereby most "V-shaped" valleys are typically formed on Earth— by water erosion through soft rock. Then the following questions might be asked:

16. Which of the following is most likely to be a V-shaped valley?
- **F.** A valley formed by glaciers
- **G.** A river valley which is cut into very hard basalt
- **H.** A valley formed by wind erosion
- **J.** A river valley in a region of soft shale rocks

17. Which of the following discoveries would most weaken the theory of V-shaped valley formation given in the passage?
- **A.** Certain parts of many valleys formed by water that are U-shaped
- **B.** A group of V-shaped valleys almost certainly formed by wind erosion
- **C.** A group of U-shaped valleys formed by water erosion in hard rock
- **D.** A group of valleys on Mars that appear to be V-shaped but that are not near any running water

In question 16, the correct answer is J, since this is consistent with the passage as described. The correct answer in question 17 is B. Finding V-shaped valleys not formed by water erosion would tend to weaken the theory that they are formed this way. The other answers do not offer evidence about V-shaped valleys on Earth, and thus are irrelevant to a theory about them.

We'll be showing you strategies for each kind of Science Reasoning question in the three Science Workouts.

TAKING CONTROL
THE TOP TEN STRATEGIES

Now that you've got some idea of the kind of adversary you face in the ACT, it's time to start developing strategies for dealing with this adversary. In other words, you've got to start developing your ACT Mindset.

THE ACT MINDSET

The ACT, as we've just seen, isn't a normal test. A normal test requires that you rely almost exclusively on your memory. On a normal test, you'd see questions like this:

> The "golden spike," which joined the Union Pacific and Central Pacific Railroads, was driven in Ogden, Utah, in May 1869. Who was President of the United States at the time?

To answer this question, you have to resort to memory dredging. Either you know the answer is Ulysses S. Grant or else you don't. No matter how hard you think, you'll never be able to answer this question if you can't remember your history.

THINK!

The ACT tests your critical thinking skills, not your memory. But the ACT isn't an IQ test either. It doesn't test "intelligence." It tests very specific problem-solving abilities that you've been developing all along in school and in life. You've got what it takes to succeed on the ACT—if you use what you've got in the right way.

But the ACT doesn't test your long-term memory. The answer to every ACT question can be found in the test. Theoretically, if you read carefully and understand the words and concepts the test uses, you can get almost any ACT question right. Notice the difference between the regular-test question above and the ACT-type question below:

1. What is the product of n and m^2, where n is an odd number and m is an even number?
   A. An odd number
   B. A multiple of four
   C. A noninteger
   D. An irrational number
   E. The square of an integer

Aside from the obvious difference (this question has answer choices, while the other one does not), there's another difference: The ACT question mostly tests your ability to *understand a situation* rather than your ability to passively *remember a fact*. Nobody expects you to know off the top of your head what the product of an odd number and the square of an even number is. But the ACT test makers do expect you to be able to roll up your sleeves and figure it out (as we'll do below).

BE CREATIVE

The mindset for the ACT is "creative problem-solving mode." Don't rely too heavily on your brain's memory cells. Instead, use your brain's *creative thinking* cells. The ACT mindset isn't too different from the one you'd use to play chess, work a crossword, or run a maze. (You run mazes all the time, don't you?)

WHAT IS THE ACT MINDSET?

Most students take the ACT with the same mindset that they use for normal tests. Their brains are on "memory mode." Students often panic and give up because they can't seem to remember enough. But you don't need to remember a ton of picky little rules for the ACT. Don't give up on an ACT question just because your memory fails.

On the ACT, if you understand what a question is really asking on the test, you can almost always answer it. For instance, take the math problem above. You might have been thrown by the way it was phrased. "How can I solve this problem?" you may have asked yourself. "It doesn't even have numbers in it!"

The key here, as in all ACT questions, is *taking control*. Take the question (by the throat, if necessary) and wrestle it into a form you can understand. Ask yourself: What's *really* being asked here? What does it *mean* when they say something like "the product of n and m^2"?

Well, you might start by putting it into words *you* might use. *You* might say something like this: "I've got to take one number times another. One of the numbers is odd and the other is an even number squared. Then I've got to see what *kind* of number I get as an answer." Once you put the question in your own terms like this, it becomes much less intimidating—and much easier to get right. You'll realize that you don't have to do complex algebraic computations with variables. All you have to do is substitute numbers.

So do it! Try picking some easy-to-use numbers. Say that n is 3 (an odd number) and m is 2 (an even number). Then m^2 would be 4, because 2^2 is 4. And $n \times m^2$ would be 3×4, which is 12—a multiple of four, but not odd, not a noninteger, not an irrational number, and not a perfect square. The only answer that can be right, then, is B.

FIGURE IT OUT

ACT questions are puzzles to solve, not quizzes for which you must *remember* the answers. Don't think: "Can I remember?" Think: "Let me figure this thing out!"

See what we mean about figuring out the answer creatively rather than passively remembering it? True, there are some things you had to remember here—what even and odd numbers are, how variables and exponents work, and maybe what integers and irrational numbers are. But these are very basic concepts. Most of what you're expected to know on the ACT is like that: basic. (By the way, you'll find such concepts gathered together in the very attractive Math Appendix at the end of this book.)

Of course, basic doesn't always mean easy. Many ACT questions are built on basic concepts, but are tough nonetheless. The problem above, for instance, is difficult because it requires some thought to figure out what's being asked. This isn't only true in Math. It's the same for every part of the ACT.

Get Into the ACT Mindset

The creative, take-control kind of thinking we call the ACT Mindset is something you want to bring to virtually every ACT question you encounter. As we'll see, being in the ACT Mindset means reshaping the test-taking experience so that *you* are in the driver's seat.

It means:

- Answering questions *if* you want to (by guessing on the impossible questions rather than wasting time on them).

- Answering questions *when* you want to (by skipping tough but "doable" questions and coming back to them after you've gotten all of the easy questions done).

- Answering questions *how* you want to (by using "unofficial" ways of getting correct answers fast).

And that's really what the ACT Mindset boils down to: Taking control. Being creative. Solving specific problems to get points as quickly and easily as you can.

What follows are the top ten strategies you need to do just that.

#1—DO QUESTION TRIAGE

In a hospital emergency room, the triage nurse is the person who evaluates each patient and decides which ones get attention first and which ones should be treated later. You should do the same thing on the ACT.

Practicing triage is one of the most important ways of controlling your test-taking experience. It's a fact that there are some questions on the ACT that most students could never answer correctly, no matter how much time or effort they spent on them. For example:

57. If $\sec^2 x = 4$, which of the following could be $\sin x$?

    A. 1.73205

    B. 3.14159

    C. $\sqrt{3}$

    D. $\frac{\sqrt{3}}{2}$

    E. Cannot be determined from the given information.

Clearly, even if you *could* manage to come up with an answer to this question, it would take some time (those of you who *insist* on doing so can refer to the Spotlight below). But would it be worth the time? We think not.

DO YOU KNOW YOUR TRIG?

Okay, since you're reading this, it's obvious that you want to know the answer to the trig question on this page. The answer is D. Here's how we got it:

$\sec^2 x = 4$	given
$\sec x = 2$ or -2	square root both sides
$\cos x = \frac{1}{2}$ or $-\frac{1}{2}$	$\cos x = \frac{1}{\sec x}$
$\cos^2 x = \frac{1}{4}$	square both sides
$\sin^2 x = 1 - \frac{1}{4}$	$\sin^2 x + \cos^2 x = 1$
	$\sin^2 x = 1 - \cos^2 x$

KAPLAN

$$\sin^2 x = \frac{3}{4}$$

$\sin x = \sqrt{\frac{3}{4}}$ or $-\sqrt{\frac{3}{4}}$ square root both sides

$\sin x = \frac{\sqrt{3}}{2}$ or $-\frac{\sqrt{3}}{2}$ $\sqrt{4} = 2$

So D—$\frac{\sqrt{3}}{2}$—is correct. But if you got it right, don't congratulate yourself quite yet. How long did it take you to get it right? So long that you could have gotten the answers to two easy questions in the same amount of time?

This question clearly illustrates our point: You should do question triage on the ACT. The first time you look at each question, make a quick decision on how hard and time-consuming it looks. Then decide whether to answer it now or skip it and do it later. Here's how:

- If the question looks comprehensible and reasonably doable, do it right away.

- If the question looks tough and time-consuming, but ultimately doable, skip it, circle the number of the question in your test booklet, and come back to it later.

- If the question looks impossible, forget about it. Guess and move on, never to return.

FOOD FOR THOUGHT

Let's say you took two-and-a-half minutes to get a tough question right. That might make you feel good, but you'd actually be better off if you had skipped the tough question and, in the same amount of time, answered two or three easier questions correctly.

This triage method is designed to make sure you spend the time needed to do all the easy questions before you risk getting bogged down with a tough problem. Remember, every question on a subject test is worth the same. You get no extra credit for test macho.

Answering easier questions first has another benefit: It gives you confidence to answer harder ones later. Doing problems in the order you choose rather than in the order imposed by the test makers gives you control over the test. Most students don't have time to do all of the problems, so you've got to make sure you do all of the ones you can easily score on!

Develop a Plan of Attack

For the English, Reading, and Science Reasoning sections, the best plan of attack is to do each passage as a block. Make a longish first pass through the questions (call it the "triage" pass), doing the easy ones, guessing on the impossible ones, and skipping any that look like they might cause particular trouble. Then, make a second pass (call it the "cleanup pass") and pick up whichever questions you think you can do with harder work.

For Math, you use essentially the same two-pass strategy, except that you move through the whole subject test twice. Work through the doable questions for the whole subject test first. Most of these will probably be toward the beginning, but not all. Then come back and attack the questions that look possible but tough or time-consuming.

No matter what subject test you're working on, you should take pains to grid your answers in the right place. It's easy to misgrid when you're skipping around, so be careful. And of course: **Make sure you have an answer gridded for every question by the time the subject test is over!**

#2—PUT THE MATERIAL INTO A FORM YOU CAN UNDERSTAND AND USE

ACT questions are rarely presented in the simplest, most helpful way. In fact, your main job for many questions is just figuring out what the question means so that you can solve it.

Since the material is presented in such an intimidating way, one of your best strategies for taking control is to recast the material into a form you can handle better. This is what we did in the math problem about "the product of n and m^2." We took the question and reworded it in a way we could understand.

Mark Up Your Test Booklet

This strategy should be employed on all four subject tests. For example, in Reading, many students find the passages overwhelming: 85 to 90 lines of dense verbiage for each one! But the secret is to put the *passages* into a form you can understand and use. Circle or underline the author's main idea, for one thing. And make yourself a road map of the passage, labeling each paragraph so you understand how it all fits together. That way, you'll also know—later, when you're doing the questions—where in the passage to find certain types of information you need. (We'll show you how to do all of these things later, in the Skill-Building Workouts.)

Reword The Questions

You'll find that you also need to do some recasting of the *questions*. For instance, take this question stem from a Science Reasoning passage.

Figure 1

15. According to Figure 1, at approximately what latitude would calculations using an estimated value at sea level of $g = 9.80$ m/sec^2 produce the least error?

A. 0°

B. 20°

C. 40°

D. 80°

At what latitude would the calculations using a value of $g = 9.80$ m/sec^2 produce the least error? Yikes! What does that mean?

Take a deep breath. Ask yourself: Where would an estimate for g of 9.80 m/sec^2 produce the least error? In a latitude where 9.80 m/sec^2 is the *real* value of g. If you find the latitude at which the real value of g is 9.80 m/sec^2, then using 9.80 m/sec^2 as an estimate there would produce no error at all!

So, in other words, what this question is asking is: At what latitude does $g = 9.80$ m/sec^2? Now *that's* a form of the question you can understand. In *that* form, you can answer it easily: choice C, which you can get just by reading the chart.

Draw Diagrams

Sometimes, putting the material into usable form involves drawing with your pencil. For instance, take a look at the following math problem.

2. Jason bought a painting with a frame 1 inch wide. If the dimensions of the outside of the frame are 5 inches by 7 inches, which of the following could be the length of one of the sides of the painting inside the frame?

F. 3 inches

G. 4 inches

H. $5\frac{1}{2}$ inches

J. $6\frac{1}{2}$ inches

K. 7 inches

Just looking at the question the first time, you might be tempted simply to subtract 1 from the outside dimensions and think that the inside dimensions are 4 by 6 (and pick G). Why isn't this correct? Because the frame goes *all* the way around—both above and below the painting, both to the right and to the left. This would have been clear if you had put the problem in a form you could understand and use.

For instance, you might have made the situation graphic by actually sketching out the painting frame (who says you don't have to be an artist to succeed at the ACT?):

When you draw the picture frame like this, you realize that if the outside dimensions are 5 by 7, the inside dimensions must be 3 by 5. Thus, the correct answer is F.

So remember: On the ACT, you've got to put everything into a form that you can understand and use.

#3—IGNORE IRRELEVANT ISSUES

It's easy to waste time on ACT questions by considering irrelevant issues. Just because an issue looks interesting, or just because you're worried about something, doesn't make it important. For example, take this English question.

...China was certainly one of the cradles

of civilization. <u>It's obvious that, China</u>
                             14
<u>has a long history.</u> As is the case with
            14
other ancient cultures, the early history

of China is lost in mythology...

14. F. NO CHANGE
    G. It's obvious that China has
       a long history.
    H. Obviously; China has
       a long history.
    J. OMIT the underlined portion.

In this question, the test makers are counting on you to waste time worrying about punctuation. Does that comma belong? Can you use a semicolon here? These issues might be worrisome, but they aren't important. There's a much bigger issue here—namely, does the sentence belong in the passage at all? No, it doesn't. If China has an ancient culture and was a cradle of civilization, it must have a long history, so the sentence really is "obvious." Redundancy is the relevant issue here, not punctuation. Choice J is correct.

Remember, you've got limited time, so don't get caught up in issues that won't get you a point.

#4—CHECK BACK

Remember, the ACT is not a test of your memory, so don't make it one. All of the information you need is in the test itself. You shouldn't be afraid to refer back to it. Much of the information is too complex to accurately remember anyway.

In Reading and Science Reasoning, always refer back to the place in the passage where the answer to a question can be found (the question stem will often contain a line reference or a reference to a specific table, graph, or experiment to help you out). Your chosen answer should match the passage—not in exact vocabulary or units of measurement, perhaps, but in *meaning*. For example:

> Isaac Newton was born in 1642 in the hamlet of Woolsthorpe in Lincolnshire, England. But he is more famous as a man of Cambridge, where he studied and taught...
>
> **7.** Which of the following does the author imply is a fact about Newton's birth?
>   **A.** It occurred in Lincoln, a small hamlet in England.
>   **B.** It took place in a part of England known for raising sheep.
>   **C.** It did not occur in a large metropolitan setting.
>   **D.** It caused Newton to seek his education at Cambridge.

You might expect the right answer to be that Newton was born in a hamlet, or in Woolsthorpe, or in Lincolnshire. But none of those is offered as a choice. Choice A is tempting, but wrong. Newton was born in Lincoln*shire*, not Lincoln. Choice B is actually true, but it's wrong here. As its name suggests, Woolsthorpe was once known for its wool—which comes from sheep. But the question asks for something implied *in the passage*.

The correct answer here is C, because a hamlet is a small village. That's not a large metropolitan setting. (It's also a famous play, but that's not among the choices.)

Checking back is especially important in Reading and Science Reasoning, because the passages leave many people feeling adrift in a sea of details. Often, the wrong answers will be "misplaced details"—details taken from different parts of the passage. They are things that don't answer the question properly but that might sound good to you if you aren't careful. By checking back with the passage, you can avoid choosing such devilishly clever wrong choices.

There's another important lesson here: Don't pick a choice just because it contains "key words" you remember from the passage. Many wrong choices, like D in the question above, are distortions—they use the right words but say the wrong things about them. Look for answer choices that contain the same *ideas* you find in the passage.

One of the best ways to avoid choosing misplaced details and distortions is to check back with the passage.

#5—ANSWER THE RIGHT QUESTION

This strategy is a natural extension of the last. As we said, the ACT test makers often include among the wrong choices for a question the correct answer to a different question. Under time pressure, it's easy for you to fall for one of these red herrings, thinking that you know what's being asked for when really you don't. For example:

7. What is the value of $3x$ if $9x = 5y + 2$ and $y + 4 = 2y - 10$?
  A. 5
  B. 8
  C. 14
  D. 24
  E. 72

To solve this problem, we need to find y first, even though the question asks about x (because x here is given only in terms of y). You could solve the second equation like this:

$$y + 4 = 2y - 10 \qquad \text{given}$$
$$4 = y - 10 \qquad \text{by subtracting } y \text{ from both sides}$$
$$14 = y \qquad \text{by adding 10 to both sides}$$

But choice C, 14, isn't the right answer here, because the question doesn't ask for the value of y—it asks about x. We can use the value of y to find x, however, by plugging the calculated value of y into the first equation:

$$9x = 5y + 2 \qquad \text{given}$$
$$9x = 5(14) + 2 \qquad \text{because } y = 14$$
$$9x = 70 + 2$$
$$9x = 72$$

KAPLAN

But E, 72, isn't the answer either, because the question doesn't ask for $9x$. It doesn't ask for x either, so if you picked B, 8, you'd be wrong as well. Remember to refer to the question! The question asks for $3x$. So we need to divide $9x$ by 3:

$9x = 72$ from above
$3x = 24$ dividing by 3

Thus, the answer is D.

Always check the question again before choosing your answer. Doing all the right work but then getting the wrong answer can be seriously depressing. So make sure you're answering the right question.

#6—LOOK FOR THE HIDDEN ANSWER

On many ACT questions, the right answer is hidden in one way or another. Don't let the answer hide from you.

An answer can be hidden by being written in a way that you aren't likely to expect. For example, you might work out a problem and get .5 as your answer, but then find that .5 isn't among the answer choices. Then you notice that one choice reads "$\frac{1}{2}$." Congratulations, Sherlock. You've found the hidden answer.

But there's another way the ACT can hide answers. Many ACT questions have more than one possible right solution, though only one correct answer choice is given. Often, the ACT will hide that answer by offering one of the less obvious possible answers to a question. For example:

2. If $3x^2 + 5 = 17$, which of the following could be the value of x?
  A. −3
  B. −2
  C. 0
  D. 1
  E. 4

You quickly solve this very straightforward problem like so:

$3x^2 + 5 = 17$ given
$3x^2 = 12$ by subtracting 5
$x^2 = 4$ dividing by 3
$x = 2$ taking square root of both sides

Having gotten an answer, you confidently look for it among the choices. But 2 isn't a choice. The explanation? This question has *two* possible solutions, not just one. The square root of 4 can be either 2 *or* −2. B is thus the answer.

Keep in mind that though there is only one right answer choice for each ACT question, that right answer may not be the one that occurs to you first. A common mistake is to pick an answer that seems "sort of" like the answer you're looking for even when you know it's wrong. Don't settle for second best. If you don't find your answer, don't assume that you're wrong. Try to think of another right way to answer the question.

#7—GUESS INTELLIGENTLY

An unanswered question is always wrong, but even a wild guess may be right. On the ACT, a guess can't hurt you, but it can help. In fact, smart guessing can make a *big* difference in your score. Always guess on every ACT question you can't answer.

NOTE

Even the luckiest guessers don't get every guessed question right, of course. But a guesser will get a higher ACT score than a nonguesser, picking up one question here and another there. It all adds up. The most important guessing advice we can give you is *never leave any question blank*.

You'll be doing two different kinds of guessing during your two sweeps through any subject test:

- Blind guessing (which you do mostly on questions you deem too hard or time-consuming even to try).
- Considered guessing (which you do mostly on questions that you do some work on, but can't make headway with).

When you guess blindly, you just choose any letter you feel like choosing (Many students like to choose B for Bart; few choose H for Homer). When you guess in a considered way, on the other hand, you've usually done enough work on a question to eliminate at least one or two choices. If you can eliminate any choices, you up the odds that you'll guess correctly.

ELIMINATION HELPS

If you guess blindly, you have one chance in four (or one in five, on the Math) of getting the question right. But if, before guessing, you can eliminate one or two choices as definitely wrong, you can improve those odds to one in three or even one in two. That translates into a higher score.

Here are some fun facts about guessing: If you were to work on only *half* of the questions on the ACT but get them all right, then guess blindly on the other half of the questions, you would probably earn a composite ACT score of around 23 (assuming you had a statistically reasonable success rate on your guesses). A 23 would put you in roughly the top quarter of all those who take the ACT. It's a good score. And all you had to do was answer half the questions correctly.

On the other hand, if you were to hurry and finish all the questions, but get only half of them right, you'd probably earn only a 19, which is below average.

How? Why are you better off answering half and getting them all right instead of answering all and getting only half right?

Here's the trick. The student who answers half the questions right and skips the others can still take guesses on the unanswered questions—and odds are this student will have enough correct guesses to move up 4 points, from a 19 to a 23. But the student who answers all the questions and gets half wrong doesn't have the luxury of taking guesses.

In short: Guess if you can't figure out an answer for any question!

SMART GUESSING

Make sure you get the points you deserve on the questions you can answer. But don't worry about the ones you have to guess on. Odds are good that you'll guess some correctly. And those correct guesses will increase your score just as much as if you'd figured out the answers.

#8—BE CAREFUL WITH THE ANSWER GRID

Your ACT score is based on the answers you select on your answer grid. Even if you work out every ACT question correctly, you'll get a low score if you misgrid your answers. So be careful! Don't disdain the process of filling in those little "bubbles" on the grid. Sure, it's pretty mindless, but under time pressure it's easy to lose control and make mistakes. Don't let that happen to you.

It's important to develop a disciplined strategy for filling in the answer grid. We find that it's smart to grid the answers in groups rather than one question at a time. What this means is this: Circle the answers you get for each question in the test booklet as you figure them out. Then transfer those answers to the answer grid in groups of five or more (until you get close to the end of the section, when you start gridding answers one by one).

Gridding in groups like this cuts down on errors because you can focus on this one task and do it right. Gridding in groups also saves time you'd otherwise spend moving papers around, finding your place, and redirecting your mind. Answering ACT questions takes deep, hard thinking. Filling out answer grids is easy, but you have to be careful, especially if you do a lot of skipping around. Shifting between "hard thinking" and "careful bookkeeping" takes time and effort.

GRID IN GROUPS

You should, of course, circle the correct answers in your test booklet *as you figure them out*. But don't transfer those answers to the grid one by one. That takes too much time. Here are our recommendations for when to grid the answers you've chosen:

- In English, Reading, and Science Reasoning: at the end of each passage.
- In Math: at the end of every page (or every two-page spread).

In English, Reading, and Science Reasoning, the test is divided naturally into groups of questions—the passages. For most students, it makes sense to circle your answers in your test booklet as you work them out. Then, when you're finished with each passage and its questions, grid the answers as a group on your answer grid.

In Math, the strategy has to be different because the Math test isn't broken up into natural groups. For most students, the best strategy for gridding Math questions is to mark your answers in the test booklet and then grid them when you reach the end of each page or every two pages. Since there are usually about five math questions per page, you'll probably be gridding math answers five or ten at a time.

No matter what test you're working on, though, you should start gridding your answers one at a time near the end of the subject test. **You don't want to be caught with ungridded answers when time is called.**

During the ACT, the proctor should warn you when you have about five minutes left on each subject test. But don't depend on proctors! Yes, they're usually nice people, but they *can* screw up once in a while. Instead, rely on you own watch. When there's five minutes left in a subject test, start gridding your answers one by one. With a minute or two left, start filling in everything you've left blank. Remember: Even one question left blank could cut your score.

#9—USE THE LETTERS OF THE CHOICES TO STAY ON TRACK

One oddity about the ACT is that even-numbered questions have F, G, H, J (and, in Math, K) as answer choices, rather than A, B, C, D (and, again, E in Math). This might be a bit confusing at first, but you can make it work *for* you. A common mistake with the answer grid is to accidentally enter an answer one row up or down. On the ACT, that won't happen if you pay attention to the letter in the answer. If you're looking for an A and you see only F, G, H, J, and K, you'll know you're in the wrong row on the answer grid.

Another advantage of having answers F through K for even-numbered questions is that it makes you less nervous about patterns in the answers. It's common to start worrying if you've picked the same letter twice or three times in a row. Since the questions have different letters, this can't happen on the ACT. Of course, you *could* pick the first choice (A or F) for several questions in a row. This shouldn't worry you. It's common for the answers in the same position to be correct three times in a row, and even four times in a row isn't unheard of.

The moral of the story is simple: Worrying about patterns in the answers is a waste of time. Don't do it.

#10—KEEP TRACK OF TIME

It's important to keep track of time while you take the ACT. During your two passes through each subject test, you really have to pace yourself. On average, English, Reading, and Science Reasoning questions should take about a half-minute each. Math questions should average less than one minute each.

SUGGESTED TIMINGS

Below is a list of suggested times for each kind of question and passage on the ACT. These are rough guidelines only! Remember to take into account the fact that you'll probably be taking two passes through the questions.

Passages
English, Reading—about 9 minutes each (including questions)
Science—about 5 minutes each (including questions)

Individual Questions
English, Reading, Science—about 30 seconds each
Math—about 1 minute each

Set your watch to 12:00 at the beginning of each subject test, so it will be easy to check your time. Again, don't rely on proctors, even if they *promise* you that they will dutifully call out the time every five, ten, or fifteen minutes. Proctors get distracted once in a while.

For English, Reading, and Science questions, it's useful to check your timing as you grid the answers for each passage. English and Reading passages should take about nine minutes each. Science passages should average about five minutes. (In the Strategic Summaries, we've written out suggested checkpoints for each subject test.)

Easier questions should take less time, but harder ones will probably take more. In Math, for instance, you need to go much faster than one per minute during your first sweep. But at the end, you may spend two or three minutes on each of the hardest problems you work out.

TAKE CONTROL

A common thread in all ten strategies above is: Take control. That's Kaplan's ACT Mindset. *You* are the master of the test-taking experience. Do the questions in the order *you* want and in the way *you* want. Use your time for one purpose—to maximize your score. Don't get bogged down or agonize. Remember, you don't earn points for suffering, but you do earn points for moving on to the next question and getting it right.

In the next section of this book—the Skill-Building Workouts—we'll provide you with the arsenal of tools and techniques you need to take control of all four subject tests on the ACT.

KAPLAN

BASIC STRATEGY REFERENCE SHEET

THE THREE COMMANDMENTS

1. Thou Shalt Learn the Test

- Learn the directions *before* test day.

- Become familiar with all four subject tests.

- Get a sense of the range of difficulty of the questions.

2. Thou Shalt Learn the Strategies

- Develop a plan of attack for each subject test.

- Develop a guessing strategy that works for you.

- Find "unofficial" ways of finding answers *fast*.

3. Thou Shalt Learn the Material

- Bone up on weak areas.

- Find out what is and isn't part of the ACT knowledge base.

- Use the Math and English Appendices to review important concepts.

TAKING CONTROL: THE TOP TEN STRATEGIES

1. Do question triage.

2. Put the material into a form you can understand and use.

3. Ignore irrelevant issues.

4. Check back.

5. Answer the right question.

6. Look for the hidden answer.

7. Guess intelligently.

8. Be careful with the answer grid.

9. Use the letters of the choices to stay on track.

10. Keep track of time.

SECTION II

SKILL-BUILDING WORKOUTS

Early tests proved that the #1 pencil would have to be abandoned.

ENGLISH WORKOUT 1
WHEN IN DOUBT, TAKE IT OUT

Think back to the last paper you had to write. Maybe your teacher assigned something like ten pages. You wrote and you wrote, and ended up with six pages. It was the night before the paper had to be turned in. You were out of research and ideas. But you knew what to do: pad it.

You're not alone. Almost all of us have padded papers at one time or another. The recipe for padding, in fact, is practically universal: You repeat yourself a few times. You trade short phrases for long-winded verbiage. You add a few offbeat ideas that don't really belong. And presto! Your six-page paper is transformed into a ten-page paper.

The ACT test makers know that most students pad. And they know how to punish you for it. In fact, almost a third of the English questions on the ACT are testing for the very same bad writing habits—long-windedness, repetitiousness, irrelevance—that padders tend to cultivate.

But there's hope. Once you know what ACT English is testing for, you can easily avoid making these common English mistakes. More than any other part of the exam, the ACT English subject test is predictable.

THINK

On recent ACTs, the shortest answer has been correct on about half of all English questions. How can you take advantage of knowing this fact? Stay tuned and we'll tell you.

On recent ACTs, the shortest answer is <u>correct,</u>
                                1

<u>and absolutely right,</u> for about half of all English
       1

1. A. NO CHANGE
   B. correct
   C. right, that is, correct,
   D. correct, absolutely, and right,

questions. Because this is <u>true</u>, a student who
2

knew no English at all could earn<u>—and justly so—</u>an
3

English subject score of about 15. Such a student

could compare the choices carefully, and choose the

<u>single shortest one</u> every time. Where the answers
4

were the same length, the student could pick at

random. On recent published ACTs, guessing

in this way would have yielded between 35 and

38 correct answers out of 75 questions.

Of course, you're going to <u>be doing</u> much
5

better than that. You actually <u>are capable of</u>
6

<u>speaking the English language.</u> You may not
6

know every little rule of English usage, but you

certainly know *something*. Obviously, getting the

question right because you know the <u>right answer</u>
7

is better than getting it right because you guessed

well. But you should always remember that the ACT

test makers <u>like</u> the shortest answers.
8

Why? Why should the ACT make life so

easy for you? <u>Why can't History or Science classes</u>
9

<u>in high school be so easy?</u> Because usually, the
9

best way to write something really is the shortest

2. F. NO CHANGE
   G. truthfully factual
   H. factually correct
   J. factual—and true too—

3. A. NO CHANGE
   B. , and justly so,
   C. and justify
   D. OMIT the underlined portion.

4. F. NO CHANGE
   G. singularly shortest one
   H. uniquely short item
   J. shortest one

5. A. NO CHANGE
   B. do
   C. achieve
   D. be, achieving,

6. F. NO CHANGE
   G. possess the capability of speaking
       that wonderful language called
       the language of England
   H. possess the capability of speaking
       in the land called England
   J. speak English

7. A. NO CHANGE
   B. best choice to select
   C. most correct answer of the
       choices given
   D. answer considered as correct

8. F. NO CHANGE
   G. have a habit of liking
   H. habitually tend to like
   J. are in the habit of liking

9. A. NO CHANGE
   B. Why isn't History or Science
       also easy to master!
   C. History and Science aren't so
       easy, either!
   D. OMIT the underlined portion.

KAPLAN

way to write it. The ACT can't help that, <u>any more</u>
                                              10
<u>than you can help the fact that you must take the</u>
                              10
<u>ACT to get into college</u>. Good writing is
    10

concise and <u>clear</u>. There are many rules of English,
             11
but many of them grow from one dominant principle:

use only the words you need to say what you

mean. [12]

10. F. NO CHANGE
  G. just as you are helpless
       to avoid the requirement of
       taking the ACT
  H. whether or not they'd want to
  J. OMIT the underlined portion and
       end the sentence with a period.

11. A. NO CHANGE
  B. clearly better
  C. translucent, like clear water
  D. clear. Thus it is short and
       to the point.

12. Suppose the author considers adding
     this final sentence: "Thus, if you
     can't say something nice, don't
     say anything at all." Would this
     be an effective conclusion for the
     paragraph?
  F. Yes, because this concept is needed
       to explain the meaning of the
       previous sentence.
  G. Yes, because it adds an uplifting
       moral tone to an otherwise
       depressing, amoral text.
  H. Yes, because this thought is
       relevant to the next paragraph.
  J. No, because the paragraph is
       not concerned with being nice.

THE ANSWERS

1. B, 2. F, 3. D, 4. J, 5. B, 6. J, 7. A, 8. F, 9. D, 10. J, 11. A, 12. J

The shortest answer happens to be correct in all twelve of the questions above. Note that "OMIT," where it is an option, is the shortest answer, since taking the material out leaves a shorter text than leaving anything in. In question 12, answer J is the "shortest" answer, since it leaves the proposed final sentence off entirely.

REDUNDANCY

In questions 1–4 above, the wrong (long) answers are redundant. This means that they make the passage say the same thing twice. The ACT is very strict about redundancy: Never let the passage repeat itself.

VERBOSITY

In questions 5–8, the wrong (long) answers are verbose. They force the reader to read more words, but they are no clearer than the short answers and don't add meaning. This is another rule the ACT is very strict about: The best way to write something is the shortest way, as long as the short way doesn't violate any rules of writing mechanics (like grammar or punctuation) or contain vulgarities inappropriate to civilized discourse.

THINK

Most ACT English questions test common sense, not tricky rules of grammar or punctuation. Remember: the ACT mindset isn't "Can I remember?" It's "I can figure it out!"

RELEVANCE

Questions 9–12 test relevance. The wrong (long) answers introduce irrelevant concepts. The paragraph is about ACT English questions and how to answer them—it's not about History or Science classes, the necessity of taking the ACT, or that lovely translucence of clear water. Ideas that are not directly and logically tied in with the purpose of the passage should be removed. The ACT is very strict about relevance.

WHEN IN DOUBT . . .

On a real ACT, more than twenty questions—almost a third of all the English items—test your awareness of redundancy, verbosity, relevance, and similar issues. For these questions—which we call Economy Questions—the shortest answer is correct with great frequency. What that means is:

• If you're not sure whether an idea is redundant, it probably is, so take it out.

• If you're not sure whether a certain way to say something is too verbose, it probably is, so take it out.

- If you're not sure whether an idea is relevant, it probably isn't, so take it out.

In other words: When in doubt, take it out.

KEEP IT SHORT—ON *ALL* ENGLISH QUESTIONS

Questions in which the lengths of the answers vary greatly, or which contain the answer choice "OMIT," are usually Economy Questions. For these questions, you should be especially inclined to choose the shortest choice. For the other questions, the shortest answer is not nearly as often correct. But even for these other questions, the shortest answer is frequently your best bet.

As we'll see in later workouts, the other English questions mostly test your ability to spot nonsense, bad grammar, and bad punctuation. But even in these cases, the rule "when in doubt, take it out" still holds. Most of the time, the best thing to do with nonsense is to take it out. And most grammatical mistakes can be solved by removing the offending words.

Because these issues of writing economy are so important to English questions of all kinds, we've made them the linchpin for our recommended approach to the English subject test. When approaching English questions, the very first question you should ask yourself is: "Does this stuff belong here? Can the passage or sentence work *without* it?"

SKIMMING ENGLISH QUESTIONS

Before launching in and starting to correct the prose on an ACT English passage, it usually pays to skim each paragraph to get a sense of how it's shaped and what it's about. For most students, that makes correcting the underlined portions a little easier, since you'll have a better sense of the context. The skimming technique is simple: You skim a paragraph, then do the questions it contains, then skim the next paragraph, do the questions *that* one contains, etc. Some students even find it helpful to skim the entire passage before starting on the questions.

In this preliminary step, you needn't read carefully—you'll be doing that when you tackle the questions—but you should at least get a sense of what the passage is about and, just as important, whether it's written in a formal or informal style (we'll talk more about the tone and style of passages in English Workout 2).

After your brief skim of a paragraph (it should only take a few seconds), it's time to start work on its questions.

THE KAPLAN THREE-STEP APPROACH

Here's our three-step (or really, three-question) approach to ACT English questions.

1. Understand

Ask: "Does this stuff belong here?" As we've seen, writing economy is very near to the hearts of ACT test makers. So ask yourself: Does the underlined section belong? Is it expressed as succinctly as possible? If the answer is no, choose the answer that gets rid of the stuff that doesn't belong. If the answer is yes, move on to . . .

2. Analyze

Ask: "Does this stuff make sense?" The ACT test makers want simple, easy-to-understand prose. They expect everything to fit together logically. Does the underlined part of the passage make logical sense? If the answer is no, select the choice that turns nonsense into sense. If the answer is yes, go on to . . .

3. Select

Ask: "Does this stuff sound like English?" Many grammar errors will sound wrong to your ear. Even the ones that don't will be recognizable to you if you study our twenty Classic Grammar Errors in English Workout 3 and create a "flag list" of the ones you're shaky on. Choose the answer that corrects the error and makes the sentence sound right.

(Note: Steps 2 and 3 will be covered more thoroughly in English Workouts 2 and 3.)

Most ACT English test takers are so worried about grammar and punctuation that they don't think about anything else. That's the wrong mindset. Don't think too much about technical rules. As indicated in the approach above, the first thing to think about is getting rid of unnecessary or irrelevant words. Only after you've decided that the underlined selection is concise and relevant do you go on to Steps 2 and 3. Note that this means you won't necessarily be going through all three steps on any English question. The answer can come at any point in the three-step approach.

BE ECONOMICAL

Now try the next practice passage, keeping in mind the approach you just learned:

The Phoenix Cardinals are the <u>oldest,</u>
                              1

<u>most long-established, longest-playing</u> football club
                   1

in the National Football League (NFL). They

began as the Racine Avenue Cardinals on Chicago's

South Side sometime in the 1870s or <u>1880s, during</u>
                     2

<u>the nineteenth century</u>. At that time, the
         2

Cardinals were an amateur team <u>that did not play</u>
                   3

<u>for money</u>.
   3

There was <u>nothing in the world which so</u>
                4

<u>much as resembled</u> pro football in those
     4

1. A. NO CHANGE
B. oldest
C. most long-established
D. longest-playing

2. F. NO CHANGE
G. 1880s
H. the nineteenth century
J. during the 1880s

3. A. NO CHANGE
B. that played for the pure joy of the sport
C. that played on a non-professional level
D. OMIT the underlined portion and end the sentence with a period.

4. F. NO CHANGE
G. nothing anything like
H. no such thing as
J. not even a dream of

KAPLAN

days. The Racine Avenue Cardinals played

amateur ball all through the late 1800s <u>and the game</u>
                                               5

<u>they played was football, no doubt about it</u>.
              5

None of the other clubs in the NFL was

formed before the league itself was established in

1919. When the NFL was first established, the

Cardinals remained <u>aloof and thumbed their noses at</u>
                                  6
<u>it</u>. Professional football had a bad reputation, and
6

the Cardinals were <u>greatly prideful</u> of their record as
                          7
amateurs. But in 1921, the Cardinals decided to

join the NFL. They were required to play a "game

to the death" with the Chicago Tigers (<u>The Detroit</u>
                                               8
<u>Tigers are a baseball team</u>). Whichever team won
                8
would be allowed to stay in Chicago; the other team

would <u>have to move</u>. The Cardinals won.
             9
The Tigers moved away and soon went

bankrupt. The Cardinals are thus the only NFL

team that won their franchise on the football field.

Ironically, the team that fought to stay in

Chicago eventually moved away. The Cardinals

were rarely as <u>successfully able to win games or</u>
                              10
<u>make money</u> as the Chicago Bears, their crosstown
      10
rivals. Fans gradually deserted the Cardinals, so the

team moved—to St. Louis in 1958 and to Phoenix in

1986, seeking a more profitable market.

5. A. NO CHANGE
B. no doubt about it
C. to be assured it was football
D. OMIT the underlined portion and end the sentence with a period.

6. F. NO CHANGE
G. aloof.
H. aloof and tried to ignore it.
J. off in their own corner.

7. A. NO CHANGE
B. full of great pride
C. proud
D. gratefully proud

8. F. NO CHANGE
G. Not to be confused with the Detroit Tigers, a baseball team
H. Not the more famous modern-day Detroit Tigers baseball team
J. OMIT the underlined portion and end the sentence with a period.

9. A. NO CHANGE
B. be forced to move along
C. be legally obliged, by injunction, to relocate their franchise
D. be obligated to be moving out

10. F. NO CHANGE
G. successful at winning
H. winning or profitable, a team,
J. successful

KAPLAN 51

Maybe Phoenix <u>is the place in which</u> the Cardinals
                    11
are destined to stay. Some people say that the name

"Cardinal" was a nineteenth-century name for a

mythical bird that arose from its own ashes <u>in the</u>
                                              12
<u>fireplace,</u> and that the Cardinals date back to 1871,
  12

the year of the great Chicago fire—which may have

begun on Racine Avenue <u>(or maybe not)</u>. Chicago
                              13
was proud to rise from its ashes like the mythical

Cardinal. The <u>name that is more common</u> for that
                        14

mythical firebird is—the Phoenix. [15]

11. A. NO CHANGE
    B. is the place at which
    C. is where
    D. OMIT the underlined portion.

12. F. NO CHANGE
    G. that had consumed it
    H. created by the fire that had
        consumed it
    J. OMIT the underlined portion.

13. A. NO CHANGE
    B. according to ironic legend
    C. resulting from violations of the
        fire code and a cow in a barn
    D. OMIT the underlined portion and
        end the sentence with a period.

14. F. NO CHANGE
    G. common name
    H. name that is famous
    J. common way of speaking

15. Suppose the author wishes to add a
new paragraph at the end of the
existing passage quickly summarizing
the history of Canadian football.
Would this be appropriate,
in light of the content and
style of the rest of the passage?
    A. Yes, because it is only fair to
        mention Canadian football at
        least once in the passage.
    B. Yes, because the Phoenix
        Cardinals now play Canadian
        football.
    C. No, because the passage does not
        focus on sports history.
    D. No, because the passage has
        nothing to do with Canadian
        football.

THE ANSWERS

1. B, 2. G, 3. D, 4. H, 5. D, 6. G, 7. C, 8. J, 9. A, 10. J, 11. C, 12. J, 13. D, 14. G, 15. D

Did you see the point? On every regular format question except number 11, you shouldn't have gotten past the first step of the three-step approach, because all of the questions test economy errors. In fact, the shortest answers are correct on every question here except that one. In 11, if you omit the phrase "is the place in which," the sentence doesn't make any sense, meaning that you'd correct it in Step 2 of the three-step approach. (Note: This passage is not typical—most ACT passages don't consist exclusively of Economy Questions—but we used this passage to drive home the point about choosing concise answers on the English subject test.)

> **HINT:** *Remember that "OMIT," when it is an option, is always the shortest answer.*
> *For instance, D is "shorter" than A and B in question 15 because not including a new*
> *paragraph makes the passage shorter than including it. (But notice that you still had to*
> *decide between C and D in that question.)*

Many students might object to answer J in question 10, because the word *successful* alone does not indicate the *kind* of success meant. But use common sense. What would make a professional football team successful? Winning, and making money. Thus, the concepts of "winning" and "profitability" are implicit in the notion that the Cardinals are (now) a successful team. The ACT expects you to cut *anything* that isn't absolutely needed.

Remember: *When in doubt, take it out.*

MATH
WORKOUT 1
THE END
JUSTIFIES THE MEANS

All that matters on the ACT is correct answers. Your goal on the Math subject test is to get as many correct answers as you can in 60 minutes. It doesn't matter what you do (short of cheating, naturally) to get those correct answers.

You don't have to do every problem the way your math teacher would. Be open to clever and original solution methods. All that matters is that your methods be quick and that they get you a good number of correct answers. How *many* correct answers you need depends on what kind of score you're aiming for, but chances are you don't have to get so many right as you might think to get a good score. Yes, it's a tough test, but it's graded "on the curve."

As we've pointed out, the ACT is different from the typical high school test. On a typical high school math test, you get a series of problems just like the ones you've been doing in class and for homework over the previous week or so. Since you're being tested on a relatively narrow scope of topics, you're expected to get almost every question right.

ACT math is different. The scope of what's tested is deliberately wide so that every student will get an opportunity to demonstrate his or her strengths, wherever they may lie.

QUESTION BREAKDOWN

Each ACT Math subject test includes:
- 24 Prealgebra and Elementary Algebra questions (corresponding roughly to the Math Appendix, #1–65)
- 10 Intermediate Algebra questions (Math Appendix, #66–70)
- 8 Coordinate Geometry questions (Math Appendix, #71–77)
- 14 Plane Geometry questions (Math Appendix, #78–95)
- 4 Trigonometry questions (Math Appendix, #96–100)

Nobody needs to get all 60 questions right. The average ACT student gets less than half of the math questions right. You need only about 40 correct answers to get your math score over 25—just two right out of every three questions gets you a great score!

BE OPEN-MINDED

According to an old legend at M.I.T., a physics professor once asked the following question on a final exam: *How could a barometer be used to determine the height of a tower?*

To answer the question, most students worked out complex equations based on the fact that air pressure (which is what a barometer measures) decreases at higher altitudes. But one student made three suggestions instead:

1. Measure the length of the barometer, then use the barometer as a ruler and measure the tower.

2. Drop the barometer and time its fall, keeping in mind that the acceleration of falling objects is about 32 ft/sec^2.

3. Find the person who built the tower and say, "I'll give you a nice barometer if you tell me how tall your tower is."

Guess which student got an A . . .

On the ACT, as in college and beyond, you'll sometimes be called upon to do more than merely regurgitate memorized facts and unquestioningly follow prepackaged procedures. True, some ACT math questions are straightforward: As soon as you understand what the question's asking, you know what to do. But more challenging—and more fun (really)—are the ACT math questions that aren't what they seem at first glance. These are the questions that call for creative solutions.

DON'T BE OBEDIENT

Too often, high school math instruction degenerates into obedience training: you show your work on tests to prove that you did everything the way it was taught in class. If you show the "right" kind of work, you get partial or even full credit, regardless of whether your answers are correct. If you're lucky, your teacher might even give you a nice pat on the back.

On the ACT, though, there's no partial credit. All that matters is the right answer. It makes no difference how you find it. In fact, as we'll see, it's sometimes safer and faster if you *don't* do ACT problems the "right" way—the way you've been taught in school. For a lot of ACT math problems there's more than one way to find the answer. And many of these other ways are faster than the so-called right way.

KAPLAN

Us, Too

When we say to do it your way, that applies to us, too. Don't blindly follow the Kaplan strategies in this book. Use your strengths. If you can think of a good way to do a problem—JUST DO IT!

Of course, old habits die hard. For years you've been subjected to obedience-training math. You've learned to waste time writing everything out. You've learned to depend on remembering "how you're supposed to do it" instead of finding ways to do it faster and smarter. Maybe you've even learned not to care much about getting right answers. It'll take something pretty drastic to break away. The drastic step we recommend is: Don't show your work.

DON'T SHOW YOUR WORK

No, we don't mean that you should try to do every ACT math problem in your head. Nobody could do that—though most people could and *should* do a lot less paper calculation than they do. Go ahead and use your pencil to calculate and organize. But don't put stuff down just for the sake of getting it on paper. *Don't* write out every step. *Don't* worry about whether you're being neat or whether anybody'd be able to understand your notes. Jot things down for *yourself*.

If you do every problem the way your algebra teacher would want you to, you may earn his or her undying gratitude, but you won't achieve your goal of getting as many correct answers as possible. You don't have *time* to use the textbook approach on every question. You don't have *time* to write out every step.

ONLY THE BUBBLES COUNT

You will not get credit for anything you write under "DO YOUR FIGURING HERE." You get credit only for correct answers correctly gridded into the "bubbles" on your answer sheet.

SECTION II: SKILL-BUILDING WORKOUTS

BE A THINKER—NOT A NUMBER CRUNCHER

One reason you're given limited time for the Math subject test is that the ACT is testing your ability to think, not your willingness to do a lot of mindless calculations. They're looking for creative thinkers, not human calculators. So, one of your guiding principles for ACT math should be: Work less, but think harder.

If you want to get the best score you can, you need to be always on the lookout for quicker ways to solve problems. Here's an example that could take a lot more time than it needs to.

1. When $\frac{4}{11}$ is converted to a decimal, the 50th digit after the decimal point is
- **A.** 2
- **B.** 3
- **C.** 4
- **D.** 5
- **E.** 6

It seems that when you convert $\frac{4}{11}$ to a decimal, there are at least 50 digits after the decimal point. The question asks for the 50th. One way to answer this question would be to divide 11 into 4, carrying the division out to 50 decimal places. That method would work, but it would take forever. It's not worth spending that much time on one question.

No ACT math question should take more than a minute to take care of, if you know what you're doing. There has to be a faster way to solve this problem. There must be some kind of pattern you can take advantage of. And what kind of pattern might there be with a decimal? How about a *repeating* decimal?!

In fact, that's exactly what you have here. The decimal equivalent of $\frac{4}{11}$ is a repeating decimal: $\frac{4}{11} = .3636363636...$

The 1st, 3rd, 5th, 7th, and 9th digits are each 3. The 2nd, 4th, 6th, 8th, and 10th digits are each 6. Put simply, odd-numbered digits are 3s and even-numbered digits are 6s. The 50th digit is an even-numbered digit, so it's a 6 and the answer is E.

What looked at first glance like a "fractions and decimals" problem turned out to be something of an "odds and evens" problem.

If you don't use creative shortcuts on problems like this one, you'll get bogged down, you'll run out of time, and you won't get a lot of correct answers.

BE CREATIVE

Be creative in the *process* you use to solve problems, not in the answer choices you pick. Don't try to select answers that somehow "look good." The ACT is not a beauty contest.

Question 1 demonstrates how the ACT designs problems to reward clever thinking and to punish students who blindly "go through the motions."

But how do you get yourself into a creative mindset on the Math subject test? For one thing, you have to take the time to understand thoroughly each problem you decide to work on. Most students are so nervous about time that they skim each math problem and almost immediately start computing with their pencils. But that's the wrong way of thinking. Sometimes on the ACT, you have to *take* time to *save* time. A few extra moments spent understanding a math problem can save many extra moments of computation or other drudgery.

KAPLAN'S THREE-STEP APPROACH TO ACT MATH PROBLEMS

At Kaplan, we've developed this take-time-to-save-time philosophy into a three-step approach to ACT math problems. The approach is designed to help you find the fast, inventive solutions that the ACT rewards. The steps are:

1. Understand
Focus first on the question stem (the part before the answer choices) and make sure you understand the problem. Sometimes you'll want to read the stem twice, or rephrase it in a way you can better understand. Think to yourself: "What kind of problem is this? What am I looking for? What am I given?" Don't pay too much attention to the answer choices yet, though you may want to give them a quick glance just to see what form they're in.

2. Analyze
Think for a moment and decide on a plan of attack. Don't start crunching numbers until you've given the problem a little thought. Ask: "What's a quick and reliable way to find the correct answer?" Look for patterns and shortcuts, using common sense and your knowledge of the test to find the creative solutions that will get you more right answers in less time. Try to solve the problem without focusing on the answer choices.

3. Select

Once you get an answer—or once you get stuck—check the answer choices. If you got an answer and it's listed as one of the choices, chances are it's right—fill in the appropriate bubble and move on. But if you didn't get an answer, narrow down the choices as best you can by a process of elimination and then guess.

THINK

Most students hate it when they solve a problem and their answer isn't among the choices. But actually, not having the answer you want among the choices helps you if you've made a mistake, because it makes you realize that you did something wrong. You can then go back and do the problem right.

Each of these steps can happen in a matter of seconds. And it may not always be clear when you've finished with one step and moved on to the next. Sometimes you'll know how to attack a problem the instant you read and understand it.

Here's how the Three-Step Approach applied to Question 1 above.

Step 1: Understand

First, we made sure we understood what the problem was asking for: the 50th digit after the decimal point in the decimal equivalent of a certain fraction. Because we knew what digit and decimal equivalent mean, it took only a second to understand what the problem was asking.

Step 2: Analyze

Second, and most crucially, we analyzed the situation and thought about a plan of attack before we tried to solve the problem. We realized that the "obvious" method would take too long, so we figured out a creative approach that got us an answer of 6 in just a few seconds.

Step 3: Select

Third, we looked at the answer choices, found 6, and selected choice E.

The Three-Step Approach isn't a rigid procedure; it's a set of guidelines that will keep you on track, moving quickly, and evading pitfalls. Just remember to think before you solve: Focus on the question stem first and save the answer choices for later.

THE FIRST STEP: UNDERSTAND

To understand an ACT math problem, you first have to understand the language. Mathematicians are generally very precise in their use of language. They choose their words carefully and mean exactly what they say. This is why they're usually no fun to talk to at parties.

In everyday life we can be a little loose with math terminology. It doesn't really matter that Harvard Square is not a square or that a batting average is not an average.

In an ACT math problem, however, words have precise meanings. You don't need to memorize definitions—you'll never have to recite one on the ACT—but you do need to understand what the question writer means.

Here's an example in which understanding the jargon is half the battle:

> **2.** If the sum of five consecutive even integers is equal to their product, what is the greatest of the five integers?
>
> **F.** 4
> **G.** 10
> **H.** 14
> **J.** 16
> **K.** 20

Step 1: Understand

Before you can begin to solve this problem, you have to figure out what it's asking, and to do that you need to know the meanings of *sum, product, consecutive, even*, and *integer*. Remember, take control. Put the question stem into words you can understand. What the question stem is really saying here is that when you add up these five consecutive even integers you get the same thing as when you multiply them.

Step 2: Analyze

How are we going to figure out what these five numbers are? We could set up an equation:
$$x + (x - 2) + (x - 4) + (x - 6) + (x - 8) = x(x - 2)(x - 4)(x - 6)(x - 8)$$

But there's no way you'll have time to solve an equation like this! So don't even try. Come up with a *better* way.

Let's stop and think logically about this one for a moment. When we think about sums and products, it's natural to think mostly of positive integers. With positive integers, we would generally expect the product to be *greater* than the sum.

But what about negative integers? Hmm. Well, the sum of five negatives is negative, and the product of five negatives is also negative, and generally the product will be "more negative" than the sum, so with negative integers the product will be *less* than the sum.

So when will the product and sum be the same? How about right at the boundary of positive and negative—that is, around 0? The five consecutive even integers with equal product and sum are: –4, –2, 0, 2, and 4.
$$(-4) \times (-2) \times 0 \times 2 \times 4 = (-4) + (-2) + 0 + 2 + 4$$

The product and sum are both 0. Ha! We've done it!

Step 3: Select
The question asks for the greatest of the five integers, which is 4, choice F.

You've probably encountered every math term that appears on the ACT sometime in your high-school math career, but you may not remember exactly what every one of them means. The Math Glossary at the back of this book is a complete but compact list of the terminology you need for ACT math problems. Look it over. Mark or jot down the ones you're not so sure of for future reference. And be sure to use the Glossary to look up any unfamiliar term you encounter while practicing with ACT math questions.

Definition Alert
As you refresh your memory of key terminology, watch out for technicalities. Here are a few examples of such technicalities (by the way, these are great for stumping your know-it-all friends):

- "Integers" include 0 and negative whole numbers. If a question says "x and y are integers," it's not ruling out numbers like 0 and -1.

- "Evens and odds" include 0 and negative whole numbers. Zero and -2 are even numbers; -1 is an odd number.

- "Prime numbers" do *not* include 1. The technical definition of a prime number is: "a positive integer with exactly two distinct positive integer factors." Two is prime because it has exactly two positive factors: 1 and 2. Four is *not* prime because it has *three* positive factors (1, 2, and 4)—too many! And 1 is *not* prime because it has only *one* positive factor (1)—too few!

- "Remainders" are integers. If a question asks for the remainder when 15 is divided by 2, don't say "15 divided by 2 is 7.5, so the remainder is .5." What you should say is: "15 divided by 2 is 7 with a remainder of 1."

- The $\sqrt{}$ symbol represents the *positive* square root only. The equation $x^2 = 9$ has two solutions: 3 and -3. But when you see $\sqrt{9}$, it means positive 3 only.

- "Rectangles" include squares. The definition of a rectangle is a four-sided figure with four right angles. It doesn't matter if the length and width are the same or not—if it has four right angles, it's a rectangle. When a question refers to "rectangle *ABCD*," it's not ruling out a square.

THE SECOND STEP: ANALYZE

Now, once you're sure you've gotten a math problem into a form you can understand, you still have to know what to *do* with the problem. Sometimes you'll know what to do the moment you understand the problem. Here's an example.

3. What is the value of $x^2 + 3x - 9$ when $x = -3$?
   A. −27
   B. −9
   C. −6
   D. 0
   E. 9

Step 1: Understand
You've probably seen dozens of problems just like this. If so, then you realize right away that what it's asking is, "What do you get when you plug $x = -3$ into $x^2 + 3x - 9$?"

Step 2: Analyze
So that's what you do—plug it in and "solve":
$$x^2 + 3x - 9 = (-3)^2 + 3(-3) - 9$$
$$= 9 + (-9) - 9$$
$$= -9$$

Step 3: Select
The answer is B.

So this is a case where you knew exactly what to do as soon as you understood what the question was asking.

But sometimes you're not so lucky. Let's look at a case where the method of solution is not so obvious, even after you "understand" the stem:

4. What is the greatest of the numbers 1^{50}, 50^1, 2^{25}, 25^2, 4^{10}?
   F. 1^{50}
   G. 50^1
   H. 2^{25}
   J. 25^2
   K. 4^{10}

Step 1: Understand
It's not hard to figure out what the question is asking: Which of five numbers is the greatest? But the five numbers are all written as powers, some of which we don't have time to calculate. Yikes! How are we going to compare them?

Step 2: Analyze
If all the powers had the same base or the same exponent, or if they could all be rewritten with a common base or exponent, we could compare all five at once. As it is, though, we should take two at a time.

Compare 1^{50} and 50^1 to start: $1^{50} = 1$, while $50^1 = 50$, so there's no way choice F could be the biggest.

Next, compare 50^1 and 2^{25}. We don't have time to calculate 2^{25}, but we can see that it doesn't take anywhere near 25 factors of 2 to get over 50. In fact, 2^6 is 64, already more than 50, so 2^{25} is much, much more than 50. That eliminates G.

Choice J, 25^2, doesn't take too long to calculate: $25 \times 25 = 625$. How does that compare to 2^{25}? Once again, with a little thought, we realize that it doesn't take 25 factors of 2 to get over 625. That eliminates J.

The last comparison is easy because choice K, 4^{10}, can be rewritten as $(2^2)^{10} = 2^{20}$, in that form clearly less than 2^{25}. That eliminates K.

Step 3: Select
So the answer is H.

ANALYSIS IS WHERE IT'S AT

As you can tell already from the few examples we've looked at, Step 2—"Analyze"—is where you'll be doing most of your serious thinking. The other two Math Workouts will address Step 2 in greater detail. Math Workout 2 will focus on analyzing Algebra and Coordinate Geometry problems. Math Workout 3 will focus on analyzing Geometry and Trigonometry problems.

KNOW WHEN TO SKIP

At any time during the Three-Step problem-solving process you could choose to cut bait and skip the question. Almost everyone should skip at least some questions the first time through.

If you know your own strengths and weaknesses, you can sometimes choose to skip a question while still in Step 1—"Understand." For example, suppose you never studied trigonometry. Maybe you think that a secant is something that sailors sing while climbing up the yardarms. Well, every form of the ACT includes exactly four trigonometry questions, and it's not hard to spot them. Why waste a second on such a question? Skip it! You don't need those four measly questions to get a great score. And since you know a second visit later won't help any, you might as well go ahead and make some random guesses.

It can be harder to decide when to skip a question if you understand it, but then get stuck in Step 2—"Analyze." Suppose you just don't see how to solve it. Don't give up *too* quickly. Sometimes it takes a half-minute or so before you see the light. But don't get bogged down either.

KAPLAN

Never spend more than a minute on a question the first time through the section. No single question is worth it. Be prepared to leave a question and come back to it later. Often, on the second try, you'll see something you didn't see before. That old light bulb will light up over your head and you'll be on your way.

Of course, eventually you're going to grid in an answer choice for every question, even the ones you don't understand. The first time through the section, however, you should concentrate on the questions you understand.

KAPLAN'S TWO-PASS PLAN FOR THE ACT MATH SUBTEST

We recommend that you plan two "passes" through the Math subtest.

- **First Pass:** Examine each problem in order. Do every problem you understand. Don't skip too hastily—sometimes it takes a few seconds of thought before you see how to do it—but don't get bogged down. Never spend more than a minute on any question in the first pass. This first pass should take about 45 minutes.

- **Second Pass:** Use the last 15 minutes to go back to the questions that stumped you the first time through. Sometimes a second look is all you need—after going away and then coming back you'll sometimes suddenly see what to do. In most cases, though, you'll still be stumped by the question stem, so it's time to give the answer choices a try. Work by process of elimination, and guess. Be sure to select an answer for every question, even if it's just a blind guess.

Never plan on visiting a question a third time. It's inefficient to go back and forth that much. Every time you leave a question and come back to it, you have to take at least a few seconds to refamiliarize yourself with the problem. Always grid in an answer choice on the second pass—even if it's just a wild guess. At the end of the second pass, every question should be answered.

DO THE ONES YOU CAN

Don't worry about the ones you can't do. Get your points where you can, and don't expect miracles in the hard problems. *Guess and move on.*

Don't worry if you don't work on every question in the section. The average ACT test taker gets fewer than half of the problems right. You can score in the top quarter of all ACT test takers if you can do just *half* of the problems on the test, get every single one of them right, and guess blindly on the other half. If you did just *one-third* of the problems and got every one right, then guessed blindly on the other forty problems, you would still earn an average score. And if you had time to make *smart* guesses—eliminating choices that are way off—you'd score even better.

DON'T WORRY. BE HAPPY!

If you skip a whole half of the test, you can double the amount of time you have to work on the problems you actually do—virtually making it certain that you make no careless errors.

DON'T MAKE CARELESS MISTAKES

Most students don't worry too much about careless errors. Since in school (where you show your work) you can still get partial credit even if you make a careless calculation error, many students think that careless errors somehow "don't count." Not so on the ACT. There are only so many problems you'll know how to do. Some of the problems will be impossible for you. So you make or break your score on the problems you *can* do. You can't afford to miss one easy problem!

Unless math is a very strong area for you, thereby giving you a real chance at almost every question, the best way to maximize your score is to make sure that you work on the ones you deserve to get correct. Don't worry about getting to every problem (though, of course, you should mark an answer for every problem on your answer grid, even if it's a blind guess).

If math *is* a strong point for you, don't give up on any of the problems. Don't get complacent on easy problems—that causes careless errors. For strong students, the easy problems may be the most challenging. You have to find a way to answer them quickly and accurately in order to have time for the tougher ones. You won't have time for the hard problems unless you save some time on the easy ones.

STUCK? TRY GUESSTIMATES AND ESTIMATES

Sometimes when you understand a problem but can't figure out how to solve it, you can at least get a general idea of how big the answer is—what is sometimes called a "ballpark estimate," "guess-estimate," or "guesstimate." You may not know whether you are looking at something the size of an African elephant or the size of an Indian elephant, but you may be pretty sure it isn't the size of a mouse and it isn't the size of a battleship.

GUESSTIMATING

Guesstimating is much cruder than the kind of estimating and rounding off you are usually taught to do in school. The purpose of using guesstimates is to quickly and easily find the smallest and largest that the answer could possibly be. It's like working on the edges of a puzzle first. Our advice: Don't bother to make a guesstimate if you can't think of an easy way to do it.

Here's a question that's not hard to understand but *is* hard to solve if you don't remember the rules for simplifying and adding radicals:

5. $\dfrac{\sqrt{32} + \sqrt{24}}{\sqrt{8}} = ?$

$$\frac{4\sqrt{2} + 2\sqrt{6}}{2\sqrt{2}}$$

- **A.** $\sqrt{7}$
- **B.** $\sqrt{2} + \sqrt{3}$
- **C.** $2 + \sqrt{3}$
- **D.** $\sqrt{2} + 3$
- **E.** 7

Step 1: Understand

The question wants you to simplify the given expression, which includes three radicals. In other words, turn the radicals into numbers you can use, then work out the fraction.

Step 2: Analyze

The best way to solve this problem would be to apply the rules of radicals—but what if you don't remember them? Don't give up; you can still guesstimate. In the question stem, the numbers under the radicals are not too far away from perfect squares. You could round $\sqrt{32}$ off to $\sqrt{36}$, which is 6. You could round $\sqrt{24}$ to $\sqrt{25}$, which is 5. And you could round $\sqrt{8}$ off to $\sqrt{9}$, which is 3. So the expression is now $\frac{6+5}{3}$, which is $3\frac{2}{3}$. That's just a guesstimate, of course—the actual value might be something a bit less or a bit more than that.

Step 3: Select

Now look at the answer choices. Choice A—$\sqrt{7}$ is less than 3, so it's too small. Choice B—$\sqrt{2} + \sqrt{3}$ is about 1.4 + 1.7, or just barely more than 3, so it seems a little small, too. Choice C—$2 + \sqrt{3}$—is about 2 + 1.7, or about 3.7—that's very close to our guesstimate! We still have to check the other choices. Choice D—$\sqrt{2} + 3$—is about 1.4 + 3, or 4.4—too big. And choice E—7—is obviously way too big. Looks like our best bet is C—and C in fact is the correct answer.

NOTE: *To review the traditional textbook methods for adding and simplifying radicals, see the Math Appendix.*

LEARN COMMON ESTIMATES

It pays to learn the approximate value of these three irrational numbers:

$$\sqrt{2} \approx 1.4$$
$$\sqrt{3} \approx 1.7$$
$$\pi \approx 3.14$$

STUCK? TRY EYEBALLING

There is another simple but powerful strategy that should give you at least a 50-50 chance on almost every diagram question: When in doubt, use your eyes. Trust common sense and careful thinking; don't worry if you've forgotten most of the geometry you ever knew. For almost half of all diagram questions you can get a reasonable answer without solving anything: Just eyeball it.

The math directions say, "Illustrative figures are NOT necessarily drawn to scale," but in fact they almost always are. You're never really *supposed* to just eyeball the figure, but it makes a lot more sense than random guessing. Occasionally, eyeballing can narrow the choices down to one likely candidate.

Here's a difficult geometry question that you might just decide to eyeball:

6. In the figure below, points *A*, *B*, and *C* lie on a circle centered at *O*. Triangle *AOC* is equilateral, and the length of *OC* is 3 inches. What is the length, in inches, of arc *ABC* ?

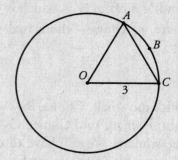

KAPLAN

F. 3

G. π

H. 2π

J. 3π

K. 6π

Step 1: Understand

There's an "equilateral" triangle that connects the center and two points on the circumference of a circle. You're looking for the length of the arc that goes from A to C.

Step 2: Analyze

What you're "supposed" to do to answer this question is recall and apply the formula for the length of an arc. But suppose you don't remember that formula (most people don't). Should you give up and take a wild guess?

No. You can eyeball it. If you understand the question well enough to realize that "equilateral" means all sides are equal, then you know immediately that side $\overline{AC}$ is 3 inches long. Now look at arc ABC compared to side $\overline{AC}$. Suppose you were an ant, and you had to walk from A to C. If you walked along line segment $\overline{AC}$, it would be a 3-inch trip. About how long a walk would it be along arc ABC? Clearly more, but not much more, than 3 inches.

Step 3: Select

Now look at the answer choices. Choice F—3—is no good: You know the arc is more than 3 inches. All the other choices are in terms of π. Just think of π as "a bit more than 3," and you will quickly see that only one answer choice is in the right ballpark. Choice G—π—would be "a bit more than 3," which sounds pretty good. Choice H—2π—would be "something more than 6." Already that's way too big. Choices J and K are even bigger. It sure looks like the answer has to be G—and it is.

> **NOTE:** *If you want to review the traditional textbook approach to arcs,*
> *see the Math Appendix.*

This is a pretty hard question. Not many ACT students would be able to solve question 6 the textbook way. If *you* could, great! That's the way to do it if you know how. Solving the problem is always more reliable than eyeballing.

But when you *don't* know how to solve a diagram problem, or if you think it would take forever to get an answer, eyeballing and eliminating answer choices sure beats wild guessing. Sometimes, as with question 6, you might even be able to narrow the choices down to the one that's probably correct.

REMINDER

If you have forgotten any of the geometry terms discussed in this Workout, look them up in the Math Glossary!

SUMMING UP

So, in this first Math Workout, we've laid out a general math strategy for you:

- First, use Kaplan's Three-Step Approach to ACT Math Problems to understand them and come up with the creative, fast solutions the ACT is looking for.

- Second, use Kaplan's Two-Pass Strategy for the ACT Math subtest to make sure you get as many correct answers as you can in 60 minutes.

In the other two Math Workouts, you'll learn a few special solution methods for some of the more intriguing ACT problems in algebra, coordinate geometry, plane geometry, and trigonometry.

READING WORKOUT 1
KNOW WHERE YOU'RE GOING

Reading skills are crucial on every part of the ACT, not just on the Reading subject test. Savvy ACT-style reading is certainly useful for the English and Science tests, and even your work on many of the Math problems will benefit from the skills discussed below. So don't ignore the Reading Workouts, even if you think you're an ace reader. You may not be an ace *ACT-style* reader.

The kind of reading rewarded by the ACT is special. You probably know how to do it already, but you may be reluctant to do it on a standardized test. You may think that success on a test like the ACT requires that you read very slowly and deliberately, making sure you remember everything before moving on. Well, we at Kaplan have found that this kind of reading won't work on the ACT. In fact, it's a sure way to run out of time halfway through the Reading subtest.

THE KEY TO ACT READING

The real key to ACT reading is to read quickly but actively, getting a sense of the gist or "main idea" of the passage and seeing how everything fits together to support that main idea. You should constantly try to think ahead. Look for the general outline of the passage—determine how it's structured. Don't worry about the details. You'll come back for those later.

REMINDER

The key to ACT success is the right mindset. Read actively, with an eye toward where the author is going. Don't worry about remembering the details of what you have read. You can (and should) always refer.

Fast, active reading, of course, requires a little more mental energy than slow, passive reading. But it pays off. Those who dwell on details—who passively let the passage reveal itself at its own pace—are sure to run out of time. Don't be that kind of reader! Again, the key is to *take control.*

Make the passage reveal itself to you on *your* schedule, by skimming the passage with an eye to structure rather than detail. Look for key words that tell you what the author is doing so that you can save yourself time. For instance, read examples very, very quickly, just glancing over the words. When an author says "for example," you know that what follows is an example of a general point. Do you need to understand that specific example? Maybe, maybe not. If you *do*, you can come back and read the verbiage when you're attacking the questions. You'll know exactly where the author gave an example of general point x (or whatever). If you *don't* need to know the example for any of the questions, great! You haven't wasted much time on something that won't get you a point.

You really have to be a "seat-of-the-pants" reader to do well under the stringent time conditions of the ACT Reading test. You must quickly assess what an author's point is, and how he or she is supporting that point. When you get good at this, you can get through passages at an amazing clip.

You actually do this kind of "reading" all the time, and not just when you're reading a book or newspaper. When you watch TV or see a movie, for instance, you can often figure out much of what's going to happen in advance. You see the bad guys run out of a bank with bags of money in their hands, and you can guess that the next thing they'll do is get into a car and drive away in excess of the speed limit. You see a character in an old sitcom bragging to his friends about how great a driver he is, and you know that he's bound to get into a fender bender before the next commercial. This ability to know where something is going is very valuable. Use it on the ACT.

To help you know where an author is going, you should pay careful attention to "structural clues." Words like *but*, *nevertheless*, and *moreover* help you get a sense of where a piece of writing is going. You also should look for signal phrases (like *clearly*, *as a result*, or *no one can deny that*) to determine the logic of the passage. The details, remember, you can come back for later, when you're doing the questions. What's important in reading the passage is getting a sense of how those details fit together to express the point or points of the passage.

IF YOU CAN READ THIS, YOU CAN READ WELL FOR THE ACT

When you buy new electronic equipment like a VCR, you know you'll probably need to check the instruction manual to figure out how to set it up and make it work. But would you read the whole manual? No way! You'd probably skip past the warranty and other pages that won't help you set things up. If the manual said something like "connect the xygupts to terminal c," you'd probably get it done even though you don't know what a xygupt is. By using the manual for a VCR, you show that you have the kind of reading skills the ACT requires. You read with a specific purpose. You refer to the right part to find the details you need. And you don't let unfamiliar words confuse you.

PRACTICE KNOWING WHERE YOU'RE GOING

In the following exercise, try to fill in the word or phrase that should come next. For most, there are many possible answers, so don't worry about getting the "right" answer.

Reading Exercise
Fill in the blanks in the following sentences:

1. You'd think that the recipe for a strawberry soufflé would be complicated, but my friend's version was ———.
2. I can't believe my good luck! The one time in my life I buy a lottery ticket, I ———.
3. A parked car burns no fuel and causes no pollution. Once the ignition is turned on, however, ———.
4. As their habitat is destroyed, wild animals ———.
5. The new word-processing program was far easier to use than the old one. Moreover, the accompanying instruction booklet explained the commands in a ——— way.
6. The new word-processing program was far easier to use than the old one. On the other hand, the accompanying instruction booklet explained the commands in a ——— way.

- In Example #1, the active reader would probably complete the sentence by saying that the friend's version was "actually quite simple" or something similar. How do you know what's coming next here? The structural clue *but* tips you off. *But* tells you that a contrast is coming up. You'd think the recipe would be complicated, *BUT* it's "actually quite simple."

- In Example #2, on the other hand, there's no real structural clue to help you out, but the *meaning* of the sentence should make clear what's coming up. The speaker here is marveling at his good luck, right? That means that he must have won some money. So, a likely completion would be something like: The one time in my life I buy a lottery ticket, I "win the jackpot."

- In Example #3, we have another contrast, signaled by the clue *however*. A parked car doesn't burn fuel or pollute. *HOWEVER*, once you turn on the ignition. . . . The answer has to be something like "the car starts burning gas and polluting." That's the clear contrast that was anticipated by the structural clue *however*.

- Example #4 demonstrates again that you don't need explicit structural clues to stay ahead. Sometimes all you need is common sense. What do you think would happen to animals whose habitat had been destroyed? Would they thrive? Celebrate? Buy a condo in Florida? No, they'd probably "start dying out." They might even "become extinct."

- Examples #5 and #6 show clearly how you can use an author's language to anticipate what point he or she is going to make next. Here, we have identical sentences, except for one small (but very important) difference. In #5, the second sentence begins with the word *moreover*, indicating a continuation, an addition of similar information. In

#6, the second sentence starts with *On the other hand*, indicating a contrast, the other side of the coin, something that stands in opposition to what has come before. The blank to #5 should be filled by a phrase like: in a "clear and easy-to-understand" way. That would allow the sentences to make sense together: The program was easy to use; moreover, the instructions were easy to understand. But the sentences in #6 only make sense together if you fill the blank with something like: in a "confusing and unclear" way (to carry out the sense of contrast). To drive the point home, try reversing the suggested completions we just gave you. #5: The program was easier to use; moreover, the instructions were confusing and unclear. Huh? That doesn't make sense. And #6: The program was easier to use; on the other hand, it was easy to understand. Again, that makes no sense.

The language in most ACT Reading passages will be pointed in the ways illustrated above. You won't be flying blind when you read actively. You'll be making educated judgments about the structure of the passage based on the words and meanings that the author uses.

Below, for your reference, we've gathered together some important ways in which an author "tells" you where a reading passage is going.

COMMON STRUCTURAL CLUES

Indicating a contrast: *but, however, on the other hand, nevertheless*

Indicating a continuation with a similar or complementary thought:
  moreover, furthermore, ; (a semicolon)

Indicating a conclusion: *therefore, thus*

Indicating reasons for a conclusion: *since, because of, due to*

Indicating an example or illustration: *for instance, for example*

Now let's see how you can use this skill of active reading to develop a plan of attack for the ACT Reading section.

THE KAPLAN THREE-STEP READING APPROACH

There are many ways to read, depending on your purpose. When you read your teacher's comments on a paper you wrote, you go very slowly and work out every word to make sure you know what you did right and what you did wrong. When you read for pleasure, you read what you like and skim what you don't. When you cram for most tests, you try to remember the facts you know you'll be asked to recall.

For the ACT, however, you have a special purpose: to answer specific multiple-choice questions. And we've found that the best way to do that is initially to read a passage quickly and actively for general understanding, then refer to the passage to answer individual questions. Not everybody should use the exact same strategy, but we find that almost every ACT test taker can succeed by following these three basic steps:

1. **Preread the passage**

2. **Consider the question stem**

3. **Refer to the passage (before looking at the choices)**

For most students, these three tasks should together take up about nine minutes per passage. Less than three of those nine minutes should be spent prereading. The remaining time should be devoted to considering the questions and referring to the passage to check your answers to the questions. As we mentioned in the ACT Basics section, you'll probably want to take two sweeps through the questions for each passage, getting the doable ones the first time around, coming back for the harder ones.

Step 1: Preread the passage

Prereading means quickly working through the passage before trying to answer the questions. Remember to "know where you're going," anticipating how the parts of the passage fit together. In this preread, the main goals are to:

- Understand the "gist" of the passage (the "main idea").

- Get an overall idea of how the passage is organized—a kind of road map—so that it will be easier to refer to later.

You may want to underline key points, jot down notes, circle structural clues—whatever it takes to accomplish the two goals above. You may even want to label each paragraph, to fix in your mind how the paragraphs relate to one another and what aspect of the main idea is discussed in each. That could be your road map.

Two important reminders: *Don't* read slowly, and *don't* get bogged down in individual details. Most of the details in the passage aren't required for answering the questions, so why waste time worrying about them?

Step 2: Consider the question stem

Approaching the questions requires self-discipline in Reading. Most test takers have an almost irresistible urge to immediately jump to the answer choices to see what "looks okay." That's not a good idea. Don't let the answer choices direct your thinking. The test makers intentionally design the answers to confuse you if they can. So, if you look at the answer choices hoping that they'll suggest something to you, you're just falling into one of their cleverly set traps.

In Reading, you should think about the question stem (the part above the answer choices) without looking at the choices. In most questions, you won't be able to remember exactly what the passage said about the matter in question. That's okay. In fact, even if you *do* think you remember, don't trust your memory. Instead . . .

Step 3: Refer to the passage

THINK

As you work on the questions, remember to refer to the passage. Don't trust your memory. But don't confine yourself to the exact words the passage uses. This is a common trap. Think about what they mean.

You won't be rereading the whole passage, of course. But refer by finding the place where the answer to a question can be found (the question stem will sometimes contain a line reference to help you out; otherwise, rely on your road map of the passage). Your chosen answer should match the passage—not in exact vocabulary, perhaps, but in *meaning*.

ANSWER THE QUESTION

In Reading, many students never even try to answer the questions. They just look at the choices and try to "feel" their way to the answer. That won't work. Don't *feel* the answers: *Find* them in the passage.

It's extremely important in Reading to make a habit of answering the question in your own words (based on your checking of the passage) *before* looking at the answer choices. Most students waste enormous amounts of time thinking about answer choices in Reading. If you do that, you'll never finish, and you'll get so confused you'll probably get many questions wrong.

KAPLAN

FILL IN THE BLANKS

One good way to practice self-discipline in Reading questions is to approach the Reading test like a "fill-in-the-blank" test instead of multiple-choice. Spend time thinking about how you'd fill in the blank before you look at the choices.

When you look at answer choices in Reading, your mental process should be "matching." You've got an answer in your head based on what you've read and rechecked in the passage. You need to match it to one of the answer choices. Avoid trying to see if they "look right." You don't want to think very hard about the choices if you can help it. They're intended to confuse you, after all, so don't think about them any more than you absolutely have to.

Practicing the Three-Step Reading Approach
Now practice the Three-Step approach on the full-length ACT passage that follows. We're going to give you added incentive to use it by first showing you the questions *without* answer choices. That way you can't give in to the temptation to look at the choices before you think about the questions. The same questions in ACT style, *with* answer choices, will follow the passage. But try to answer them in "fill-in-the-blank" format first.

TIMING

Keep track of time. If you can, try to devote only nine minutes to each passage and its questions.

Questions	Your Answers
1. The author states that "on many manors meadow land was even more valuable than the arable" (lines 55–56) because:	it allowed oxen to regain their strength
2. According to the passage, the fact that the peasants' individual strips of land were unfenced subdivisions of larger fields required each peasant to:	plant the same crop
3. According to the second paragraph (lines 3–22), the fallow part of the arable had to be plowed a total of how many times in any given calendar year?	2
4. The passage suggests that the practice of peasants owning strips "scattered through the three fields in different parts" (lines 26–27) was instituted in order to:	assure that each peasant would have strips plowed partly @ take whatever imported animals
5. On the basis of the information in the passage, it may be inferred that people in medieval times did not think of sowing hay because:	harvested
6. As it is used in line 38, the word "garnered" means:	planted with grain the next year
7. According to the passage, if one of the arable's three great fields were left fallow one year, it would be:	
8. Which of the following conclusions is suggested by the fourth paragraph (lines 30–42)?	medieval peasants were restricted by custom
9. According to the passage, a manor's value might be judged according to the number of its plows because:	more plows = more tilled land
10. According to the passage, summer pasture for a manor's geese would be provided:	by whatsl

Passage I

By the tenth century most of northern Europe was divided into farming units known as manors . . . .

Almost always a manor comprised four parts: arable, meadow, waste, and the village area itself. The arable was of course the land
5   which grew the crops on which the inhabitants of the manor subsisted. To maintain fertility and keep down weeds it was necessary to fallow a part of the cultivated land each year. It was, therefore, usual (though not universal) to divide the arable into three fields. One such field was planted with winter grain, a second with spring grain, and
10   the third left fallow; the following year, the fallow field would be planted with winter grain, the field in which winter grain had been raised was planted with spring grain, and the third field left fallow. By following such a rotation, the cycle was completed every three years. Since the fallow field had to be plowed twice in the year in order to
15   keep down the weeds, and the others had to be plowed once, work for the plow teams extended almost throughout the year. Plowing stopped only at times when all hands were needed to bring in the harvest, or when the soil was too wet to be plowed, or was frozen. The amount of land that could be tilled was fixed fairly definitely by
20   the number of plows and plow teams which the manor could muster; and official documents sometimes estimated the wealth and value of a manor in terms of the number of plows it possessed.

The three great fields lay open, without fences, but were subdivided into numerous small strips (often one acre in size, i.e., the amount
25   of one day's plowing) which individual peasants "owned". The strips belonging to any one individual were scattered through the three fields in different parts, perhaps in order to assure that each peasant would have strips plowed early and late, in fertile and infertile parts of the arable land.

30   Custom severely restricted the individual's rights over his land. The time for plowing and planting was fixed by custom and each peasant had to conform, since he needed his neighbor's help to plow his strips and they needed his. Uniform cropping was imperative, since on a given day the village animals were turned into the fields to
35   graze after the harvest had been gathered, and if some individual planted a crop which did not ripen as early as that of his neighbors, he had no means of defending his field from the hungry animals. If his crop ripened sooner, on the other hand, it could not be garnered without trampling neighboring fields. Moreover, the very idea of
40   innovation was lacking: men did what custom prescribed, cooperated in the plowing and to some extent in the harvesting, and for many generations did not dream of trying to change.

The meadow was almost as important as the arable for the economy of the village. Hay from the meadow supported the
45 indispensable draught animals through the winter. The idea that hay might be sown did not occur to men in medieval times; consequently they were compelled to rely on natural meadows alone. One result was that in many manors shortage of winter fodder for the plow teams was a constant danger. It was com-
50 mon practice to feed oxen on leaves picked from trees, and on straw from the grain harvest; but despite such supplements the draught animals often nearly starved in winter. In some cases oxen actually had to be carried out from their winter stalls to spring pastures until some of their strength was recovered and
55 plowing could begin. Thus on many manors meadow land was even more valuable than the arable and was divided into much smaller strips (often the width of a scythe stroke).

The waste provided summer pasture for various animals of the manor: pigs, geese, cattle, and sheep. The animals of the
60 whole manor normally grazed together under the watchful eyes of some young children or other attendants who could keep them from wandering too far afield, and bring them back to the village at night. The waste also was the source of wood for fuel and for building purposes, and helped to supplement the food
65 supply with such things as nuts, berries, honey, and rabbits....

The fourth segment of the manor was the village itself, usually located in the center of the arable near a source of drinking water, and perhaps along a road or path or footpath leading to the outside world. The cottages of medieval peasants were
70 extremely humble, usually consisting of a single room, with earthen floor and thatched roof. Around each cottage normally lay a small garden in which various vegetables and sometimes fruit trees were planted. In the village streets chickens, ducks, and dogs picked up a precarious living.

From History of Western Civilization, a Handbook, *Sixth Edition, Copyright ©1986 by William H. McNeill; The University of Chicago Press, Chicago.*

1. The author states that "on many manors meadow land was even more valuable than the arable" (lines 55–56) because:

   A. the meadow produced the leaves and straw that fed the manor's various animals through the winter months.

   B. when necessary, the meadow could be used to grow supplementary crops.

   C. the strength of the manor's draught animals depended upon the meadow's production of winter fodder.

   D. profit could be made selling hay to manors with insufficient winter fodder for their draught animals.

2. According to the passage, the fact that the peasants' individual strips of land were unfenced subdivisions of larger fields required each peasant to:

   F. follow a fixed planting schedule so as to be able to harvest crops at the same time as the other peasants.

   G. harvest crops independently of his neighbors.

   H. limit the size of strips to what could be plowed in a single day.

   J. maintain small garden plots in order to provide his family with enough food.

3. According to the second paragraph (lines 3–22), the fallow part of the arable had to be plowed a total of how many times in any given calendar year?

   A. one

   B. two

   C. four

   D. six

4. The passage suggests that the practice of peasants owning strips "scattered through the three fields in different parts" (lines 26–27) was instituted in order to:

   F. divide resources fairly evenly.

   G. preserve the wealth of elite landowners.

   H. protect the three fields from overuse.

   J. force neighbors to work only their own lands.

5. On the basis of the information in the passage, it may be inferred that people in medieval times did not think of sowing hay because:

   A. hay sowing had not been done in the past.

   B. the need for more hay was not great enough to warrant the extra work.

   C. northern Europeans did not yet have the necessary farming techniques for successful hay cultivation.

   D. the tight schedule of cultivating the arable meant that the peasants had no time to cultivate extra crops.

6. As it is used in line 38, the word "garnered" means:

   F. planted

   G. watered

   H. gathered

   J. plowed

        Ⓕ Ⓖ Ⓗ Ⓙ

7. According to the passage, if one of the arable's three great fields were left fallow one year, it would be:

   A. left fallow for two more years in succession.

   B. planted the next year with winter grain only.

   C. planted the next year with spring grain only.

   D. planted with either winter or spring grain the next year.

        Ⓐ Ⓑ Ⓒ Ⓓ

8. Which of the following conclusions is suggested by the fourth paragraph (lines 30–42)?

     I. An individual was free to cultivate his own land in any way he wished.

     II. The manor was run according to tradition.

     III. Successful farming required cooperative methods.

   F. I and II only

   G. I and III only

   H. II and III only

   J. I, II, and III

        Ⓕ Ⓖ Ⓗ Ⓙ

9. According to the passage, a manor's value might be judged according to the number of its plows because:

   A. the more plows a manor had, the less land had to be left fallow.

   B. plows, while not in themselves valuable, symbolized great wealth.

   C. manors with sufficient plows could continue plowing throughout the year.

   D. the number of plows a manor owned determined how much land could be cultivated.

        Ⓐ Ⓑ Ⓒ Ⓓ

10. According to the passage, summer pasture for a manor's geese would be provided:

   F. next to cottages, within the village.

   G. on the fallow field of the arable.

   H. on the communal ground of the waste.

   J. on the whole of the meadow.

        Ⓕ Ⓖ Ⓗ Ⓙ

WHAT ABOUT ROMAN NUMERALS?

A small percentage of questions on the ACT—like question 8 in this passage—are Roman numeral questions. You're given three (sometimes four) statements, each labeled with a Roman numeral. The idea is to treat each one as a true-false statement. Decide which statements are true, and then choose the choice that includes those statements and *only* those statements. Often you can save yourself some time on these questions. For instance, in question 8: Once you decide that Statement I is *false*, you can eliminate choices F, G, and J, all of which include Statement I. Thus, you can get your answer, choice H, without even looking at Statements II and III! Always watch the answer choices in Roman numeral questions.

The Lay of the Land

Well, how'd you do? Did you remember to *refer* to the passage? You probably found that you had to do a more thorough check for some questions than for others. For relatively easy questions like 3 and 7, for instance, you might have been able to find your answer with real certainty just by reading and understanding the question, with only a quick double-check of the passage. Other questions, like question 5, might have required a more detailed check of the passage. Still other questions, like 1 and 8, might have given you real trouble unless you went back and studied the passage more thoroughly.

This passage, like most nonfiction passages on the ACT, was organized in a fairly logical way around the main idea, which you might have expressed as "the structure and common practices of the medieval manor." Here's one possible road map you might have come up with:

- Paragraph 1 (just a single sentence, really): Intro to the topic of medieval manors (divided, as cited in the first line of next paragraph, into arable, meadow, waste, and village)

- Paragraphs 2, 3, and 4: Discussion of the arable and the practices associated with it

- Paragraph 5: Discussion of the meadow

- Paragraph 6: Discussion of the waste

- Paragraph 7: Discussion of the village

It should be obvious why, in your prereading step, you really need to get some sense of the layout of the passage like this. Many questions don't contain specific line references to help you locate information, and if you don't have a road map of the passage in your head or on paper, you might get lost.

Below is a key to the 10 questions attached to this passage.

Key to Passage I
(Nonfiction—Social Studies)

	ANSWER	REFER TO	TYPE	COMMENTS
1.	C	Lines 43–56	Detail	The entire paragraph supports this claim.
2.	F	Lines 33–39	Detail	"Uniform cropping was imperative . . ."
3.	B	Lines 14–15	Detail	Don't confuse fallow with planted fields.
4.	F	Lines 25–39	Inference	Every peasant got some fertile and some infertile land—inferably, to be fair to each.
5.	A	Lines 39–42, 45–47	Inference	No line ref, so you had to have a sense of the structure to find this.
6.	H	Line 37–38	Detail	Use context. The crop is ripe, and so must be ready to be gathered.
7.	B	Lines 10–11	Detail	No line reference; otherwise no problem.
8.	H	Lines 30–42	Inference	I—lines 31 says the opposite II—lines 30–34 III—line 34–40
9.	D	Lines 19–20	Detail	No line reference; number of plows = amount of land.
10.	H	Lines 57–58	Detail	Whole paragraph devoted to describing waste.

NOTE: *We'll focus more on the individual question types in Reading Workout 2, at which time we'll show you a fast, effective approach to answering individual questions.*

As you continue in your ACT training, don't forget the very first piece of Reading advice we offered: read actively. Always know where you're going in a passage, and keep an eye on the structure. Use this habit whenever you read on the ACT, not just in the section called Reading. It helps on all four subject tests.

KAPLAN

SCIENCE WORKOUT 1
LOOK FOR PATTERNS

The Science Reasoning subject test causes a lot of unnecessary anxiety among ACT takers. Many people get so overwhelmed by the terminology and technicality of the passages that they just give up. What they fail to realize is that Science Reasoning is a little like the reverse of Math. In Math, you'll remember, we said that many of the questions are difficult problems based on elementary principles. In Science, on the other hand, many of the questions are elementary problems based on difficult material. So it's important that you never panic if you don't understand the passage in Science Reasoning. You can often get many of the questions right on a passage, even if you find it virtually incomprehensible!

Many ACT takers also tend to rely too heavily on what they've learned in school when approaching the Science Reasoning subject test. But as we've said, "remembering" is not the mind-set the ACT will reward. You couldn't possibly know the answers to ACT Science Reasoning questions in advance: You have to pull them out of the passages. All the information you need to answer the questions is right on the page. You just have to find it and use it.

Worrying about science knowledge can be a problem no matter how good or bad your science background is. Students who have done poorly in science tend to panic because they think they don't know enough. Students who have done well in science might know *too* much. Some questions include wrong choices that are scientifically correct but don't relate to the passages. Choosing such answers will get you no points on the ACT. So try not to rely primarily on your knowledge of science. Instead, use your ability to refer to the passages. It's your ability to reason and think critically that's being tested.

YOU DON'T NEED
TO KNOW SCIENCE

Knowing science is great, and it certainly can help your work in the Science Reasoning subject test. But you don't need to know a truckload of scientific facts to answer ACT Science questions. The questions are answerable from the information *in the passage*.

READING SKILLS AND "READING" SKILLS

ACT Science Reasoning requires many of the same skills that ACT Reading does. The strategies discussed in Reading Workout I will therefore also work well for many Science Reasoning passages. The most important difference between Reading and Science is that the "details" you have to find in the Science Reasoning passages almost all relate to numbers or scientific processes or both, and they are often contained in graphs and tables rather than in paragraph form. The secrets to finding most of these details are:

- **Reading graphs, tables, and research summaries** Many questions involve only accurately retrieving data from a single graph or table. Others involve combining knowledge from two different graphs or tables. Still others involve understanding experimental methods well enough to evaluate information contained in summaries of experiments.

- **Looking for patterns in the numbers that appear** Do these numbers get bigger or smaller? Where are the highest numbers? Where are the lowest numbers? At what point do the numbers change? A little calculation is sometimes required, but not much. In Science, you won't be *computing* with numbers so much as thinking about what they *mean*.

ANSWER THE QUESTION

As in Reading, it's tempting to avoid the process of actually answering the question and instead to just look at the answer choices and see which sounds best. Don't do it.

In Science, as in Reading, it's crucial to consider the questions and at least try to answer them before looking at the answer choices. Refer to the passage to find the answer, and try to match it with one of the choices. Use the process of elimination as a fallback strategy for hard questions—but don't make it your main approach.

THE THREE-STEP APPROACH TO READING IN SCIENCE

The same Three-Step Approach for Reading is also useful in Science. The three steps, you'll remember, are:

1. **Preread the passage**

2. **Consider the question stem**

3. **Refer to the passage (before looking at the choices)**

But in Science Reasoning, you have seven shorter passages to do instead of the four longer ones in Reading. Each passage should average five minutes. We recommend using just about one minute or so to preread the passage, and then a total of about four minutes to consider the questions and refer to the passage (that's about 40 seconds per question). Notice that this is less time prereading than in the Reading test.

Preread the Passage

It's especially important in Science Reasoning not to get bogged down in the details (we'll see that this is also critical in the Natural Sciences passage in Reading). Some of the material covered is extremely technical, and you'll just get frustrated trying to understand it completely. So it's crucial that you skim, to get a general idea of what's going on and—just as important—to get a sense of where certain types of data can be found.

Almost all Science Reasoning passages have the same general structure. They begin with an introduction. Always read through the introduction first to orient yourself. Some passages relate to material you may have already studied in high school. If you're familiar with the concepts in the passage, you may not need to do more than skim the introduction. If not, you'll want to read the introduction somewhat more carefully. But remember, don't focus on details. Try to get a sense of the overall situation.

After reviewing the introduction, quickly scan the rest of the passage. How is the information presented? Graphs? Diagrams? Are there experiments? What seems to be important? Size? Shape? Temperature? Speed? Chemical composition? Don't worry about details and don't try to remember it all. Plan to refer to the passage just as you would in Reading.

Consider the following introduction:

> Scientists researching the relationship between birds and dinosaurs have chosen to carefully examine three fossils dating from the Jurassic period: an *archaeopteryx* (the oldest known bird) at the British Museum in London, a *composognathus* (a dinosaur) at the Field Museum in Chicago, and a *teleosaurus* (a crocodile) at the National Museum in Beijing. All three creatures were about the same size as a turkey.

SCIENTIFIC TERMS

Scientific terms can be intimidating. But don't worry if you've never heard of things like *archaeopteryx* or *teleosaurus* before. The introduction tells you what they are. On the ACT, if you need to know the meaning of a special scientific term, the test will normally define it for you. If the test doesn't tell you what a word means, you can usually figure it out from the context (or else you won't need to know it).

Remember to read actively. Ask yourself: Why would the scientists choose these three creatures? Since the scientists are studying birds and dinosaurs, the first two choices seem natural. But why should they include a crocodile? Maybe the National Museum in Beijing had a special deal on crocodile bones? More likely it's because crocodiles are somewhat like dinosaurs, but not extinct.

As you preread the passage, you also want to make sure you know what any tables and graphs in the passage are meant to represent. Feel free to take notes, mark up the test booklet, or circle important information. Get a sense of what kind of data is contained in each graph and table, but don't read the data carefully yet! You may want to take note of general trends in the data, but don't waste time taking in information that may not be relevant to the questions. Remember, your goal is to answer questions, *NOT* to learn and remember everything that goes on in the passage.

Consider the Question Stem

Most of your time in Science Reasoning will be spent considering questions and referring to the passage to find the answers. Here's where you should do most of your really careful reading. It's essential that you understand exactly what the question is asking. Then, go back to the passage and get a sense of what the answer should be *before* looking at the choices.

There are really three basic kinds of Science questions:

- **Data Analysis Questions** For these questions, you'll almost certainly be going back to the graphs and tables in the passage to read and analyze their data. Look for patterns in the data (you'll get some practice reading graphs and tables later in this Workout). And try to get a sense of what the answer should be before looking at the choices.

- **Experiment Questions** Make sure you understand the purpose of the experiments. What are these scientists trying to prove? Try to identify the *control group*, if any, in each experiment, and the *factor* that is being varied from one trial to the next. (Experiments will be covered more fully in Science Workout 2.)

- **Principle Questions** These questions ask you to apply a scientific principle, or to identify ways of defending or attacking a principle. This includes making predictions based on a given theory, or showing how a hypothesis might be strengthened or weakened by particular findings. (These questions will be especially important for the Conflicting Viewpoints passage, discussed in Science Workout 3.)

As we mentioned, one possible pitfall in answering the questions is relying too heavily on your own knowledge of science. For example, the following question might have appeared with the passage excerpted above:

1. The dinosaur studied by the scientists, *composognathus*, was:
   A. definitely a reptile.
   B. definitely a bird.
   C. about the size of a turkey.
   D. larger than *archaeopteryx* or *teleosaurus*.

If you know that dinosaurs are usually classified as reptiles, choice A would be very tempting. But it's wrong. The passage doesn't say that. In fact, if we had read the rest of this passage, we would have learned that the researchers were questioning whether dinosaurs should be classified as reptiles or birds. What the passage *does* say is that all three of the creatures tested are turkey sized, making the correct choice C.

In answering questions, you should use your knowledge of scientific *methods* and *procedures*. But don't rely heavily on any knowledge of specific *facts*.

Refer to the Passage

As in Reading, you have to be diligent about referring to the passage. Your prereading of the passage should have given you an idea of where particular kinds of data can be found. Sometimes the questions themselves will direct you to the right place.

Be careful not to mix up units when taking information from graphs, tables, and summaries. Make sure you don't confuse *decreases* and *increases*. Many questions will hinge on whether you can correctly identify the factors that decrease and the ones that increase. The difference between a correct and an incorrect answer will often be a "decrease" where an "increase" should be. Read the questions carefully!

Once you've paraphrased the information and matched it to an answer choice, you might want to double-check the question to make sure that you've actually answered the question asked. Many of the questions in Science Reasoning are reversal questions. Always look for words like *not* and *except* in the questions.

READING TABLES AND GRAPHS

Most of the specific information in ACT Science passages is contained in tables or graphs, usually accompanied by explanatory material. Knowing how to read data from tables and graphs is critical to success on the Science Reasoning subject test!

In order to read most graphs and tables, you have to do four things:

- **Determine what is being represented**
- **Determine what the axes (or columns and rows) represent**
- **Take note of units of measurement**
- **Look for trends in the data**

Let's say you saw the graph on the following page in a Science Reasoning passage.

AIR TEMPERATURE AT VARIOUS
ALTITUDES AT TEST SITE #3

- **Determine what is being represented.** Most graphs and tables have titles that tell you what they represent. For some, though, you may have to get that information from the introduction. Here, the graph is representing how cold or hot the air is at various altitudes above a certain Test Site #3.

- **Determine what the axes represent.** These, too, are usually labeled. In the graph above, the *x*-axis represents distance above sea level in kilometers, while the *y*-axis represents the air temperature in degrees Celsius.

- **Take note of units of measurement.** Note that distance here is measured in *kilometers*, not miles or feet. Temperature is measured in degrees *Celsius*, not Fahrenheit.

- **Look for trends in the data.** The "pattern" of the data in this graph is pretty clear. As you rise in altitude, the temperature drops—the higher the altitude, the lower the temperature. (As we'll see later, this kind of trend is called an *inverse variation*.)

The sloping line on the graph represents the various temperatures measured at the various altitudes. To find what the measured temperature was at, say, 2 km above sea level, find the 2 km point on the *x*-axis and trace your finger directly up from it until it hits the line. It does so at about the level of 3° C. In other words, at an altitude of 2 km above sea level at Test Site #3, the air temperature was about 3° C.

Be careful with units of measurement! Most passages use the metric system, but a few may use traditional or British units of measure. You won't be expected to remember oddball unit conversions like 8 furlongs = 1 mile or 2.54 cm = 1 in, and passages that use special units of measure such as microns or parsecs will define these units if necessary. But don't assume that all the units in the graphs match the units in the questions. For instance, try the following question.

KAPLAN

2. At what altitude did the meteorologists measure an air temperature of
   10° C?
   F. 1.4 m
   G. 140 m
   H. 1400 m
   J. 14 km

Many test takers solving the problem above would find the point on the line at the level of 10° C on the *y*-axis, trace their fingers down to the *x*-axis, see that the altitude would be about halfway between 1 and 2 (a little closer to 1, maybe), and then quickly choose F. But F is wrong, since F gives you 1.4 *meters*, while the graph figures are given in *kilometers*. Remember to translate the data! A kilometer is 1,000 meters, so 1.4 kilometers would be 1.4 times 1,000 meters = 1,400 meters. That's choice H.

You should follow a similar procedure with tables of information. For instance, in the introduction to the passage in which the following table might have appeared, you would have learned that scientists were trying to determine the effects of two pollutants (Pb and Hg, lead and mercury) on the trout populations of a particular river:

Location	Water temperature (°C)	Presence of Pb (parts per million)	Presence of Hg (parts per million)	Population Density of Speckled Trout (# per 100 m³)
1	15.4	0	3	7.9
2	16.1	0	1	3.5
3	16.3	1	67	0
4	15.8	54	3	5.7
5	16.0	2	4	9.5

- **Determine what is being represented.** There's no informative title for this table, but the introduction would have told you what the table represents.

- **Determine what the columns and rows represent.** In tables, you get columns and rows instead of *x*-and *y*-axes. But the principle is the same. Here, each row represents the data from a different numbered location on the river. Each column represents different data—water temperature, presence of the first pollutant, presence of the second pollutant, population of one kind of trout, population of another kind of trout.

- **Take note of units of measurement.** Temperature is measured in degrees Celsius. The two pollutants are measured in parts per million (or ppm). The trout populations are measured in average number per 100 cubic meters of river.

• **Look for trends in the data.** Glancing at the table, it looks like locations where the Hg concentration is high (as in Location 3), the trout population is virtually nonexistent. This would seem to indicate that trout find a high Hg concentration incompatible. But notice the location where the other pollutant is abundant—in Location 4. Here, both trout populations seem to be more in line with other locations. That would seem to indicate that this other pollutant—Pb—is NOT quite so detrimental to trout populations (though we'd have to do more studies if it turned out that all of the trout in that location had three eyes).

HOW TABLES AND GRAPHS RELATE

To really understand tables and graphs, it helps to see how the same information can be represented in both. For instance, look at the following table and graph.

Concentration of *E. coli* in Cooling Pool B	
DISTANCE FROM EFFLUENT PIPE 3	1000s OF E. COLI PER CENTILITRE
zero m.	4
5 m.	56
10 m.	276
15 m.	140
20 m.	75

Concentration of *E. coli* in Cooling Pool B

The table and graph above represent the exact same data. And here's yet another way of depicting the same data, in a bar chart.

Concentration of *E. coli* in Cooling Pool B

Remember that data can be represented in many different ways. But however it appears in the passage—in tables, graphs, or charts—you'll have to read and translate it to answer the questions.

LOOK FOR PATTERNS AND TRENDS

When you first examine a graph or table, don't focus on exact numbers. Look for *patterns* in the numbers. But don't assume that there is *always* a pattern or trend: Finding that there *isn't* a pattern is just as important as finding that there *is* one. When looking for patterns and trends, you should keep three specific things in mind:

- **Extremes** (maximums and minimums)

- **Critical points** (or points of change)

- **Direct** or **inverse variation**

Extremes

Extremes—or maximums and minimums—are merely the highest and lowest points that things reach. In tables, the minimums and maximums will be represented by relatively high and low numbers. In graphs, they will be represented by highs and lows on the *x*- and *y*-axes. In bar charts, they will be represented by the tallest and shortest bars.

In Table 1, what location on the river has the maximum concentration of Hg? Of Pb?

Location	Water temperature (°C)	Presence of Pb (parts per million)	Presence of Hg (parts per million)	Population Density of Speckled Trout (# per 100 m^3)
1	15.4	0	3	7.9
2	16.1	0	1	3.5
3	16.3	1	67	0
4	15.8	54	3	5.7
5	16.0	2	4	9.5

A glance at the numbers tells you that Location 3—with 67 ppm—represents the maximum for Hg, while Location 4—with 54 ppm—represents the maximum for Pb.

How can taking note of maximums and minimums help you spot patterns in the data? Look again at Table 1 above. Notice that the maximum concentration of Hg—67 ppm—just happens to coincide with the *minimums* for trout population—0 per 100 m^3 for both. That's a good indication that there's some cause and effect going on here. Somehow, a maximum of Hg concentration correlates with a minimum of trout population. The obvious (though not airtight) conclusion is that a high concentration of Hg is detrimental to trout populations. And this kind of finding is much more readily evident when you look at maximums and minimums.

Critical Points

Critical points—or points of change—are values at which something dramatic happens. For example, at atmospheric pressure water freezes at 0° C and boils at about 100° C. If you examined water at various temperatures below the lower of these two critical points, it would be solid. If you examined water at various temperatures between the two points, it would be liquid. If you examined water above the higher critical point, it would be a gas.

When you scan the numbers in a chart or points on a graph, look for places where values bunch together or where suddenly something special happens. At atmosphere pressure 0° C is a critical point for water—as is 100° C—since something special happens: The substance changes form.

To find out how critical points can help you evaluate data, turn the page and take another look at the graph representing the concentration of *E. coli* (a common type of bacterium) in Cooling Pool B.

Meters distant from Effluent Pipe 3

Notice how the concentration is low very near Effluent Pipe 3. From there, it rises until about 10 meters away from the pipe, then it falls again, tapering off as you get farther from the pipe. There's a critical point, then, right around 10 meters from Effluent Pipe 3. Somehow, that vicinity is most conducive to the growth of *E. coli*. As you move closer to or farther away from that point, the concentration falls off. So, in looking to explain the data, you'd want to focus on that location—10 meters from the pipe. What is it about that location that's so special? What makes it the hot new place for *E. coli* to see and be seen?

Variation

Variation is a bit more complex than extremes or critical points. Variation refers to the way two different things change *in relation to each other*. Direct variation means that two things vary in the same way: When one gets bigger, the other does too; when one gets smaller, so does the other. Inverse variation means that two things vary in *opposite* ways: When one gets bigger, the other gets smaller, and vice versa. We saw an example of inverse variation in the air temperature graph, where altitude and air temperature varied inversely—as altitude *in*creased, air temperature *de*creased.

But here's a more familiar example for nonscientists: As you walk home from school at a constant rate, time varies directly with the distance from school and indirectly with the distance from home. As time passes (as the amount of time *in*creases) you move farther away from school (the distance from school *in*creases). Both increase in the same direction. That's direct variation.

But as the amount of time *in*creases, the distance to your house *de*creases. The two change in opposite ways. That's inverse variation.

Many of the graphs on the ACT are intended to display variation. As we've just seen, graphs with *x-y* coordinates (horizontal and vertical axes) are used for this purpose. On such a graph, direct variation will be displayed by lines moving upward to the right. Inverse variations will plot out to lines moving downward to the right.

In the two graphs above, both variations make straight lines. This is because the speed at which you walked was constant. Sometimes, direct or inverse variations can be more complicated because the rates are *not* constant. Such variation could be called "nonlinear," because when plotted on a graph, it produces wavy, zigzag, broken, or curved lines. For example, if you started out from school running, then gradually slowed down as you got tired, then stopped for a while about halfway home to smell some roses before finally continuing home at a steady pace, the variation would not be linear. Distance from school would increase more slowly as time progressed, and for a while the distance wouldn't increase *at all*. Distance to home would decrease more slowly as you slowed down, and would also stop decreasing during the time you stopped to smell the roses.

Graphs of this kind often look strange, but they can represent very ordinary activities. If you know how to walk home from school, you can probably understand the kinds of relationships and number patterns the ACT uses.

The Real Thing

Now that you've had some practice with graphs and tables, let's take a look at a full-fledged Science Reasoning passage that requires these skills. Give yourself about seven minutes to do the passage and the questions (on the actual test, you'll want to move a bit faster).

Passage I

Although the effective acceleration due to gravity at the earth's surface is often treated as a constant ($g = 9.80$ m/sec^2) its actual value varies from place to place because of several factors.

First, a body on the surface of any rotating spheroid experiences an effective force perpendicular to the rotational axis and proportional to the speed of rotation. This centrifugal force, which counteracts gravity, varies with latitude, increasing from zero at the poles to a maximum at the equator. In addition, because the earth "bulges" at the equator, a body at equatorial sea level is farther from the center of the earth than is a body at polar sea level. Figure 1 shows the variation of mean values of g at sea level resulting from both effects; the contribution from "bulging" is about half that from rotation.

Figure 1

Measurements of g also vary depending on local rock density and altitude. Table 1 shows the effect of altitude on g at various points above sea level.

Table 1

Change in Altitude (km)	g (m/sec$_2$)
1	-0.0031
5	-0.0154
10	-0.0309
25	-0.0772
30	-0.1543

3. If the earth's density were uniform, at approximately what latitude would calculations using an estimated value at sea level of $g = 9.80$ m/sec^2 produce the least error?

    A.   0°

    B.   20°

    C.   40°

    D.   80°
                               Ⓐ Ⓑ Ⓒ Ⓓ

4. According to the passage, the effective acceleration due to gravity at the surface of a rotating but non-"bulging" sphere would tend to be greatest at the:

    F.   equator, where the rotation effect is strongest.

    G.   equator, where the rotation effect is weakest.

    H.   poles, where the rotation effect is strongest.

    J.   poles, where the rotation effect is weakest.
                               Ⓕ Ⓖ Ⓗ Ⓙ

5. Given the information in the passage, which of the following figures most closely approximates the value of g at a point 10 km high along the equator?

    A.   9.75 m/sec^2

    B.   9.80 m/sec^2

    C.   9.81 m/sec^2

    D.   9.87 m/sec^2
                               Ⓐ Ⓑ Ⓒ Ⓓ

6. Given the information presented in the passage, an increase in the speed of the earth's rotation would most likely cause which of the following results at sea level?

      I.   An increase in g only along the equator

      II.   A decrease in g at all nonpolar points

      III.   No change in g at the poles

      IV.   An increase in g at the poles

    F.   II only

    G.   I and III only

    H.   II and III only

    J.   II and IV only
                               Ⓕ Ⓖ Ⓗ Ⓙ

7. Suppose that the earth stopped rotating but still "bulged." Based on information from the passage, the value of g at sea level at the equator would be:

    A.   exactly 9.80 m/sec^2.

    B.   greater than 9.78 m/sec^2.

    C.   exactly 9.78 m/sec^2.

    D.   less than 9.78 m/sec^2.
                               Ⓐ Ⓑ Ⓒ Ⓓ

8. According to the information in Figure 1, the value of g :

    F.   changes by a greater average amount per degree latitude between 30° and 60° than it does near the equator or poles.

    G.   changes by a greater average amount per degree latitude near the equator or poles than it does between 30° and 60°.

H. increases by an average of 5.8 m/sec² per degree latitude from the equator to the poles.

J. decreases by an average of 3.1 x 10⁻³ m/sec² per degree latitude from the equator to the poles.

Ⓕ Ⓖ Ⓗ Ⓙ

CONFUSED?

Remember, you score points by answering the questions right, not by understanding the passages completely. You *can* get points on a Science Reasoning passage, even if you don't understand it!

Don't Freak!

This was actually a relatively simple, straightforward Science Reasoning passage, but the terminology may have been intimidating nonetheless. The introduction tells you that the issue here is gravity, and how its pull (in other words, the acceleration due to gravity) changes because of several factors. Those factors—and the changes they cause—are represented in Figure 1 (which deals with the factor of latitude, which has an effect because of global "bulge" and the rotation effect) and Table 1 (which deals with the factor of altitude).

Analyzing Figure 1 as described above, you should have seen that the graph is supposed to show how *g* (the acceleration due to gravity) is affected by latitude (i.e., north-south location on the globe). The higher the latitude (the greater the distance from the equator), the greater the value of *g*. Thus, there's a *direct variation* between the two, though the variation isn't constant. As the curves at the beginning and ending of the line in Figure 1 tell you, the increase in *g* is "slower" near the equator and near the poles.

Notice how you could have answered **Question 3** just by understanding Figure 1. Question 3 asks, assuming the earth's density were uniform, "at what latitude would calculations using an estimated value at sea level of *g* = 9.80 m/sec² produce the least error?" First, figure out what that question is asking. You remember this question; we mentioned it in ACT Basics. It's simply asking you: Where would you get an actual value of *g* closest to 9.80 m/sec²? Find 9.80 on the *y*-axis of the graph, follow across until you intersect with the curved line, and see where you are on the *x*-axis. That turns out to be about a third of the way from 30° to 60° latitude. In other words, choice C, 40°, is the answer.

Similarly, **Question 4** can be knocked off pretty easily. Where is the "effective acceleration due to gravity"(*g*, in other words) greatest (on a rotating but nonbulging sphere)? To answer this question you need to understand Figure 1. Although Figure 1 includes the effects of both rotation and bulging, it's clear that both factors cause the effective acceleration due to gravity to increase as the latitude increases from 0° to 90°. So the effective acceleration would be the greatest at 90° latitude —the poles. But that only narrows the choices down to H and J. To decide between them, we have to infer further whether the rotation effect is weakest or greatest at the poles. The second paragraph of the introduction gives you the answer: The effect of rotation ("centrifugal force") is zero at the poles. You can't get weaker than zero, so the answer is choice J.

We'll get to **Question 5** below.

To answer **Question 6**, you again need only understand the introduction and Figure 1. This is a Principle question, asking you to apply the principles about rotational effects on g to a hypothetical situation in which rotation *in*creased. Well, as you learned in the introduction, the effects of the earth's rotation tend to lessen the effects of gravity, so increasing the speed of rotation would lessen the effects of gravity even more—i.e., a lesser value for g except at the poles, where the effect of gravity is zero. So g would *de*crease everywhere but at the poles. Statements II and III are true, while Statements I and IV are false. Choice H is correct.

Question 7 requires more applications of principles, and is yet another question that can be answered by simply reading Figure 1. It asks you to suppose that rotation effects (one of the two factors affected by latitude) ceased, but that the earth still bulged at the equator. What would be the value of g? Well, again, rotation tends to "counteract" gravity, so it would have a depressing effect on g. *Without* rotation, then, g would be less depressed—it would go up, in other words. That means (reading from Figure 1 again) that g at 0° latitude (the equator) would, in the absence of rotation, go up from its current value of 9.78. That's why B is correct.

Question 8 (not to get monotonous) is still another that can be answered just by a proper reading of Figure 1. It asks you to describe what the graph tells you about the value of g. As we saw, the value rises slowly as you head away from 0° latitude (the equator), rises more rapidly in the middle latitudes, and slows down again near 90° latitude (the poles). That's best described by choice F. (Choice G gets it backwards—remember to read the choices carefully!) Choices H and J would involve you in some extensive calculations, at the end of which you'd realize that they were not true. But there's no reason to get that far. If you find yourself doing extensive calculation, you should know that you're on the wrong track. ACT Science Reasoning will involve simple calculation only.

Notice how you could have answered five of the six questions with just a rudimentary grasp of the introduction and an understanding of how to "read" Figure 1.

The other question, **Question 5**, requires that you read both Figure 1 and Table 1 properly. It asks for the value of g at the equator (that information comes from Figure 1), but at an altitude of 10 km above sea level (that information comes from Table 1). Figure 1 tells you that the value of g at the equator *at sea level* would be 9.78 m/sec². But at 10 km above sea level, according to Table 1, g would be slightly lower—0.0309 m/sec² lower, to be precise. So, 9.78 minus 0.0309 would be about 9.75 m/sec². That's choice A.

Look for Patterns

The passage and questions above should convince you of one thing: To do well on Science Reasoning, you have to be able to read graphs and tables, paying special attention to trends and patterns in the data. Sometimes, that's ALL you need to do to get most of the points on a passage.

ENGLISH WORKOUT 2
MAKE IT MAKE SENSE

In English Workout 1, we saw that the ACT expects you to use your words efficiently, and that, in fact, the shortest answer is correct remarkably often. But, obviously, the shortest answer is often wrong. What could make it wrong? It may not mean what it says.

REMINDER

Should you always pick the shortest answer in English? NO! All things being equal, lean toward choosing the shortest answer, but don't just pick the shortest answer without thinking.

Take this example: "Abraham Lincoln's father was a model of hard-working self-sufficiency. He was born in a log cabin he built with his own hands." Well, that's a cute trick, being born in a cabin you built yourself. Presumably the writer means that *Abe* was born in a cabin that his *father* built. But the literal meaning of the example is that the father somehow managed to be born in a cabin that he himself had built.

DON'T TAKE ANY NONSENSE!

It's possible, of course, to analyze this example in terms of the rules of apostrophe use and pronoun reference. But that's not practical for the ACT, even for a student who has good grammar skills. There isn't time to carefully analyze every question, consider all the rules involved, and decide on an answer. You have to do seventy English questions in only forty minutes—that's almost two questions per minute.

But there *is* plenty of time to approach examples like this one in a more pragmatic way. Ask yourself, *Does this stuff make sense?*

THINK

What you read always has two possible meanings: an intended meaning, and a literal meaning. The intended meaning is what the writer was trying to say. The literal meaning is what the author actually did say. The ACT demands that the intended and literal meanings of every passage be exactly the same.

Most of the time, we may not notice mistakes in which writers fail to say what they mean because we've taught ourselves to read for intended meaning only. We try to figure out what the author was *trying* to say, and we don't really care much if an author isn't exactly clear.

But for the ACT, it's important to care. You need to adjust your mindset. After deciding whether or not the selection in a question is concise and relevant (Step 1 in the Three-Step Approach), the next step isn't to remember lots of rules; it's to make sure that the sentence says exactly what it's supposed to *mean*. If not, your job is to make it so. Your job, in other words, is to make it make sense.

SENSE QUESTIONS

We at Kaplan have a name for questions that test meaning errors—Sense Questions. Once you get the hang of them, these questions can actually be fun. Errors of meaning are often funny once you see them. The following passage gives examples of the most common kinds of Sense Questions you'll find on the ACT.

Passage I

Most people—even those who've never read

Daniel Defoe's *Robinson Crusoe*—are familiar

with the strange story of the sailor shipwrecked on

a far-flung Pacific island. Relatively few of them,

however, know that Crusoe's <u>story. It was</u> actually
                                    1

based on the real-life adventures of a Scottish

seaman, Alexander Selkirk. Selkirk came to the

Pacific as a member of a 1703 privateering

expedition led by a captain named William Dampier.

During the voyage, Selkirk became dissatisfied

with conditions aboard ship. <u>After a bitter quarrel</u>
                                          2
<u>with his captain, he put Selkirk ashore</u> on tiny Mas a
                    2
Tierra, one of the islands of Juan Fernandez, off

the coast of Chile. Stranded, Selkirk lived there

alone—in much the <u>same manner as</u> Defoe's
                              3

Crusoe—until 1709, when he was finally rescued by

another English privateer.

Upon his return to England, Selkirk found

himself a <u>celebrity, his</u> strange tale had already
                  4

1. A. NO CHANGE
   B. story: was
   C. story, was
   D. story was

   Ⓐ Ⓑ Ⓒ Ⓓ

2. F. NO CHANGE
   G. Quarreling with his captain, the boat was put ashore
   H. Having quarreled with his captain, Selkirk was put ashore
   J. Having quarreled with his captain, they put Selkirk ashore

   Ⓕ Ⓖ Ⓗ Ⓙ

3. A. NO CHANGE
   B. same manner that
   C. identical manner that
   D. identical way as

   Ⓐ Ⓑ Ⓒ Ⓓ

4. F. NO CHANGE
   G. celebrity, but his
   H. celebrity. His
   J. celebrity his

   Ⓕ Ⓖ Ⓗ Ⓙ

KAPLAN 103

become the talk of pubs and coffeehouses

throughout the British Isles. The story even

reached the ears of Richard Steele, who featured it

in his periodical, *The Tatler*. Eventually, <u>he became</u> the
                                              5
subject of a bestselling book, *A Cruizing Voyage Round*

the World, by Woodes Rogers. <u>And while</u> there is some
                                    6
evidence that Defoe, a journalist, may actually have

interviewed Selkirk personally, most literary historians

believe that it was the reprinting of the Rogers book

in 1718 that served as the real stimulus for Defoe's

novel.

    In *Crusoe*, which <u>has been published</u> in
                                    7
1719, Defoe took substantial liberties with the Selkirk

story. For example, while Selkirk's presence on the

island was of course <u>known for many people</u> (certainly
                                8
everyone in the crew that stranded him there), no one

in the novel is aware of Crusoe's survival of the wreck

and presence on the island. Moreover, while Selkirk's

exile lasted just six years, Crusoe's goes on for a much

more dramatic, though less credible, twenty-eight

<u>(over four times as long)</u>. But Defoe's most blatant
                9
embellishment of the tale is the invention of the

character of Friday, for whom there was no

5. A. NO CHANGE
   B. Selkirk became
   C. his became
   D. he becomes

Ⓐ Ⓑ Ⓒ Ⓓ

6. F. NO CHANGE
   G. But since
   H. And therefore
   J. OMIT the underlined portion and start the sentence with "There."

Ⓕ Ⓖ Ⓗ Ⓙ

7. A. NO CHANGE
   B. was published
   C. had been published
   D. will have been published

Ⓐ Ⓑ Ⓒ Ⓓ

8. F. NO CHANGE
   G. widely known among people
   H. known about many people
   J. known to many people

Ⓕ Ⓖ Ⓗ Ⓙ

9. A. NO CHANGE
   B. (much longer)
   C. (a much longer time, of course)
   D. OMIT the underlined portion

Ⓐ Ⓑ Ⓒ Ⓓ

counterpart whatsoever in the real-life story.

Because of its basis in fact, *Robinson Crusoe*
    10
is often regarded as the first major novel in English

literature. Still popular today, contemporary
                    11
audiences enjoyed the book as well. In fact, two
           11
sequels, in which Crusoe returns to the island after

his rescue, were eventually published. Though to
                    12
little acclaim. Meanwhile, Selkirk himself never

gave a hoot about returning to the island that
        13
had made him famous. Legend has it that he never

gave up his eccentric living habits, spending his last

years in a cave teaching alley cats to dance in his

spare time. One wonders if even Defoe himself could

have invented a more fitting end to the bizarre story

of his shipwrecked sailor. ⬛14 ⬛15

10. F. NO CHANGE
    G. Despite
    H. Resulting from
    J. As a consequence of

Ⓕ Ⓖ Ⓗ Ⓙ

11. A. NO CHANGE
    B. Still read today, Defoe's contemporaries also enjoyed it.
    C. Viewed by many even then as a classic, the book is still popular to this day.
    D. Much read in its day, modern audiences still find the book compelling.

Ⓐ Ⓑ Ⓒ Ⓓ

12. F. NO CHANGE
    G. published, though
    H. published although
    J. published; although

Ⓕ Ⓖ Ⓗ Ⓙ

13. A. NO CHANGE
    B. evinced himself as desirous of returning
    C. could whip up a head of steam to return
    D. expressed any desire to return

Ⓐ Ⓑ Ⓒ Ⓓ

> Items 14 and 15 pose questions about the passage as a whole.

14. Considering the tone and subject matter of the preceding paragraphs, is the last sentence an appropriate way to end the essay?
    F. Yes, because it is necessary to shed some doubt on Defoe's creativity.
    G. Yes, because the essay is about the relationship between the real Selkirk and Defoe's fictionalized version of him.
    H. No, because there is nothing "bizarre" about Selkirk's story as it is related in the essay.
    J. No, because the focus of the essay is more on Selkirk himself than on Defoe's fictionalized version of him.

Ⓕ Ⓖ Ⓗ Ⓙ

15. This essay would be most appropriate as part of a:
    A. scholarly study of eighteenth-century maritime history.
    B. study of the geography of the islands off of Chile.
    C. history of privateering in the Pacific.
    D. popular history of English literature.

Ⓐ Ⓑ Ⓒ Ⓓ

ANSWERS

1. D, 2. H, 3. A, 4. H, 5. B, 6. F, 7. B, 8. J, 9. D, 10. G, 11. C, 12. G,
13. D, 14. G, 15. D

You may have found these Sense Questions harder than the Economy Questions in English Workout 1. The shortest answers here aren't right nearly as often. But, all other things being equal, the shortest answer is still your best bet. It's correct about half of the time—eight out of fifteen questions: numbers 1, 3, 7, 8, 9, 10, 12, and 13.

On some of the questions in Passage I above, you may not have gotten past Step 1 in the Three-Step Approach. Question 9, for example, presented material that was clearly redundant. We certainly know that 28 years is longer than 6 (and if we're really up on our math we can even figure out that 28 is "more than four times" 6), so including any parenthetical aside like the ones given would be unnecessary. Remember, when in doubt, take it out. As we saw in English Workout 1, questions that include an "OMIT" option, and those in which some of the answers are much longer than others, are usually testing writing economy.

In the rest of the questions in this passage, the answers differ in other ways. They may join or fragment sentences, rearrange things, or add words that affect the meaning of the sentences. When the answers are all about the same length, as in most of the questions here, the question is more likely to test sense. Consider the shortest answer first, but don't be as quick to select it and move on. Think about the effect each choice has on the *meaning* of the sentence and pick longer answers if the shortest one doesn't make sense.

> **HINT:** *Students tend to reject informal writing as "incorrect." But ACT passages are written at various levels of formality. Some are as stiff as textbooks. Others are as casual as a talk with friends. Pay attention to the tone of the words. Are they serious? Are they laid back? Stay with the author's tone. Don't always stay formal.*

GOOD GRAMMAR MAKES GOOD SENSE

The ACT test makers include questions like those in Passage I to test many different rules of writing mechanics. Though it's not *necessary* to think about rules to answer the questions, familiarity with the rules can give you an alternative approach. The more ways to think about a question you have, the more likely you are to find the right answer.

We'll discuss some of these examples in groups based on what they're designed to test. That way we can briefly discuss the rules, but also show you how the basic strategic approach of "make it make sense" can get you the answers without a lot of technical analysis. Let's start with **Question 1**.

...Relatively few of them,

however, know that Crusoe's <u>story. It was</u> actually
                              1
based on the real-life adventures of a Scottish

seaman, Alexander Selkirk.

1. A. NO CHANGE
   B. story: was
   C. story, was
   D. story was

If the underlined section for Question 1 were left as it is, the second sentence of the passage would be incomplete. It wouldn't make sense. "Relatively few people know that Crusoe's story" *what*? To make it make sense, you've got to continue the sentence so that it can tell us what it is that few people know about Crusoe's story. The three alternatives all do that, but B introduces a nonsensical colon, while C adds a comma when there's no pause in the sentence. D, however, continues the sentence—adding nothing unnecessary, but making it complete.

COMPLETENESS

What Question 1 is testing is something we call completeness—the requirement that every sentence should consist of an entire thought. Don't just blindly judge the completeness of a sentence by whether or not it contains a subject and a verb. The alleged sentence—"Relatively few of them, however, know that Crusoe's story."—actually *does* contain a subject and a verb, but it's still not complete. It leaves a thought hanging. Don't leave thoughts hanging on the ACT. The test makers don't like it one bit.

Question 12 tests the same concept:

...In fact, two

sequels, in which Crusoe returns to the island after

his rescue, were eventually <u>published. Though to</u>
                                              12
little acclaim.

12. F. NO CHANGE
    G. published, though
    H. published although
    J. published; although

Here, however, the fragment should be more obvious, since the clause that's trying to pass itself off as a sentence—"Though to little acclaim."—contains neither a subject nor a verb. That's the technical reason it's wrong, and if you recognized this, great. But on a more intuitive level, it just doesn't make sense to say, as a complete thought: "Though to little acclaim." So, you've got to make it make sense.

Clearly, that fragment has to be connected to the sentence before it, so F and J are wrong, since both would leave the fragment isolated. H goes too far in the other direction, omitting any punctuation at all between the fragment and the main body of the sentence, and that's no good. But the

KAPLAN 107

correct choice, G, does just what we need it to do: It connects the fragment logically to the main sentence, but it provides a comma to represent the pause between the two.

Again, knowing the rules of grammar certainly helps here, but you could have gotten this answer by just using common sense.

SENTENCE STRUCTURE

Technically, of course, Questions 1 and 12 test sentence structure, which is a broader topic of which completeness is one part. The "rules" of good sentence structure require that every sentence contain a complete thought. A "sentence" without a complete thought is called a *fragment*. A "sentence" with *too many* complete thoughts (usually connected by commas) is called a *run-on*. That's what we find in **Question 4**:

Upon his return to England, Selkirk found himself a

<u>celebrity, his</u> strange tale had already become the talk
    4
of pubs and coffeehouses throughout the British Isles.

4. **F.** NO CHANGE
   G. celebrity, but his
   H. celebrity. His
   J. celebrity his

Here we have two complete thoughts: (1) Selkirk found himself a celebrity upon his return, and (2) his tale was bandied about the pubs and coffeehouses. You can't just run these two complete thoughts together with a comma, as the underlined portion does. And you certainly can't just run them together *without* a comma or anything else, as choice J does. You *can* relate the two thoughts with a comma and a linking word (*and,* for instance), but choice G's inclusion of the word *but* makes no sense. It implies a contrast, while the two complete thoughts are actually very similar. Thus, you should create two sentences, one for each thought. That's what correct choice H does.

Remember to make sure all of the sentences in a passage contain at least one, but not more than one, complete thought. Fragments and run-ons appear frequently on the English section of the ACT. Both are sense problems that need to be corrected.

MODIFIERS

Question 2 tests modifier problems:

…<u>After a bitter quarrel with his captain, he put Selkirk</u>
                            2
<u>ashore</u> on tiny Mas a Tierra, one of the islands of Juan
    2
Fernandez…

2. **F.** NO CHANGE
   G. Quarreling with his captain, the boat was put ashore
   H. Having quarreled with his captain, Selkirk was put ashore
   J. Having quarreled with his captain, they put Selkirk ashore

In a well-written sentence, it must be clear exactly what words or phrases in the sentence are modifying (or referring to) what other words or phrases in the sentence. In the underlined portion here, the clause "after a bitter quarrel with his captain" *should* modify the pronoun that follows it— *he*. But it doesn't. The *he* who put Selkirk ashore must be the captain, but it can't be the captain who had "a bitter quarrel with his captain." That doesn't make sense (unless the captain quarrels with himself). So put the thing modified next to the thing modifying it. The person who quarreled with his captain was Selkirk—not the boat and not "they," whoever they are—so H is correct.

If you recognized the problem with Question 2 as a "misplaced modifier," that's great. Fantastic, even. But you didn't have to know the technicalities to get the right answer here. You just had to make the sentence make sense.

Question 11 tests a similar problem:

...Still popular today, contemporary
                11
audiences enjoyed the book as well.
                11

11. A. NO CHANGE

B. Still read today, Defoe's contemporaries also enjoyed it.

C. Viewed by many even then as a classic, the book is still popular to this day.

D. Much read in its day, modern audiences still find the book compelling.

The way the sentence is written, it basically means that contemporary audiences are "still popular today." That doesn't make sense. The *intended* meaning is that the *book* is still popular today, as it was then. Choice C fixes the sense problem by putting its modifier—"viewed by many even then as a classic"—next to the thing it modifies—"the book." Notice that the other choices all misplace their modifiers in the same way, making them modify "Defoe's contemporaries" (in B) and "modern audiences" (in D).

As a rule of thumb, you should always make sure that modifiers are as close as possible to the things they modify.

IDIOM (PROPER WORD FORM AND CHOICE)

Question 3 tests a rather hazy linguistic concept known as *idiom*. The word "idiomatic" refers to language that, well, uses words in the right way. Many words have special rules. If you're a native speaker of the language, you probably picked up many of these rules by ear before your eighth birthday; if you're not a native speaker, you had to learn them one by one.

...Stranded, Selkirk lived there alone—

in much the <u>same manner as</u> Defoe's Crusoe—until
                    3
1709, when he was finally rescued by another...

3. A. NO CHANGE

B. same manner that

C. identical manner that

D. identical way as

The sentence as written actually makes perfect sense. Selkirk lived in "much the same manner as" Defoe's Crusoe. The phrase *much the same* calls for *as* to complete the comparison between Selkirk's and Crusoe's ways of life. Note how B and C would create completeness problems—in much the same (or identical) manner that Defoe's Crusoe *what*? Choice D, meanwhile, is just plain unidiomatic. In English, we just don't say "in much the *identical* way," because the word identical is an absolute. You can't be *more* or *partially* identical; either you are or aren't identical to something else. But even if you didn't analyze D this carefully, it should have just sounded wrong to your ear. (In English Workout 3 we'll show you how "trusting your ear" can be a great way to get correct answers on the English subject test.)

THINK

The rules of grammar evolved to make sure that language expresses ideas clearly and efficiently. Thus, you can "bypass" the rules by making sure that the writing really does express the meaning. If the words do a good job of expressing meaning, they probably follow the rules. But if the words don't make sense, they probably break a rule somewhere.

Question 8 tests another idiom problem:

…For example, while Selkirk's presence on the

island was of course <u>known for many people</u>
                                      8
(certainly everyone in the crew that stranded

him there), no one in the novel is aware of

Crusoe's survival of the wreck and presence on the

island.

8. F. NO CHANGE
G. widely known among people
H. known about many people
J. known to many people

The underlined portion as written is unidiomatic. Selkirk's presence wasn't known *for* many people—it was known *by,* or known *to,* many people. When you're "known *for*" something, that means you have a reputation for doing such and such. That makes no sense in this context. But J *does* make sense, since it points out that Selkirk's presence on the island was known *to* many people—that is, it was something that many people knew about. G is unidiomatic; we just wouldn't say "among people" here, since it's not specific enough. That sounds as if we're talking about people as a species. H would have been acceptable if it had read "known about *by* many people," but without the *by* the correction just wouldn't make sense.

KAPLAN

Idiom is a tough topic if you're not a native speaker. You have to think very carefully about the meaning of every word. But if you *are* a native speaker, use your seventeen years of hearing English as a guide. Choose the correction that makes sense *and* doesn't sound weird.

PRONOUNS

Remember, the object of grammar rules is to make sure that the meaning of language is clearly conveyed. Sometimes, the test will throw you a sentence in which the meaning of a pronoun is *un*clear. You won't be sure whom or what the pronoun is referring to. That's the kind of problem you were given in **Question 5**:

...The story even reached the ears of Richard Steele,

who featured it in his periodical, *The Tatler*. Eventually,

<u>he became</u> the subject of a best-selling book...
    5

5. A. NO CHANGE
   B. Selkirk became
   C. his became
   D. he becomes

> **HINT:** *Mistakes of sense often involve pronouns. Make a habit of checking every underlined pronoun as you go along. What does the pronoun stand for? Can you tell? If not, there's an error. Does it make sense? If not, there's an error.*

The *intended* meaning of the pronoun *he* here is as a substitute for "Selkirk." But what's the closest male name to the pronoun? Richard Steele, the publisher of *The Tatler*. That creates an unclear situation. Make it clear! Choice B takes care of the problem by naming Selkirk explicitly. C would create a sense problem—his *what* became the subject of a book? Meanwhile, D shifts the verb tense into the present, which makes no sense since this book was written over 250 years ago!

Make sure it's perfectly clear to what or to whom all pronouns refer.

LOGIC

Remember when we talked about structural clues back in Reading Workout 1? (C'mon, it wasn't *that* long ago!) Structural clues are signal words that an author uses to show where he or she is going in a piece of writing. They show how all of the pieces logically fit together. If the author uses the structural clue *on the other hand*, that means a contrast is coming up; if he or she uses the clue *moreover*, that means that a continuation is coming up—an addition that is more or less in the same vein as what came before.

Many ACT English questions mix up the logic of a piece of writing by giving you the wrong structural clue or other logic word. That's what happened in **Question 10**.

...<u>Because of</u> its basis in fact, *Robinson Crusoe*
     10
is often regarded as the first major novel in English

literature.

10. F. NO CHANGE
   G. Despite
   H. Resulting from
   J. As a consequence of

As written, this sentence means that *Crusoe* was regarded as the first major novel *because* it was based on fact. But that makes no sense. If it was based on fact, that would work *against* its being regarded as a novel. There's a contrast between basis in "fact" (which implies nonfiction) and "first major novel" (which implies fiction). To show that contrast logically, you need a contrast word like *despite*. That's why G is correct here. G makes the sentence make sense.

Question 6 also tests logic:

. . . the subject of a best-selling book,

A Cruizing Voyage Round the World,

by Woodes Rogers. <u>And while</u> there is some
           6
evidence that Defoe, a journalist, may actually have

interviewed Selkirk personally, most literary

historians believe that it was the reprinting of the

Rogers book in 1718 that served as the real stimulus

for Defoe's novel.

6. F. NO CHANGE
   G. but since
   H. and therefore
   J. OMIT the underlined portion and start the sentence with "There."

The structural clue should convey a sense of continuation from the preceding sentence (since we're still talking about the book *A Cruizing Voyage*), but also a sense of contrast with the latter part of the sentence of which it's a part (since there is a contrast there between one possible stimulus versus another). *And while* does the trick (or both tricks, actually). *And* provides the continuation; *while* provides the needed contrast.

G and H, however, introduce structural clues (*since, therefore*) that imply a cause-and-effect relationship between the two impulses—Defoe's interview and the appearance of *A Cruizing Voyage*—which makes no sense in context. Meanwhile, omitting the portion would create a run-on sentence with two complete thoughts—about Defoe's interview and about the opinion of "most literary historians"—without subordinating one to the other or connecting them with a linking word. Remember, don't always pick "OMIT" just because it's there!

VERB USAGE

Verbs have an annoying habit of changing form depending on who's doing the action and when he or she is doing it. Example: "I *hate* verbs; he *hates* verbs; and we both *have hated* verbs ever since we were kids." You have to be very careful to make sure verbs match their subject and the tense of the surrounding context. Take **Question 7**:

...In *Crusoe*, which <u>has been published in</u>
                                    7
1719, Defoe took substantial liberties with the

Selkirk story.

7. A. NO CHANGE
   B. was published
   C. had been published
   D. will have been published

The publication of *Robinson Crusoe* is something that took place in 1719—the past, in other words. So the underlined portion, which puts the verb in the present perfect tense, is flawed. Choices C and D, meanwhile, would put the verb into several bizarre tenses normally used to convey a complex time relationship. C makes it seem as if publication of the book happened *before* Defoe took his liberties with the story. But that's nonsensical. The liberties were taken in the writing of the book. D, meanwhile, does very strange things with the time sequence. But keep things simple. The book was published in the past; Defoe also took his substantial liberties in more or less the same past. So just use the simple past tense. The book was published in 1719, choice B.

Make sure verbs are in the right case and tense. Put them in the case and tense that make the most sense. The test makers just love to throw verb problems at you.

TONE

As we said earlier, the passages in the English subject test vary in tone. Some are formal; others are informal. Usually, you'll know which is which without having to think about it. If a passage contains slang, a few exclamation points, and a joke or two, the tone is informal; if it sounds like something a Latin instructor would say, it's probably formal.

Good style requires that the tone of a piece of writing be at the same level throughout. Sometimes the underlined portion might not fit the tone of the rest of the passage. If so, it's up to you to correct it.

Look at **Question 13**:

...Meanwhile, Selkirk himself never

<u>gave a hoot about returning</u> to the island that had
              13
made him famous.

13.A. NO CHANGE
   B. evinced himself as desirous of returning
   C. could whip up a head of steam to return
   D. expressed any desire to return

WATCH OUT

Don't pick an answer just because it sounds "fancy." The word "desirous" in Question 13 might be tempting—but don't give in to the temptation. Pick commonsense, everyday words that express the meaning the author intends. Don't worry if it sounds plain.

Selkirk "never gave a hoot" about going back? No way! Slang doesn't belong in this passage. This isn't the most formally written passage in the world, but it's certainly no place for a phrase like *gave a hoot* or (just as bad) *whip up a head of steam* (that's choice C). B, meanwhile, goes too far in the opposite direction. "Evinced himself as desirous of returning" sounds like something no human being would say. But the rest of the passage sounds human. It makes no sense to shift tonal gears in the middle of a passage. So keep the tone consistent. Choose D.

NONSTANDARD-FORMAT ENGLISH QUESTIONS

The Nonstandard-Format questions ask about the passage as a whole. Keep in mind the main point of the passage—the "gist"—as well as the overall tone and style. For an entire passage to "make sense," it has to be consistent throughout, both in content and in tone and style.

Judging the Passage

Question 14 asks you to judge the passage. Was the last sentence an appropriate ending or not? Generally speaking, the correct answer to a question of this type is usually one that approves of the passage. So, unless you're pretty sure that the passage is badly written, give it the "benefit of the doubt." As a rule of thumb, on questions that ask you to judge the passage, lean toward selecting a choice that approves of it.

14. Considering the tone and subject matter of the preceding para-graphs, is the last sentence an appropriate way to end the essay?

   F. Yes, because it is necessary to shed some doubt on Defoe's cre-ativity.

   G. Yes, because the essay is about the relationship between the real Selkirk and Defoe's fictionalized version of him.

   H. No, because there is nothing "bizarre" about Selkirk's story as it is related in the essay.

   J. No, because the focus of the essay is more on Selkirk himself than on Defoe's fictionalized version of him.

Think of the passage as a whole. It's been comparing Selkirk's real life with the one that Defoe made up for the character of Robinson Crusoe. Therefore, ending in this way, with an ironic reference to Defoe as writing a more fitting end to Selkirk's life, is perfectly appropriate. The answer to the question, then, should be yes (eliminating choices H and J). F says yes, but gives a nonsensical reason for saying yes. Why is it necessary to shed doubt on Defoe's creativity? Does the author hold a grudge against Defoe? Not that we can tell. So G is the best answer here.

Reading-Type Questions

If you thought **Question 15** looked like a Reading question hiding in the English part of the exam, you were right. As mentioned in ACT Basics, one reason that you should keep thinking about what the passage means—rather than focusing on picky rules of grammar or punctuation—is that the ACT often asks Reading-type questions. Take Question 15:

15. This essay would be most appropriate as part of a:
   A. scholarly study of eighteenth-century maritime history.
   B. study of the geography of the islands off of Chile.
   C. history of privateering in the Pacific.
   D. popular history of English literature.

Remember what we said above: Keep the main idea, style, and tone of the whole passage in mind. What was this passage principally about? How Defoe's *Robinson Crusoe* was loosely based on the life of a real shipwrecked sailor, Alexander Selkirk. Would that kind of thing belong in a study of geography (choice B)? No. The focus is on the fictionalization of a historical life, not on the physical features of the islands off Chile. The passage isn't principally about privateering or maritime history either, so C and A are wrong as well. This passage is about the relationship between a true story and a famous fictionalized story. And its tone isn't overly scholarly either. So it probably belongs in a popular history of English literature (choice D).

Structure and Purpose

In English, there will also be questions that test your grasp of overall structure and purpose in a piece of prose. The test makers scramble the order of the sentences in a paragraph (or of the paragraphs in a passage). The question then asks you to decide on the best order for the scrambled parts. Take the following example.

[1] Only recently has new evidence led many scientists to question the accepted division between birds and dinosaurs. [2] Traditionally, they have been placed in entirely separate classes within the subphylum *Vertebrata*. [3] Birds and dinosaurs don't have many obvious similarities. [4] Birds formed the class *Aves*, while dinosaurs constituted two orders, *Saurischia* and *Ornithischia*, within the class *Reptilia*.

16. To best fulfill the author's purpose, the order of the sentences in the paragraph above should be:
   F. 1, 2, 3, 4
   G. 2, 3, 4, 1
   H. 3, 2, 4, 1
   J. 3, 2, 1, 4

Here again, the goal is to make it make sense. All of the sentences in this paragraph relate to the differences between birds and dinosaurs. Sentence 3 best introduces this idea. Notice that two of the answer choices begin with Sentence 3—H and J. The other two can be eliminated.

Look again at the logic of the sentences. Clearly, Sentence 4 elaborates on the distinction introduced in Sentence 2, describing the two separate classes into which birds and dinosaurs have traditionally been placed. In order for the paragraph to make sense, then, Sentence 4 must immediately follow Sentence 2. Only H has them in that order, so H looks like the answer.

Just to check, you'll want to read the entire paragraph in the order suggested by H. And if you do, you'll notice that the paragraph makes perfect sense, with Sentence 3 introducing the topic, Sentences 2 and 4 showing how that topic has been traditionally viewed, and Sentence 1 coming in naturally to show how that traditional view is no longer valid.

GUESSING HINT

In Question 16, two of the answer choices listed Sentence 3 first and two of the choices listed Sentence 1 last. If the same sentence is listed as first or last in two answers, it's actually more likely than the others to belong at the beginning or ending of the passage. If a question had the following answers, what would be the best blind guess?

A. 1, 2, 3, 4, 5
B. 2, 5, 4, 3, 1
C. 3, 1, 2, 5, 4
D. 3, 4, 2, 5, 1

D is the best blind guess. Sentence 3 is the best bet to be first, and Sentence 1 is the best bet to be last, since they appear in these positions most. Note: Questions like this one, in which blind guessing would narrow the choices down to just one, are rare on real ACTs. But you can often narrow the choices to two.

For questions like this, it's usually a good idea to start by trying to figure out the first (and sometimes the last) sentence, because first and last sentences usually have the most obvious functions in an ACT-style paragraph.

To sum up, the questions in the passage above, as in any ACT English passage, test many specific issues—sentence structure, word form, style, idiom, logic, transitions, modifiers, pronouns, tone, etc. But always remember that many of them can be resolved by merely trying to . . . *make it make sense.*

KAPLAN

MATH
WORKOUT 2
SHAKE IT UP!

The main idea of Math Workout 1 was: Don't jump in head first and start crunching numbers until you've given the problem some thought. Make sure you know what you're doing—*and* that what you're doing won't take too long.

As we saw in Math Workout 1, sometimes you'll know how to proceed as soon as you understand the question. A good number of ACT algebra and coordinate geometry questions are straightforward textbook questions you may already be prepared for.

TEN TEXTBOOK QUESTIONS

When you take the ACT, you can be sure you'll see some of the following questions with only slight variations. You'll find answers and explanations for these questions in the Math Appendix.

1. Evaluate an algebraic expression. (*See Math Appendix, #52*)

    Example: If $x = -2$, then $x^2 + 5x - 6 = ?$

2. Multiply binomials. (*See Math Appendix, #56*)

    Example: $(x + 3)(x + 4) = ?$

3. Factor a polynomial. (*See Math Appendix, #61*)

    Example: What is the complete factorization of $x^2 - 5x + 6$?

4. Simplify an algebraic fraction. (*See Math Appendix, #62*)

    Example: For all $x \neq \pm 3$, $\frac{x^2 - x - 12}{x^2 - 9} = ?$

5. Solve a linear equation. (*See Math Appendix, #63*)

    Example: If $5x - 12 = -2x + 9$, then $x = ?$

6. Solve a quadratic equation. (*See Math Appendix, #66*)

    Example: If $x^2 + 12 = 7x$, what are the two possible values of x?

7. Solve a system of equations. (*See Math Appendix, #67*)

   Example: If $4x + 3y = 8$, and $x + y = 3$, what is the value of x?

8. Solve an inequality. (*See Math Appendix, #69*)

   Example: What are all the values of x for which $-5x + 7 < -3$?

9. Find the distance between two points in the (x, y) coordinate plane. (*See Math Appendix, #71*)

   Example: What is the distance between the points with (x, y) coordinates $(-2, 2)$ and $(1, -2)$?

10. Find the slope of a line from its equation. (*See Math Appendix, #73*)

    Example: What is the slope of the line with the equation $2x + 3y = 4$?

These questions are all so straightforward and traditional, they could have come out of a high school algebra textbook. These are the questions you should do the way you were taught.

NONTRADITIONAL QUESTIONS

The techniques you'd use in questions like the ten listed above are the techniques they've been teaching you all along in high school math classes. In case you'd like to review them, you'll find all the standard approaches you might need for the ACT succinctly summarized in the Math Appendix. We're not so concerned in these Workouts with problems you may already know how to solve. *Here in Workout 2 we're going to focus on several Algebra and Coordinate Geometry situations where the quick and reliable solution method is not so obvious, where often the best method is one your algebra teacher never told you about.*

IF AT FIRST YOU DON'T SUCCEED, SHAKE IT UP!

It's bound to happen at some point on Test Day. You look at a math problem and you don't see what to do. Don't freak out at first glance. Think about the problem for a few seconds before you give up. When you don't see the quick and reliable approach right away, shake the problem up a little. Try one of these "shake-it-up" techniques:

1. **Restate**

2. **Remove the disguise**

3. **Pick numbers**

4. **Backsolve**

#1—RESTATE

Often, the way to get over that stymied feeling is to change your perspective. Have you ever watched people playing Scrabble®? In their search for high-scoring words that can be formed using the letters on their seven tiles, they continually move the tiles around in their rack. Sometimes a good word becomes apparent only after rearranging the tiles. One might not see the seven-letter word in this arrangement:

R E B A G L A

But reverse the tiles and a word almost reveals itself:

A L G A B E R

The tiles can spell "ALGEBRA."

The same gimmick works a lot on the ACT, too. When you get stuck, try looking at the problem from a different angle. Try rearranging the numbers, or changing fractions to decimals, or factoring, or multiplying out, or redrawing the diagram, or anything that might give you the fresh perspective you need to uncover a good solution method.

Here's a question you might not know what to do with at first glance:

1. Which of the following is equivalent to $7^{77} - 7^{76}$?
   A. 7
   B. 7^{77-76}
   C. $7^{77} \div 76$
   D. $7(77 - 76)$
   E. $7^{76}(6)$

Here's a hint: *Think of an easier problem testing the same principles.* The important thing to look for is the basic relationships involved—here, we have exponents and subtraction. That subtraction sign causes trouble, because none of the ordinary rules of exponents (see Math Appendix, #47–48) seem to apply when there is subtraction of "unlike" terms.

Another hint: How would you work with $x^2 - x$? Most test takers could come up with another expression for $x^2 - x$: they'd factor to $x(x - 1)$. Or if the problem asked for $x^{77} - x^{76}$, they'd factor to $x^{76}(x - 1)$. The rule is no different for 7 than for x. Factoring out the 7^{76} gives you: $7^{76}(7 - 1)$, which is $7^{76}(6)$, or choice E.

Sometimes an ACT algebra question will include an expression that isn't of much use in its given form. The breakthrough in such a case may be to restate the expression by either simplifying it or factoring it. For example:

2. If $\frac{x}{2} - \frac{x}{6}$ is an integer, which of the following statements must be true?
   F. x is positive.
   G. x is odd.
   H. x is even.
   J. x is a multiple of 3.
   K. x is a multiple of 6.

Re-express: $\frac{x}{2} - \frac{x}{6} = \frac{3x}{6} - \frac{x}{6} = \frac{2x}{6} = \frac{x}{3}$

This form of the expression tells us a lot more. If $\frac{x}{3}$ is an integer, then x is equal to 3 times an integer:

$\frac{x}{3}$ = an integer
$x = 3 \cdot$ (an integer)

In other words, x is a multiple of 3, choice J.

#2—REMOVE THE DISGUISE

Sometimes it's hard to see the quick and reliable method immediately because the true nature of the problem is hidden behind a disguise. Look at this example:

3. What are the (x, y) coordinates of the point of intersection of the line representing the equation $5x + 2y = 4$ and the line representing the equation $x - 2y = 8$?
   A. $(2, 3)$
   B. $(-2, 3)$
   C. $(2, -3)$
   D. $(-3, 2)$
   E. $(3, -2)$

This may look like a coordinate geometry question, but do you really have to graph the lines to find the point of intersection? Remember, the ACT is looking for creative thinkers, not mindless calculators! Think about it for a moment—what's the special significance of the point of intersection, the one point that the two lines have in common? That's the one point whose coordinates will satisfy *both* equations.

COORDINATE GEOMETRY

Although this question turned out not to be a real coordinate geometry problem, the test makers do have a soft spot in their hearts for coordinate geometry. Typically 8 or more of the 60 math questions involve coordinate geometry. It's hard to get a top score without getting at least some coordinate geometry questions right. Use Math Appendix #71–77 to review the relevant rules and formulas.

KAPLAN

So what we realize now is that this is not a coordinate geometry question at all, but a "system-of-equations" question. All it's really asking you to do is solve the pair of equations for *x* and *y*. The question has *nothing* to do with slopes, intercepts, axes, or quadrants. It's a pure algebra question in disguise.

Now that we know we're looking at a system of equations, the method of solution presents itself more clearly. The first equation has a +2*y*, and the second equation has a −2*y*. If we just "add" the equations, the *y* terms cancel:

$$5x + 2y = 4$$
$$\underline{x - 2y = 8}$$
$$6x \qquad = 12$$

If $6x = 12$, then $x = 2$. Plug that back into either of the original equations and you'll find that $y = -3$. The point of intersection is $(2, -3)$, and the answer is C.

Here's another disguised question:

4. A geometer uses the following formula to estimate the area *A* of the shaded portion of a circle as shown in the figure below when only the height *h* and the length of the chord *c* are known:

$$A = \frac{2ch}{3} + \frac{h^3}{2c}$$

What is the geometer's estimate of the area, in square inches, of the shaded region if the height is 2 inches and the length of the chord is 6 inches?

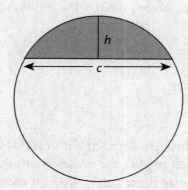

    F.   6

    G. $6\frac{2}{3}$

    H. $7\frac{1}{2}$

    J. $8\frac{2}{3}$

    K.   12

At first glance, this looks like a horrendously esoteric geometry question. Who ever heard of such a formula?

But when you think about the question a bit, you realize that you don't really have to understand the formula. You certainly don't have to remember it—it's right there in the question.

In fact, this is not really a geometry question at all. It's really just an "evaluate the algebraic expression" question in disguise. All you have to do is plug the given values $h = 2$ and $c = 6$ into the given formula:

$$A = \frac{2ch}{3} + \frac{h^3}{2c}$$

$$= \frac{2(6)(2)}{3} + \frac{(2)^3}{2(6)}$$

$$= 8 + \frac{2}{3} = 8\frac{2}{3}$$

Choice J is correct.

The people who wrote this question wanted you to freak out at first sight and give up. Don't give up on a question too quickly just because it looks like it's testing something you never saw before. In many such cases it's really a familiar problem in disguise.

#3—PICK NUMBERS

Sometimes you can get stuck on an algebra problem just because it's too general or abstract. A good way to get a handle on such a problem is to bring it down to earth and make it more explicit by temporarily substituting particular numbers for the variables. For example:

> **5.** If a is an odd integer and b is an even integer, which of the following
>   must be odd?
>   **A.** $2a + b$
>   **B.** $a + 2b$
>   **C.** ab
>   **D.** a^2b
>   **E.** ab^2

Rather than try to think this one through abstractly, it's easier for most people simply to pick numbers for a and b. There are rules that predict the evenness or oddness of sums, differences, and products, but there's no need to memorize those rules. When it comes to adding, subtracting, and multiplying evens and odds, what happens with one pair of numbers generally happens with all similar pairs.

Just say, for the time being, that $a = 1$ and $b = 2$. Plug those values into the answer choices, and there's a good chance only one choice will be odd:

A. $2a + b = 2(1) + 2 = 4$
B. $a + 2b = 1 + 2(2) = 5$
C. $ab = (1)(2) = 2$
D. $a^2b = (1)^2(2) = 2$
E. $ab^2 = (1)(2)^2 = 4$

Choice B was the only odd one for $a = 1$ and $b = 2$, so it *must* be the one that's odd no matter *what* odd number a actually stands for and even number b actually stands for.

#4—BACKSOLVE

With some ACT math problems, rather than try to solve the problem and then look among the choices for the answer, it may actually be easier to take each answer choice and try it out until you find the one that works. Since this approach involves working backwards from the answer choices to the question stem, it's called "backsolving." Here's a good example:

6. All 200 tickets were sold for a particular concert. Some tickets cost $10 apiece, and the others cost $5 apiece. If total ticket sales were $1,750, how many of the more expensive tickets were sold?

    F. 20
    G. 75
    H. 100
    J. 150
    K. 175

There are ways to solve this problem by setting up an equation or two, but if you're not comfortable with the algebraic approach to this one, why not just try out each answer choice?

BACKSOLVING

When backsolving, start with the middle choices—that is, C or H. The answer choices are generally listed in numerical order, and if the first number you try doesn't work, the process of trying out that first number might tell you whether to go for a smaller one or a larger one.

Start with choice H. If 100 tickets went for $10, then the other 100 went for $5. One hundred tickets at $10 is $1,000, and 100 tickets at $5 is $500, for a total of $1,500—too small. There must have been more than one hundred, $10 tickets.

So let's try choice J next. If 150 tickets went for $10, then the other 50 went for $5. So 150 tickets at $10 is $1,500, and 50 tickets at $5 is $250, for a total of $1,750—that's it! The answer is J.

Backsolving your way to the answer may not be a method you'd show your algebra teacher with pride—but your algebra teacher won't be watching on Test Day. Remember, all that matters is right answers—it doesn't matter how you get them.

ADVICE FOR SOME SPECIFIC STORY-PROBLEM SITUATIONS

We find that about one-third of the questions in the math subtest are story problems. Although some story problems present unique situations that must be analyzed on the spot, other story problems are just variations on familiar themes. Experience with a few of the more common story problems and their standard solution set-ups will certainly come in handy on Test Day.

Percent Problems

In percent problems, you're usually given two numbers and asked to find a third. The key is to identify what you have and what you're looking for.

KEY: *Identify the Part, the Percent, and the Whole.*

(Usually the Part is associated with the word *is* and the Whole is associated with the word *of*.) Put the numbers and the unknown into the general form:

Part = Percent × Whole

For example:

7. In a group of 250 students, 40 are seniors. What percentage of the group are seniors?
   A. 1.6%
   B. 6.25%
   C. 10%
   D. 16%
   E. 40%

The Percent is what we're looking for ("What percentage . . ."); the Whole is 250 (". . . of the group . . ."); and the Part is 40 (". . . are seniors"). Plug these into the general formula:

$$\text{Part} = \text{Percent} \times \text{Whole}$$
$$40 = 250x$$
$$x = \frac{40}{250} = .16 = 16\%$$

The answer is D.

Percent Increase/Decrease Problems

Many ACT percent problems concern percent change. To increase a number by a certain percent, calculate that percent of the original number and add it on. To decrease a number by a certain percent, calculate that percent of the original number and then subtract. For example, to answer the question, "What number is 30% greater than 80?" first find 30% of 80—that's 24—and add that on to 80: 80 + 24 = 104.

The ACT has ways of complicating percent change problems. Especially tricky are problems with multiple changes, such as a percent increase followed by another percent increase, or a percent increase followed by a percent decrease.

PERCENT CHANGE TRAP

When a quantity is increased or decreased by a percent more than once, you cannot simply add and subtract the percents to get the answer. In this kind of percent problem:

• The first percent change is a percent of the starting amount, but

• The second percent change is a percent of the new amount.

Here's a question, for example, that's not so simple as it seems at first:

8. If a positive number is increased by 70 percent, and then the result is decreased by 50 percent, which of the following accurately describes the net change?

   F. a 20 percent decrease

   G. a 15 percent decrease

   H. a 12 percent increase

   J. a 20 percent increase

   K. a 120 percent increase

To get a handle on this one, pick a number. Suppose the original number is 100. After a 70 percent increase it rises to 170. That number, 170, is decreased by 50 percent, which means it's reduced by half to 85. The net change from 100 to 85 is a 15 percent decrease—choice G.

PICK 100 ON PERCENT PROBLEMS

Picking numbers is a good strategy when the answer choices are all percents. And 99 percent of the time the best number to pick—the easiest to work with—will be 100.

AVERAGE PROBLEMS

Instead of giving you a list of values to plug into the average formula, ACT average questions often put a slight spin on the problem. They tell you the average of a group of terms and ask you to find the value of the missing term. Here's a classic example:

> **9.** To earn a B for the semester, Linda needs an average of at least 80 on the five tests. Her average for the first four test scores is 79. What is the minimum score she must get on the fifth test to earn a B for the semester?
> **A.** 80
> **B.** 81
> **C.** 82
> **D.** 83
> **E.** 84

The key to almost every average question is to use the sum. Sums can be combined much more readily than averages. An average of 80 on five tests is more usefully thought of as a combined score of 400. To get a B for the semester, Linda's five test scores have to add up to 400 or more. The first four scores add up to $4 \times 79 = 316$. She needs another 84 to get that 316 up to 400. The answer is E.

WEIGHTED AVERAGE PROBLEMS

Another spin ACT test makers put on average problems is to give you an average for part of a group and an average for the rest of the group and then ask for the combined average.

WEIGHTED AVERAGE TRAP

To get a combined average, it's usually *wrong* simply to average the averages.

For example:

10. In a class of 10 boys and 15 girls, the boys' average score on the final exam was 80 and the girls' average score was 90. What was the average score for the whole class?

   F. 83

   G. 84

   H. 85

   J. 86

   K. 87

Don't just average 80 and 90 to get 85. That would work only if the class had exactly the same number of girls as boys. In this case, there are more girls, so they carry more "weight" in the overall class average. In other words, the class average should be somewhat closer to 90 (the girls' average) than to 80 (the boys' average).

As usual with averages, the key is to use the sum. The average score for the whole class is the total of the 25 individual scores divided by 25. We don't have 25 scores to add up, but we can use the boys' average and the girls' average to get two subtotals.

If 10 boys average 80, then their 10 scores add up to 10×80, or 800. If 15 girls average 90, then their 15 scores add up to 15×90, or 1,350. Add the boys' total to the girls' total: $800 + 1,350 = 2,150$. That's the class total, which can be divided by 25 to get the class average: $\frac{2,150}{25} = 86$. The answer is J.

PROBABILITY PROBLEMS

Probabilities are part-to-whole ratios. The whole is the total number of possible outcomes. The part is the number of "favorable" outcomes. For example, if a drawer contains two black ties and five other ties, and you want a black tie, the total number of possible outcomes is 7 (the total number of ties) and the number of "favorable" outcomes is 2 (the number of black ties). The probability of choosing a black tie at random is $\frac{2}{7}$.

PROBABILITY TRAP

The probability of what *will* happen is not affected by what already *has* happened. *Whenever* you flip a fair coin, the probability is $\frac{1}{2}$ that it will be heads. Even if you flip the coin and get heads ten times in a row, the probability is still $\frac{1}{2}$ on the eleventh flip. Of course, the odds against eleven heads in a row are huge, but once the first ten flips are history they're no longer relevant. Only the flips yet to come matter.

WHAT TO DO NEXT

Because more than half the math questions on the ACT involve algebra, it's a good idea to take some time before Test Day to solidify your understanding of the basics. Focus on #52–70 in the Math Appendix. Keep things in perspective. Geometry questions are important, too, but algebra questions are more important.

KAPLAN

READING WORKOUT 2
LOOK IT UP!

In Reading Workout 1, we discussed general strategies for approaching ACT Reading. Now let's look more closely at the major types of *questions* you'll encounter. As we mentioned in ACT Basics, there are really three main types of Reading questions on the test: Specific Detail Questions and Inference Questions (which make up the bulk of any Reading subtest), as well as Big Picture Questions (of which there are usually just a few).

REMEMBER

The three-Step Approach to Reading is:

1. Preread the passage.
2. Consider the questions.
3. Refer to the passage.

The following passage is a typical ACT nonfiction passage, this one from the Humanities. Do the passage and its questions, using the three-step approach. Afterward, we'll discuss selected questions from this set as examples of Specific Detail, Inference, and Big Picture Questions.

Passage II

Tragedy was the invention of the Greeks. In their Golden Age, the fifth century before Christ, they produced the world's greatest drama-tists, new forms of tragedy and comedy that have been models ever since, and a theatre that every age goes back to for rediscovery of
5 some basic principle....

Since it derived from primitive religious rites, with masks and cere-monial costumes, and made use of music, dance, and poetry, the Greek drama was at the opposite pole from the modern realistic stage. In fact, probably no other theatre in history has made fuller use
10 of the intensities of art. The masks, made of painted linen, wood, and plaster, brought down from primitive days the atmosphere of gods, heroes, and demons. Our nineteenth- and twentieth-century grandfa-thers thought masks must have been very artificial. Today, however, we appreciate their exciting intensity and can see that in a large the-
15 atre they were indispensable. If they allowed no fleeting change of expression during a single episode, they could give for each episode in turn more intense expression than any human face could. When Oedipus comes back with bleeding eyes, the new mask could be more terrible than any facial makeup the audience could endure, yet
20 in its sculpted intensity more beautiful than a real face.

Most essential of all intensities, and hardest for us to understand, was the chorus. Yet many playwrights today are trying to find some equivalent to do for a modern play what the chorus did for the Greeks. During the episodes played by the actors, the chorus would
25 only provide a background of group response, enlarging and rever-berating the emotions of the actors, sometimes protesting and opposing but in general serving as ideal spectators to stir and lead the reactions of the audience. But between episodes, with the actors out of the way, the chorus took over. We have only the words, not
30 the music or dance, and some translations of the odes are in such for-mal, old-fashioned language that it is hard to guess that they were accompanied by vigorous, sometimes even wild dances and symbolic actions that filled an orchestra which in some cities was sixty to ninety feet in diameter. Sometimes the chorus expressed simple horror or
35 lament. Sometimes it chanted and acted out, in unison and in precise formations of rows and lines, the acts of violence the characters were enacting offstage. When Phaedra rushes offstage in *Hippolytus* to hang herself from the rafters, the members of the chorus, all fifteen of them, perform in mime and chant the act of tying the rope and
40 swinging from the rafters. Sometimes the chorus tells or reenacts an incident of history or legend that throws light on the situation in the play. Sometimes the chorus puts into specific action what is a general intention in the mind of the main character.

When Oedipus resolves to hunt out the guilty person and cleanse the
45 city, he is speaking metaphorically, but the chorus invokes the gods
of vengeance and dances a wild pursuit.

On the printed page, the choral odes seem static and formal, lyric
and philosophical, emotional let-downs that punctuate the series of
episodes, like intermissions between two acts of a play. The reader
50 who skips the odes can get the main points of the play. A few are
worth reading as independent poems, notably the famous one in
Antigone beginning, "Many are the wonders of the world, but none is
more wonderful than man." Some modern acting versions omit the
chorus or reduce it to a few background figures. Yet to the Greeks the
55 odes were certainly more than mere poetic interludes: the wild
Dionysian words and movements evoked primitive levels of the subconscious and at the same time served to transform primitive violence
into charm and beauty and to add philosophical reflections on the
meaning of human destiny.

60 For production today, we can only improvise some partial equivalent. In Athens the entire population was familiar with choral perfor-
mances. Every year each of the tribes entered a dithyramb in a contest, rehearsing five hundred men and boys for weeks. Some modern
composers have tried to write dramatic music for choruses: the most
65 notable examples are the French composer Darius Milhaud, in the
primitive rhythms, shouts, and chants of his operatic version of the
Oresteia; George Gershwin, in the Negro funeral scenes of *Porgy and
Bess*; and Kurt Weill, in the African choruses for *Lost in the Stars*, the
musical dramatization of Alan Paton's novel, *Cry, the Beloved Country*.
70 For revivals of Greek tragedies we have not dared use much music
beyond a few phrases half shouted, half sung, and drumbeats and
suggestive melodies in the background.

From Invitation to the Theatre, © 1967 by George Kernodle; Harcourt, Brace, & World Inc.,
publisher.

1. Combined with the passage's additional information, the fact that
some Greek orchestras were sixty to ninety feet across suggests that:
   A. few spectators were able to see the stage.
   B. no one performer could dominate a performance.
   C. choruses and masks helped overcome the distance between
   actors and audience.
   D. Greek tragedies lacked the emotional force of modern theatrical
   productions.

SECTION II: SKILL-BUILDING WORKOUTS

2. Which of the following claims expresses the writer's opinion and not a fact?

    F. The Greek odes contained Dionysian words and movements.

    G. Greek theater has made greater use of the intensities of art than has any other theater in history.

    H. Many modern playwrights are trying to find an equivalent to the Greek chorus.

    J. The chorus was an essential part of Greek tragedy.

    Ⓕ Ⓖ Ⓗ Ⓙ

3. The description of the chorus' enactment of Phaedra's offstage suicide (lines 37–40) shows that, in contrast to modern theater, ancient Greek theater was:

    A. more violent.

    B. more concerned with satisfying an audience.

    C. more apt to be historically accurate.

    D. less concerned with a realistic portrayal of events.

    Ⓐ Ⓑ Ⓒ Ⓓ

4. It can be inferred that one consequence of the Greeks' use of masks was that:

    F. the actors often had to change masks between episodes.

    G. the characters in the play could not convey emotion.

    H. the actors wearing masks played non-speaking roles.

    J. good acting ability was not important to the Greeks.

    Ⓕ Ⓖ Ⓗ Ⓙ

5. Which of the following is supported by the information in the second paragraph (lines 6–20)?

    A. Masks in Greek drama combined artistic beauty with emotional intensity.

    B. The use of masks in Greek drama was better appreciated in the nineteenth century than it is now.

    C. Masks in Greek drama were used to portray gods but never human beings.

    D. Contemporary scholars seriously doubt the importance of masks to Greek theater.

    Ⓐ Ⓑ Ⓒ Ⓓ

6. The author indicates in lines 44–45 that Oedipus's resolution "to hunt out the guilty person and cleanse the city" was:

    F. at odds with what he actually does later in the performance.

    G. misinterpreted by the chorus.

    H. dramatized by the actions of the chorus.

    J. angrily condemned by the chorus.

    Ⓕ Ⓖ Ⓗ Ⓙ

7. According to the passage, when actors were present on stage, the chorus would:

    A. look on as silently as spectators.

    B. inevitably agree with the actors' actions.

    C. communicate to the audience solely through mime.

    D. react to the performance as an audience might.

    Ⓐ Ⓑ Ⓒ Ⓓ

KAPLAN

8. The main point of the fourth paragraph (lines 47–59) is that choral odes:

   F. should not be performed by modern choruses.

   G. have a meaning and beauty that are lost in modern adaptations.

   H. can be safely ignored by a modern-day reader.

   J. are only worthwhile in *Antigone*.

9. The passage suggests that modern revivals of Greek tragedies "have not dared use much music" (lines 70–72) because:

   A. modern instruments would appear out of place.

   B. to do so would require a greater understanding of how choral odes were performed.

   C. music would distract the audience from listening to the words of choral odes.

   D. such music is considered far too primitive for modern audiences.

10. *Porgy and Bess* and *Lost in the Stars* are modern plays that:

   F. are revivals of Greek tragedies.

   G. use music to evoke the subconscious.

   H. perform primitive Greek music.

   J. have made use of musical choruses.

THE GENERAL OUTLINE

A quick preread of the passage should have given you a sense of its general organization:

- First paragraph—introduces the topic of Greek tragedy

- Second paragraph—discusses use of masks (artificial but intense)

- Third paragraph—discusses use of chorus (also artificial but intense)

- Fourth paragraph—expands discussion to chorus odes

- Fifth paragraph—concludes with discussion of how Greek tragedy is performed today, and how it has influenced some modern art

That's really all the road map you need going into the questions. Aside from that, you should take a sense of the author's main point: Greek tragedy included many artificial devices, but these devices allowed it to rise to a high level of intensity.

LOOK IT UP

The answers are in the passage. Focus your attention on locating them. Your mindset should be: "Find the answer," not "Remember the answer."

SPECIFIC DETAIL QUESTIONS

Questions 6 and 7 in the passage above are typical Detail Questions. As you've seen, some Detail Questions (such as 6) give you a line reference to help you out; others (such as 7) don't, forcing you either to start tearing your hair out (if you're an unprepared test taker) or else to seek out the answer based on your own sense of how the passage is laid out (one of the two key reasons to pre-read the passage). With either type of Detail Question, once you've found the part of the passage that a question refers to, the answer is often (though not always) pretty obvious.

Question 6 provides a line reference (lines 44–45), but to answer the question confidently, you should have also read a few lines before and a few lines after the cited lines. There you would have read: "Sometimes the chorus puts into action what is a general intention in the mind of the main character. When Oedipus resolves . . ." Clearly, the Oedipus example is meant to illustrate the point about the chorus acting out a character's intentions. So H is correct—they are "dramatizing" (or acting out) Oedipus's resolution. (By the way, G might have been tempting, but there's no real evidence that the chorus is "misinterpreting," just that they're "putting a general intention into specific action.")

Question 7 is a Detail Question *without* a line reference. Such questions are common on the ACT, and they require that you have a good sense of the structure of the passage as a whole, so that you can locate the place where the question is answered. This question's mention of the chorus should have sent you to paragraph 3, but that's a long paragraph, so you probably had to skim it to find the answer in lines 24–28, where the author claims that the chorus serves to "lead the reactions of the audience"—captured by correct choice D.

THINK

When given a specific line reference, always read a few sentences before and after the cited lines, to get a sense of the context.

KAPLAN

INFERENCE QUESTIONS

In ACT Basics, you learned that, in Inference Questions, your job is to combine ideas logically to make an inference—something that's not stated explicitly in the passage but that is definitely said *im*plicitly. Often, Inference Questions have a word like *suggest, infer, inference,* or *imply* in the question stem to tip you off.

To succeed on Inference Questions, you have to "read between the lines." Common sense is your best tool here. You use various bits of information in the passage as evidence for your own logical conclusion.

Like Detail Questions, Inference Questions sometimes do and sometimes don't contain line references. **Question 9** does, referring you to lines 70–72, but you really have to keep the context of the entire paragraph in mind when you make your inference. Why would modern revivals not have "dared" to use much music? Well, the paragraph opens by saying that modern productions "can only improvise some partial equivalent" to the choral odes. Inferably, since we can only improvise the odes, we don't understand very much about them. That's why the use of music would be considered daring, and why choice B is correct.

NOTE

Think of the passages as references, not as textbooks. You don't try to memorize dictionaries or encyclopedias (unless you're a very strange person). You use them to check information that you don't know or can't remember. Use ACT passages in the same way. *Refer* to the passage to find the information you need to answer the questions.

Question 4 provides no line reference, but the mention of masks should have sent you to the second paragraph of the passage, where (according to your trusty road map) masks are discussed. Lines 15–16 explain that masks "allowed no fleeting change of expression during a single episode." Treat that as your first piece of evidence. Your second comes in lines 16–17: "they [the masks] could give for each episode in turn more intense expression than any human face could." Put those two pieces of evidence together—masks can't change expression *during* a single episode, but they can give expression for each episode *in turn*.

Clearly, the actors must have changed masks between episodes, so that they could express the different emotions that different episodes required. Choice F is correct.

PUT TWO AND TWO TOGETHER

Making inferences often requires that you take bits of information from different parts of the passage and combine them. Common sense will then lead you to an appropriate inference—one that's not too extreme.

One warning for Inference Questions: Be careful to keep your inferences as "close" to the passage as possible. Don't make wild inferential leaps. An inference should seem to follow naturally and inevitably from the evidence provided in the passage.

BIG-PICTURE QUESTIONS

We find that about one-third of the ACT Reading questions are Detail Questions and most of the rest are Inference Questions. But there are also a few questions that test your understanding of the theme, purpose, and organization of the passage as a whole. For these Big-Picture Questions, your main task is different from what it is for Detail or Inference Questions, though you should still plan to find the answer in the passages. Big-Picture Questions tend to look for:

- Main point or purpose of a passage or part of a passage

- Author's attitude or tone

- Logic underlying the author's argument

- How ideas in different parts of the passage relate to each other

- Difference between fact and opinion

One way to see the Big Picture is to read actively. As you read, ask yourself, "What's this all about? What's the point of this? Why is the author saying this?"

MISSING THE BIG PICTURE?

If you're still stumped after reading the passage, try doing the Detail and Inference questions first. They can help you fill in the Big Picture.

Question 8 asks for the main idea of a particular paragraph—namely, the fourth, which our general outline of the passage indicates as the paragraph about choral odes. Skimming that paragraph, you find reference to how the odes seem to us modern people—"static and formal" (line 47), "like intermissions between two acts of a play" (line 49). Later, the author states, by way of contrast (note the use of the clue word *yet*): "Yet to the Greeks the odes were certainly more than mere poetic interludes." Clearly, the author in this paragraph wants to contrast our modern static view of the odes with the Greeks' view of them as something more. That idea is best captured by choice G.

Question 2, meanwhile, is another common type of Big Picture Question—one that requires that you distinguish between expressions of fact and opinion in the passage. A simple test for fact (versus opinion) is this: Can it be proven objectively? If yes, it's a fact.

The content of Greek odes (choice F) is a matter of fact; you can go to a Greek ode and find out whether it does or doesn't contain Dionysian words. Similarly, the efforts of modern playwrights to find an equivalent to the Greek chorus (choice H), and the central importance of the chorus to Greek tragedy (choice J) can be factually verified.

But the "intensities of art" are a subjective matter. What one person thinks is intense might strike another as boring. So G is the expression of opinion the question is looking for.

FACT OR OPINION?

A good way to distinguish fact from an author's opinion is to picture yourself as a fact checker for a newspaper or magazine. Is the point in question something you could verify in a book or with an expert? If not, it's probably not a fact.

FIND AND PARAPHRASE

The examples above show that your real task in Reading is not what you might expect. Your main job is to *find* the answers. Perhaps a better name for the Reading subtest would be "find and paraphrase." But students tend to think that their task in Reading is to "comprehend and remember." That's the wrong mindset.

Here's a key to the Greek tragedy passage, so that you can check the answers to the questions not discussed above.

Key to Passage II
(Nonfiction—Humanities)

	ANSWER	REFER TO	TYPE	COMMENTS
1.	C	Lines 14–18, 24–26	Inference	Q-stem emphasizes distance between audience and stage; masks and choruses help to "enlarge" the action, so that it can be understood from a distance.
2.	G	Throughout	Big Picture	Discussed above.
3.	D	Lines 37–40	Inference	Combine info from lines 6–12, 37–40, 56–59.
4.	F	Lines 15–17	Inference	Discussed above.
5.	A	Lines 6–20	Inference	Combine info from lines 9–10, 18–20.
6.	H	Lines 44–45	Detail	Discussed above.
7.	D	Lines 24–28	Detail	Discussed above.
8.	G	Lines 47–49	Big Picture	Discussed above.
9.	B	Lines 70–72	Inference	Discussed above.
10.	J	Lines 67–73	Detail	"Some modern composers have tried to write dramatic music for choruses."

DON'T BE AFRAID TO SKIP

Now that you've done a couple of full-length passages and questions, you've probably encountered at least a few questions that you found unanswerable. What do you do if you can't find the answer in the passage, or if you *can* find it but don't understand, or if you *do* understand but can't see an answer choice that makes sense? Skip the question. Skipping is probably more important in Reading than in any other ACT question type. Remember to *take control*. Many students find it useful to skip as many as half of the questions on the first pass through a set of Reading questions. That's fine.

SKIP

Remember, answer the easy questions for each passage first. Skip the tough ones and come back to them later. Sometimes the thinking you do on an easy question will help you work out a hard one. When students can't finish on time, it's usually because they stubbornly refuse to skip.

When you come back to a Reading question the second time, it usually makes sense to use the process of elimination. The first time around, you tried to find the *right* answer but you couldn't. So, now try to identify the three *wrong* answers. Eliminating three choices is slower than finding one right choice, so don't make it your main strategy for Reading. But it's a good way to try a second attack on a question.

ELIMINATE, DON'T COMPARE

When you use the process of elimination, treat each choice as a "true-false" statement. In your mind, you are distinguishing between wrong answers and a right answer—*not* between better and worse answers. Don't compare the answers to each other. Compare them to the passage. Pick the choice that's closest to what the passage says.

Another thing to consider when attacking a question for a second time is that the right answer may have been hidden. Maybe it's written in an unexpected way, with different vocabulary. Or maybe there is another good way that you haven't thought of to answer the question. But remember that it's still important to avoid getting bogged down when you come back to a question. Be willing to admit that there are some problems you just can't answer. Guess if you have to.

MORE PRACTICE WITH READING

In the first two Reading Workouts, you've worked on two full-length nonfiction passages—one in Social Studies and one in the Humanities. In Reading Workout 3 we'll talk about some special strategies for the two other kinds of passages—Prose Fiction and (the third nonfiction type) Natural Sciences.

SCIENCE WORKOUT 2
ALWAYS KNOW
YOUR DIRECTION

In Science Workout 1 you learned that to succeed on the ACT Science Reasoning subtest, you've got to be able to spot trends and patterns in the data of graphs and tables. But that's not all you need to do well. You've also got to learn how to think like a scientist. You don't have to know very much science (although it certainly helps), but you should at least be familiar with how scientists go about getting and testing knowledge.

HOW SCIENTISTS THINK

Scientists use two very different kinds of logic, which (to keep things nontechnical) we'll call:

- General-to-Specific Thinking
- Specific-to-General Thinking

General-to-Specific

In some cases, scientists have already discovered a law of nature and wish to apply their knowledge to a specific case. For example, a scientist may wish to know how fast a pebble (call it Pebble A) will be falling when it hits the ground three seconds after being dropped. There is a law of physics from which it can be determined that: On Earth, falling objects accelerate at a rate of about 9.8 m/sec^2. The scientist could use this known general principle to calculate the specific information she needs: After three seconds, the object would be falling at a rate of about 3 sec $\times$ 9.8 m/sec^2, or roughly 30 m/sec. You could think of this kind of logic as *general-to-specific*. The scientist uses a *general* principle (the acceleration of any object falling on Earth) to find a *specific* fact (the speed of Pebble A).

Specific-to-General

But scientists use a different kind of thinking in order to discover a new law of nature. In this case, they examine many specific facts and then draw a general conclusion about what they've seen. For example, a scientist might watch hundreds of different kinds of frogs live and die, and might notice that all of them developed from tadpoles. She might then announce a theory: All frogs develop from tadpoles. You could think of this kind of logic as *specific-to-general*. The scientist looks at many *specific* frogs to find a *general* rule about all frogs.

This conclusion is called a "theory," not a fact or a truth, because the scientist has not checked every single frog in the universe. She knows that there theoretically *could* be a frog somewhere that grows from pond scum or from a Dalmatian puppy. But until she finds such a frog, it is reasonable for her to think that her theory is correct. Many theories, in fact, are so well documented that they become the equivalent of laws of nature.

THINK

When working on ACT Science questions, ask yourself whether you should be doing general-to-specific or specific-to-general thinking.

In your science classes in school, you mostly learn about general-to-specific thinking. Your teachers explain general rules of science to you and then expect you to apply these rules to answer questions and solve problems. Some ACT Science questions are like that as well. But a majority are not. Most ACT Science questions test specific-to-general thinking. The questions test your ability to see the kinds of patterns in specific data that, as a scientist, you would use to formulate your own general theories. We did something like this in Science Workout 1, when we theorized—based on the trends we found in a table of data—that the pollutant Hg was in some way detrimental to trout populations.

HOW EXPERIMENTS WORK

Many ACT passages describe experiments and expect you to understand how they're designed. Experiments help scientists do specific-to-general thinking in a reliable and efficient way. Consider the tadpole researcher above. In a real-world situation, what would probably happen is that she would notice some of the frogs develop from tadpoles and wonder if maybe they all did. Then she'd know what to look for and could check all the frogs systematically. This process contains the two basic steps of any experiment:

- Forming a theory (guessing that all frogs come from tadpoles)

- Testing a theory (checking the frogs to see if this guess was right)

Scientists are often interested in cause-and-effect relationships. Having formed her theory about tadpoles, a scientist might wonder what *causes* a tadpole to become a frog. To test causal relationships, a special kind of experiment is needed. She must test one possible cause at a time in order to isolate which one actually produces the effect in question. For example, the scientist might inject tadpoles with several different kinds of hormones. Some of these tadpoles might die. Others might turn into frogs normally. But a few—those injected with Hormone X, say—might remain tadpoles for an indefinite time. One reasonable explanation is that Hormone X in some way inhibited whatever causes normal frog development. In other words, the scientist would hypothesize a causal relationship between Hormone X and frog development.

EXPERIMENTS

The experimental method requires that the researcher focus on one factor that varies while other factors remain constant. Experiments often use some sort of control group to make sure that the factor investigated really is significant.

Watch Your Tadpoles' Diets

The relationship between Hormone X and frog development, however, would not be demonstrated very well if the scientist also fed different diets to different tadpoles, kept some in warmer water, or allowed some to have more room to swim than others—or if she didn't also watch tadpoles who were injected with no hormones at all but who otherwise were kept under the same conditions as the treated tadpoles. Why? Because if the "eternal tadpoles" had diets that differed from that of the others, the scientist wouldn't know whether it was Hormone X or the special diet that kept the eternal tadpoles from becoming frogs. Moreover, if their water was warmer than that of the others, maybe it was the warmth that somehow kept the tadpoles from developing. And if she didn't watch untreated tadpoles (a "control group"), she couldn't be sure whether under the same conditions a normal, untreated tadpole would also remain undeveloped.

THE VARYING FACTOR

Many ACT Science questions ask you to determine the purpose of an experiment or to design one yourself. To figure out the purpose of an experiment, look to see what factor was allowed to change: That's what's being tested. To design an experiment yourself, keep everything constant except the factor you must investigate.

Thus, a scientist creating a well-designed experiment will:

- Ensure that there's a single factor (like Hormone X) that varies from test to test or group to group

- Ensure that all other factors (diet, temperature, space, etcetera) remain the same

- (Often) ensure that there is a control group (tadpoles who don't get any Hormone X at all) for comparison purposes (though a control group isn't always necessary)

Find What Varies

One of the advantages of knowing how experiments work is that you can tell what a researcher is trying to find out about by checking to see what she allows to vary. That's what is being researched—in this case, Hormone X. Data about things other than hormones and tadpole-to-frog development would be outside the design of the experiment. Information about other factors might be interesting, but could not be part of a scientific proof.

For example, if some of the injected tadpoles that did grow into frogs later actually turned into princes, the data from experiments about the hormone they were given would not prove what causes frogs to become princes, though the data *could* be used to design *another* experiment intended to explore what could make a frog become a prince.

Therefore, whenever you see an experiment in Science Reasoning, you should ask yourself:

- **What's the factor that's being varied?** That is what is being tested.

- **What's the control group?** It's the group that has nothing special done to it (again, there won't *always* be a control group).

- **What do the results show?** What differences exist between the results for the control group and those for the other group or groups? Or between the results for one treated group and those for another, differently treated group?

HANDLING EXPERIMENT QUESTIONS

The following is a full-fledged Science Reasoning passage organized around two experiments. Use the three-Step Approach as usual (pre-read the passage; consider the question stem; refer to the passage before looking at the choices), but this time, since this is a passage that centers on experiments, remember to ask yourself the three questions above. Take about 5 or 6 minutes to do the passage and its questions.

Passage II

A *mutualistic* relationship between two species increases the chances of growth or survival for both of them. Several species of fungi form mutualistic relationships called *mycorrhizae* with the roots of plants. The benefits to each species are shown in the figure below.

Some of the plant species that require or benefit from the presence of mycorrhizal fungi are noted below.

Cannot survive without mycorrhizae	Grow better with mycorrhizae
All conifers Some deciduous trees (e.g. birch, beech) Orchids	Citrus trees Ericaceae (heath, rhododendrons, azaleas) Grapes Soybeans

Agronomists investigated the effects of mycorrhizae on plant growth and survival in the following studies.

Study 1

Three 4-acre plots were prepared with soil from a pine forest. The soil for Plot A was mixed with substantial quantities of cultured mycorrhizal fungi. The soil for Plot B contained only naturally occurring mycorrhizal fungi. The soil for Plot C was sterilized in order to kill any mycorrhizal fungi. Additionally, Plot C was lined with concrete. After planting, Plot C was covered with a fabric that filtered out microorganisms while permitting air and light to penetrate, as shown below. 250 pine seedlings were planted in each of the 3 plots. All plots received the same amount of water. The 6-month survival rates were recorded in the table below.

Cross-section of Plot C

SECTION II: SKILL-BUILDING WORKOUTS

	# Seedlings alive after 6 months	Utilization of available K (average)	Utilization of available P (average)
Plot A	107	18%	62%
Plot B	34	10%	13%
Plot C	0	N/A	N/A

N/A = not applicable

Study 2

The roots of surviving seedlings from Plots A and B were analyzed to determine how efficiently they absorbed potassium (K) and phosphorus (P) from the soil. The results were added to the table above.

1. The most likely purpose of the concrete liner was:
   A. to block the seedlings from sending out taproots to water below the plot.
   B. to prevent mycorrhizal fungi in the surrounding soil from colonizing the plot.
   C. to absorb potassium and phosphorus from the soil for later analysis.
   D. to provide a firm foundation for mycorrhizal fungi in the plot.

   (A) (B) (C) (D)

2. Mycorrhizae are highly susceptible to acid rain. Given the information from the passage, acid rain is probably most harmful to:
   F. wheat fields.
   G. birch forests.
   H. orange groves.
   J. grape vines.

   (F) (G) (H) (J)

3. In a third study, pine seedlings were planted in soil from a different location. The soil was prepared as in Study 1. This time, the survival rates for seedlings planted in Plot A and Plot B were almost identical to each other. Which of the following theories would NOT help to explain these results?
   A. Sterilization killed all the naturally occurring mycorrhizal fungi in the new soil.
   B. The new soil was so mineral-deficient that it could not sustain life.
   C. The new soil was naturally more fertile for pine seedlings than that used in Study 1.
   D. Large quantities of mycorrhizal fungi occurred naturally in the new soil.

   (A) (B) (C) (D)

4. According to the passage, in which of the following ways do plants benefit from mycorrhizal associations?

   I. More efficient sugar production

   II. Enhanced ability to survive drought

   III. Increased mineral absorption

   F. I only

   G. III only

   H. II and III only

   J. I, II, and III

   Ⓕ Ⓖ Ⓗ Ⓙ

5. Which of the following generalizations is supported by the results of Study 2?

   A. Mycorrhizal fungi are essential for the survival of pine seedlings.

   B. Growth rates for pine seedlings may be improved by adding mycorrhizal fungi to the soil.

   C. Mycorrhizal fungi contain minerals that are not normally found in pine forest soil.

   D. Pine seedlings cannot absorb all the potassium that is present in the soil.

   Ⓐ Ⓑ Ⓒ Ⓓ

ANSWERS

1. B, 2. G, 3. A, 4. H, 5. D

A Beneficial Fungus

Notice how many diagrams and tables were used here. That's common in experiment passages, where information is given to you in a wide variety of forms. Typically, though, the experiments themselves are clearly labeled, as Study 1 and Study 2 were here.

A quick prereading of the introduction would have revealed the topic of the experiments here—the "mutualistic relationship" between some fungi and some plant roots, the relationship called mycorrhiza ("myco" for short). The first diagram just shows you who gets what out of this relationship. The benefit accruing to the plant (the arrow pointing to the word *plant*) is an increased ability to absorb water and minerals. The benefit accruing to the fungus (the other arrow) is the plant-synthesized sugars on which the fungus feeds. That's the mutual benefit that the myco association creates.

Notice, by the way, that reading this first diagram alone is enough to answer **Question 4**, which we'll do right now. The question is asking: What do the plants get out of the association? And we just answered that—increased ability to absorb water and minerals. Statement III is obviously correct, but so is Statement II, since increased water absorption would indeed enhance the plant's ability to survive drought (a drought is a shortage of water, after all). Statement I, though, is a distortion. We know that the *fungi* benefit from sugars produced by the plants, but we don't have any evidence that the association actually causes plants to produce sugar more efficiently. So I is out; II and III are in, making H the answer to question 4.

Can't Live Without Those Fungi

But let's get back to the passage. We've just learned who gets what out of the myco association. Now we get a chart that shows what *kind* of plants enter into such associations. Some (those in the first column) are so dependent on myco associations that they can't live without them. Others (those in the second column) merely grow better with them; presumably they could live without them.

Here again, there's a question we can answer based solely on information in this one table. **Question 2** tells us that mycos are highly susceptible to acid rain, and then asks what kind of plant communities would be most harmed by acid rain. Well, if acid rain hurts mycos, then the plants that are *most* dependent on myco fungi (that is, the ones listed in the first column) would be the *most* harmed by acid rain. Of the four choices, only birch forests—choice G—correspond to something in column 1 of the table. Birch trees can't even *survive* without myco fungi, so anything that hurts myco fungi would inferably hurt birch forests. (Grapevines and orange groves—which are citrus trees—would *also* be hurt by acid rain, but not as much, since they *can* survive without myco fungi; meanwhile, we're told nothing about wheat in the passage.)

Well, we've answered two of the five questions already and we haven't even gotten to the first experiment. That brings up an important point—namely, that even in passages that center around experiments, there are plenty of Data Analysis questions. Don't expect there to be passages that have only Data Analysis Questions, other passages that have only Experiment Questions, and others that have only Principle Questions. Most passages will have a mixture of all three.

SOME POINTS ARE QUICKER THAN OTHERS

Many questions on experiment passages will be answerable based solely on the data contained in a single graph or table. You can get these points with relative ease, even if you don't have time for, or don't fully understand, the experiments.

Study 1

Now look at the first experiment. Three plots, each with differently treated soil, are planted with pine seedlings. Plot A gets soil with cultivated myco fungi; Plot B gets untreated soil with only naturally occurring myco fungi; and Plot C gets no myco fungi at all, since the soil has been sterilized and isolated (via the concrete lining and the fabric covering). Now ask yourself the three important experiment questions.

KAPLAN

- **What's the factor being varied?** The factor being varied is the amount of myco fungi in the soil. Plot A gets lots; Plot B gets just the normal amount; Plot C gets none at all. It's clear, then, that the scientists are testing the effects of myco fungi on the growth of pine seedlings.

- **What's the control group?** The plants in Plot B, since they get untreated soil. To learn the effects of the fungi, the scientists will then compare the results from fungi-rich Plot A with the control, and the results from fungi-poor Plot C with the same control.

- **What do the results show?** The results are listed in the first column of the table below the illustration of Plot C. And they are decisive: No seedlings at all survived in Plot C; 34 did in Plot B; and 107 did in Plot A. The minimums and maximums coincide. Minimum fungi = minimum number of surviving seedlings; maximum fungi = maximum number of surviving seedlings. Clearly there's a cause-and-effect relationship here. Myco fungi probably help pine seedlings survive.

Questions 1 and 3 can be answered solely on the basis of Study 1. **Question 1** is merely a procedural question: Why the concrete liner in Plot C? Well, in the analysis of the experiment above, we saw that the factor being varied was the amount of myco fungi. Plot C was designed to have none at all. Thus, one can safely assume that the concrete liner was probably there to prevent any stray myco fungi from entering the sterilized soil—choice B.

Question 3 actually sets up an extra experiment based on Study 1. The soils were prepared in the exact same way, except that the soil came from a different location. The results? The number of surviving seedlings from Plots A and B were almost identical. What can that mean? Well, Plot A was supposed to be the fungi-rich plot, whereas Plot B (the control) was supposed to be the fungi-normal plot. But here they have the same results. However, notice that we're *not* told what those results are; it could be that no seedlings survived in any plots this time around.

WATCH FOR REVERSALS

Some questions on the ACT are reversal questions—that is, they ask for the one choice that *isn't* true. Question 3 is a classic example. The wrong choices are things that *could* explain the results; the correct answer is the one that *can't*. It's easy to get mixed up on these questions. Remember: Always double-check the question stem to make sure you're answering the right question!

The question—a reversal question—is phrased so that the three wrong choices are things that *could* explain the results; the correct choice will be the one that *can't*. Choices B, C, and D all *can* explain the results, since they all show how similar results could have been obtained from Plots A and B. If the new soil just couldn't support life—fungi or no fungi—well, Plots A and B would have gotten similar results; namely, no seedlings survive. On the other end of the spectrum, choices C and D show how the two plots might have gotten similar *high* survival rates. If there were lots of myco fungi naturally in this soil (that's choice D), then there wouldn't be all that much difference between the soils in Plots A and B. And if the soil were naturally extremely fertile for the pine seedlings (that's choice C), there must have been lots of fungi naturally present in the soil because pine tress (conifers) don't grow without fungi. So all three of these answers would help to explain similar results in Plots A and B.

Choice A, however, wouldn't help, since it talks about the sterilized soil that's in Plot C. The soil in Plot C won't affect the results in Plots A and B, so choice A is the answer here—the factor that *doesn't* help to explain the results.

Study 2

This study takes the surviving seedlings from Plots A and B in Study 1 and just tests how much potassium (K) and phosphorus (P) the roots have used. The results are listed in the second and third columns of the table. (Notice the "N/A"—not applicable—for Plot C in these columns, since there were no surviving seedlings to test in Plot C!) The data show much better utilization of both substances in the Plot-A seedlings, the seedlings that grew in a fungi-rich soil. This data would tend to support a theory that the myco fungi aid in the utilization of K and P, and that this in turn aids survival in pine seedlings.

The only question that hinges on Study 2 is **Question 5**. It asks what generalization would be supported by the specific results of Study 2. Notice that Study 2 involved only measuring K and P. It did not involve survival rates (that was Study 1), so Choice A can't be right. And *neither* study measured growth rates, so B is out. The minerals K and P were in the control group's soil, which was natural, untreated pine forest soil, so choice C is clearly unsupported.

But the data *did* show that not all of the potassium (K) could be absorbed by pine seedlings. Only 18 percent was absorbed in Plot A, while only 10 percent was absorbed in Plot B. That's a long way from 100 percent, so choice D seems a safe generalization to make.

PRACTICE WITH EXPERIMENT QUESTIONS

Now that we've taken you step by step through a Science Reasoning passage based on an experiment, it's time to try one on your own. Give yourself about 6 minutes for the following passage and questions. This time the explanations at the end will be very short:

Passage III

The flowchart on the next page shows the steps used by a chemist in testing sample solutions for positive ions of silver (Ag), lead (Pb), and mercury (Hg).

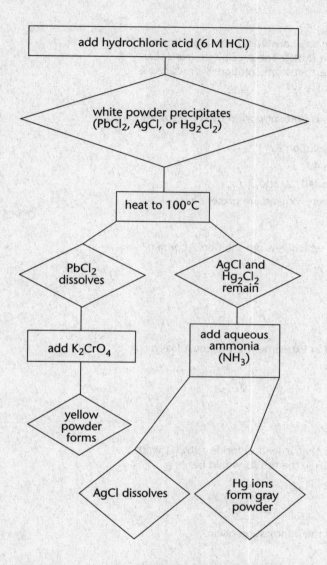

The following experiments were performed by the chemist:

Experiment 1

Hydrochloric acid (6 M HCl) was added to samples of four unknown solutions labeled 1, 2, 3, and 4. A white powder precipitated out of solutions 1, 2, and 3; no precipitate formed in solution 4.

Experiment 2

Each of the sample solutions from Experiment 1 was placed in a 100°C water bath for 15 minutes. The precipitate in solution 1 redissolved completely; solutions 2 and 3 still contained a white powder; solution 4 was unchanged. Solutions 2 and 3 were centrifuged to remove the precipitates, which were retained for further testing. Potassium chromate (K_2CrO_4) was then added to each sample. A bright yellow precipitate formed in solutions 1 and 2; none formed in solutions 3 or 4.

Experiment 3

The white powder centrifuged from solutions 2 and 3 in Experiment 2 was treated with aqueous ammonia (NH_3). The precipitate from solution 2 returned into solution, while that from solution 3 produced a gray powder.

6. Which of the following conclusions is best supported by the results of Experiment 1 alone?

   F. Silver ions are present only in solution 3.

   G. No ions are present in solution 4.

   H. Lead ions are present in solutions 1, 2, and 3.

   J. No positive ions of silver, mercury, or lead are present in solution 4.

7. Based on the experimental results, which ions did solution 2 contain?

   A. Lead ions only

   B. Lead and silver ions only

   C. Silver and mercury ions only

   D. Silver ions only

8. The yellow precipitate that formed in Experiment 2 was most likely:

   F. AgCl

   G. Hg_2Cl_2

   H. $PbCrO_4$

   J. Ag_2CrO_4

9. The experimental results suggest that if lead chloride ($PbCl_2$) were treated with aqueous ammonia (NH_3), the results would be:

   A. a bright yellow precipitate.

   B. a light gray precipitate.

   C. a powdery white precipitate.

   D. impossible to determine from the information given.

10. A student proposed that the analysis could be carried out more efficiently by heating the samples to 100° C before adding the 6 M HCl. This suggestion is:

   F. a bad idea; since $PbCl_2$ will not precipitate out of solution at this temperature, lead ions would be undetectable.

   G. a bad idea; the hot solutions could not be safely centrifuged.

   H. a good idea; the number of steps would be reduced from 3 to 2, saving much time and effort.

   J. a good idea; the chloride-forming reaction would proceed faster, eliminating the necessity for a 15-minute water bath.

KAPLAN

ANSWERS

6. J, 7. B, 8. H, 9. D, 10. F

Precipitating Ions

This experiment passage was somewhat different from the preceding one. In the mycorrhiza experiment, the scientists were thinking in specific-to-general terms (observing the growth of *specific* pine seedlings to come to a conclusion about the *general* effect of myco fungi on pine seedlings). In this series of experiments, the general principle is known—silver, lead, and mercury will precipitate or dissolve when certain things are done to them—and the scientists are using this principle to test certain specific substances in order to identify them. In fact, this is more like a procedure than an experiment, since there's no control group. But the same kind of experimental thinking—using the results of varying procedures to make reasonable inferences about what's happening—will get you your answers.

This passage also introduces the idea of a flowchart. Basically, the flowchart indicates an order of procedures. You follow the flowchart from top to bottom. The things in squares indicate what's done to a specimen; the things in diamonds indicate possible results.

FLOWCHARTS

Flowcharts are just what their name implies—charts depicting the "flow" of procedures. Follow a flowchart, either across or down, to find out what procedures come first, which come next, etcetera. Where flowcharts branch into two or more different arms, these represent alternative results. If one result occurs, you follow that "arm"; if the other result occurs, you follow the other "arm."

So, let's say you have an unknown substance. Following the flowchart, the first thing you do is add hydrochloric acid. If a white powder precipitates, that means there are positive ions of silver, lead, and/or mercury. (If nothing precipitates, the experiment is over; the substance is not of interest here.)

But, assuming you do get a white powder, how do you identify exactly which kind of white powder you have? You do the next procedure—heat it to 100°C. When you do this, any lead ions will dissolve, but any silver or mercury ions will remain as a powder. So, the flowchart has to divide here.

If part of your specimen dissolved when heated, that doesn't necessarily mean you have lead ions. To test for that, you add K_2CrO_4. If a yellow powder forms, then you know you've got lead; if not, you've got something else.

But what about the other branch? That tells you what has to be done if you *do* have some powder remaining after heating. And what you do is add NH_3. If the powder dissolves, you've got silver ions. If it forms a gray powder, on the other hand, what you've got are mercury (Hg) ions.

The Experiments

The three experiments here are actually three parts of a single experiment or procedure, each one using the results of the former in the way outlined in the flowchart. The questions ask for results at various points in the procedure, so let's look at them briefly now:

Key to Passage III

	ANSWER	REFER TO	COMMENTS
6.	J	Experiment 1 only	If any Ag, Pb, or Hg ions were present, they would have precipitated out as powder. Note that G is too extreme (could be ions of a fourth type not within scope of the experiment). Not enough testing in Exp. 1 to determine F or H.
7.	B	All 3 experiments	Heating left powder, so has to have Ag or Hg or both, so cut A. Addition of K_2CrO_4 left yellow precipitate, so must contain Pb (cut C and D).
8.	H	Experiment 2	Must be lead-based, because Ag and Hg precipitates were already removed (cut F, G, and J).
9.	D	Flowchart	No evidence for what would happen—two different branches of the flowchart.
10.	F	Flowchart	If the solutions were heated first, and then the HCl was added, the $PbCl_2$ would never form, and the chemist would not know whether lead ions were present.

As you've seen, not all experiments on the ACT Science Reasoning subject test are specific-to-general experiments; some are general-to-specific procedures. But the same kind of strict thinking—manipulating factors to narrow down possibilities—can get you points, no matter what direction you're thinking in.

ENGLISH WORKOUT 3
TRUST YOUR EAR—
MAKE IT ALL MATCH

In the first two English workouts, we discussed English questions that hinged mostly on common sense. But there are also some English questions—we call them Technicality Questions—that may seem harder because they test for the technical rules of grammar, requiring you to correct errors that don't necessarily harm the economy or sense of the sentence. But don't worry. You don't have to be a grammar whiz to get these questions right. Luckily, you can often detect these errors because they "sound funny." Most of the time on the ACT, it's safe to *trust your ear*.

THINK

Technicality Questions test specific rules of grammar. With questions of this type, there's no strong bias toward shorter answers, so trust your ear, not your eyes, on these questions.

For example, which of the following "sounds right" and which "sounds funny"?

• Bob doesn't know the value of the house he lives in.

• Bob don't know the value of the house he lives in.

The first sounds a lot better, right? And for many of these questions, all you need to do is "listen" carefully in this way. You may not know the formal rules of grammar, punctuation, and diction, but you communicate in English every day. You wouldn't be communicating unless you had a decent feel for the rules.

> **HINT:** *In questions testing specific rules of grammar, the answers tend to all be about the same length. "OMIT" is not usually a choice.*

FORMAL OR INFORMAL?

Some of you may have caught an apparent error in *both* of the examples above—ending a sentence with a preposition such as "in." This is undesirable in extremely formal writing. But ACT passages aren't usually that formal. The ACT test writers expect you to have a feel for the level of formality in writing. If the passage is informal, pick informal answers. If the passage is slightly formal (as most ACT passages are), pick slightly formal answers. If the passage is extremely formal, pick extremely formal answers. For example, if the passage starts off "You'll just love Bermuda—great beaches, good living . . . ." it won't end like this: "and an infinitely fascinating array of flora and fauna which may conceivably exceed, in range and scope, that of any alternative . . . ." It's too formal. Pick something like this: "You'll just love Bermuda—great beaches, good living, and lots of awesome plants and animals."

REGIONAL AND ETHNIC DIALECTS

Although ACT passages differ in level of formality, they all are designed to test "standard" English—the kind used by middle-class people in most of America. Test takers who speak regional or ethnic dialects may therefore find it more difficult to follow their ears on some ACT questions. In much of the South, for instance, it's common to use the word "in" with the word "rate," like this: "Mortality declined in a rate of almost 2 percent per year." Most speakers of English, however, use the word "at" with "rate," like this: "Mortality declined *at* a rate of . . . ." Fortunately, ACT questions testing issues like this are rare. And even if you do speak a "nonstandard" dialect, you probably know what standard English sounds like. The dialect used on most television and radio programs would be considered "standard."

THINK

Some students are offended that the ACT expects them to talk like somebody else. That feeling is justified, but it won't help improve your ACT score. Don't stubbornly pick an answer that "sounds" right to you but which you know wouldn't sound right to a "standard" English speaker. Your goal should be to get the best ACT score you can, not to prove a point about regional or ethnic biases.

LISTEN CAREFULLY

In the following short passage, many students will be able to determine a large number of correct answers by "listening" carefully to each choice.

KAPLAN

Passage II

Halloween was first celebrated <u>among various</u> Celtic
1
tribes in Ireland in the fifth century B.C. It traditionally

took place on the official last day of summer—

October <u>31, and</u> was named "All-Hallows' Eve." It
2
was believed that all persons who had died during

the previous year returned on this day to select a

person or animal to inhabit for the next twelve months,

until they could <u>pass peaceful</u> into the afterlife.
3

On All-Hallows' Eve, the Celts <u>were dressing</u> up as
4
demons and monsters to frighten the spirits away,

and tried to make their homes <u>as coldest</u> as possible
5
to prevent any stray ghosts from crossing their

thresholds. Late at night, the townspeople typically

gathered outside the village, where a druidic priest

would light a huge bonfire to frighten away ghosts and

to honor the sun god for the past summer's harvest.

Any villager <u>whom was</u> suspected of being possessed
6

would be captured, after which <u>they</u> might be
7
sacrificed in the bonfire as a warning to other spirits

seeking to possess the living.

When the Romans invaded the British Isles,

they adopted Celtic—not Saxon—Halloween

rituals, but outlawed human sacrifice

1. A. NO CHANGE
   B. among varied
   C. between the various
   D. between various

Ⓐ Ⓑ Ⓒ Ⓓ

2. F. NO CHANGE
   G. 31—and
   H. 31. And
   J. 31; and

Ⓕ Ⓖ Ⓗ Ⓙ

3. A. NO CHANGE
   B. pass peacefully
   C. passed peacefully
   D. be passing peaceful

Ⓐ Ⓑ Ⓒ Ⓓ

4. F. NO CHANGE
   G. were dressed
   H. dressed
   J. are dressed

Ⓕ Ⓖ Ⓗ Ⓙ

5. A. NO CHANGE
   B. colder
   C. coldest
   D. as cold

Ⓐ Ⓑ Ⓒ Ⓓ

6. F. NO CHANGE
   G. whom were
   H. who was
   J. who were

Ⓕ Ⓖ Ⓗ Ⓙ

7. A. NO CHANGE
   B. it
   C. he or she
   D. those

Ⓐ Ⓑ Ⓒ Ⓓ

SECTION II: SKILL-BUILDING WORKOUTS

in A.D. 61. Instead, they used effigies for their

sacrifices. In time, as <u>belief in</u> spirit possession waned,
8

Halloween rituals lost their serious aspect and

<u>had been</u> instead performed for amusement.
9

    Irish immigrants, fleeing from the

potato famine in the 1840s, <u>brought there</u>
10

Halloween customs to the United States. In New

England, Halloween became a night of costumes and

practical jokes. Some favorite pranks <u>included</u>
11

<u>unhinging</u> front gates and overturning outhouses.
11

The Irish also introduced the custom of carving jack-o'-

lanterns. The ancient Celts probably began the

tradition by hollowing out a large turnip, carving it

with a demon's face, and lighting it from inside with a

candle. Since there were <u>far less</u> turnips in New
12

England than in Ireland, the Irish immigrants were

forced to settle for pumpkins.

    Gradually, Halloween celebrations spread to other

regions of the United States. Halloween has been a

popular holiday ever since, <u>although these days it's</u>
13

principal celebrants are children <u>rather than</u> adults.
14

8. F. NO CHANGE
   G. belief for
   H. believing about
   J. belief of

9. A. NO CHANGE
   B. having been
   C. have been
   D. were

Ⓐ Ⓑ Ⓒ ●

10. F. NO CHANGE
   G. brought they're
   H. brought their
   J. their brought-in

Ⓕ Ⓖ ● Ⓙ

11. A. NO CHANGE
   B. include unhinging
   C. had included unhinged
   D. includes unhinged

● Ⓑ Ⓒ Ⓓ

12. F. NO CHANGE
   G. lots less
   H. not as much
   J. far fewer

Ⓕ Ⓖ Ⓗ ●

13. A. NO CHANGE
   B. although these days its
   C. while now it's
   D. while not it is

Ⓐ ● Ⓒ Ⓓ

14. F. NO CHANGE
   G. rather then
   H. rather
   J. else then

● Ⓖ Ⓗ Ⓙ

<table>
<tr><td colspan="3" align="center">Key</td></tr>
<tr><td>ANSWER</td><td>PROBLEM</td><td>SOLUTION</td></tr>
<tr><td>1. A</td><td>among/between distinction</td><td>See Error 18 below</td></tr>
<tr><td>2. G</td><td>commas and dashes mixed</td><td>See Error 6 below</td></tr>
<tr><td>3. B</td><td>use of adjectives and adverbs</td><td>See Error 7 below</td></tr>
<tr><td>4. H</td><td>unnecessary-ing ending</td><td>See Error 16 below</td></tr>
<tr><td>5. D</td><td>comparative/superlative</td><td>See Error 17 below</td></tr>
<tr><td>6. H</td><td>who/whom confusion</td><td>See Error 11 below</td></tr>
<tr><td>7. C</td><td>pronoun usage error</td><td>See Error 1 below</td></tr>
<tr><td>8. F</td><td>preposition error</td><td>See Error 10 below</td></tr>
<tr><td>9. D</td><td>tense problem with to be</td><td>See Error 15 below</td></tr>
<tr><td>10. H</td><td>they're/there/their mixup</td><td>See Error 13 below</td></tr>
<tr><td>11. A</td><td>verb tense problem</td><td>See Error 14 below</td></tr>
<tr><td>12. J</td><td>less/fewer confusion</td><td>See Error 19 below</td></tr>
<tr><td>13. B</td><td>it's/its confusion</td><td>See Error 12 below</td></tr>
<tr><td>14. F</td><td>then/than confusion</td><td>See Error 17 below</td></tr>
</table>

MAKE IT ALL MATCH

Many students could rely almost exclusively on their ear to correct many of the above errors. But there are a few English questions on every ACT that test errors your ear probably won't or can't catch. If you've got a good ear for English, there might be only a handful of such questions on the test. If not, there might be many more. For these, you'll have to think about the rules more formally. But fortunately, only a small number of rules are typically involved, and we'll discuss them all in this workout. Even more fortunately, most of the technicalities tested on the ACT boil down to one general principle: *Make it all match.*

CLASSIC GRAMMAR ERRORS

The rest of this workout is designed to help you build your own "flag list" of common errors on the ACT that your ear might not catch. Consider each classic error. If it seems like common sense to you (or, better, if the error just *sounds* like bad English to you, while the correction *sounds* like good English), you probably don't have to add it to your flag list. On the other hand, if it doesn't seem obvious, add it to your list.

As we'll see, making things match works in two ways. Some rules force you to match one part of the sentence with another part. Other rules force you to match the right word or word form with the intended meaning.

Classic Grammar Error 1: *they* **and** *it* **(singulars and plurals)**

The most tested "matching" rule on the ACT is this: Singular nouns must match with singular verbs and pronouns, and plural nouns must match with plural verbs and pronouns. The most common error in this area involves the use of the word *they.* It's plural, but in everyday speech, we often use it as a singular.

Sentence—"If a student won't study, they won't do well."

Problem—*A student* (singular) and *they* (plural) don't match.

Correction—"If students won't study, they won't do well," or "If a student won't study, he or she won't do well."

Classic Grammar Error 2: *and* **(compound subjects)**

Another common matching error concerns "compound subjects" (lists).

Sentence—"The fool gave the wrong tickets to Bob and I."

Problem—*I* is a subject; it can't be the object of the preposition *to.*

Correction—"The fool gave the wrong tickets to Bob and me."

> **HINT:** *Try dropping the rest of the list* (Bob and). *"The fool gave the wrong tickets to I" should sound funny to you.*

Classic Grammar Error 3: commas or dashes (parenthetical phrases)

One rule of punctuation is tested far more often than any other on the ACT. Parenthetical phrases must begin and end with the same punctuation mark. Such phrases can be recognized because without them the sentence would still be complete. For instance: "Bob, on his way to the store, saw a large lizard in the street." If you dropped the phrase "on his way to the store," the sentence would still be complete. Thus, this phrase is parenthetical. It could be marked off with commas, parentheses, or dashes. But the same mark is needed at both ends of the phrase.

Sentence—"Bob—on his way to the store, saw a lizard."

Problem—The parenthetical phrase starts with a dash but finishes with a comma.

Correction—"Bob, on his way to the store, saw a lizard."

Classic Grammar Error 4: commas (run-ons and comma splices)

The ACT test makers expect you to understand what makes a sentence and what doesn't. You can't combine two sentences into one with a comma (though you can with a semicolon or conjunction).

Sentence—"Ed's a slacker, Sara isn't."

Problem—Two sentences are spliced together with a comma.

Correction—"Ed's a slacker, but Sara isn't." or "Ed's a slacker; Sara isn't." or "Ed, unlike Sara, is a slacker."

Usually, only one thing should happen in each sentence. There should be one "major event." There are only a few ways to put more than one event in a sentence. One way is to connect the sentences with a conjunction (a word like *and* or *but*), as in the first correction. Or, as in the second, a semicolon can stand for such a word. The other way is to "subordinate" one event to the other in a clause, as in the third correction.

Classic Grammar Error 5: fragment

This rule goes hand in hand with the one above. A sentence must have at least one "major event." A "fragment" is writing that could be a subordinate part of a sentence, but not a whole sentence itself.

Sentence—"Emily listened to music. While she studied."

Problem—"She studied" would be a sentence, but *while* makes this a fragment.

Correction—"Emily listened to music while she studied."

Classic Grammar Error 6: any punctuation mark

The ACT doesn't test tricky rules of punctuation. But it does expect you to know what the punctuation marks mean and to match their use to their meanings. Here are some common punctuation marks and their meanings:

Period (.)—means "full stop" or "end of sentence."

Question mark (?)—serves the same purpose, but for questions.

Exclamation mark (!)—can be used instead of a period, but is generally inappropriate for all but very informal writing because it indicates extreme emotion.

Comma (,)—means "little stop." In many cases a comma is optional. But never use a comma where a stop would be confusing, as in: "I want to go, to the, store."

Semicolon (;)—used to separate two complete, but closely related thoughts.

Colon (:)—works like an "=" sign, connecting two equivalent things. Colons are usually used to begin a list.

Dash (—)—can be used for any kind of pause, usually a long one or one indicating a significant shift in thought.

Classic Grammar Error 7: -*ly* endings (adverbs and adjectives)

The ACT expects you to understand the difference between adverbs (the -*ly* words) and adjectives. The two are similar because they're both "modifiers." They modify, or refer to, or describe, another word or phrase in the sentence. The trick is that nouns and pronouns must be modified by adjectives, while other words, especially verbs and adjectives themselves, must be modified by adverbs.

Sentence—"Anna is an extreme gifted child, and she speaks beautiful too."

Problem—*Extreme* and *beautiful* are adjectives, but they're supposed to modify an adjective (*gifted*) and a verb (*speaks*) here, so they should be adverbs.

Correction—"Anna is an extremely gifted child, and she speaks beautifully too."

Classic Grammar Error 8: *good* or *well*

In everyday speech, we often confuse the words *good* and *well*. But *good* is an adjective (it modifies a noun or pronoun); *well* is an adverb (it can modify verbs and adjectives).

Sentence—"Joe did good on the ACT."

Problem—*Good* is an adjective, but here it's modifying a verb (*did*), so use an adverb.

Correction—"Joe did well on the ACT."

One exception: "Well" can also be used as an adjective, when it means "healthy." So: "Joe was well again by the morning of the ACT" is correct, even though "well" is modifying the noun Joe.

Classic Grammar Error 9: *lie, lay, laid, lain*

The words *lay* and *lie* are easy to confuse because they look alike and have similar meanings. The key difference in meaning is point of view. If the speaker is doing something without a direct object, he is "lying." If the speaker is doing it to something else, he is "laying." So, for example, "I will go lie down" (not *lay down*), but "I will lay this pencil on the desk" (not *lie it*).

It gets worse. The past tense of *lay* is *laid*. That's not too hard. The confusing word is *lie*. The past tense of *lie* is *lay*; when used for special tenses (with the words *had, have,* or *been,* for example), the form is *lain*. Thus, you'd say "I lay down" (meaning you, yourself, took a rest at some time in the past), or "I have lain down for a nap every afternoon for years now." But you'd say, "I laid that pencil on the desk yesterday, just as I have laid it on the desk every day for years now."

Don't confuse *lie* with the word *lie* that relates to dishonesty. The past tense of *lie* (meaning to tell an untruth) is *lied*.

Sentence—"I lied. I said that I had lain down, but I hadn't. In fact, I had just laid the pencil down. After I lied, though, I lay down to repent for having lied."

Problem—None. All uses of *lie, lied, lay, laid*, and *lain* above are **correct**.

Try not to get bogged down with *lie* and *lay*. If you don't get it, don't sweat it. It will account for one point if it appears at all.

Classic Grammar Error 10: *in, of, to, for* (idiomatic preposition use)

Whenever you see a preposition, double check to make sure it makes sense and that it "matches" the other words. Many words require particular prepositions.

Sentences—"She tried to instill on me a respect to the law."
"I want to protect you in all dangers."

Problem—The prepositions don't match the verbs.

Corrections—"She tried to instill in me a respect for the law."
"I want to protect you from all dangers."

Classic Grammar Error 11: *who* or *whom*

Many students fear the words *who* and *whom* more than any other grammatical conundrum. Fear no more. There's an easy way to remember when to use them: They work the same way *he* and *him*

work. Turn the sentence into a question as we've done in the example below. If the answer to the question is *he*, the form should be *who*. If the answer is *him*, the form should be *whom*. Notice that the *m*'s go together.

Sentence—"Always remember who you're speaking to."

Problem—*Who* is wrong. Ask: Speaking to who? Speaking to him, not to he. So, it should be *whom*.

Correction—"Always remember whom you're speaking to."

Some students try to avoid the who/whom problem by using the word *which* instead. Nope. It's not nice to call people "whiches." Never use the word *which* for a person.

Classic Grammar Error 12: *its* or *it's* (apostrophe use)
Probably the trickiest rule on the ACT is the proper use of apostrophes. Apostrophes are used primarily for two purposes: possessives and contractions. When you make a *noun* (not a pronoun) possessive by adding an "s," you use an apostrophe. Examples: Bob's, the water's, a noodle's. You NEVER use an apostrophe to make a pronoun possessive—pronouns have special possessive forms. You'd never write "her's." When you run two words together to form a single word, you use an apostrophe to join them. For example: You'd, he's, they're.

Apostrophes also have a few unusual uses, but luckily they're almost never tested on the ACT. So, master the basics and you're in good shape. The most common apostrophe issue on the ACT is usage of the words *its* and *it's*. A good way to remember which is which is that *its* and *it's* follow the same rule as do *his* and *he's*. Both *its* and *his* are possessive pronouns—so they have *no* apostrophes. Both *it's* and *he's* are contractions—so they *do* have apostrophes.

Sentence—"The company claims its illegal to use it's name that way."

Problem—*It's* is a contraction of *it is*; its is the possessive form of *it*.

Correction—"The company claims it's illegal to use its name that way."

Classic Grammar Error 13: *there, their*, or *they're* and *are* or *our* (proper word usage)
Some students confuse the words *there, their*, and *they're*. A good way to remember which is *they're* is to remember that contractions use apostrophes—so *they're* is the contraction for *they are*. You can tell which is *there* because it's spelled like *here*, and the words *here* and *there* match. (*Their* means of or belonging to them"; you'll just have to remember that one the old-fashioned way.)

Students also frequently confuse the words *are* (a verb) and *our* (a possessive). You can remember that *our* is spelled like *your*, another, less confusing possessive.

Classic Grammar Error 14: *sang, sung, brang, brung*, etcetera. (Verb forms)
When the answers differ because of different forms of the same or similar verbs (for example, *live, lives, lived*), ask yourself *who* did it and *when* did they do it? We would say "I now live" but "he now lives." In these sentences, the *who* is different—and so the verb changes. Similarly, we would say "I now live" but "I lived in the past." In these sentences, the *when* is different—so the verb changes.

Most verbs are "regular" in this way, with only the endings "s" and "d" to worry about. You use the "s" when the point of view is "he," "she," or "it" and the time is now (present tense). You use the "d" for times in the past. For times in the future, or several steps backward in time, there are no special endings. You use the words *will, will have, have,* and *had* for these time sequences. "I *will* live. I *will have* lived for twenty-five years by the time the next century begins. I *had* lived in Nebraska, but we moved. I *have* lived in Indiana since then."

But a few verbs are irregular. They have special forms. For example, we say "sang" rather than "singed" and "have sung" rather than "have singed" or "have sang." Each of these verbs must be learned separately.

One irregular verb commonly tested on the ACT is *bring.*

Sentence—"I've brung my umbrella to work."

Problem—*Brang* and *brung* aren't used in standard English.

Correction—"I've brought my umbrella to work."

Classic Grammar Error 15: *be* and *was* (forms of the verb *to be*)

The ACT tests the use of proper verb forms, especially of the verb *to be.* You *must* use the following forms. Memorize them if you have to:

PRESENT TENSE:	I *am*, we *are*, you *are*, they *are*, he *is*, she *is*, it *is*
PAST TENSE:	I *was*, we *were*, you *were*, they *were*, he/she/it *was*
FUTURE TENSE:	I/we/you/they/he/she/it *will be*
PERFECT TENSE:	I/we/you *have been*, he/she/it *has been*
PAST PERFECT:	I/we/you/he/she/it *had been*
FUTURE PERFECT:	I/we/you/he/she/it *will have been*

Notice that different forms of the verb (*am, are, is, were, was, will be, have been, had been, will have been*) are used depending on point of view (called "case" in grammar) and whether the action is now, in the past, or in the future (called "tense" in grammar). In many dialects, the words *be* and *was* are used instead of the special forms given. For example, many speakers might say "They *be* going home," or "They *was* going home." But the ACT would require you to write "They *are* (or *were*) going home."

Classic Grammar Error 16: *-ing* endings (unidiomatic verb use)

Don't use -ing endings where they aren't needed. They are used to indicate repeated or continuous action and shouldn't be used for a single action that occurs once.

Sentence—"When I left for the store, I was forgetting my list."

Problem—The *-ing* ending isn't necessary.

Correction—"When I left for the store, I forgot my list."

Classic Grammar Error 17: *-er* and *-est*, *more* and *most* (comparatives and superlatives)

Whenever you see the endings *-er* or *-est*, or the words *more* or *most*, double-check to make sure they're used logically. Words with *-er* or with *more* should be used to compare two only things. If there are more than two things involved, use *-est* or *most*.

Sentence—"Bob is the fastest of the two runners."

Problem—The comparison is between just two things, so *-est* is inappropriate.

Correction—"Bob is the faster of the two runners."

Don't use the words *more* or *most* if you can use the endings instead. Say "I think vanilla is tastier than chocolate," not "I think vanilla is more tasty than chocolate." Never use both *more* or *most* *and* an ending. Don't say "Of the five flavors of frozen yogurt I've eaten, strawberry delight is the most tastiest." Just say it's "the tastiest."

Classic Grammar Error 18: *between* or *among*
Make sure that you use the word *between* only when there are two things involved. When there are more than two things, or an unknown number of things, use *among*.

Sentence—"I will walk among the two halves of the class." "I will walk between the many students in class."

Problem—Use *between* for two things; *among* for more than two.

Correction—"I will walk between the two halves of the class." "I will walk among the many students in class."

Classic Grammar Error 19: *less* or *fewer*
Make sure that you use the word *less* only for uncountable things. When things can be counted, they are *fewer*.

Sentence—"I have fewer water than I thought, so I can fill less buckets."

Problem—You can count buckets; you can't count water.

Correction—"I have less water than I thought, so I can fill fewer buckets."

HINT: People are always countable, so use fewer *when writing about them.*

Classic Grammar Error 20: *hopefully*
Don't use the word *hopefully* to mean "I hope" or "let's hope." *Hopefully* means only "in a manner full of hope," and can be used only as an adverb.

Sentence—"Hopefully, I'll remember every item on my flag list."

Problem—*Hopefully* is not a substitute for *I hope*.

Correction—"I hope I'll remember every item on my flag list."

And let's hope that you do. As we've seen in the three English Workouts, common sense is all you need for most English questions, but some rules it pays to learn cold.

For a more thorough account of the grammar points you should know for the ACT, refer to the English Appendix.

MATH WORKOUT 3
FIGURING IT OUT

Every ACT Math subject test has 14 geometry questions and 4 trigonometry questions. Depending on what kind of score you're aiming for, you might be able to blow off those few trigonometry questions. But you probably don't want to blow off that many geometry questions.

Fortunately, a good number of the geometry questions are straightforward textbook questions. Nothing's distorted or disguised: They are what they seem. You know what to do with these questions—if you know your geometry—the instant you understand them.

TEN TEXTBOOK QUESTIONS

Here's a set of ten such questions. When you take the ACT you will see quite a few questions just like these—possibly reworded and certainly with different numbers and figures. Use these questions to find out how well you remember your geometry.

1. In the figure below, line *t* crosses parallel lines *m* and *n*. What is the degree measure of ∠*x* ?

    A.   40
    B.   50
    C.   60
    D.   130
    E.   140

Ⓐ Ⓑ Ⓒ Ⓓ Ⓔ

2. In the figure below, △ABC is isosceles with AB = BC. What is the degree measure of ∠x ?

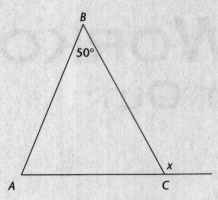

F. 50
G. 65
H. 100
J. 115
K. 130

Ⓕ Ⓖ Ⓗ Ⓙ Ⓚ

3. In the figure below, ∠B is a right angle and the lengths of $\overline{AB}$, $\overline{BC}$, and $\overline{CD}$ are given in units. What is the area of △ACD, in square units?

A. 10
B. 12
C. 16
D. 20
E. 32

Ⓐ Ⓑ Ⓒ Ⓓ Ⓔ

4. In the figure below, △ABC is similar to △DEF. ∠A corresponds to ∠D, ∠B corresponds to ∠E, and ∠C corresponds to ∠F. If the given lengths are of the same unit of measure, what is the value of x ?

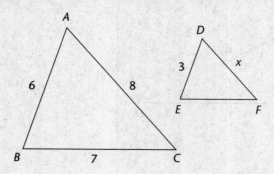

F. 3

G. 3.5

H. 4

J. 5

K. 6

Ⓕ Ⓖ Ⓗ Ⓙ Ⓚ

5. In △ABC below, ∠B is a right angle. If $\overline{AB}$ is 1 unit long and $\overline{BC}$ is 2 units long, how many units long is $\overline{AC}$?

A. $\sqrt{2}$

B. $\sqrt{3}$

C. 2

D. $\sqrt{5}$

E. 3

Ⓐ Ⓑ Ⓒ Ⓓ Ⓔ

6. In the figure below, $\overline{AC}$ is perpendicular to $\overline{BD}$, the measure of $\angle D$ is 30° and the measure of $\angle B$ is 45°. If $\overline{AD}$ is 6 units long, how many units long is $\overline{AB}$?

F. 3

G. $3\sqrt{2}$

H. $2\sqrt{6}$

J. $3\sqrt{3}$

K. 6

Ⓕ Ⓖ Ⓗ Ⓙ Ⓚ

7. In the figure below, $\overline{BE}$ is perpendicular to $\overline{AD}$, and the lengths of $\overline{AB}$, $\overline{BC}$, $\overline{CD}$, and $\overline{BE}$ are given in inches. What is the area, in square inches, of trapezoid *ABCD* ?

A. 24

B. 30

C. 32

D. 34

E. 36

Ⓐ Ⓑ Ⓒ Ⓓ Ⓔ

8. What is the area, in square inches, of a circle with a diameter of 8 inches?

F. 4π

G. 8π

H. 16π

J. 32π

K. 64π

Ⓕ Ⓖ Ⓗ Ⓙ Ⓚ

9. In the circle centered at *O* in the figure below, the measure of ∠*AOB* is 40°. If $\overline{OA}$ is 9 units long, how many units long is minor arc *AB* ?

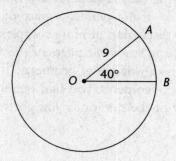

A. π
B. 2π
C. 9
D. 9π
E. 40

Ⓐ Ⓑ Ⓒ Ⓓ Ⓔ

10. In the figure below, *ABCD* is a square and $\overline{AB}$ is a diameter of the circle centered at *O*. If $\overline{AD}$ is 10 units long, what is the area, in square units, of the shaded region?

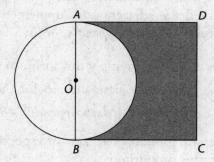

F. $100 - 50\pi$
G. $100 - 25\pi$
H. $100 - \frac{25\pi}{2}$
J. $100 - 10\pi$
K. $100 - 5\pi$

Ⓕ Ⓖ Ⓗ Ⓙ Ⓚ

ANSWERS

1. E, 2. J, 3. A, 4. H, 5. D, 6. G, 7. E, 8. H, 9. B, 10. H

SECTION II: SKILL-BUILDING WORKOUTS

10 correct: You have a solid grounding in geometry. Straightforward textbook geometry questions are no problem for you. Skip ahead to the section called More Complex Geometry Questions.

8–9 correct: You have a pretty good—if not perfect—grasp of the geometry you need to know for the ACT. Before moving on to the discussion of more complex geometry, read the explanations below of the questions you got wrong, and study the pages of the Appendix they direct you to.

0–7 correct: You have gaps in your knowledge of geometry. Before you can hope to get much out of our discussion of more complex geometry, you had better solidify your geometry foundations. Look at the explanations below of the questions you got wrong and study the pages of the Appendix they direct you to.

Explanations for the Textbook Ten

1. When a transversal crosses parallel lines, the four acute angles formed are all equal, the four obtuse angles formed are all equal, and any angles that are not equal are supplementary. The angle marked x is obtuse, so it's supplementary to the given 40° angle. $180 - 40 = 140$. The answer is E. (*Math Appendix, #79*)

2. The three angles of any triangle add up to 180°. Furthermore, the two angles opposite the equal sides of an isosceles triangle are equal. The given angle measures 50°, so the other two angles split the remaining 130°. Since those other two angles are equal, they each measure 65°. The angle marked x is adjacent and supplementary to a 65° angle, so $x = 180 - 65 = 115$. The answer is J. (*Math Appendix, #80*)

3. The formula for the area of a triangle is $A = \frac{1}{2}bh$. To apply this formula, you need the base and the height. Here you can use $\overline{CD}$ for the base and $\overline{AB}$ for the height. So: Area $= \frac{1}{2}(CD)(AB) = \frac{1}{2}(5)(4) = 10$. The answer is A. (*Math Appendix, #83*)

4. In similar triangles, corresponding sides are proportional. $\overline{DE}$ corresponds to $\overline{AB}$, and $\overline{DF}$ corresponds to $\overline{AC}$, so we can set up this proportion:

$$\frac{AB}{DE} = \frac{AC}{DF}$$

$$\frac{6}{3} = \frac{8}{x}$$

$$6x = 3 \times 8$$

$$6x = 24$$

$$x = 4$$

The answer is H. (*Math Appendix, #82*)

5. The Pythagorean theorem says: $(\text{leg}_1)^2 + (\text{leg}_2)^2 = (\text{hypotenuse})^2$. Here the legs have lengths of 1 and 2, so plug them into the formula:

$$
\begin{aligned}
(1)^2 + (2)^2 &= (\text{hypotenuse})^2 \\
1 + 4 &= x^2 \\
x^2 &= 5 \\
x &= \sqrt{5}
\end{aligned}
$$

The answer is D. (*Math Appendix, #84*)

6. The indicated angles tell you that ΔABC is a 45-45-90 triangle and that ΔACD is a 30-60-90 triangle. $\overline{AD}$ is the hypotenuse and $\overline{AC}$ is the shorter leg of the 30-60-90 triangle, so $AC = \frac{1}{2}(AD) = 3$. $\overline{AC}$ is also the shorter leg of the 45-45-90, and $\overline{AB}$, the side we're looking for, is the hypotenuse. Therefore, $AB = (AC)\sqrt{2} = 3\sqrt{2}$. The answer is G. (*Math Appendix, #85*)

7. The formula for the area of a trapezoid is $A = (\frac{b_1 + b_2}{2})h$, where b_1 and b_2 are the lengths of the parallel sides. You could think of it as the height times the *average* of the bases. In this case you're given the height (3 inches), one base (8 inches), and enough information to figure out the other base. Notice that ΔABE is a 3-4-5 triangle, so $AE =$ 4 inches. And if you were to drop an altitude down from point C, you'd get another 3-4-5 triangle on the right:

Now you can see that the bottom base is 16 inches. Plug these numbers into the formula:

$$
\begin{aligned}
A &= (\tfrac{b_1 + b_2}{2})h \\[6pt]
&= (\tfrac{8 + 16}{2}) \times 3 \\[6pt]
&= 12 \times 3 = 36
\end{aligned}
$$

The answer is E. (*Math Appendix, #87*)

8. The formula for the area of a circle is $A = \pi r^2$, where r is the radius. If the diameter is 8 inches, then the radius is 4 inches, which we plug into the formula:

$$A = \pi r^2$$
$$= \pi (4)^2$$
$$= 16\pi$$

The answer is H. (*Math Appendix, #91*)

9. The central angle of minor arc AB is $40°$, which is $\frac{1}{9}$ of the whole circle's $360°$. The length of minor arc AB, therefore, is $\frac{1}{9}$ of the whole circle's circumference.

$$C = 2\pi r = 2\pi (9) = 18\pi$$
$$\tfrac{1}{9} C = \tfrac{1}{9}(18\pi) = 2\pi$$

The answer is B. (*Math Appendix, #90*)

10. The shaded region is equal to the area of the square minus the area of the *semi*circle. The area of the square is $10 \times 10 = 100$. The radius of the circle is half of 10, or 5, so the area of the whole circle is $\pi(5)^2 = 25\pi$, and the area of the semicircle is $\frac{25\pi}{2}$. The square minus the semicircle, then, is: $100 - \frac{25\pi}{2}$. The answer is H. (*See Math Appendix, #87, #91*)

MORE COMPLICATED GEOMETRY QUESTIONS

ACT geometry questions are not all as straightforward as the above. As if it weren't hard enough to remember all the facts and formulas needed for problems like the Textbook Ten above, the test writers have ways of further complicating geometry questions.

ACT geometry questions are not all what they seem. It's not always obvious at first what the question is getting at. Sometimes you really have to think about the figure and the given information before that light bulb goes on in your head. Often the inspiration that brings illumination is finding the hidden information.

Here's an example that doesn't come right out and say what it's all about.

1. In the figure below, ΔABC is a right triangle and $\overline{AC}$ is perpendicular to $\overline{BD}$. If $\overline{AB}$ is 6 units long, and $\overline{AC}$ is 10 units long, how many units long is $\overline{AD}$?

A. 3

B. $2\sqrt{3}$

C. 3.6

D. 4

E. $3\sqrt{2}$

At first this looks like a Pythagorean theorem question. In fact, the two given sides of ΔABC identify it as the 6-8-10 version of the 3-4-5 special right triangle. (*Math Appendix, #85*) So we know that $BC = 8$. So what? What good does that do us? How's that going to help us find AD?

The inspiration here is to realize that this is a "similar triangles" problem. We don't see the word *similar* anywhere in the question stem, but the stem and the figure combined actually tell us that all three triangles in the figure—ΔABC, ΔADB, and ΔBDC—are similar. We know the triangles are similar because they all have the same three angles. Here are the three triangles separated and oriented to show the correspondences:

In this orientation it's easy to see the proportion setup that will solve the problem:

$$\frac{10}{6} = \frac{6}{x}$$
$$10x = 36$$
$$x = 3.6$$

The answer is C.

Here's another example with hidden information:

2. In the figure below, the area of the circle centered at O is 25π, and $\overline{AC}$ is perpendicular to $\overline{DB}$. If $\overline{AC}$ is 8 units long, how many units long is $\overline{BD}$?

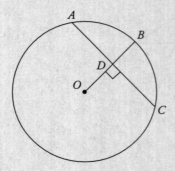

F. 2

G. 2.5

H. 3

J. 3.125

K. 4

This is a tough one. It's not easy to see how to get BD from the given information. You can use the area—25π—to figure out the radius, and then you'd know the length of $\overline{OB}$:

$$\text{Area} = \pi r^2$$
$$25\pi = \pi r^2$$
$$25 = r^2$$
$$r = 5$$

So you know $OB = 5$, but what about BD? If you knew OD, you could subtract that from OB to get what you want. But do you know OD? This is the place where most people get stuck.

The inspiration that will lead to a solution is that you can take advantage of the right angle at D. Look what happens when you take a pencil and physically add $\overline{OA}$ and $\overline{OC}$ to the figure:

KAPLAN

$\triangle OAD$ and $\triangle OCD$ are right triangles. And when we write in the lengths, we discover some special right triangles:

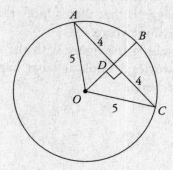

Now it's apparent that $OD = 3$. Since $OB = 5$, BD is $5 - 3 = 2$. The answer is F.

FIGURELESS PROBLEMS

Some ACT geometry problems present an extra challenge because they don't provide a figure. You have to "figure it out" for yourself. Try this one:

3. If one side of a right triangle is 3 units long, and a second side is 4 units long, which of the following could be the length, in units, of the third side?
   A. 1
   B. 2
   C. $\sqrt{7}$
   D. $3\sqrt{2}$
   E. $3\sqrt{3}$

The key to solving most figureless problems is to sketch a diagram, but sometimes that's not so easy because the test makers deliberately give you less information than you might like. Question 3 is the perfect example. It gives you two sides of a right triangle and asks for the third. Sounds familiar. And the two sides it gives you—3 and 4—*really* sound familiar. It's a 3-4-5, right?

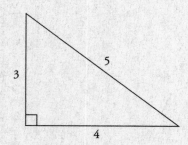

So the answer's 5...

Whoops! There's no 5 among the answer choices! What's going on?!

Better check back. Notice that the question asks, "Which of the following *could* be the length . . . . " That *could* is crucial. It suggests that there's more than one possibility. Our answer of 5 was too obvious. There's another one somewhere.

Can you think of another way of sketching the figure with the same given information? Who says that the 3 and 4 have to be the two legs? Look at what happens when you make one of them—the larger one, of course—the *hypotenuse* :

This is not a 3-4-5 triangle, because in a 3-4-5 the 3 and the 4 are the legs. This is no special right triangle; to figure out the length of the third side, resort to the Pythagorean theorem:

$$(\text{leg}_1)^2 + (\text{leg}_2)^2 = (\text{hypotenuse})^2$$
$$3^2 + x^2 = 4^2$$
$$9 + x^2 = 16$$
$$x^2 = 7$$
$$x = \sqrt{7}$$

The answer is C.

MANY STEPS AND MANY CONCEPTS

Some of the toughest ACT geometry questions are ones that take many steps to solve and combine many different geometry concepts. The following is an example.

4. In the figure below, $\overline{AB}$ is tangent to the circle at A. If the circumference of the circle is 12π units and $\overline{OB}$ is 12 units long, what is the area, in square units, of the shaded region?

F. $18\sqrt{3} - 6\pi$
G. $24\sqrt{3} - 6\pi$
H. $18\sqrt{3} - 2\pi$
J. $12\pi - 12$
K. $24\sqrt{3} - 2\pi$

This is about as hard as they come on the ACT. It is by no means clear how the given inform tion—the circumference of the circle and the length of $\overline{OB}$—will lead you to the area of the shaded region. The way through this problem has too many twists and turns for you to be able to see straight through it.

So what do you do? Give up? No. *Don't* give up immediately unless you're really short on time or you know for sure you can't do the problem.

So then should you just plow ahead blindly and figure out every length, angle, and area you can and see where that leads you? *Well, not exactly.* It would be better to be more systematic.

The key to success with a circuitous problem like question 4 is to focus on your destination—what you're looking for—and think about what you need to get there. Then go back to the given information and see what you can do with it to get you going in the right direction. Think about where you're headed before you take even one step; otherwise you may just have to backtrack.

Your destination in question 4 is "the area of the shaded region." That region is a shape that has no name, let alone an area formula. Like most shaded regions, this one is in fact the difference between two familiar shapes with names and area formulas. Think of the shaded region in question 4 as:

$$(\text{the area of } \triangle AOB) - (\text{the area of sector } AOC)$$

With that in mind, you know you need to figure out the area of the triangle and the area of the sector.

First, the triangle. You are explicitly given $OB = 12$. You are also given that $\overline{AB}$ is tangent to the circle at A, which tells you that $\overline{OA}$ is a radius and that $\angle OAB$ is a right angle. So if you can figure out the radius of the circle, you'll have two sides of a right triangle, which will enable you to figure out the third side, and then figure out the area.

You can get the radius from the given circumference. Plug what you know into the formula and solve for r:

$$\text{Circumference} = 2\pi r$$
$$12\pi = 2\pi r$$
$$r = \frac{12\pi}{2\pi} = 6$$
$$OA = 6$$

Aha! So it turns out that $\triangle AOB$ is no ordinary right triangle. Since one leg—6—is exactly half the hypotenuse—12—you're looking at a 30-60-90 triangle. By applying the well-known side ratios $(1:\sqrt{3}:2)$ for a 30-60-90 triangle (*Appendix B, #85*), you determine that $AB = 6\sqrt{3}$. Now you can plug the lengths of the legs in for the base and altitude in the formula for the area of a triangle, and this is what you'll get:

$$\text{Area} = \frac{1}{2}bh$$
$$= \frac{1}{2}(6\sqrt{3})(6)$$
$$= 18\sqrt{3}$$

Already it looks like the answer is going to be F or H—they're the choices that begin with $18\sqrt{3}$. You could just guess F or H and move on, but if you've come this far, you might as well go all the way.

Next, you need to determine the area of the sector. Fortunately, while working on the triangle, you figured out the two things you need to get the area of the sector: the radius of the circle (6) and the measure of the central angle (60°). The radius tells you that the area of the whole circle (πr^2) is 36π. And the central angle tells you that the sector is $\frac{60}{360}$ or $\frac{1}{6}$ of the circle. One sixth of 36π is 6π. So the area of the shaded region is $18\sqrt{3} - 6\pi$, choice F.

TRIGONOMETRY

It's always obvious when you've come to one of the trigonometry questions. There are only four of them, so you can still get a good score without them. But trigonometry questions are generally among the most straightforward and predictable math questions on the ACT. "SOHCAHTOA" alone is usually enough to get you two right answers. If you can master Math Appendix #96–100, you can get all four. It's up to you. You are in control. No one knows your strengths and weaknesses better than you. If you've never studied trigonometry, or if you know you never "got" it, SKIP THE TRIG QUESTIONS. If trigonometry is your favorite math topic, go for it! If, like most people, you're somewhere between those extremes, pick your spots. Do the ones you understand; guess on the ones you don't.

WHAT TO DO NEXT

If you worked through this chapter and you discovered any rusty areas in your geometry knowledge, check out Math Appendix #78–95. If you have time, you should also review trigonometry in Math Appendix #96–100.

READING WORKOUT 3
ARTS AND SCIENCES

Now that you've learned the general approach to ACT Reading (in Reading Workout 1) and the approach for each of the specific question-types (in Reading Workout 2), let's look more closely at the two kinds of ACT passage that give students the most trouble—the Prose Fiction passage and the Natural Sciences passage.

As shown in ACT Basics, the passage breakdown for every ACT Reading test is as follows:

Prose Fiction—one passage per test

Nonfiction—three passages per test, one each in:

- Social Studies

- Natural Sciences

- Humanities

Your approach will be essentially the same for all three nonfiction passages, since they're all well-organized essays. Your approach to the Prose Fiction passage, however, will be somewhat different.

What follows are two full ACT Reading passages—one Prose Fiction passage and one Natural Sciences passage (which, for convenience, we'll call just Science)—complete with questions. We'll talk about specific strategies for each, but, just as important, we'll talk about how you can bring together everything you've learned so far and combine this knowledge into a plan of attack for *all* Reading passages. At the end of the Workout, we'll also show you how to salvage a few extra points if you find yourself near the end of the test with not enough time to read the final passage.

THE PROSE FICTION PASSAGE

The Prose Fiction passage differs from the three nonfiction passages in that it is not a well-structured essay designed to communicate ideas in a logical, orderly way. It is, usually, a story in which characters fully equipped with their own motivations and emotions interact with each other in revealing ways. For that reason, the Prose Fiction passage won't break down into an orderly outline or road map, so don't even try to characterize the function of each paragraph. Pay attention instead to the *story*.

WITHOUT A MAP

Prose Fiction passages aren't constructed in an orderly way, as the nonfiction passages are. So don't try to construct a mental road map for the Prose Fiction passage. Instead, *pay attention to the story and the characters.*

In the Prose Fiction passage, almost all of the questions relate to the characters. Your job is to find the answers to the following questions:

- **Who are these people?** What are they like? How are they related to each other?

- **What is their state of mind?** Are they angry? Sad? Reflective? Excited?

- **What's going on?** What's happening on the surface? What's happening *beneath* the surface?

Most of the passages focus on one person, or are written from the point of view of one of the characters. Figure out who this main character is and pay special attention to what he or she is like. Read between the lines to determine unspoken emotions and attitudes. Little hints—a momentary frown, a pointed or sarcastic comment—are sometimes all you have to go on, so *pay attention*. In fact, you'll probably want to spend more time prereading the Prose Fiction passage than you do any of the other three passages. It's important to get a good feel for the tone and style of the passage as a whole before going to the questions.

WHAT A CHARACTER!

In the Prose Fiction passage, you want to focus on the *characters*. Who are they? What are they like? The author won't usually tell you outright. You have to figure it out for yourself, judging from what they say and do.

Fortunately, the questions in these passages tend to go quicker than in the other passages, so you'll be able to make up some of that extra time you spend on the passage.

KAPLAN

MAKE IT A MOVIE IN YOUR HEAD

Try to make the passage into a movie! Imagine the scenes, the characters, the events. In the Prose Fiction passage, it should be easy to imagine the story unfolding like a movie. Pay careful attention not only to what the characters say but how they say it as well.

And don't forget to read actively, as always. Don't just read and then react. Once you have an idea of the personality of the characters, you should be able to anticipate how they will react to the events of the passage.

ATTACKING THE PROSE FICTION PASSAGE

What follows is a typical ACT Prose Fiction passage, complete with questions. Before trying it, you might want to glance back at the techniques discussed in our first Reading Workout. Review the three-Step Reading Strategy. Recall that you should probably plan to spend about three minutes prereading (a little more, actually, since this is the Prose Fiction passage). Then do whichever questions you can figure out quickly. Skip any hard or time-consuming problems and come back for them later.

When you work on the questions, constantly refer to the passage. Plan to spend much more time with your eyeball pointed at the passage than at the questions. And don't forget to answer the questions in your own words (based on what you've preread and reread in the passage) before you look at the answers.

Passage III

I recall a mist starting in as I crossed the lawn that afternoon. I was making my way up to the summer house for the purpose of clearing away the remains of his lordship's taking tea there with some guest a little while earlier. I can recall spotting from some distance . . . .
5 Miss Kenton's figure moving about inside the summerhouse. When I entered she had seated herself on one of the wicker chairs scattered around its interior, evidently engaged in some needlework. On closer inspection, I saw she was performing repairs to a cushion. I went about gathering up the various items of crockery from amidst the
10 plants and the cane furniture, and as I did so, I believe we exchanged a few pleasantries, perhaps discussed one or two professional matters. For the truth was, it was extremely refreshing to be out in the summerhouse after many continuous days in the main building and neither of us was inclined to hurry with our tasks . . . . In fact, I was looking
15 out over the lawn to where the mist was thickening down around the poplar trees planted along the cart-track, when I finally introduced the topic of the previous year's dismissals. Perhaps a little predictably, I did so by saying:

"I was just thinking earlier, Miss Kenton. It's rather funny to
remember now, but you know, only this time a year ago, you were still
insisting you were going to resign. It rather amused me to think of it."
When I finally turned to look at her, she was gazing through the glass
at the great expanse of fog outside.

"You probably have no idea, Mr. Stevens," she said eventually,
"how seriously I really thought of leaving this house. I felt so strongly
about what happened. Had I been anyone worthy of any respect at all,
I dare say I would have left Darlington Hall long ago." She paused for
a while, and I turned my gaze back out to the poplar trees down in the
distance. Then she continued in a tired voice: "It was cowardice, Mr.
Stevens. Simple cowardice. Where could I have gone? I have no family.
Only my aunt. I love her dearly, but I can't live with her for a day without feeling my whole life is wasting away. I did tell myself, of course, I
would soon find some situation.

"But I was so frightened, Mr. Stevens. Whenever I thought of leaving, I just saw myself going out there and finding nobody who knew
or cared about me. There, that's all my high principles amount to. I
feel so ashamed of myself. But I just couldn't leave, Mr. Stevens. I just
couldn't bring myself to leave."

Miss Kenton paused again and seemed to be deep in thought. I
thus thought it opportune to relate at this point, as precisely as possible, what had taken place earlier between myself and Lord Darlington.
I proceeded to do so and concluded by saying:

"What's done can hardly be undone. But it is at least a great comfort to hear his lordship declare so unequivocally that it was all a terrible misunderstanding. I just thought you'd like to know, Miss Kenton,
since I recall you were as distressed by the episode as I was."

"I'm sorry, Mr. Stevens," Miss Kenton said behind me in an entirely
new voice, as though she had just been jolted from a dream, "I don't
understand you." Then as I turned to her, she went on: "As I recall,
you thought it was only right and proper that Ruth and Sarah be sent
packing. You were positively cheerful about it."

"Now really, Miss Kenton, that is quite incorrect and unfair. The
whole matter caused me great concern, great concern indeed. It is
hardly the sort of thing I like to see happen in this house."

"Then why, Mr. Stevens, did you not tell me so at the time?"

I gave a laugh, but for a moment was rather at a loss for an
answer. Before I could formulate one, Miss Kenton put down her
sewing and said:

"Do you realize, Mr. Stevens, how much it would have meant to
me if you had thought to share your feelings last year? You knew how
upset I was when my girls were dismissed. Do you realize how much it
would have helped me? Why, Mr. Stevens, why, why, why do you
always have to pretend?"

I gave another laugh at the ridiculous turn the conversation had
65 suddenly taken. "Really, Miss Kenton," I said, "I'm not sure I know
what you mean. Pretend? Why, really . . . ."

"I suffered so much over Ruth and Sarah leaving us. And I suffered
all the more because I believed I suffered alone."

From The Remains of the Day, © *1989 by Kazuo Ishiguro; Alfred A. Knopf, Inc., publisher.*

1. Based on the details in the passage, it can be inferred that Mr.
   Stevens and Miss Kenton are Lord Darlington's:
   A. guests.
   B. relatives.
   C. acquaintances.
   D. employees.   Ⓐ Ⓑ Ⓒ Ⓓ

2. The statement "Had I been anyone worthy of any respect at all, I dare
   say I would have left Darlington Hall long ago" (lines 26–27) can be
   interpreted to mean:
   F. no one at Darlington Hall truly respects Miss Kenton.
   G. Miss Kenton has little respect for Mr. Stevens.
   H. Miss Kenton feels she betrayed her principles by staying.
   J. Miss Kenton senses that Mr. Stevens feels superior to her.   Ⓕ Ⓖ Ⓗ Ⓙ

3. According to the passage, the intent of Mr. Stevens's recollection of
   Miss Kenton's desire to resign (lines 19–22) is most likely to:
   A. open up a discussion of an event that had upset Miss Kenton.
   B. turn the conversation to the professional topic of furniture repair.
   C. indulge in nostalgic reminiscences of happier days.
   D. irritate Miss Kenton by mocking the seriousness of that desire.   Ⓐ Ⓑ Ⓒ Ⓓ

4. Mr. Stevens gives "a laugh" (line 56) because he is suddenly:
   F. amused.
   G. insecure.
   H. suspicious.
   J. sarcastic.   Ⓕ Ⓖ Ⓗ Ⓙ

5. The main point of Miss Kenton's references to her own family (lines
   31–34) is that:
   A. she would have nowhere to turn if she left her job.
   B. children often reject those they should love.
   C. she was afraid of discovering that she did not love her aunt.
   D. life becomes very tedious when one visits relatives.   Ⓐ Ⓑ Ⓒ Ⓓ

6. What is it that Mr. Stevens describes as "done" (line 43)?

   F. Lord Darlington's earlier conversation with him

   G. Miss Kenton's talk of leaving Darlington hall

   H. Ruth and Sarah's dismissal

   J. Any talk of Miss Kenton's dismissal

   Ⓕ Ⓖ Ⓗ Ⓙ

7. As he is revealed in the passage, Mr. Stevens is:

   A. bored with their conversation in the summer house.

   B. increasingly hostile to Miss Kenton's depiction of his actions.

   C. uncomfortable with expressing his deep affection for Miss Kenton.

   D. unaware of how his past behavior had affected Miss Kenton.

   Ⓐ Ⓑ Ⓒ Ⓓ

8. Which of the following would be out of character for the narrator?

   I. Pointing out to Miss Kenton why she was unfairly characterizing his actions

   II. Spending time thinking about Miss Kenton's accusations

   III. Ridiculing Miss Kenton for poorly repairing the cushion

   F. I only

   G. II only

   H. I and II only

   J. III only

   Ⓕ Ⓖ Ⓗ Ⓙ

9. Miss Kenton interacts with Mr. Stevens in a way that can best be described as:

   A. sincere but formal.

   B. indifferent but polite.

   C. timid but angry.

   D. patronizing but kindly.

   Ⓐ Ⓑ Ⓒ Ⓓ

10. At the end of the passage, Miss Kenton asks "Why, Mr. Stevens, why, why, why do you always have to *pretend*?" (lines 62–63) What specific action of Mr. Stevens does she have in mind?

   F. His apparent cheerfulness at Ruth and Sarah's dismissal

   G. His simulation of great affection for her

   H. His phony concern for her own future employment

   J. His empty expressions of sympathy for her own suffering

   Ⓕ Ⓖ Ⓗ Ⓙ

Tight-Lipped Servants

It should be clear now why trying to build a mental road map of the Prose Fiction passage is not such a good idea. Unlike the paragraphs in the nonfiction passages, those in the Prose Fiction passage tend not to be organized around a single topic. They just move the story forward. Instead of building a road map, then, your prereading step should have been spent finding answers to the important questions about character and action.

- **Who are these people?** The first paragraphs of the passage are peppered with hints about who these people are. Lines 3–4 discuss Mr. Stevens "clearing away the remains of his lordship's taking tea." Line 8 describes Miss Kenton "performing repairs to a cushion." Line 21 discusses her previous plans for resigning. Clearly, Mr. Stevens and Miss Kenton are servants (we later learn—in line 41—that their employer is Lord Darlington). Notice how, by answering this basic question, you've already answered Question 1.

- **What is their state of mind?** We read of "the previous year's dismissals" (line 17) and Miss Kenton's intentions to leave the house (line 25) as a result of them. She "felt so strongly about what happened" (lines 25–26) but she was afraid to take the step of actually leaving in protest ("It was cowardice," she admits in lines 29–30). It sounds like some other servants were dismissed unfairly last year, and that this upset Miss Kenton. Apparently, Mr. Stevens also found the incident distressing (lines 52–54), but Miss Kenton hadn't realized this at the time.

- **What's going on?** These are obviously very formal people, but there are strong emotions rumbling beneath the surface. It's clear that Miss Kenton is very upset because she didn't realize that Mr. Stevens disapproved of the dismissals, too ("Do you realize, Mr. Stevens, how much it would have meant to me if you had thought to share your feelings last year?"—lines 59–60. And later: "Why, Mr. Stevens, why, why, why do you always have to *pretend*?"—lines 62–63). We get the impression that Mr. Stevens is not a man who very readily shows his feelings and emotions—as Miss Kenton puts it, he always *pretends*.

As for the questions, notice how many inference-type questions there are. This is typical of the Prose Fiction passage, where so much information is conveyed implicitly—"between the lines." In most cases, you have to read *around* the specific line references in order to find your answer. If you've done your prereading step properly, however, you should be able to knock off most of the questions quickly.

Key to Passage III
(Prose Fiction)

	ANSWER	REFER TO	TYPE	COMMENTS
1.	D	First 2 paragraphs	Inference	Discussed above
2.	H	Lines 26–27, 36	Inference	"There that's all my high principles amount to," she says.
3.	A	Lines 19–22, 39–42	Inference	Lines 39–42 show that Mr. Stevens has just been discussing this subject with Lord Darlington, and now wants to discuss it with Miss Kenton.
4.	G	Lines 56–57	Inference	He is "at a loss for an answer," and clearly not laughing out of amusement.
5.	A	Lines 30–38	Detail	"Where could I have gone? I have no family."
6.	H	Lines 43–46	Detail	Refers back to "the previous year's dismissals," first mentioned in line 17.
7.	D	Throughout	Big Picture	Mr. Stevens' nervous laughs hint that he had no idea how deeply Miss Kenton was affected.
8.	J	Throughout	Inference	I—He does this in lines 52–54. II—He wishes to respond to the accusations in lines 49–51. III—This kind of blatant harshness would be uncharacteristic of so discreet and proper a man.
9.	A	Throughout	Big Picture	Miss Kenton freely expresses her feelings to him throughout, so she is sincere. But she never loses her formal language and demeanor.
10.	F	Lines 59–64, 49–51	Inference	She wishes that he "had thought to share [his] feelings;" she was under the impression that he was "positively cheerful about [the dismissals]."

THE NATURAL SCIENCES PASSAGE

The Science passage in the Reading subject test is often similar in outward appearance to a passage on the Science Reasoning subject test. Illustrations, graphs, and tables of information may be included. Usually, though, the emphasis in Reading is more on understanding ideas rather than reading and analyzing experiments and data.

KAPLAN

Approaching the Science passage is really not any different from approaching the other nonfiction passages, since all are well-organized essays that lay out ideas in a straightforward, logical way. But you may be more likely to find unfamiliar vocabulary in Science passages. *Don't panic*. Any unfamiliar terms will usually be defined explicitly in the passage, or else will have definitions inferable from context.

YOU DON'T HAVE TO BE AN EINSTEIN

As in the Science Reasoning subject test, you don't have to be a science whiz to get a decent score. The same advice that helps on the other passages—know where you're going; look it up—will get you points on the Science passage.

DON'T GET LOST!

In the Science passage, it's easy to lose yourself in complex details. Don't do it. It's *especially* important not to get bogged down in the Science passage! Many students try to understand and remember everything as they read. But that's not the right ACT mindset. In your prereading of the passage, just get the "gist" and the outline; don't sweat the details. As always, use line references in the questions when possible. They will lead you back to the details that are important. You'd be surprised how many questions you can answer on a passage you don't really understand.

WEAK IN SCIENCE?

Don't freak out if you find yourself in a fog as you read the Science passage. Keep your head, and quickly get to the questions. Focus on the detail questions with line references. You *can* score points on the Science passage, even if you don't get it.

ATTACKING THE NATURAL SCIENCES PASSAGE

The next passage is a typical ACT-style Science passage with questions. Try to attack it with the same Three-Step Approach you use for other passages. Remember: Don't get bogged down in the details! And don't worry if you don't understand everything, particularly just after prereading. Your only goal is to get a sense of the passage and its outline.

Passage IV

Atoms can be excited in many ways other than by absorbing a photon. The element phosphorous spontaneously combines with oxygen when exposed to air. There is a transfer of energy to the phosphorous electrons during this chemical reaction which excites
5 them to sufficiently high energy states that they can subsequently emit light when dropping into a lower state. This is an example of what is termed chemiluminescence, the emission of light as a result of chemical reaction.

A related effect is bioluminescence, when light is produced by
10 chemical reactions associated with biological activity. Bioluminescence occurs in a variety of life forms and is more common in marine organisms than in terrestrial or freshwater life. Examples include certain bacteria, jellyfish, clams, fungi, worms, ants, and fire-flies. There is considerable diversity in how light is produced. Most
15 processes involve the reaction of a protein with oxygen, catalyzed by an enzyme. The protein varies from one organism to another, but all are grouped under the generic name luciferin. The enzymes are known as luciferase. Both words stem from the Latin lucifer meaning light-bearing. The various chemical steps leading to bioluminescence
20 are yet to be explained in detail, but in some higher organisms the process is known to be activated by the nervous system.

The firefly is best understood. Its light organ is located near the end of the abdomen. Within it luciferin is combined with other atom-ic groups in a series of processes in which oxygen is converted into
25 carbon dioxide. The sequence culminates when the luciferin is split off from the rest, leaving it in an excited state. The excess energy is released as a photon. The peak in the emission spectrum lies between 550 and 600 nm depending on the type of luciferase. This flash pro-duced by the simultaneous emission of many photons serves to
30 attract mates, and females also use it to attract males of other species, which they devour.

Certain bacteria also produce light when stimulated by motion. This is why the breaking sea or a passing boat generate the greenish light seen in some bodies of water such as Phosphorescent Bay in
35 Puerto Rico. Some fish have a symbiotic relationship with bacteria. The "flashlight fish" takes advantage of the light created by bacteria lodged beneath each eye. Certain other fish produce their own biolu-minescence, which serves as identification. However, the biological advantage if any of bioluminescence in some other organisms such as
40 fungi remains a mystery.

Triboluminescence is the emission of light when one hard object is sharply struck against another. This contact, when atom scrapes against atom, excites electrons and disrupts electrical bonds. Light is then created when the electrons find their way to lower states.

45 Triboluminescence is not to be confused with the glow of small particles that may be broken off by the impact. Such "sparks" are seen as a result of their high temperature. Light given off by hot objects is known as thermoluminescence, or incandescence.

Another form of thermoluminescence is the basis for dating 50 ancient ceramic objects. Quartz and other constituents of clay are continually irradiated by naturally occurring radioactive elements (e.g., uranium and thorium) and by cosmic rays. This produces defects in the material where electrons may be trapped. Heating pottery to 500°C releases the trapped electrons, which can then migrate 55 back to their original atoms, where on returning to an atomic orbit they then emit a photon. The intensity of thermoluminescence is therefore a measure of the duration of irradiation since the time when the pottery had been previously fired.

Excitation is also possible by other means. The passage of an elec- 60 trical current (electroluminescence) is one. The impact of high energy particles is another. The aurora borealis and its southern counterpart the aurora australis arise when a stream of high energy particles from the sun enters the earth's upper atmosphere and literally shatters some of the molecules of the air. This leaves their atoms in excited 65 states, and the light subsequently given off is characteristic of the atoms. Although the oxygen molecule, a major constituent of our atmosphere, has no emission in the visible, the oxygen atom can emit photons in either the red or green portions of the spectrum. Other atoms contribute to light at other wavelengths.

From Light and Color in Nature and Art, *© 1983 by Samuel J. Williamson; John Wiley & Sons, publisher.*

11. According to the information in the sixth paragraph (lines 49–58), the brighter the thermoluminescence of a heated piece of ancient pottery:

A. the younger the piece is.

B. the older the piece is.

C. the less irradiation has occurred within the piece's clay.

D. the fewer electrons have become trapped within the clay.

Ⓐ Ⓑ Ⓒ Ⓓ

SECTION II: SKILL-BUILDING WORKOUT

12. If an ancient ceramic bowl is heated to 500° C, light is emitted when certain electrons:

   F. release radioactive elements found in the clay.

   G. scrape against other electrons.

   H. become superheated.

   J. return to their former atoms.   Ⓕ Ⓖ Ⓗ Ⓙ

13. Compared to bioluminescence, chemiluminescence is NOT produced by:

   A. organic proteins that have been catalyzed.

   B. a chemical reaction.

   C. any reaction involving oxygen.

   D. a change in energy states.   Ⓐ Ⓑ Ⓒ Ⓓ

14. It can be inferred from the passage that the description of the firefly's production of light is a good example of the degree to which researchers understand:

   F. why light attracts fireflies.

   G. how a chemical process can trigger bioluminescence.

   H. how female fireflies attack male fireflies.

   J. how to measure the intensity of a firefly's bioluminescence.   Ⓕ Ⓖ Ⓗ Ⓙ

15. In both chemiluminescence and bioluminescence, photons are emitted:

   A. as excess energy.

   B. only by certain marine organisms.

   C. only when luciferase are present.

   D. only when phosphorous is present.   Ⓐ Ⓑ Ⓒ Ⓓ

16. Based on details in the passage, the word "excited" as used in line 1 means:

   F. split off from a molecule.

   G. agitated until glowing.

   H. raised to a higher energy level.

   J. heated to the point of disintegration.   Ⓕ Ⓖ Ⓗ Ⓙ

17. In discussing the creation of the two kinds of *aurora*, the passage asserts that the oxygen molecule "has no emission in the visible [spectrum]" (line 68) but also states that "the oxygen atom can emit photons in either the red or the green portions of the spectrum" (lines 67–68). Is the passage logically consistent?

   A. Yes, because visible light is emitted after the oxygen molecules have been broken apart into oxygen atoms.

   B. Yes, because the passage presents factual information and therefore cannot be illogical.

   C. No, because the oxygen molecule forms the largest part of the atmosphere and scientific theories must account for its invisible emissions.

D. No, because the writer has failed to adequately differentiate between the oxygen molecule's behavior and that of the oxygen atom.   Ⓐ Ⓑ Ⓒ Ⓓ

18. Assume that two meteors have collided and shattered. Astronomers see both a burst of light and then a subsequent glow. Such a visual phenomenon could best be explained as the result of:
    I. chemiluminescence
    II. triboluminescence
    III. thermoluminescence
    F. II only
    G. II and III only
    H. I and III only
    J. I, II, and III   Ⓕ Ⓖ Ⓗ Ⓙ

19. Based on information presented in the passage, which of the following is a hypothesis, rather than a fact?
    A. Fireflies use bioluminescence to attract mates.
    B. Thermoluminescence and triboluminescence are two distinctly different kinds of light emission.
    C. A firefly's type of luciferase determines the peak of its light emission's intensity.
    D. All organisms that produce bioluminescence do so for some biological advantage.   Ⓐ Ⓑ Ⓒ Ⓓ

20. According to the last paragraph (lines 59–69), both the *aurora borealis* and the *aurora australis*:
    F. demonstrate the effects on atoms of high energy particles.
    G. occur in the presence of oxygen.
    H. emit light due to the presence of electrical currents.
    J. are visible from the surface of the earth.   Ⓕ Ⓖ Ⓗ Ⓙ

Exciting Atoms

Feeling a little numb? Unless you're a real science buff, you probably found this passage a lot less exciting than the atoms did. And you may have found yourself adrift in a sea of bewildering terms—*chemiluminescence, luciferin, aurora australis*.

We hope, though, that you didn't panic. You could still get points—and lots of them—from this passage even if all that you took away from your prereading was a sense that the passage was mainly about things in nature glowing when their atoms are excited. That, and a sense of a road map, was really all you needed. Most of the questions were answerable by referring back to the appropriate lines in the passage and paraphrasing what you read there.

Here's a possible road map for the passage:

• First paragraph: Introduction of idea of excited atoms releasing photons (i.e., luminescence). Discusses *chemiluminescence* (resulting from a chemical reaction).

- Second paragraph: Discusses *bioluminescence* (associated with biological activity—that is, with things that are alive).

- Third paragraph: Example of *bioluminescence*—fireflies.

- Fourth paragraph: More examples of *bioluminescence*—sea life.

- Fifth paragraph: Discusses *triboluminescence* (things hitting each other) and *thermoluminescence* (hot objects).

- Sixth paragraph: Example of *thermoluminescence*—refired ceramic objects.

- Seventh paragraph: Concludes with discussion of *electroluminescence* (associated with electrical currents).

Basically, the author is giving us a rundown on the various kinds of luminescence in nature. When the questions ask about one kind or another, you simply refer to the appropriate paragraph and lines.

Below is a key to the answers for this passage. Notice how you could have gotten an answer to number 12, for instance, *even if you were totally confused.* If you found "500°" in the passage (line 54), the sentence more or less spelled out the answer for you, requiring a minimum of paraphrasing. Again, never panic if you don't understand the passage as a whole! Just find the questions you *can* understand, and find the answers in the passage.

Key to Passage IV
(Nonfiction—Natural Sciences)

	ANSWER	REFER TO	TYPE	COMMENTS
11.	B	Lines 50–59	Inference	More time since last firing to trap more electrons, creating brighter glow.
12.	J	Lines 54–55	Detail	"migrate back to their original atoms"
13.	A	Paragraph 2	Detail	Be careful with the reversal word "NOT" in the question. "Organic" means "having to do with life."
14.	G	Lines 23–32	Inference	Remember, passage is about luminescence, not fireflies.
15.	A	Lines 3–8, 29–32	Inference	B and C aren't chemi-; D isn't bio-. Only A is both.
16.	H	Line 2–8, 42–49	Detail	Lines 5–6 say it all.
17.	A	Lines 59–69	Big Picture	Remember, you should usually select a choice that approves of the passage. Note difference between oxygen molecule and oxygen atom.
18.	G	Lines 41–48	Inference	I—No, since no chemical reaction II—Yes, since impact reaction III—Yes, since "subsequent glow" (probably a heat reaction)
19.	D	Throughout	Big Picture	Any statement about "all organisms" is probably a hypothesis, since no one can verify what's true of every organism in existence.
20.	F	Lines 59–69	Detail	"a stream of high energy particles from the sun."

WHAT TO DO WHEN YOU'RE RUNNING OUT OF TIME

If you're nearly out of time and you've still got an entire passage untouched, you need to shift to last-minute strategies. Don't try to preread the passage; you'll just run out of time before you answer any questions. Instead, scan the questions without reading the passage and look first for the ones that mention line numbers or specific paragraphs. You can often get quick points on these questions by referring back to the passage as the question stem directs, reading a few lines around the reference, and taking your best shot.

FINISHING ISN'T THAT IMPORTANT

Don't worry if you don't have time to look at all the questions. You can earn scores in the top 15 percent of all ACT test takers even if you never look at a *whole passage* in Reading—if almost all the questions you do answer on the other three passages are right and if you remember to guess on the rest.

Of course, the most important thing is to make sure you have gridded in at least a random guess on every question. If some of your blind guesses are right (as some of them statistically *should* be), they'll boost your score just as much as well-reasoned, thought-out answers would!

KAPLAN

SCIENCE WORKOUT 3
KEEP YOUR VIEWPOINTS STRAIGHT

On every Science Reasoning subject test you'll find one "Conflicting Viewpoints" passage, in which two scientists propose different theories about a particular scientific phenomenon. Often, the two theories are just differing interpretations of the same data; other times, each scientist offers his own data to support his own opinion. In either case, it's essential that you know more or less what theory each scientist is proposing, and that you pay careful attention to how and where their theories differ.

In Science Workout 2, we talked about how scientists think, and you should bring all of that information to bear on the Conflicting Viewpoints passage. Since the scientists are disagreeing on interpretation, it's usually the case that they're engaging in specific-to-general thinking. They're each using specific data, sometimes the *same* specific data, but they're coming to very different general conclusions.

It's important to remember that your job is *not* to figure out which scientist is right and which is wrong. Instead, you'll be tested on whether you *understand* each scientist's position and the thinking behind it. That's what the questions will hinge on.

POINTS AND VIEWPOINTS

Sometimes you may find yourself understanding one scientist's viewpoint but not the other's. Don't let that upset you. Many of the questions will involve just one scientist's theory, so even if Scientist 2 has totally lost you, you can still do well on questions that involve Scientist 1 only. Remember: You get points for answering individual questions, not for understanding everything!

HOW TO PREREAD THE CONFLICTING VIEWPOINTS PASSAGE

When tackling the Conflicting Viewpoints passage, you'll probably want to spend a little more time than usual on the prereading step of the Three-Step Approach. As we saw on other Science Reasoning passages, your goal in prereading is to get a general idea of what's going on so that you can focus when you do the questions. But we find that it pays to spend a little extra time with the Conflicting Viewpoints passage in order to get a clearer idea of the opposing theories and the data behind them.

REMEMBER

The Three-Step Approach goes like this:
1. Preread the passage
2. Consider the question stem
3. Refer to the passage (before looking at the choices)

The passage will usually consist of a short introduction laying out the scientific issue in question, followed by two different viewpoints on that issue. Sometimes these viewpoints are presented under the headings Scientist 1 and Scientist 2, or else the headings might be Theory 1 and Theory 2, Hypothesis 1 and Hypothesis 2, or something similar.

A scientific viewpoint on the ACT will typically consist of two parts:

- A statement of the general theory

- A summary of the data behind the theory

Usually, the very first line of each viewpoint expresses the general theory. So, for instance, Scientist 1's first sentence might be something like: *The universe will continue to expand indefinitely*. This is Scientist 1's viewpoint boiled down to a single statement. Scientist 2's first sentence might be: *The force of gravity will eventually force the universe to stop expanding and to begin contracting*. This is Scientist 2's viewpoint, and it is clearly in direct contradiction to Scientist 1's opinion.

It's very important that you understand these basic statements of theory, and, just as important, that you see how they're opposed to each other. In fact, you might want to circle the theory statement for each viewpoint, right there in the test booklet, to fix the two positions in your mind.

After each statement of theory will come the data that's behind it. As we said, sometimes the scientists are just drawing different interpretations from the same data. But usually, each will have different supporting data. There are two different kinds of data:

- Data that support the scientist's own theory

- Data that weaken the opposing scientist's theory

KAPLAN

It's normally a good idea to identify the major points of data for each theory. You might under-line a phrase or sentence that crystallizes each, or even take note of whether it primarily supports the scientist's own theory or shoots holes in the opposing theory.

Once you understand each scientist's theory and the data behind it, you'll be ready to move on to the questions. Remember that some of the questions will refer to only one of the viewpoints. Whatever you do, *don't mix up the two viewpoints!* A question asking about the data supporting Theory *2* may have wrong answers that perfectly describe the data for Theory *1*. If you're careless, you can easily fall for one of these wrong answers.

KEEP YOUR THEORIES STRAIGHT

In the heat of the moment, it's easy to confuse the two opposing theories. Don't do it. Always double check to make sure you haven't assigned the ideas of Scientist 1 to Scientist 2, and vice versa.

THE REAL THING

What follows is a full-fledged, ACT-style Conflicting Viewpoints passage. Give yourself six min-utes or so to do the passage and all seven questions.

Passage IV

Tektites are natural, glassy objects that range in size from the diame-ter of a grain of sand to that of a human fist. They are found in only a few well-defined areas, called strewn fields. Two theories about the origin of tektites are presented below.

Scientist 1
Tektites almost certainly are extraterrestrial, probably lunar, in origin. Their forms show the characteristics of air-friction melting. In one study, flanged, "flying saucer" shapes similar to those of australites (a common tektite form) were produced by ablating lenses of tektite glass in a heated airstream that simulated atmospheric entry.

Atmospheric forces also make terrestrial origin extremely improba-ble. Aerodynamic studies have shown that because of atmospheric density, tektite-like material ejected from the earth's surface would never attain a velocity much higher than that of the surrounding air, and therefore would not be shaped by atmospheric friction. Most likely, tektites were formed either from meteorites or from lunar mate-rial ejected in volcanic eruptions.

Analysis of specimen #14425 from the *Apollo 12* lunar mission shows that the sample strongly resembles some of the tektites from the Australasian strewn field. Also, tektites contain only a small fraction of the water that is locked into the structure of terrestrial volcanic glass. And tektites never contain unmelted crystalline material; the otherwise similar terrestrial glass produced by some meteorite impacts always does.

Scientist 2

Nonlocal origin is extremely unlikely, given the narrow distribution of tektite strewn fields. Even if a tightly focused jet of lunar matter were to strike the earth, whatever was deflected by the atmosphere would remain in a solar orbit. The next time its orbit coincided with that of the earth, some of the matter would be captured by earth's gravity and fall over a wide area.

There are striking similarities not only between the composition of the earth's crust and that of most tektites but between the proportions of various gases found in the earth's atmosphere and in the vesicles of certain tektites.

Tektites were probably formed by meteorite impacts. The shock wave produced by a major collision could temporarily displace the atmosphere above. Terrestrial material might then splatter to suborbital heights and undergo air-friction melting upon reentry. And tektite fields in the Ivory Coast and Ghana can be correlated with known impact craters.

1. The discovery that many tektites contain unmelted, crystalline material would:
   A. tend to weaken Scientist 1's argument.
   B. tend to weaken Scientist 2's argument.
   C. be incompatible with both scientists' views.
   D. be irrelevant to the controversy.

   Ⓐ Ⓑ Ⓒ Ⓓ

2. Which of the following is a reason given by Scientist 2 for believing that tektites originate on the earth?
   F. The density of the earth's atmosphere would prevent any similar lunar or extraterrestrial material from reaching the earth's surface.
   G. Tektites have a composition totally unlike that of any material ever brought back from the Moon.
   H. Extraterrestrial material could not have been as widely dispersed as tektites are.
   J. Material ejected from the Moon or beyond would eventually have been much more widely distributed on earth.

   Ⓕ Ⓖ Ⓗ Ⓙ

3. Scientist 1 could best answer the point that some tektites have vesicles filled with gases in the same proportion as the earth's atmosphere by:

   A. countering that not all tektites have such gas-filled vesicles.

   B. demonstrating that molten material would be likely to trap some gases while falling through the terrestrial atmosphere.

   C. suggesting that those gases might occur in the same proportions in the Moon's atmosphere.

   D. showing that similar vesicles, filled with these gases in the same proportions, are also found in some terrestrial volcanic glass.

     Ⓐ Ⓑ Ⓒ Ⓓ

4. How did Scientist 2 answer the argument that tektitelike material ejected from the earth could not reach a high enough velocity relative to the atmosphere to undergo air-friction melting?

   F. By asserting that a shock wave might cause a momentary change in atmosphere density, permitting subsequent aerodynamic heating

   G. By pointing out that periodic meteorite impacts have caused gradual changes in atmospheric density over the eons

   H. By attacking the validity of the aerodynamic studies cited by Scientist 1

   J. By referring to the correlation between tektite fields and known impact craters in the Ivory Coast and Ghana

     Ⓕ Ⓖ Ⓗ Ⓙ

5. The point of subjecting lenses of tektite glass to a heated airstream was to:

   A. determine their water content.

   B. see if gases became trapped in their vesicles.

   C. reproduce the effects of atmospheric entry.

   D. simulate the mechanism of meteorite formation.

     Ⓐ Ⓑ Ⓒ Ⓓ

6. Researchers could best counter the objections of Scientist 2 to Scientist 1's argument by:

   F. discovering some phenomenon that would quickly remove tektite-sized objects from orbit.

   G. proving that most common tektite shapes can be produced by aerodynamic heating.

   H. confirming that active volcanoes once existed on the moon.

   J. mapping the locations of all known tektite fields and impact craters.

     Ⓕ Ⓖ Ⓗ Ⓙ

7. Which of the following characteristics of tektites is LEAST consistent with the theory that tektites are of extraterrestrial origin?

   A. Low water content

   B. "Flying saucer" shapes

   C. Narrow distribution

   D. Absence of unmelted material

     Ⓐ Ⓑ Ⓒ Ⓓ

ANSWERS

1. A, 2. J, 3. B, 4. F, 5. C, 6. F, 7. C

WHAT'S THE CONFLICT?

Your prereading of the introduction should have revealed the issue at hand—namely, tektites, which are small glassy objects found in certain areas known as strewn fields. The conflict is about the *origin* of these objects: In other words, where did they come from?

Scientist 1's theory is expressed in his first sentence: "Tektites almost certainly are extraterrestrial, probably lunar, in origin." Put that into a form you can understand: In other words, Scientist 1 believes that tektites come from space, probably the moon. Scientist 2, on the other hand, has an opposing theory, also expressed in her first sentence: "Nonlocal origin is extremely unlikely." In other words, it's unlikely that tektites came from a nonlocal source; instead, they probably came from a *local* source, i.e., right here on Earth. The conflict is clear. One says that tektites come from space; the other says they come from Earth. You might have even labeled the two positions: "space origin" and "Earth origin."

But how do these scientists support their theories? Scientist 1 presents three points of data:

1. Tektite shapes show characteristics of "air-friction melting" (supporting the theory of space origin).

2. "Atmospheric forces" wouldn't be great enough to shape tektitelike material ejected from Earth's surface (weakening the theory of earth origin).

3. Tektites resemble moon rocks gathered by *Apollo 12* but not Earth rocks (strengthening the theory of space origin).

Scientist 2 also presents three points of data:

1. Any matter coming from space would "fall over a wide area" instead of being concentrated in strewn fields (weakening the theory of space origin).

2. There are "striking similarities" between tektites and the composition of the earth's crust (strengthening the theory of Earth origin).

3. "Meteorite impacts" could create shock waves, explaining how terrestrial material could undergo air-friction melting (strengthening the theory of Earth origin by counteracting Scientist 1's first point).

Obviously, you wouldn't want to write out the supporting data for each theory the way we've done above. But it probably would be a good idea to underline the key phrases in the data descriptions ("air-friction melting," "*Apollo 12*," etcetera) and number them. What's important is that you have an idea of what data supports which theory. The questions, once you get to them, will then force you to focus.

ATTACKING THE QUESTIONS

Now let's quickly attack the questions:

Question 1 asks how it would affect the scientists' arguments if it were discovered that many tektites contain unmelted crystalline material. Well, Scientist 1 says that tektites *never* contain unmelted crystalline material, and that the terrestrial glass produced by some meteorite impacts *always* does. Therefore, by showing a resemblance between tektites and earth materials, this discovery would weaken Scientist 1's argument for extraterrestrial origin. Choice A is correct.

For **Question 2**, you had to identify which answer choice was used by Scientist 2 to support the argument that tektites are terrestrial in origin. You should have been immediately drawn to choice J, which expresses what we've identified above as Scientist 2's first data point. Notice how choice F is a piece of evidence that Scientist *1* cites. (Remember not to confuse the viewpoints!) As for G, Scientist 2 says that tektites *do* resemble earth materials, but never says that they *don't* resemble lunar materials. And choice H gets it backwards; Scientist 2 says that extraterrestrial material *would* be widely dispersed, and that the tektites are *not* widely dispersed, rather than vice versa.

Countering Evidence

For **Question 3**, you need to find the best way for Scientist 1 to counter the point that some tektites have vesicles filled with gases in the same proportion as the earth's atmosphere. First, make sure you understand the meaning of that point. The idea that these gases must have been trapped in the vesicles (little holes) while the rock was actually being formed is being used by Scientist 2 to suggest that tektites are of terrestrial origin. Scientist 1 *could* say that not all tektites have such gas-filled vesicles—Choice A—but that's not a great argument. If any reasonable number of them *do*, Scientist 1 would have to come up with an alternative explanation (Scientist 2 never claimed that *all* tektites contained these vesicles). But if, as B suggests, Scientist 1 could demonstrate that molten material would be likely to trap some terrestrial gases while falling through earth's atmosphere, this would explain how tektites might have come from beyond the earth and still contain vesicles filled with Earthlike gases. Choice C is easy to eliminate if you know that the moon's atmosphere is extremely thin and totally different in composition from the earth's atmosphere, so it doesn't make much sense to suggest that those gases might occur in the same proportions as in the moon's atmosphere. Finally, since it's Scientist *2* who claims that tektites are terrestrial in origin, choice D, showing that similar gas-filled vesicles occur in some terrestrial volcanic glass, wouldn't help Scientist *1* at all.

In **Question 4**, you're asked how Scientist 2 answered the argument that tektitelike material ejected from the earth could not reach a high enough velocity to undergo air-friction melting. Well, that was Scientist 2's third data point. The shock wave produced by a major meteorite collision could momentarily displace the atmosphere right above the impact site (meaning the air moved out of the way for a brief time). So, when the splattered material reentered the atmosphere, it would undergo air-friction melting. That's basically what choice F says, so F is correct.

Question 5: The concept of subjecting lenses of tektite glass to a heated airstream was mentioned toward the beginning of Scientist 1's argument. The point was to simulate the entry of extraterrestrial tektite material through Earth's atmosphere, and that's closest to choice C.

Keeping Your Scientists Straight

Question 6 shows again why it pays to keep each scientist's viewpoint straight. You can't counter the objections of Scientist 2 to Scientist 1's argument unless you know what Scientist 2 was objecting to. Scientist 2's first data point is the only one designed to shoot holes in the opposing viewpoint. There, Scientist 2 takes issue with the idea that lunar material could strike the earth without being dispersed over a far wider area than the known strewn fields. But if, as correct choice F says, researchers found some force capable of removing tektite-sized objects from orbit *quickly*, it would demolish the objection that Scientist 2 raises in her first paragraph. The tektite material would strike the earth or be pulled away quickly, instead of remaining in a solar orbit long enough to be captured by the earth's gravity and subsequently be distributed over a wide area of the earth.

Question 7 wasn't too tough if you read the question stem carefully. You want to find the tektite characteristic that is LEAST consistent with the theory that tektites came from the moon or beyond. This is Scientist 1's theory, so you want to pick the answer choice that doesn't go with his argument. Scientist 1's evidence *does* include tektites' low water content, "flying saucer" shapes, and absence of unmelted material. The only answer choice that he didn't mention was the narrow distribution of the strewn fields. And with good reason. That's part of Scientist 2's argument *against* an extraterrestrial origin. So the correct answer is choice C.

KNOW YOUR EVIDENCE

As you can see, many questions on the Conflicting Viewpoints passage involve evidence: what evidence was presented, what evidence would hurt or help one scientist's views, what evidence was used for what purpose. It's important that you take note of the evidence (data) each scientist uses.

TOTAL AND UTTER CONFUSION

Now we're going to do something very cruel. We're going to to throw you a Science Reasoning passage of such technical difficulty that many of you will want to go screaming for the exits before you finish reading it.

But we're doing this for a reason. Sometimes on the ACT Science Reasoning test, you'll find yourself encountering a bear of a passage—one that seems entirely incomprehensible. The secret to success with these passages is: *Don't panic*. As we'll show you, you can get points on even the most difficult Science Reasoning passage in the entire history of the ACT—as long as you keep your cool and approach it in a savvy, practical way. Here's the passage.

Passage V

Neutrinos (ν) are subatomic particles that travel at approximately the speed of light. They can penetrate most matter, because they are electrically neutral and effectively massless.

Generally accepted theory holds that the nuclear reactions that power the Sun create vast quantities of neutrinos as by-products. Three proposed stages (PPI, PPII, and PPIII) of the most important solar reaction are shown in Figure 1, along with their neutrino-producing subpaths. Equations for the subpaths are shown in Table 1, as are the predicted neutrino energies and fluxes.

Figure 1

Table 1

Subpath name	Subpath equation	Neutrino energy (MeV)	Expected flux on Earth (10^{10}cm^{-2}sec^{-1})
P-p	$_1H^1 + {_1}H^1 \longrightarrow {_1}H^2 + \beta^+ + \gamma$	0.42*	6.06781
p-e-p	$_1H^1 + \beta^- + {_1}H^1 \longrightarrow {_1}H^2 + \gamma$	1.44	0.01524
Be^7†	$_4Be^7 + \beta^- \longrightarrow {_3}Li^7 + \gamma$	0.87	0.43924
Be^7††	$_4Be^7 + \beta^- \longrightarrow {_3}Li^7 + \gamma$	0.38	0.04880
B^8	$_5B^8 \longrightarrow {_4}Be^8 + \beta^+ + \gamma$	14.06*	0.00054

†Be^7 subpath 1
††Be^7 subpath 2

*Maximum

8. According to the information presented in the passage, which of the following stages or subpaths should contribute the smallest portion of the total solar neutrino flux on Earth?

F. p-p

G. PPI

H. PPII

J. PPIII

(F) (G) (H) (J)

9. Of the neutrinos that are produced in the subpaths described in the passage, which type can have the greatest energy?

A. ν_1

B. ν_2

C. ν_3

D. ν_4

(A) (B) (C) (D)

10. Based on the information presented in the passage, the percentage of solar neutrinos produced by Be^7 subpath 2 is approximately:

F. 1.2%

G. 10%

H. 12%

J. 90%

(F) (G) (H) (J)

11. Solar neutrinos are detected through a reaction with $_{37}$Cl for which the minimum neutrino energy is approximately 0.8 MeV. Of the neutrinos discussed in the passage, this method would detect:

A. all of the neutrinos produced in PPI and PPII.

B. some of the neutrinos produced in PPI, PPII, and PPIII.

C. only neutrinos produced in Be^7 subpath 1 of PPII.

D. only neutrinos produced in PPIII.

(A) (B) (C) (D)

12. The symbol β represents a beta particle, a particle emitted during nuclear decay. Beta particles may be positively or negatively charged. During which of the following subpaths are beta particles emitted?

  I.   p-p

  II. p-e-p

  III. B^8

F. II only

G. I and III only

H. II and III only

J. I, II, and III

ANSWERS

8. J, 9. D, 10. F, 11. B, 12. G

Confused? If you aren't, you should stick close to your phone, because the Nobel Prize committee will probably be calling sometime soon! On the other hand, if you *were* confused, don't sweat it. As we said in ACT Basics, some ACT questions are so hard that even your *teachers* would have a hard time getting them correct.

The good news is that you don't have to understand a passage to get a few questions right. For instance, here's how you might have approached the passage above.

GETTING POINTS EVEN IF YOU DON'T GET *THE* POINT

Your prereading of the introduction should have told you that the passage is about neutrinos coming from the sun. But that may be all you were able to get from this gibberish. You may have been in a total fog looking at Figure 1 and Table 1. But if you didn't panic, you might have noticed a few things: First, that whatever Figure 1 illustrates, there are some really big parts and some really small parts. If you look at the *x*-axis of the chart, you'll see that, whatever PPI, PPII, and PPIII are, the first is 88%, the second only 12%, and the third only .01%.

Is that tiny, vague insight enough to get a point? Yes! Look at **Question 8**. It asks which stage or subpath contributes the *smallest* portion of flux. Well, look for a small portion. PPIII's figure of 0.01% is a very small number, whatever it's supposed to be referring to, so PPIII would be a good guess here. And indeed, choice J is correct for Question 8.

You could have gotten a point here without even understanding what the passage was all about!

What about Table 1? This is a little easier to understand, especially if you ignore the column about subpath equations. But "neutrino energy" sounds like something we can comprehend.

Apparently, each subpath produces a different level of neutrino energy. Some have high energy (like B^8, with 14.06) and some have low energy (like B^7++, with only 0.38). Energy is mentioned in **Question 9**. Which type of neutrinos can have the greatest energy? Well, if B^8 were a choice, we'd pick that. But the choices are these funny νs, not Bs. Well, try to find B^8 somewhere in the other chart—Figure 1. There we find it somehow associated with ν_4 neutrinos. So take a gamble; choose ν_4—which is choice D—for this question. If you did that, you'd still have gotten another point, still without really understanding much more than before.

You're hot; keep it going. **Question 10** refers to Be^7 subpath 2. You may have noticed in the note under Table 1 that the Be^7 with two little dagger marks signifies subpath 2. So far, so good. Notice that the choices are all percentages. Where are percentages mentioned? In Figure 1. So find Be^7 with two dagger marks in Figure 1. You find it in the area of PPII, which is 12 percent of the x-axis in that chart. But notice that Be^7 with two dagger marks represents only *part* of that part of the figure—10 percent, to be exact. So, 10 percent of 12 percent would be 1.2%. That's choice F. It's also the correct answer.

Things get a little harder with **Question 11**, but you still might have gotten the answer if you used common sense. Here we get some mumbo jumbo about $_{37}Cl$, but the part of the question that should have caught your eye was the bit about a minimum neutrino energy of 0.8 MeV. Neutrino energy was represented in the third column of Table 1. According to that table, only three subpaths have an energy greater than 0.8—p-e-p (with 1.44), Be^7 with one dagger mark (with 0.87), and B^8 (the champion, with 14.06). Unfortunately, the answer choices aren't expressed in those terms; they're expressed in terms of PPI, II, and III, so we're going to have to translate from table to figure again, just as we did with Question 9.

Take p-e-p first. That's part (but not all) of the PPI portion of Figure 1. Be^7 with one dagger mark, similarly, is part (but not all) of the PPII portion. And B^8 is all of the PPIII portion. So there are at least parts of PPI, PPII, and PPIII implicated here. That should have led you to Choice B, which would have gotten you yet another point. Notice that choice A is inaccurate because it talks about *all* of something in PPI and PPII, and doesn't mention PPIII at all. Choices C and D, meanwhile, seem too limited, since they only mention one of the PP areas (whatever they are). So B was definitely the closest answer choice.

Finally, **Question 12** talks about beta particles. Well, that little beta symbol appears only in the subpath column of Table 1. There we find beta symbols in the equations for *all* of the subpaths in the table. That may have led you to believe that all three Roman numerals should be included, and no one would have blamed you for choosing choice J (I, II, and III). You would have been wrong, but you can't win them all when you're winging questions you don't really understand.

Of course, if you noticed that the question was asking for beta particles *emitted*, and if you knew that in the subpath equations everything *before* the arrow is what you start with while everything *after* the arrow is what you finish with, you might have been able to make a better guess. You would have realized that those equations with a beta symbol *before* the arrow were ones in which a beta particle was *absorbed*, while those with a beta symbol *after* the arrow were ones in which a beta particle was *emitted*. In that case, then, you would have seen that the equations for p-p and B^8 *do* have beta particles emitted, while the equation for p-e-p does not. That might have led you to choice G—I and III only—which *is* the correct answer.

Six questions, six points—and all without understanding the passage in any deep or thorough way. Of course, if you understand the mysteries of neutrino flux and p-e-p subpaths, congratulations. You're probably enough of a science whiz to ace the subject test anyway. But if you're like most ACT test takers, you won't understand everything the passages talk about. Sometimes you'll even find yourself totally lost.

The moral of the story, of course, is don't give up on a passage just because you don't understand it. You may not be able to get *every* point associated with the passage, but you may be able to get at least one or two (or three or four). Remember: The test is designed in such a way that you can *figure out* many of the questions, even if you don't know the subject area.

WHAT TO DO WHEN YOU'RE RUNNING OUT OF TIME

Let's conclude now with another quick point about getting quick points. If you're nearly out of time and you've still got a whole Science Reasoning passage left, you need to shift to last-minute strategies. As in Reading, don't try to preread the passage, or you'll just run out of time before you answer any questions. Instead, scan the questions without reading the passage and look first for the ones that require only reading data off of a graph or table. You can often get a couple of quick points just by knowing how to find data quickly.

FINISHING ISN'T THAT IMPORTANT

Don't worry if you don't have time to look at all the questions. You can earn high scores in the ACT Science Reasoning section—even if you never look at a *whole passage*—if almost all the questions you *do* answer are right and if you remember to guess on the rest.

Again, the most important thing is to make sure you have gridded in at least a random guess on every question.

SECTION III

STRATEGIC SUMMARIES

"Excuse me, I think I need another test booklet. My Verbal section looks like it's in Swedish or something."

ENGLISH SUMMARY

THE FORMAT

The English subject test:

- Is 45 minutes long.

- Includes 5 passages, representing a range of writing styles and levels of formality.

- Consists of 75 questions, divided among the 5 passages. They test many different points of grammar, punctuation, writing mechanics, usage, and rhetorical skills, by proposing alternative ways of expressing information underlined at various points in the passages. We divide the questions strategically into three groups:

    1. Economy Questions

    2. Sense Questions

    3. Technicality Questions

There are also a few *Out-of-Format* Questions that require different strategies, as outlined in Special Strategies below.

The questions do NOT get harder as you proceed through the section.

THE MINDSET

- *When in doubt, take it out.* Make sure that everything is written as concisely as possible. If you think something doesn't belong in a sentence, it probably doesn't, so choose an answer that leaves it out.

- *Make it make sense.* Grammar allows language to communicate meaning clearly. Most grammatically faulty sentences on the ACT don't say what the author obviously intended to say. If a sentence has more than one possible meaning, figure out what the author intended to say, and fix the sentence so it conveys that meaning properly.

• *Trust your ear.* Mistakes in grammar often sound bad to your ear. Trust that instinct. Don't choose the answer that "sounds fancy," choose the one that "sounds right." But keep in mind that there are some errors your ear won't catch. For these errors, use your flag list.

THE APPROACH

For each question, ask yourself three things. Note that you may actually have your answer before getting to all three questions:

1. Ask: *Does this stuff belong here?* Is it redundant? Is it relevant? Is this a long way to say a short idea? If so, choose an answer that gets rid of the stuff that doesn't belong.

2. Ask: *Does this stuff make sense?* The ACT test makers want short, simple, easy-to-understand prose. They expect everything to fit together logically. Choose the answer that turns nonsense into sense.

3. Ask: *Does this stuff sound like English?* If not, choose the answer that does. Recognize items on your "flag list" from English Workout 3 and let them help out when your ear isn't sure. These classic errors appear again and again on ACT English subject tests.

SPECIAL STRATEGIES

Out-of-Format Questions: A few questions will require you to rearrange the words in a sentence, the sentences in a paragraph, or even the paragraphs in a passage. Others may ask questions about the meaning of all or part of the passage, or to describe its structure. Your approach to these questions should be:

1. *Determine your task.* What is the question asking you to do?

2. *Consider the passage as a whole.* Most passages will have a well-defined theme, laid out in a logical way. Choose the answer that expresses this theme, or the arrangement of elements that best continues the logical "flow" of the passage.

3. *Prephrase your answer.* As in Reading, you should have an idea of what the answer is before looking at the choices.

KAPLAN

TIMING

We recommend that you NOT skip around in the English subject test. Although you can certainly use the usual two-Pass Approach, you might prefer to go straight from beginning to end, answering all of the questions as you go. Unlike in other sections, in English you'll usually have at least a sense of what the right answer should be right away. Remember, even the correct answer will start to sound wrong if you think about it too much!

Set your watch to 12:00 at the beginning of the subject test. Although you should go faster if you can, here's roughly where you should be at the following checkpoints:

12:09..........One passage finished and answers gridded in

12:18..........Two passages finished and answers gridded in

12:27..........Three passages finished and answers gridded in

12:36..........Four passages finished and answers gridded in

12:45..........Five passages finished and answers for the entire section gridded in.

Note that you should do at least some work on all 75 English questions, and make sure you have at least one guess gridded in for every question when time is called.

WHEN YOU'RE RUNNING OUT OF TIME

If you have no time left even to read the last few questions, choose the shortest answer for each one. Remember that "OMIT," when it appears, counts as the shortest answer.

SCORING

Your performance on the English subject test will be averaged into your ACT Composite Score, weighted equally with your scores on the other three subject tests. You will also receive:

• English subject score—from 1 to 36—for the entire English subject test

• Usage/Mechanics subscore—from 1 to 18—based on your performance on the questions testing grammar, usage, punctuation, and sentence structure

• Rhetorical Skills subscore—from 1 to 18—based on your performance on the questions testing strategy, organization, and style

MATH
SUMMARY

THE FORMAT

The Math subject test:

- Is 60 minutes long.

- Consists of 60 questions, which test your grasp of pre-algebra, algebra, coordinate geometry, plane geometry, and trigonometry. We break down the questions into the following strategic categories:

    1. Diagram Questions

    2. Story Questions

    3. Concept Questions

    The questions tend to test more advanced math concepts as you proceed through the section.

THE MINDSET

- *The end justifies the means.* Remember that what's important on the ACT is getting as many correct answers as quickly as possible. If that means doing straightforward questions in a straightforward way, that's fine. But many questions can be solved faster by unorthodox methods.

- *Take time to save time.* It sounds paradoxical, but to go your fastest on the ACT Math test you've got to slow down. Never dive in headlong, wildly crunching numbers, manipulating equations, or filling out figures without first giving the problem a few seconds of thought.

- *When in doubt, shake it up.* ACT Math questions are not always what they seem at first sight. Sometimes all you need is a new perspective to break through the disguise.

SECTION III: STRATEGIC SUMMARIES

THE APPROACH

1. *Understand*. First focus on the question stem and make sure you understand the problem. Sometimes you'll want to read the stem twice, or rephrase it in a way you can better understand. Think to yourself: "What kind of problem is this? What am I looking for? What am I given?" When you begin, don't pay too much attention to the answer choices, though you may want to give them a quick glance just to see what form they're in.

2. *Analyze*. Think for a moment and decide on a plan of attack. Don't start crunching numbers until you've given the problem a little thought. "What's a quick and reliable way to find the correct answer?" Look for patterns and shortcuts, using common sense and your knowledge of the test to find the creative solutions that will get you more right answers in less time. Try to solve the problem without focusing on the answer choices.

3. *Select*. Once you get an answer—or once you get stuck—check the answer choices. If you got an answer and it's listed as one of the choices, chances are it's right—fill in the appropriate bubble and move on. But if you *didn't* get an answer, narrow down the choices as best you can by a process of elimination, and then guess.

SPECIAL STRATEGIES

We offer several recommendations for what to do when you get stuck. If after a few moments of thought you find you still can't come up with a reasonable way of doing the problem, try one of these techniques:

1. *Backsolve*. We recommend that you normally attempt to solve a problem before looking at the answer choices. But when you're stuck, take advantage of the multiple-choice format. In some of the questions, you can just try out each answer choice until you find the one that works.

2. *Pick numbers*. Some problems are hard because they're general or abstract. Bring these down to earth by temporarily replacing variables with specific numbers.

3. *Guesstimate*. Sometimes you'll understand what a problem is asking for, but you just won't know what algorithm, formula, or theorem to apply. If you can figure out some ballpark estimate for the correct answer, you'll probably be able to eliminate at least one or two answer choices.

4. *Eyeball*. Even though the directions warn you that diagrams are "*not* necessarily" drawn to scale, eyeballing is a surprisingly effective guessing strategy. When you don't fully fathom the geometry of a situation, but you *do* have a diagram to work with, see how many answer choices you can eliminate just by sizing things up with your eyes.

TIMING

Remember the two-Pass Approach. Spend about 45 minutes on your first pass through the Math subject test, doing the easier questions, guessing on the questions you know you'll never get, and marking the tough ones that you'll want to come back to. Spend the last 15 minutes picking up those questions that you skipped on the first pass.

We recommend that you grid your answers at the end of every page or every two-page spread. In the last five minutes or so, start gridding your answers one by one. And make sure that you have an answer (even if it's a blind guess) gridded for every question by the time the subject test is over.

Don't worry if you have to guess on a lot of the math questions. You can miss a lot of questions on the subject test and still get a great score. Remember that the average ACT test taker gets less than half the math questions right!

WHEN YOU'RE RUNNING OUT OF TIME

If at some point you realize you have more questions left than you have time for, be extra willing to skip around, looking for questions you understand right away. Pick your spots. Concentrate on the questions you have the best chance of correctly answering. Just be sure to grid an answer—even if it's just a wild guess—for *every* question.

SCORING

Your performance on the Math subject test will be averaged into your ACT Composite Score, equally weighted with your scores on the other three subject tests. You will also receive:

- Math subject score—from 1 to 36—for the entire Math subject test

- Prealgebra/Elementary Algebra subscore—from 1 to 18

- Intermediate Algebra/Coordinate Geometry subscore—from 1 to 18

- Plane Geometry/Trigonometry subscore—from 1 to 18

READING
SUMMARY

THE FORMAT

The Reading subject test:

- Is 35 minutes long.

- Includes four passages:

    - Three Nonfiction passages (one each in Social Studies, Natural Sciences, and Humanities, though there is no significant difference among them except subject matter)

    - One Prose Fiction passage (an excerpt from a short story or novel)

- Consists of 40 questions, 10 on each passage. They include:

    1. Specific Detail Questions

    2. Inference Questions

    3. Big Picture Questions

  The questions do NOT get harder as you go through the section.

THE MINDSET

- *Know where you're going.* Try to read passages actively, anticipating where the author is going by paying attention to structural clues and common sense. Pay attention to the structure of each passage and don't get bogged down in the details.

- *Look it up.* Find the answers, don't remember them. Think of the passages as reference books, not textbooks. Refer.

SECTION III: STRATEGIC SUMMARIES

THE APPROACH

1. *Preread the passage.* Try to understand the "gist" of the passage. Get a sense of the overall structure of the passage. Create a mental road map (except on the Prose Fiction passage) to make referring back easier.

2. *Consider the question stem.* Understand the question first, without looking at the array of answer choices. Remember that many wrong choices are designed to mislead test takers who just jump past the question stem and start comparing choices to each other.

3. *Refer to the passage before looking at the choices.* Always refer to the passage before answering the question. If the question includes a line reference, use it. Only then look at the choices. Make sure your answer matches the passage in meaning, and that it doesn't just use the same words as the passage.

SPECIAL STRATEGIES

Prose Fiction Passage

When you preread the passage, pay attention to the characters, especially the main character. Read between the lines to determine unspoken emotions and attitudes. Ask yourself:

- Who are these people? What are they like? How are they related to each other?

- What is their state of mind? Are they angry, sad, reflective, excited?

- What's going on? What's happening on the surface? What's happening *beneath* the surface?

Nonfiction Passages

Don't be thrown by unfamiliar vocabulary. If you find a difficult term, odds are the definition will be given to you in context (or else it simply might not matter what the word means). Remember, you can still get lots of questions right, even if you don't fully understand the passage. The answers to all of the questions can be found.

TIMING

You might want to take a few seconds at the beginning of the subject test to page through the passages, gauging the difficulty of each one. At first glance you may wish to skip an entire passage if it seems very difficult.

We recommend that you treat each passage and its questions as a block. Take two passes through each block before moving on to the next (skip around if you like, but watch your answer grid if you do!). Get the easy questions on the first pass through and save the tougher ones for the second pass. Just make sure to keep track of time.

Set your watch to 12:00 at the beginning of the subject test. Although you should go faster if you can, here's roughly where you should be at the following checkpoints.

12:09 ....One passage finished and answers gridded in

12:18 ....Two passages finished and answers gridded in

12:27 ....Three passages finished and answers gridded in

12:35 ....Four passages finished and answers for entire section gridded in

Don't spend time agonizing over specific questions. Avoid thinking long and hard about the answer choices. Once you've spent a minute or so on a question, make your best guess and keep moving on.

Don't panic if you can't finish all four passages. Make sure you do a good job on at least three passages—and remember to grid answers (even if they're blind guesses) for all questions by the end. Even if you try all four passages, you probably won't really work on all forty *questions*. For many questions, you'll just have to guess. Just make sure you guess on the tough ones and actually work on the easy ones!

WHEN YOU'RE RUNNING OUT OF TIME

If you have less than 5 minutes left for the last passage, do the following:

1. Skip the prereading step.

2. Look for questions with specific line references and do them.

3. Refer to the cited location in the passage and answer the question as best you can, based on what you see there.

4. Make sure you have gridded in an answer for every question before time is called.

SCORING

Your performance on the Reading subject test will be averaged into your ACT Composite Score, weighted equally with your scores on the other three subject tests. You will also receive:

• Reading subject score—from 1 to 36—for the entire Reading subject test

• Social Science/Sciences subscore—from 1 to 18—based on your performance on the nonfiction passages drawn from Social Studies and Natural Sciences

• Arts/Literature subscore—from 1 to 18—based on your performance on the nonfiction passage (drawn from the Humanities) and on the Prose Fiction passage

SCIENCE REASONING SUMMARY

THE FORMAT

The Science Reasoning subject test:

- Is 35 minutes long.

- Includes 7 "passages," or sets of scientific information, involving graphs, tables, and research summaries. Typically, one of the passages involves two conflicting viewpoints on a single scientific issue.

- Consists of 40 questions, divided among the 7 passages. We divide the questions strategically into three categories:

    1. Data Analysis Questions

    2. Experiment Questions

    3. Principle Questions

    The questions do NOT get harder as you proceed through the section.

THE MINDSET

- *Look for patterns.* Usually, the exact data contained in Science Reasoning passages are not as important as are *changes* in the data. Look for extremes (maximums and minimums), critical points (points of change), and variation (direct and inverse).

- *Know your direction.* There are two kinds of scientific reasoning—general-to-specific and specific-to-general. Always be aware of when scientists are inferring a specific case from a general rule, and when they are using specific data to form a (general) theory.

- *Refer, don't remember.* Don't even *think* of trying to remember data. It's always there, right on the page, for you to refer to when needed.

THE APPROACH

1. *Preread the passage.* Look for the overall topic. What is being researched? Look for the purpose of each experiment. How do the experiments differ? Don't get bogged down in details and don't worry about understanding everything.

2. *Consider the question stem.* Make sure you understand exactly what the question is asking. Get a sense of what the answer should be without looking at the choices, many of which are designed to mislead you if you're indecisive.

3. *Refer to the passage before looking at the choices.* Always refer back to the passage before looking at the choices and selecting one. Make sure you read charts and graphs accurately, and that you do not confuse different kinds of units.

SPECIAL STRATEGIES

Reading Tables and Graphs

When reading tables and graphs, you should:

- Determine what is being represented

- Determine what the axes (or columns and rows) represent

- Take note of units of measurement

- Look for trends in the data

Experiments

Remember how experiments work. There is typically (though not always) a control group plus an experimental group or groups. In a well-designed experiment, the only difference between the groups will be a variation in the factor that's being tested. Ask yourself:

- What's the factor that's being varied?

- What's the control group, if any?

- What do the results show? What differences exist between the results for one group and those for another?

Conflicting Viewpoints Passage

Spend a little more time than usual on the pre-reading step of this passage. Focus on the two points of view. What are the scientists arguing about? What do they agree on, if anything? What do they differ on? Identify the following for each scientist:

- Basic theory statement (usually the first sentence of each scientist's presentation)

- Major pieces of data behind the theory (keeping in mind whether each supports the scientist's own theory or weakens the opposing scientist's theory)

TIMING

Some Science Reasoning passages are a lot harder than others, and they're not arranged in order of difficulty, so you might want to take a few seconds at the beginning of the subject test to page through the passages, gauging the difficulty of each one. You may wish to skip an entire passage if it seems very difficult (but remember that a very difficult passage may have very easy questions).

As in Reading, treat each passage and its questions as a block, taking two passes through each block before moving on to the next. Get the easy questions on the first pass through and save the tougher ones for the second pass. Some questions will probably be impossible for you to answer; take an intuitive guess on these.

Set your watch to 12:00 at the beginning of the subject test. Although you should go faster if you can, here's where you should be at the following checkpoints:

12:05 ....One passage finished and answers gridded in

12:10 ....Two passages finished and answers gridded in

12:15 ....Three passages finished and answers gridded in

12:20 ....Four passages finished and answers gridded in

12:25 ....Five passages finished and answers gridded in

12:30 ....Six passages finished and answers gridded in

12:35 ....Seven passages finished and answers for the entire section gridded in

Don't spend time agonizing over specific questions. Avoid thinking long and hard about the answer choices. If you've spent a minute or so on a question and don't seem to be making any headway, make your best guess and move on.

Don't panic if you can't finish all seven passages, but try to do a good job on at least five of them. And make sure you remember to grid answers (even if they're blind guesses) for all questions by the end.

WHEN YOU'RE RUNNING OUT OF TIME

If you have less than three minutes left for the last passage, do the following:

1. Skip the prereading step.

2. Look for questions that refer to specific experiments or to specific graphs or tables.

3. Refer to the cited location in the passage and answer the question as best you can, based on what you see there.

4. Make sure you have gridded in an answer for every question before time is called.

SCORING

Your performance on the Science Reasoning subject test will be averaged into your ACT Composite Score, weighted equally with your scores on the other three subject tests. You will also receive:

• Science Reasoning subject score—from 1 to 36—for the entire Science Reasoning subject test

Unlike the other three subject scores, the Science Reasoning score is *not* divided into subscores.

SECTION IV

READY, SET, GO

CALCULATORS ON THE ACT

TO CALCULATE OR NOT TO CALCULATE

Since fall 1996, students have been permitted to use calculators on the Math section of the ACT. The good news for noncalculator users is that you never *absolutely need* to use a calculator on the ACT. No math question on the ACT requires messy or tedious calculations. But while the calculator can't answer questions for you, it can keep you from making computational errors on questions you know how to solve. The bad news, however, is that a calculator can actually *cost* you time if you overuse it. Take a look at this example:

1. The sum of all the integers from 1 to 44, inclusive, is subtracted from the sum of all the integers from 7 to 50, inclusive. What is the result?

   A.   6
   B.   44
   C.   50
   D. 264
   E. 300

You could . . . add all the integers from 1 through 44, and then all the integers from 7 through 50, and then subtract the first sum from the second. And then punch in all the numbers into the calculator. And then hope you didn't hit any wrong buttons.

TRAP

If a problem seems to involve a lot of calculation, look for a quicker way.

But that's the long way . . . and the wrong way. That way involves hitting over 250 keys on your calculator. It'll take too long, and you're too likely to make a mistake. The amount of computation involved in solving this problem tells you that there must be an easier way. Remember, no ACT problem absolutely requires the use of a calculator.

THE RIGHT WAY—THINK FIRST

Let's look at that problem again:

1. The sum of all the integers from 1 to 44, inclusive, is subtracted from the sum of all the integers from 7 to 50, inclusive. What is the result?
  A.   6
  B.   44
  C.   50
  D.   264
  E.   300

A calculator *can* help you on this question, but you have to think first. Both sums contain the same number of consecutive integers, and each integer in the first sum has a corresponding integer 6 greater than it in the second sum. Here's the scratchwork:

$$
\begin{array}{ll}
1 & 7 \\
+2 & +8 \\
+3 & +9 \\
\cdot & \cdot \\
\cdot & \cdot \\
\cdot & \cdot \\
+42 & +48 \\
+43 & +49 \\
+44 & +50 \\
\end{array}
$$

This means there are 44 pairs of integers which are each 6 apart. So the total difference between the two sums will be the difference between each pair of integers, times the number of pairs. Now you can pull out your calculator, punch "6 × 44 =" and get the correct answer of 264 with little or no time wasted. Mark (D) in your test booklet and move on.

FIND THE PATTERN, SAVE SOME TIME

Spotting the pattern shows you how a calculator can save time.

KAPLAN

USING THE CALCULATOR TO SAVE TIME

Of course, there will be many situations on the ACT in which using a calculator can *save* you time. Here's an ACT trig question that's much easier with a calculator:

2. sin 495° =

    F. $-\dfrac{\sqrt{2}}{2}$

    G. $-\dfrac{1}{2}$

    H. $\dfrac{1}{2}$

    J. $\dfrac{\sqrt{2}}{2}$

    K. $\dfrac{3\sqrt{2}}{2}$

Without a calculator this is a very difficult problem. To find a trigonometric function of an angle greater than or equal to 90°, sketch a circle of radius 1 and centered at the origin of the coordinate grid. Start from the point (1, 0) and rotate the appropriate number of degrees counterclockwise. When you rotate counterclockwise 495°, you rotate 360° (which brings you back to where you started), and then an additional 135°. That puts you 45° into the second quadrant. Now you need to know whether sine is positive or negative in the second quadrant. Pretty scary, huh?

With a calculator this problem becomes simple. Just punch in "sin 495°" and you get 0.7071067811865. (A) and (B) are negative, so they're out, and 0.7071067811865 is clearly not equal to $\frac{1}{2}$, so (C) is also wrong. That leaves only (D) or (E). Now, is greater than 1, so if you multiply it by another number greater than 1 (namely $\frac{3}{2}$), the result is obviously greater than 1. So you can eliminate (E), leaving (D) as the correct answer. With a calculator, you can get this question right without really understanding it.

CALCULATORS: THE GAME PLAN

The key to effective calculator use is practice, so don't run out the night before the test to buy a fancy new calculator. If you don't already have a calculator (and intend to use one on the test), buy one now. Unless you're doing Math or Science in college, you won't need anything more complex than trig functions. Bear in mind that you're better off bringing a straightforward model you're familiar with than an esoteric model you don't know how to use.

CALCULATORS **NOT** ALLOWED ON THE TEST

Pocket organizers, computers, models with writing pads, computers with QWERTY keyboards, paper tapes, power cords, wireless transmitters, noisy calculators, Kray supercomputers.

LEARNING THE DO'S AND DON'TS

Practicing with your calculator is the best way to get a sense of where it can help and save time. It's important to develop a sense of the most effective ways in which to use your calculator on the test. Here's a brief guide to spotting those calculator-friendly Math questions:

3. $(7.3 + 0.8) - 3(1.98 + 0.69) =$
   A. −0.99
   B. −0.09
   C. 0
   D. 0.09
   E. 0.99

This problem basically involves straightforward computation, so you'd be right if you reached for your calculator. However, if you just start punching the numbers in as they appear in the question, you might come up with the wrong answer. When you're performing a string of computations you know that you need to follow the order of operations. The problem is, your calculator might not know this. Some calculators have parentheses keys and do follow PEMDAS, so it's important to know your machine and what its capabilities are.

KNOW YOUR CALCULATOR

Some calculators automatically follow the order of operations but others don't. It's important to feel comfortable with your calculator, and know what it can and cannot do.

KAPLAN

If your calculator doesn't follow the order of operations, you'd need to perform the operations within parentheses separately. You'd get 8.1 − 3(2.67). Multiplication comes before subtraction, so you'd get 8.1 − 8.01, and then finally .09, choice D.

4. A certain bank issues 3-letter identification codes to its customers. If each letter can be used only once per code, how many different codes are possible?

F.   26

G.   78

H.   326

J. 15,600

K. 17,576

Just manipulating the numbers in this problem will get you nowhere, but once you arrive at the setup, a calculator is very useful.

For the first letter in the code you can choose any of the 26 letters in the alphabet. For the second letter, you can choose from all the letters in the alphabet except the one you used in the first spot, so there are 26 − 1 = 25 possibilities. For the third there are 26 − 2 = 24 possibilities. So the total number of different codes possible is equal to 26 × 25 × 24. Using your calculator you find there are 15,600 codes—choice J.

BACKSOLVE

A calculator can help you in backsolving (plugging the answer choices back into the question stem) and picking numbers (substituting numbers for the variables in the question).

5. Which of the following fractions is greater than 0.68 and less than 0.72 ?

A. $\dfrac{5}{9}$

B. $\dfrac{3}{5}$

C. $\dfrac{7}{11}$

D. $\dfrac{2}{3}$

E. $\dfrac{5}{7}$

Here you have to convert the fractions in the answer choices to decimals and see which one falls in the range of values given to you in the question. If you're familiar with common decimal/fraction conversions you might know that choice B, $\frac{3}{5} = .6$ (too small) and choice D, $\frac{2}{3}$ is approximately .67 (also too small). But you'd still have to check out the other three choices. Your calculator can make short work of this, showing you that choice A, $\frac{5}{9} = .5\overline{5}$, choice C, $\frac{7}{11} = .\overline{63}$, and choice E, $\frac{5}{7}$ is approximately .71. Only 0.71 falls between 0.68 and 0.72, so E is correct.

THE KAPLAN ADVANTAGE™ STRESS MANAGEMENT SYSTEM

The countdown has begun. Your date with THE TEST is looming on the horizon. Anxiety is on the rise. The butterflies in your stomach have gone ballistic. Perhaps you feel as if the last thing you ate has turned into a lead ball. Your thinking is getting cloudy. Maybe you think you won't be ready. Maybe you already know your stuff, but you're going into panic mode anyway. Worst of all, you're not sure of what to do about it.

Don't freak! It is possible to tame that anxiety and stress—before *and* during the test. We'll show you how. You won't believe how quickly and easily you can deal with that killer anxiety.

MAKING THE MOST OF YOUR PREP TIME

Lack of control is one of the prime causes of stress. A ton of research shows that if you don't have a sense of control over what's happening in your life you can easily end up feeling helpless and hopeless. So, just having concrete things to do and to think about—taking control—will help reduce your stress. This section shows you how to take control during the days leading up to taking the ACT—or any other test.

IDENTIFY THE SOURCES OF STRESS

In the space provided, jot down (in pencil) anything you identify as a source of your test-related stress. The idea is to pin down that free-floating anxiety so that you can take control of it. Here are some common examples to get you started:

- I always freeze up on tests.
- I'm nervous about the math (or the grammar or reading comp, etc.).
- I need a good/great score to go to Acme College.

STRESS TIP

Don't forget that your school probably has counseling available. If you can't conquer test stress on your own, make an appointment at the counseling center. That's what counselors are there for.

- My older brother/sister/best friend/girl- or boyfriend did really well. I *must* match their scores or do better.
- My parents, who are paying for school, will be really disappointed if I don't test well.
- I'm afraid of losing my focus and concentration.
- I'm afraid I'm not spending enough time preparing.
- I study like crazy but nothing seems to stick in my mind.
- I always run out of time and get panicky.
- I feel as though thinking is becoming like wading through thick mud.

Sources of Stress

_____

_____

_____

_____

_____

_____

_____

_____

_____

Take a few minutes to think about the things you've just written down. Then rewrite them in some sort of order. List the statements you most associate with your stress and anxiety first, and put the least disturbing items last. Chances are, the top of the list is a fairly accurate description of exactly how you react to test anxiety, both physically and mentally. The later items usually describe your fears (disappointing Mom and Dad, looking bad, etc.). As you write the list, you're forming a hierarchy of items so you can deal first with the anxiety provokers that bug you most. Very often, taking care of the major items from the top of the list goes a long way toward relieving overall testing anxiety. You probably won't have to bother with the stuff you placed last.

TAKE STOCK OF YOUR STRENGTHS AND WEAKNESSES

Take one minute to list the areas of the test that you are good at. They can be general ("world history") or specific ("Nevada from 1850 to 1875"). Put down as many as you can think of, and if possible, time yourself. Write for the entire time; don't stop writing until you've reached the one-minute stopping point.

Strong Test Subjects

_____
_____
_____
_____
_____
_____
_____
_____
_____

Next, take one minute to list areas of the test you're not so good at, just plain bad at, have failed at, or keep failing at. Again, keep it to one minute, and continue writing until you reach the cutoff. Don't be afraid to identify and write down your weak spots! In all probability, as you do both lists you'll find you are strong in some areas and not so strong in others. Taking stock of your assets *and* liabilities lets you know the areas you don't have to worry about, and the ones that will demand extra attention and effort.

Weak Test Subjects

_____
_____
_____
_____
_____
_____

VERY SUPERSTITIOUS

Stress expert Stephen Sideroff, Ph.D., tells of a client who always stressed out before, during, and even after taking tests. Yet she always got outstanding scores. It became obvious that she was thinking superstitiously—subconsciously believing that the great scores were a result of her worrying. She also didn't trust herself, and believed that if she didn't worry she wouldn't study hard enough. Sideroff convinced her to take a risk and work on relaxing before her next test. She did, and her test results were still as good as ever—which broke her cycle of superstitious thinking.

continued

_____

_____

_____

Now, go back to the "good" list, and expand it for two minutes. Take the general items on that first list and make them more specific; take the specific items and expand them into more general conclusions. Naturally, if anything new comes to mind jot it down. Focus all of your attention and effort on your strengths. Don't underestimate yourself or your abilities. Give yourself full credit. At the same time, don't list strengths you don't really have; you'll only be fooling yourself.

Expanding from general to specific might go as follows. If you listed "world history" as a broad topic you feel strong in, you would then narrow your focus to include areas of this subject about which you are particularly knowledgeable. Your areas of strength might include modern European history, the events leading up to World War I, the Bolshevik revolution, etc. You could then break these general categories down to specific areas you know really well. World War I includes the socioeconomic conditions, politics, the rising discontent and rebellion of the population, and all the other factors and events that led up to Archduke Ferdinand becoming an assassin's target.

Suppose your list includes a narrow topic, such as the history of the state of Nevada, 1850 to 1875. Expanding this item from the specific to the overall could include: a chronology of gold and silver mining in the state, how mining production affected both the state and federal economies, harm to the environment because of mining and smelting, and so on, in a continually expanding range of connected issues.

Whatever you know comfortably (that is, almost as well as you know the back of your hand) goes on your "good" list. Okay. You've got the picture. Now, get ready, check your starting time, and start writing down items on your expanded "good" list.

Strong Test Subjects: An Expanded List

_____

_____

_____

_____

continued

_____

_____

_____

_____

_____

_____

_____

After you've stopped, check your time. Did you find yourself going beyond the two minutes allotted? Did you write down more things than you thought you knew? Is it possible you know more than you've given yourself credit for? Could that mean you've found a number of areas in which you feel strong?

You just took an active step toward helping yourself. Notice any increased feelings of confidence? Enjoy them.

Here's another way to think about your writing exercise. Every area of strength and confidence you can identify is much like having a reserve of solid gold at Fort Knox. You'll be able to draw on your reserves as you need them. You can use your reserves to solve difficult questions, maintain confidence, and keep test stress and anxiety at a distance. The encouraging thing is that every time you recognize another area of strength, succeed at coming up with a solution, or get a good score on a test, you increase your reserves. And, there is absolutely no limit to how much self-confidence you can have or how good you can feel about yourself.

WHAT DO YOU WANT TO ACCOMPLISH IN THE TIME REMAINING?

The whole point to this next exercise is sort of like checking out a used car you might want to buy. You'd want to know up front what the car's weak points are, right? Knowing that influences your whole shopping-for-a-used-car campaign. So it is with your conquering-test-stress campaign: Knowing what your weak points are ahead of time helps you prepare.

So let's get back to the list of your weak points. Take two minutes to expand it just as you did with your "good" list. Be honest with yourself without going overboard. It's an accurate appraisal of the test areas that give you troubles. So, pick up your pencil, check the clock, and start writing.

LINK YOUR THOUGHTS

When you're committing new information to memory, link one fact to another, much as elephants are linked trunk to tail in a circus parade. Visualize an image (preferably a bizarre one) that connects the thoughts. You'll remember them in the same linked way, with one thought easily bringing the next to your mind.

THE "NEW AGE" OF RELAXATION

Here are some more tips for beating stress:

• Find out if massage, especially shiatsu, is offered through your school's phys ed department, or at the local "Y."

• Check out a book on acupressure, and find those points on your body where you can press a "relax button."

• If you're especially sensitive to smells, you might want to try some aromatherapy. Lavender oil, for example, is said to have relaxing properties. Health food stores, drug stores, and New Age bookstores may carry aromatherapy oils.

• Many health food stores carry herbs and supplies that have relaxing properties, and they often have a specialist on staff who can tell you about them.

Weak Test Subjects: An Expanded List

_____

_____

_____

_____

_____

_____

_____

_____

_____

_____

How did you do? Were you able to keep writing for the full two minutes? Has making this "weak" list helped you become more clear about the specific areas you need to address?

Facing your weak spots gives you some distinct advantages. It helps a lot to find out where you need to spend extra effort. Increased exposure to tough material makes it more familiar and less intimidating. (After all, we mostly fear what we don't know and are probably afraid to face.) You'll feel better about yourself because you're dealing directly with areas of the test that bring on your anxiety. You can't help feeling more confident when you know you're actively strengthening your chances of earning a higher overall test score.

IMAGINE YOURSELF SUCCEEDING

This next little group of exercises is both physical and mental. It's a natural followup to what you've just accomplished with your lists.

First, get yourself into a comfortable sitting position in a quiet setting. Wear loose clothes. If you wear glasses, take them off. Then, close your eyes and breathe in a deep, satisfying breath of air. Really fill your lungs until your rib cage is fully expanded and you can't take in any more. Then, exhale the air completely. Imagine you're blowing out a candle with your last little puff of air. Do this two or three more times, filling your lungs to their maximum and emptying them totally. Keep your eyes closed, comfortably but not tightly. Let your body sink deeper into the chair as you become even more comfortable.

With your eyes shut you can notice something very interesting. You're no longer dealing with the worrisome stuff going on in the world *outside* of you. Now you can concentrate on what happens *inside* you. The more you recognize your own physical reactions to stress and anxiety, the more you can do about them. You may not realize it, but you've begun to regain a sense of being in control.

Let images begin to form on the "viewing screens" on the back of your eyelids. You're experiencing visualizations from the place in your mind that makes pictures. Allow the images to come easily and naturally; don't force them. Imagine yourself in a relaxing situation. It might be in a special place you've visited before or one you've read about. It can be a fictional location that you create in your imagination, but a real-life memory of a place or situation you know is usually better. Make it as detailed as possible and notice as much as you can.

If you don't see this relaxing place sharply or in living color, it doesn't mean the exercise won't work for you. Some people can visualize in great detail, while others get only a sense of an image. What's important is not how sharp the details or colors, but how well you're able to manipulate the images. If you can conjure up finely detailed images, great. If you only have a faint sense of the images, that's okay—you'll still experience all the benefits of the exercise.

Think about the sights, the sounds, the smells, even the tastes and textures associated with your relaxing situation. *See* and *feel* yourself in this special place. Say you're special place is the beach, for example. Feel how warm the sand is. Are you lying on a blanket, or sitting up and looking out at the water? Hear the waves hitting the shore, and the occasional seagull. Feel a comfortable breeze. If your special place is a garden or park, look up and see the way sunlight filters through the trees. Smell your favorite flowers. Hear some chimes gently playing and birds chirping.

Stay focused on the images as you sink farther back into your chair. Breathe easily and naturally. You might have the sensations of any stress or tension draining from your muscles and flowing downward, out your feet and away from you.

Take a moment to check how you're feeling. Notice how comfortable you've become. Imagine how much easier it would be if you could take the test feeling this relaxed and in this state of ease. You've coupled the images of your special place with sensations of comfort and relaxation. You've also found a way to become relaxed simply by visualizing your own safe, special place.

OCEAN DUMPING

Visualize a beautiful beach, with white sand, blue skies, sparkling water, a warm sun, and seagulls. See yourself walking on the beach, carrying a small plastic pail. Stop at a good spot and put your worries and whatever may be bugging you into the pail. Drop it at the water's edge and watch it drift out to sea. When the pail is out of sight, walk on.

Now, close your eyes and start remembering a real-life situation in which you did well on a test. If you can't come up with one, remember a situation in which you did something (academic or otherwise) that you were really proud of—a genuine accomplishment. Make the memory as detailed as possible. Think about the sights, the sounds, the smells, even the tastes associated with this remembered experience. Remember how confident you felt as you accomplished your goal. Now start thinking about the upcoming test. Keep your thoughts and feelings in line with that successful experience. Don't make comparisons between them. Just imagine taking the upcoming test with the same feelings of confidence and relaxed control.

This exercise is a great way to bring the test down to earth. You should practice this exercise often, especially when the prospect of taking the exam starts to bum you out. The more you practice it, the more effective the exercise will be for you.

EXERCISE YOUR FRUSTRATIONS AWAY

Whether it is jogging, walking, biking, mild aerobics, pushups, or a pickup basketball game, physical exercise is a very effective way to stimulate both your mind and body and to improve your ability to think and concentrate. A surprising number of students get out of the habit of regular exercise, ironically because they're spending so much time prepping for exams. Also, sedentary people—this is medical fact—get less oxygen to the blood and hence to the head than active people. You can live fine with a little less oxygen; you just can't think as well.

Any big test is a bit like a race. Thinking clearly at the end is just as important as having a quick mind early on. If you can't sustain your energy level in the last sections of the exam, there's too good a chance you could blow it. You need a fit body that can weather the demands any big exam puts on you. Along with a good diet and adequate sleep, exercise is an important part of keeping yourself in fighting shape and thinking clearly for the long haul.

There's another thing that happens when students don't make exercise an integral part of their test preparation. Like any organism in nature, you operate best if all your "energy systems" are in balance. Studying uses a lot of energy, but it's all mental. When you take a study break, do something active instead of raiding the fridge or vegging out in front of the TV. Take a five- to ten-minute activity break for every 50 or 60 minutes that you study. The physical exertion gets your body into the act which helps to keep your mind and body in sync. Then, when you finish studying for the night and hit the sack, you won't lie there, tense and unable to sleep, because your head is overtired and your body wants to pump iron or run a marathon.

One warning about exercise, however: It's not a good idea to exercise vigorously right before you go to bed. This could easily cause sleep-onset problems. For the same reason, it's also not a good idea to study right up to bedtime. Make time for a "buffer period" before you go to bed: For 30 to 60 minutes, just take a hot shower, meditate, simply veg out.

GET HIGH . . . NATURALLY

Exercise can give you a natural high, which is the only kind of high you can afford right now. Using drugs (prescription or recreational) specifically to prepare for and take a big test is definitely self-defeating. Except for the drugs that occur naturally in your brain, *every* drug has major drawbacks—and a false sense of security is only one of them.

You may have heard that popping uppers helps you study by keeping you alert. If they're illegal, definitely forget about it. You're just wasting your time. Amphetamines make it hard to retain information. So you'll stay awake, but you probably won't remember much of what you read. And, taking an upper before you take the test could really mess things up. You're already going to be a little anxious and hyper; adding a strong stimulant could easily push you over the edge into panic. Remember, a little anxiety is a good thing. The adrenaline that gets pumped into your bloodstream helps you stay alert and think more clearly. But, too much anxiety and you can't think straight at all.

Mild stimulants, such as coffee, cola, or over-the-counter caffeine pills can sometimes help as you study, since they keep you alert. On the down side, they can also lead to agitation, restlessness, and insomnia. Some people can drink a pot of high-octane coffee and sleep like a baby. Others have one cup and start to vibrate. It all depends on your tolerance for caffeine.

Alcohol and other depressants are out, too. Again, if they're illegal, forget about it. Depressants wouldn't work, anyway, since they lead to the inevitable hangover/crash, the fuzzy thinking, and lousy sense of judgment. These are not going to help you ace the test.

Instead, go for endorphins—the "natural morphine." Endorphins have no side effects and they're free—you've already got them in your brain. It just takes some exercise to release them.

CYBERSTRESS

If you spend a lot of time in cyberspace anyway, do a search for the phrase *stress management*. There's a ton of stress advice on the Net, including material specifically for students.

NUTRITION AND STRESS: THE DOS AND DON'TS

Do eat:

- Fruits and vegetables (raw is best, or just lightly steamed or nuked)

- Low-fat protein such as fish, skinless poultry, beans, and legumes (like lentils)

- Whole grains such as brown rice, whole wheat bread, and pastas (no bleached flour)

Don't eat:

- Refined sugar; sweet, high-fat snacks (simple carbohydrates like sugar make stress worse, and fatty foods lower your immunity)

- Salty foods (they can deplete potassium, which you need for nerve functions)

Running around on the basketball court, bicycling, swimming, aerobics, power walking—these activities cause endorphins to occupy certain spots in your brain's neural synapses. In addition, exercise develops staying power and increases the oxygen transfer to your brain. Go into the test naturally.

TAKE A DEEP BREATH . . .

Here's another natural route to relaxation and invigoration. It's a classic isometric exercise that you can do whenever you get stressed out—just before the test begins, even *during* the test. It's very simple and takes just a few minutes.

Close your eyes. Starting with your eyes and—*without holding your breath*—gradually tighten every muscle in your body (but not to the point of pain) in the following sequence:

1. Close your eyes tightly.
2. Squeeze your nose and mouth together so that your whole face is scrunched up. (If it makes you self-conscious to do this in the test room, skip the face-scrunching part.)
3. Pull your chin into your chest, and pull your shoulders together.
4. Tighten your arms to your body, then clench your hands into tight fists.
5. Pull in your stomach.
6. Squeeze your thighs and buttocks together, and tighten your calves.
7. Stretch your feet, then curl your toes (watch out for cramping in this part).

At this point, every muscle should be tightened. Now, relax your body, one part at a time, *in reverse order*, starting with your toes. Let the tension drop out of each muscle. The entire process might take five minutes from start to finish (maybe a couple of minutes during the test). This clenching and unclenching exercise should help you to feel very relaxed.

AND KEEP BREATHING

Conscious attention to breathing is an excellent way of managing test stress (or any stress, for that matter). The majority of people who get into trouble during tests take shallow breaths. They breathe using only their upper chests and shoulder muscles, and may even hold their breath for long periods of time. Conversely, the test taker who by accident or design keeps breathing normally and rhythmically is likely to be more relaxed and in better control during the entire test experience.

So, now is the time to get into the habit of relaxed breathing. Do the next exercise to learn to breathe in a natural, easy rhythm. By the way, this is another technique you can use during the test to collect your thoughts and ward off excess stress. The entire exercise should take no more than three to five minutes.

With your eyes still closed, breathe in slowly and *deeply* through your nose. Hold the breath for a bit, and then release it through your mouth. The key is to breathe slowly and deeply by using your diaphragm (the big band of muscle that spans your body just above your waist) to draw air in and out naturally and effortlessly. Breathing with your diaphragm encourages relaxation and helps minimize tension.

As you breathe, imagine that colored air is flowing into your lungs. Choose any color you like, from a single color to a rainbow. With each breath, the air fills your body from the top of your head to the tips of your toes. Continue inhaling the colored air until it occupies every part of you, bones and muscles included. Once you have completely filled yourself with the colored air, picture an opening somewhere on your body, either natural or imagined. Now, with each breath you exhale, some of the colored air will pass out the opening and leave your body. The level of the air (much like the water in a glass as it is emptied) will begin to drop. It will descend progressively lower, from your head down to your feet. As you continue to exhale the colored air, watch the level go lower and lower, farther and farther down your body. As the last of the colored air passes out of the opening, the level will drop down to your toes and disappear. Stay quiet for just a moment. Then notice how relaxed and comfortable you feel.

THUMBS UP FOR MEDITATION

Once relegated to the fringes of the medical world, meditation, biofeedback, and hypnosis are increasingly recommended by medical researchers to reduce pain from headaches, back problems— even cancer. Think of what these powerful techniques could do for your test-related stress and anxiety.

Effective meditation is based primarily on two relaxation methods you've already learned: body awareness and breathing. A couple of different meditation techniques follow. Experience them both, and choose the one that works best for you.

BREATHE LIKE A BABY

A baby or young child is the best model for demonstrating how to breathe most efficiently and comfortably. Only her stomach moves as she inhales and exhales. The action is virtually effortless.

DRESS FOR SUCCESS

When you dress on test day, do it in loose layers. That way you'll be prepared no matter what the temperature of the room is. (An uncomfortable temperature will just distract you from the job at hand.)

And, if you have an item of clothing that you tend to feel "lucky" or confident in—a shirt, a pair of jeans, whatever—wear it. A little totem couldn't hurt.

THINK GOOD THOUGHTS

Create a set of positive, but brief affirmations and mentally repeat them to yourself just before you fall asleep at night. (That's when your mind is very open to suggestion.) You'll find yourself feeling a lot more positive in the morning. Periodically repeating your affirmations during the day makes them even more effective.

Breath Meditation

Make yourself comfortable, either sitting or lying down. For this meditation you can keep your eyes open or close them. You're going to concentrate on your breathing. The goal of the meditation is to notice everything you can about your breath as it enters and leaves your body. Take three to five breaths each time you practice the meditation, which should take about a minute for the entire procedure.

Take a deep breath and hold it for five to ten seconds. When you exhale, let the breath out very slowly. Feel the tension flowing out of you along with the breath that leaves your body. Pay close attention to the air as it flows in and out of your nostrils. Observe how cool it is as you inhale and how warm your breath is when you exhale. As you expel the air, say a cue word such as "calm" or "relax" to yourself. Once you've exhaled all the air from your lungs, start the next long, slow inhale. Notice how relaxed feelings increase as you slowly exhale and again hear your cue words.

Mantra Meditation

For this type of meditation experience you'll need a mental device (a mantra), a passive attitude (don't *try* to do anything), and a position in which you can be comfortable. You're going to focus your total attention on a mantra you create. It should be emotionally neutral, repetitive, and monotonous, and your aim is to fully occupy your mind with it. Furthermore, you want to do the meditation passively, with no goal in your head of how relaxed you're supposed to be. This is a great way to prepare for studying or taking the test. It clears your head of extraneous thoughts and gets you focused and at ease.

Sit comfortably and close your eyes. Begin to relax by letting your body go limp. Create a relaxed mental attitude and know there's no need for you to force anything. You're simply going to let something happen. Breathe through your nose. Take calm, easy breaths and as you exhale, say your mantra (*one, ohhm, aah, soup*—whatever is emotionally neutral for you) to yourself. Repeat the mantra each time you breathe out. Let feelings of relaxation grow as you focus on the mantra and your slow breathing. Don't worry if your mind wanders. Simply return to the mantra and continue letting go. Experience this meditation for ten to fifteen minutes.

QUICK TIPS FOR THE DAYS
JUST BEFORE THE EXAM

• The best test takers do less and less as Test Day approaches. Taper off on your study schedule and take it easy on yourself. You want to be relaxed and ready on test day. Give yourself time off, especially the evening before the exam. By that time, if you've studied well, everything you need to know is firmly stored in your memory banks.

• Positive self-talk can be extremely liberating and invigorating, especially as the test looms closer. Tell yourself things such as, "I choose to take this test" rather than "I have to"; "I will do well" rather than "I hope things go well"; "I can" rather than "I cannot." Be aware of negative, self-defeating thoughts and images and immediately counter any you become aware of. Replace them with affirming statements that encourage your self-esteem and confidence. Create and practice doing visualizations that build on your positive statements.

• Get your act together sooner rather than later. Have everything (including choice of clothing) laid out days in advance. Most important, know where the test will be held and the easiest, quickest way to get there. You will gain great peace of mind if you know that all the little details—gas in the car, directions, etc.—are firmly in your control before Test Day.

• Experience the test site a few days in advance. This is very helpful if you are especially anxious. If at all possible, find out what room your part of the alphabet is assigned to, and try to sit there (by yourself) for a while. Better yet, bring some practice material and do at least a section or two, if not an entire practice test, in that room. In this case, familiarity doesn't breed contempt; it generates comfort and confidence.

• Forego any practice on the day before the test. It's in your best interest to marshal your physical and psychological resources for twenty-four hours or so. Even race horses are kept in the paddock and treated like princes the day before a race. Keep the upcoming test out of your consciousness; go to a movie, take a pleasant hike, or just relax. Don't eat junk food or tons of sugar. And—of course—get plenty of rest the night before. Just don't go to bed too early. It's hard to fall asleep earlier than you're used to, and you don't want to lie there thinking about the test.

STRESS TIP

A lamp with a 75-watt bulb is optimal for studying. But don't put it so close to your study material that you create a glare.

WHAT ARE "SIGNS OF A WINNER," ALEX?

Here's some advice from a Kaplan instructor who won big on *Jeopardy!*™ In the green room before the show, he noticed that the contestants who were quiet and "within themselves" were the ones who did great on the show. The contestants who did not perform as well were the ones who were fact-cramming, talking a lot, and generally being manic before the show. Lesson: Spend the final hours leading up to the test getting sleep, meditating, and generally relaxing.

DON'T FORCE IT

Never try to force relaxation. You'll only get frustrated and find yourself even more uptight. Be passive.

AVOID MUST-Y THINKING

Let go of "must-y" thoughts, those notions that you must do something in a certain way—for example, "I must get a great score, or else!" or "I must meet Mom and Dad's expectations."

HANDLING STRESS DURING THE TEST

The biggest stress monster will be Test Day itself. Fear not; there are methods of quelling your stress during the test.

- Keep moving forward instead of getting bogged down in a difficult question, game, or passage. You don't have to get everything right to achieve a fine score. So, don't linger out of desperation on a question that is going nowhere even after you've spent considerable time on it. The best test takers skip (temporarily) difficult material in search of the easier stuff. They mark the ones that require extra time and thought. This strategy buys time and builds confidence so you can handle the tough stuff later.

- Don't be thrown if other test takers seem to be working more busily and furiously than you are. Continue to spend your time patiently but doggedly thinking through your answers; it's going to lead to higher-quality test taking and better results. Don't mistake the other people's sheer activity as signs of progress and higher scores.

- *Keep breathing!* Weak test takers tend to share one major trait: They forget to breathe properly as the test proceeds. They start holding their breath without realizing it, or they breathe erratically or arrhythmically. Improper breathing hurts confidence and accuracy. Just as important, it interferes with clear thinking.

- Some quick isometrics during the test—especially if concentration is wandering or energy is waning—can help. Try this: Put your palms together and press intensely for a few seconds. Concentrate on the tension you feel through your palms, wrists, forearms, and up into your biceps and shoulders. Then, quickly release the pressure. Feel the difference as you let go. Focus on the warm relaxation that floods through the muscles. Now you're ready to return to the task.

- Here's another isometric that will relieve tension in both your neck and eye muscles. Slowly rotate your head from side to side, turning your head and eyes to look as far back over each shoulder as you can. Feel the muscles stretch on one side of your neck as they contract on the other. Repeat five times in each direction.

With what you've just learned here, you're armed and ready to do battle with the test. This book and your studies will give you the information you'll need to answer the questions. It's all firmly planted in your mind. You also know how to deal with any excess tension that might come along, both when you're studying for and taking the exam. You've experienced everything you need to tame your test anxiety and stress. You are going to get a great score.

LAST-MINUTE TIPS

Is it starting to feel like your whole life is a buildup to the ACT? You've known about it for years, worried about it for months, and now spent at least a few hours in solid preparation for it. As the test gets closer, you may find your anxiety is on the rise. You shouldn't worry. After the preparation you've received from this book, you're in good shape for Test Day.

To calm any pretest jitters you may have (and assuming you've left yourself at least some breathing time before your ACT), let's go over a few last-minute strategies for the couple of days before and after the test.

Three Days Before the Test

- If you haven't already done so, take the full-length practice test in this book under timed conditions. If you have already done so, try an actual published ACT (your guidance counselor might have one).

- Try to use all of the techniques and tips you've learned in this book. Take control. Approach the test *strategically* and *creatively*.

> *WARNING: Don't take a full practice ACT unless you have at least forty-eight hours left before the test! Doing so will probably exhaust you, hurting your scoring potential on the actual test! You wouldn't run a marathon the day before the real thing, would you?*

Two Days Before the Test

- Go over the results of your practice test. Don't worry too much about your score or whether you got a specific question right or wrong. Remember the practice test doesn't count. But do examine your performance on specific questions with an eye to how you might get through each one faster and with greater accuracy on the actual test to come.

- After reviewing your test, look over the Strategic Summaries. If you feel a little shaky about any of the areas mentioned, quickly read the relevant workouts.

SECTION IV: READY, SET, GO

- This is the day to do your last studying—review a couple of the more difficult principles we've covered, do a few more practice problems, and call it quits. It doesn't pay to make yourself crazy right before the test. Besides, you've prepared. You'll do well.

The Day Before the Test

- Don't study.

- Get together an "ACT survival kit" containing the following items:

  - Watch

  - At least 3 sharpened No. 2 pencils

  - Pencil sharpener

  - 2 erasers

  - Photo ID card (if you're not taking the test at your high school, make sure your ID is official)

  - Your admission ticket

  - Snack—there's a break, and you'll probably get hungry

  - Your lucky rabbit's foot

- Know exactly where you're going and how you're getting there. It's probably a good idea to visit your test center sometime before test day, so that you know what expect on the big day.

- Relax the day before the test. Read a good book, take a bubble bath, watch TV. Exercise can be a good idea early in the afternoon. Working out makes it easier to sleep when you're nervous, and it also makes many people feel better. Of course, don't work so hard that you can't get up the next day!

- Get a good night's sleep. Go to bed early and allow for some extra time to get ready in the morning.

The Morning of the Test

- Eat breakfast. Make it something substantial, but not anything too heavy or greasy. Don't drink a lot of coffee if you're not used to it; bathroom breaks cut into your time, and too much caffeine—or any other kind of drug—is a bad idea.

- Dress in layers so that you can adjust to the temperature of the test room.

254 **KAPLAN**

- Read something. Warm up your brain with a newspaper or a magazine. You shouldn't let the ACT be the first thing you read that day.

- Be sure to get there early. Allow yourself extra time for traffic, mass-transit delays, and any other possible problems.

- If you can, go to the test with a friend (even if he or she isn't taking the test). It's nice to have somebody supporting you right up to the last minute.

During the Test

- Don't get rattled. If you find your confidence slipping, remind yourself how well you've prepared. You've followed the Three Commandments of ACT Success. You know the test; you know the strategies; you know the material tested. You're in great shape, as long as you *relax!*

- Even if something goes really wrong, don't panic. If the test booklet is defective—two pages are stuck together or the ink has run—try to stay calm. Raise your hand, and tell the proctor you need a new book. If you accidentally misgrid your answer page or put the answers in the wrong section, again don't panic. Raise your hand, and tell the proctor. He or she might be able to arrange for you to regrid your test after it's over, when it won't cost you any time.

After the Test

Once the test is over, put it out of your mind. If you don't plan to take the ACT again, shelve this book and start thinking about more interesting things.

You might walk out of the ACT thinking that you blew it. This is a normal reaction. Lots of people—even the highest scorers—feel that way. You tend to remember the questions that stumped you, not the many that you knew. If you're really concerned, call us for advice. Also call us if you had any problems with your test experience—a proctor who called time early, a testing room whose temperature hovered just below freezing. We'll do everything we can to make sure that your rights as a test taker are preserved!

But remember, unless you've ignored our recommendation about NOT listing any schools to receive your scores automatically, you've got nothing to worry about (provided that there is still time to get the scores there before the deadline). If you really did blow the test, you can take it again and no admissions officer will be the wiser.

Odds are, though, you didn't really blow it. Most people only remember their disasters on the test; they don't remember the numerous small victories that kept piling up the points.

Don't Freak!

It pays to read through the Kaplan Advantage™ Stress Management System in the front of this book. You will want the latest scientific principles working for you—helping you relax, retain more information, and excel on the ACT. Identify the stress tips that work well for you—from calming beverages and snacks to brain-boosting study techniques—and add them to your arsenal for testing success.

REMEMBER

If you had any significant problems with your testing experience, or if you just feel that for reasons beyond your control you didn't do as well as you should have, call Kaplan at 1-800-KAP-TEST and we'll help!

But For Now . . .

Just relax. You've prepared for the ACT with Kaplan. You're going to do well.

SECTION V

PRACTICE TEST

PRACTICE TEST

What follows is a Kaplan-created test similar to the actual ACT test booklet.

Before taking this test, find a quiet room where you can work uninterrupted for three hours. Make sure you have a comfortable desk, several No. 2 pencils, and a piece of paper to record your answers.

Once you start this practice test, don't stop until you've finished. Remember: You can review any questions within a section, but you may not jump from one section to another.

You'll find the answers and explanations to the test questions immediately following the test.

Good luck.

ENGLISH TEST

45 Minutes—75 Questions

DIRECTIONS: In the following five passages, certain words and phrases have been underlined and numbered. You will find alternatives for each underlined portion in the right-hand column. Select the one that best expresses the idea, that makes the statement acceptable in standard written English, or that is phrased most consistently with the style and tone of the entire passage. If you feel that the original version is best, select "NO CHANGE." You will also find questions asking about a section of the passage or about the entire passage. For these questions, decide which choice gives the most appropriate response to the given question. For each question in the test, select the best choice, and fill in the corresponding space on the answer folder. You may wish to read each passage through before you begin to answer the questions associated with it. Most answers cannot be determined without reading several sentences around the phrases in question. Make sure to read far enough ahead each time you choose an alternative.

Passage I

Many people enjoy the hobby of aquarium keeping.

It has several advantages. <u>As pets they are very quiet,</u>
<u>not worrying too much about pats on the head or 4:00</u>
<u>A.M. walks.</u> Yet even many avid aquarists are unaware
of the fact that their hobby has a fascinating history.

1. **A.** NO CHANGE
   B. Fish make quiet pets; they do not need to be patted on the head or walked at 4:00 A.M.
   C. Their owner who did not pat them on the head is not worried about walking these quiet pets at 4:00 A.M.
   D. These quiet pets without a pat on the head from their owners are not to be walked at 4:00 A.M. by necessity.

Fish keeping actually has ancient origins, <u>who</u>
<u>beginning with</u> the Sumerians over 4,500 years ago.
They kept fishes in artificial ponds. The ancient
Assyrians and Egyptians also kept fish. In addition to
<u>keeping and having</u> fish as pets, the Chinese used them
for practical purposes, raising carp for food as early as

2. **F.** NO CHANGE
   G. which begins with
   H. beginning with
   J. who, beginning at

3. **A.** NO CHANGE
   B. keeping and possessing
   C. keep and have
   D. keeping

100 B.C. They were probably the first people to <u>breeds</u>
fish with any degree of success. Their selective breeding of ornamental goldfish was introduced in Japan,
where the breeding of ornamental carp was perfected.
<u>The ancient Romans</u> kept fish for food and
entertainment. They were the were the first known

4. **F.** NO CHANGE
   G. breeded
   H. breed
   J. bred

5. **A.** NO CHANGE
   B. These are the ancient Romans
   C. Yes, one can find ancient Romans which
   D. The ancient Romans, nevertheless,

GO ON TO NEXT PAGE

seawater aquarists, constructing ponds supplied with
fresh ocean water. The Romans were also the first to use
open-air tanks to preserve and fatten fish for market.

In seventeenth-century England, goldfish were
<u>being</u> kept in glass containers, but aquarium keeping did
  6
not become well established until the relationship among

animals, oxygen, and plants <u>became known</u> a century
                   7
later. In the eighteenth century, France's importation of
goldfish from the Orient created a need for small
aquariums. Ceramic bowls, occasionally fitted with
transparent panels, were produced. 8

By 1850, the keeping of fish, reptiles, and
amphibians had become a useful method of study for
naturalists. Philip Gosse, a British ornithologist, first
coined the term "aquarium." The first display aquariums

opened in 1853 at Regent's Park in <u>London aquariums</u>
                                    9
soon appeared in Naples, Berlin, and Paris. The first
aquarium to serve as a financial enterprise was opened by
the circus entrepreneur P. T. Barnum at the American
Museum in New York City. By 1928, forty-five public or
commercial aquariums were open. <u>Then it slowed and</u>
                                    10
<u>few new large aquariums appeared until after World</u>
                            10
<u>War II</u>. Marineland of Florida, built in 1956, was the first
 10

oceanarium. <u>*Flipper* was a popular television show about</u>
                                    11
<u>a dolphin.</u>
 11

6. **F.** NO CHANGE
   G. to have been
   H. sometimes being
   J. OMIT the underlined portion.

7. **A.** NO CHANGE
   B. which became known
   C. becoming known
   D. were known almost

8. The purpose of the preceding sentence is to:
   F. emphasize the inappropriateness of the aquariums produced at that time.
   G. illustrate the fact that the importation of goldfish produced a corresponding need for small containers.
   H. contradict the assertion made earlier in the paragraph that the English kept goldfish in glass containers.
   J. explain why goldfish could not live for long in small containers.

9. **A.** NO CHANGE
   B. London, which
   C. London, where it
   D. London, and

10. **F.** NO CHANGE
   G. Then its growth having slowed; few new large ones appeared until after World War II.
   H. Then having slowed, few new large ones appeared until after World War II was over.
   J. Then growth slowed, and few new large aquariums appeared until after World War II.

11. **A.** NO CHANGE
   B. A popular television show about a dolphin was *Flipper*.
   C. (A popular television show, *Flipper*, was about a dolphin.)
   D. OMIT the underlined portion.

GO ON TO NEXT PAGE

So next time you meet an aquarist you might share some of this "fish trivia." For fish keeping is not only an entertaining hobby; it also has a rich and long history,
^{12}

have playing a role in many diverse cultures since ancient
^{13}
times.

> Items 14–15 pose questions about the passage as a whole.

14. Which of the following best summarizes the conclusion made by the essay as a whole?
    F. The study of history is a valuable task.
    G. People who keep aquariums must learn "fish trivia."
    H. The hobby of keeping aquariums has an intriguing past.
    J. Maintaining an aquarium is a big responsibility.

12. F. NO CHANGE
    G. —fish trivia. For
    H. "fish trivia," and
    J. "fish trivia! For

13. A. NO CHANGE
    B. having played
    C. has
    D. had played

15. The essay is made up of five paragraphs. Which of the following is the best description of how the paragraphs are organized?
    A. First example, second example, third example, definition, argument.
    B. Introduction, earliest examples, later examples, most recent examples, conclusion.
    C. Historical survey, first example, second example, third example, fourth example.
    D. Introduction, background information, argument, counterargument, personal account.

Passage II

The late twentieth century may well be remembered as the Age of the "Yuppie" (young urban professional). Our society seems obsessed with the notion of social mobility. There are two different types of social mobility:
^{16}
horizontal and vertical. If there is a change in occupation,
^{16}
but no change in social class, it is called "horizontal mobility." One example of this would be a lawyer who changes law firms that are comparable in pay salary and
^{17}
prestige. A change in role involving a change in social
^{17}
standing is called "vertical mobility" and can be either
^{18}
upward or downward.

The extent of change can vary greatly. At one pole, social mobility may affect only one member of a society. At the one pole, social mobility may affect only one

16. F. NO CHANGE
    G. mobility horizontal, and vertical.
    H. mobility; horizontal and vertical.
    J. mobility: being horizontal and vertical.

17. A. NO CHANGE
    B. in pay and prestige.
    C. with pay, salary and prestige.
    D. pay in terms of salary and prestige.

18. F. NO CHANGE
    G. it's called "vertical mobility"
    H. they're called "vertical mobility"
    J. it is called "vertical mobility"

GO ON TO NEXT PAGE

member of a society. At the other extreme, it may change

the entire social system. The Russian Revolution of

1917, <u>therefore</u>, altered an entire class structure.
19

[1] <u>In addition to involving degrees of change,</u> social
20

mobility occurs at a variety of rates. [2] The "American

dream" is based in part on the notion of rapid social

mobility, in which an unknown individual becomes an

"overnight success." [3] One example of rapid social

mobility would be the young guitar player who becomes

an instant rock star. [4] The athlete who wins an Olympic

gold medal <u>too</u> [5] For instance, each generation in a
21

family may be a little better off than the generation

before it. [6] Social mobility may also be accomplished

by more gradual changes. 22

The results of mobility are difficult to measure <u>in</u>
23

<u>that.</u> Some view large-scale mobility in a negative light,
23

claiming that it disintegrates class structure and puts an

end to meaningful traditions. <u>Accordingly</u> others claim
24

that <u>they're</u> attempting to rise validate and therefore
25

reinforce the class system. They see mobility as a

positive thing, enabling individuals to improve their own

---

19. **A.** NO CHANGE
B. nonetheless
C. for instance
D. consequently

20. **F.** NO CHANGE
G. In addition, it involved differing degrees of change,
H. In addition to the fact that it involved change's differing degrees,
J. It involves degrees of change,

21. **A.** NO CHANGE
B. is another example.
C. is too.
D. OMIT the underlined portion and end with a period.

22. For the sake of unity and coherence, sentence 6 should be placed:
F. where it is now.
G. after sentence 2.
H. after sentence 4.
J. at the beginning of the next paragraph.

23. **A.** NO CHANGE
B. in.
C. on.
D. OMIT the underlined portion and end the sentence with a period.

24. **F.** NO CHANGE
G. (Begin new paragraph) Similarly,
H. (Begin new paragraph) Likewise,
J. (Do NOT begin new paragraph) On the other hand,

25. **A.** NO CHANGE
B. they
C. those who are
D. their

GO ON TO NEXT PAGE

lives and the lives of their families. $\boxed{26}$

Still others see social mobility as destroying, rather

than <u>reinforced—the class system yet</u> they feel this is a
₂₇

positive change. According to them, society will benefit

from the breakdown <u>like a flat tire</u> of a social system in
₂₈

which material wealth is given so much importance.

Whether we view it positively or negatively, social

mobility is a basic fact of modern industrial society. The

crowd of yuppies hitting the shopping malls, credit cards

in hand, <u>show</u> that vertical mobility is very much with us
₂₉

<u>and so will a lot of other things be</u>.
₃₀

26. Suppose that at this point in the passage the writer wanted to add more information. Which of the following additions would be most relevant to the paragraph?
   F. A discussion of the problems of the educational system in America
   G. A listing of average salaries for different occupations
   H. Some examples of the benefits of social mobility
   J. A discussion of a rock star's new video

27. A. NO CHANGE
   B. reinforcing, the class system; yet
   C. reinforced. The class system; and
   D. that it reinforces the class system

28. F. NO CHANGE
   G. (such as a flat tire)
   H. (like the kind a flat tire gets)
   J. OMIT the underlined portion.

29. A. NO CHANGE
   B. shows
   C. showing
   D. to show

30. F. NO CHANGE
   G. and there they will be for some time to come.
   H. and will be for some time to come.
   J. OMIT the underlined portion and end the sentence with a period.

GO ON TO NEXT PAGE

Passage III

> The following paragraphs may or may not be in the most logical order. Each paragraph is numbered in parentheses, and item 45 will ask you to choose the sequence of paragraph numbers that is in the most logical order.

[1]

The critic George Moore once said of this artist <u>that</u>
31
<u>is</u> "her pictures are the only pictures painted by a woman
31
that could not be destroyed without creating a blank, a
hiatus in the history of art." In part a tribute to Morisot,
Moore's <u>statement are also one</u> that shows the prejudices
32
Morisot faced as a woman in a male-dominated
discipline.

[2]

The Impressionist painter Berthe Morisot was born
in1841 to a wealthy family that had connections to the
French government. Yet it was no surprise to anyone
when Morisot <u>showed little interest in it, and instead took</u>
33
<u>after her grandfather</u> the painter Jean Honoré Fragonard.
33

<u>Being her earliest</u> childhood, she had the desire to be an
34
artist. At the age of twenty-one, she began seven years of
study with Corot. She had her first work accepted at the
Paris Salon in 1864. In 1868 she met the Impressionist
painter Edouard <u>Manet and</u> served as his model for
35
several portraits. She was actively involved with the
Impressionist exhibiting society of the 1870s and 1880s.

31. A. NO CHANGE
    B. that being that
    C. is
    D. that

32. F. NO CHANGE
    G. statement's is also one
    H. statement is also one
    J. statements are also among those

33. A. NO CHANGE
    B. showed little interest in politics and instead took after her grandfather,
    C. with little interest in it—politics—took up after her grandfather instead
    D. was little interested in it, taking after her grandfather

34. F. NO CHANGE
    G. From, her being in earliest
    H. Being in early
    J. From her earliest

35. A. NO CHANGE
    B. Manet (who was neither Belgian nor Dutch) and
    C. Manet (a man not Belgian and not Dutch) and
    D. Manet—a man of neither Belgian nor Dutch extraction, and

GO ON TO NEXT PAGE

265

[3]

Either Morisot's subject matter nor her style is
36

distinctive. As a woman, she lacked the freedom enjoyed

by her male colleagues, who face no threat of social
37

disapproval in their journeys through Parisian cafes,

theaters, and parks. Therefore, Morisot turned her
38

limitations to her advantage, creating a unique vantage

point. Unlike her fellow Impressionists, who painted

scenes of Parisian night life, Morisot concentrated on her

own private sphere. Portraying women performing
39

domestic and social activities. 40

[4]

Morisot's paintings frequently feature female

members of her family, especially her daughter. She

often captures her models at thoughtful moments in their

chores. In contrast to the vast landscapes of her male

colleagues, Morisot's figures are generally enclosed by

some device: such as a balustrade, balcony, veranda, or
41

embankment. The sense of confinement conveyed by

many of her paintings may be in part a reflection of the

barriers Morisot faced as a woman artist. But despite the

---

36. F. NO CHANGE
G. Neither Morisot's subject matter nor her style is
H. Neither Morisot's subject matter or her style are
J. Neither Morisot's subject matter nor her style

37. A. NO CHANGE
B. colleagues, whom faced
C. colleagues, who faced
D. colleagues, and faced

38. F. NO CHANGE
G. Similarly,
H. Likewise,
J. However,

39. A. NO CHANGE
B. sphere. She began to portray
C. sphere insofar portraying
D. sphere, which were

40. Paragraph 3 makes the point that Morisot's painting did not include subject matter available to her male colleagues. The author wants to revise the whole paragraph to emphasize a more positive judgment of her work's value and a less negative view of its limitations. Which of the following revisions of the paragraph's first sentence would best allow her to express this changed perspective?
F. While Morisot's subject matter lacks originality, her style, in fact, is quite suited to expressing her distinctive interests.
G. Morisot's subject matter and style are somewhat limited by her society's confining standards, but her work takes on a greater meaning in its social context.
H. Morisot's subject matter may not appear particularly distinctive, but her work has great meaning in its social context.
J. Few can say that Morisot is one of the great Impressionists, but there are not many great Impressionists in any case.

41. A. NO CHANGE
B. some device—
C. some device:
D. some such device such as,

GO ON TO NEXT PAGE

obstacles, Morisot managed to achieve the recognition she deserved, helping to ease the way for her successors the people who followed after her.
42

42. **F.** NO CHANGE
G. those who came after.
H. which followed her.
J. OMIT the underlined portion and end the sentence with a period.

Items 43–45 pose questions about the passage as a whole.

---

43. The writer could best continue this essay by:
A. discussing how Morisot's success influenced social attitudes toward later women artists.
B. comparing several Impressionist landscape paintings by various artists.
C. providing background information on the art critic George Moore.
D. listing, by title and author, a series of articles on important Impressionists.

44. In the second paragraph, is the writer's reference to specific dates appropriate?
F. No, because the information interferes with the biographical purpose of this essay.
G. No, because the information, while it does not interfere with the biographical purpose of the essay, is out of place since the rest of the essay does not cite dates.
H. Yes, because the information helps to make the story of Morisot believable.
J. Yes, because the information helps to carry out the biographical purpose of this essay.

45. Choose the sequence of paragraph numbers that will make the passage's structure most logical.
A. NO CHANGE
B. 2, 1, 3, 4
C. 2, 3, 1, 4
D. 3, 2, 4, 1

GO ON TO NEXT PAGE

SECTION V: PRACTICE TEST

Passage IV

It used to be that when people wanted to see a scary movie they could choose from films such as *Dracula* and *Frankenstein*. But these classic monster movies, with an occasional exception, <u>has been replaced</u> by a new breed

46

of horror <u>film the</u> slasher movie. It is interesting and

47
perhaps somewhat disturbing to examine what such changes in taste may indicate about some of the values at work in our nation.

<u>First:</u> commercially successful low-budget chiller

48
was *Halloween*, and in its wake psycho-slasher films have the movie market <u>glutted.</u> The formula for these

49
movies consists of the serial murder of teenagers by a ruthless psychotic, with some humor thrown in. <u>The fact</u>

50
<u>of the matter being that the popularity of the series</u> of

50
Friday the Thirteenth movies and of their hundreds of silly imitators indicates that there is a huge market for such portrayals of random violence. Indeed, filmgoers appear to cast their votes for more and more graphic forms of violence. As a result, filmmakers—<u>those who</u>

51
<u>actually made films</u>—generate

51

<u>increasing gory</u> productions.

52

46. F. NO CHANGE
    G. have been replaced
    H. were being replaced
    J. replaced

47. A. NO CHANGE
    B. film, which is the
    C. film: the
    D. film known, as the

48. F. NO CHANGE
    G. First;
    H. The first
    J. First—

49. A. NO CHANGE
    B. (Place after *have*)
    C. (Place after *movie*)
    D. (Place after *wake*)

50. F. NO CHANGE
    G. The fact of the matter being
    H. The popularity of the
    J. Factually speaking, in terms of popularity,

51. A. NO CHANGE
    B. —those making the films, actually
    C. (which are the people making the films)
    D. OMIT the underlined portion.

52. F. NO CHANGE
    G. increasing, gory,
    H. increasingly full of gore,
    J. increasingly gory

GO ON TO NEXT PAGE

As a result of this <u>trend</u> slasher films now represent
⁵³
mainstream Hollywood movies. Once limited only to the

<u>periphery (fringe)</u> of the movie industry, the exploitation
⁵⁴
of gore has become a major box office attraction. Older

slasher films, such as *Psycho* and *The Texas Chainsaw*

Massacre, actually seem like classics in comparison to

the countless imitators filling video stores and movie

screens. <u>They're</u> so many of these low-budget imitators
⁵⁵
in distribution that, in 1981 alone, they accounted for half

of the fifty top-grossing movies. That's a big wad of

cash! 56

Although the popularity of such films has declined

somewhat as their novelty has worn <u>off. However,</u> they
⁵⁷
remain a standard feature of the yearly production

schedule. Even many high-budget horror films have

adopted the slasher formula of chills and violence. Are

these movies a means of harmless fun, as some fans

claim? Are they a reflection of an <u>increasingly and</u>
⁵⁸
<u>evermore violent?</u> Or do such movies perhaps even
⁵⁸
encourage violence? Considering the great changes both

within the movie industry and in <u>public (human)</u> taste,
⁵⁹
these are questions that we must begin to consider. 60

53. A. NO CHANGE
    B. trend:
    C. trend—
    D. —trend—

54. F. NO CHANGE
    G. periphery
    H. periphery (that is, the fringe)
    J. periphery, fringe,

55. A. NO CHANGE
    B. They are
    C. There's
    D. There are

56. Is the final sentence of this paragraph appropriate?
    F. No, because its reference to money is irrelevant to the topic of the paragraph.
    G. No, because its reference to money, while relevant to the topic of the paragraph, is conveyed through an inappropriate image.
    H. Yes, because the exclamation with which the sentence ends heightens the drama of the paragraph.
    J. Yes, because its specific image helps to clarify the preceding sentence.

57. A. NO CHANGE
    B. off, and they
    C. off, so
    D. off, they

58. F. NO CHANGE
    G. more, and more, and more violent society
    H. increasingly violent society
    J. increasingly violent society, full of anger, blood and shooting

59. A. NO CHANGE
    B. public, and human
    C. public
    D. human's

GO ON TO NEXT PAGE

60. How can the tone and purpose of this essay best be described?
- **F.** The tone is serious; the purpose is to point out a significant change in entertainment.
- **G.** The tone is lighthearted; the purpose is to recommend a new form of entertainment.
- **H.** The tone is sarcastic; the purpose is to show how contemporary movies lack value.
- **J.** The tone is harsh; the purpose is to urge people not to attend slasher films.

Passage V

> The following paragraphs may or may not be in the most logical order. Each paragraph is numbered in parentheses, and item 75 will ask you to choose the sequence of paragraph numbers that is in the most logical order.

[1]

The strangest of these events all involve <u>unexplained</u> ₆₁ <u>disappearances—the kind that haven't been fully</u> ₆₁ <u>explained.</u> Ships have been found ₆₁

<u>abandoned and deserted</u> for no apparent reason. ₆₂

<u>Without transmitting distress signals, some ships having</u> ₆₃ <u>vanished forever.</u> Planes have reported their position and ₆₃ then disappeared. Even rescue missions are said to have vanished while flying in the area. Theories accounting for such occurrences <u>ranging towards</u> the interference of ₆₄ UFOs to the existence of powerful fields of some the existence of powerful fields of some unknown force. So far, no conclusions <u>have been reached.</u> ₆₅

61. A. NO CHANGE
B. unexplained disappearances, which haven't been explained, fully.
C. unexplained disappearances.
D. unexplained disappearances that have not been explained.

62. F. NO CHANGE
G. abandoned
H. abandoned, including left
J. abandoned (deserted)

63. A. NO CHANGE
B. They've not transmitted distress signals, and they've vanished forever, never to return.
C. Transmitting no distress signals, having vanished forever, have been some ships.
D. Some ships have vanished forever without transmitting any distress signal.

64. F. NO CHANGE
G. range to
H. ranging from
J. range from

65. A. NO CHANGE
B. have (yet) been reached.
C. having yet been reached.
D. yet reached.

GO ON TO NEXT PAGE

[2]

In the North Atlantic Ocean, the Bermuda Islands—a jumble of 300 islets, rocks, and islands—form part of a roughly triangular <u>region (England is roughly triangular,</u> <u>too)</u> whose other boundaries are the southern U.S.
66

<u>coast and</u> the Greater Antilles. Perhaps the first
67
European to explore this area was Juan de Bermudez in

1515. <u>They wonder who</u> whether he ever experienced
68
anything strange back then, for this is the region known today as the Bermuda Triangle. Extremely strange events <u>had been</u> frequently reported from this area. [70]
69

[3]

Others are critical of the claims posed about the Bermuda Triangle. They point out that wreckage has not been found and that scientific searches have uncovered nothing to substantiate the strange events attributed to the region. Also, they question <u>so</u> it can be that boaters and
71
fliers continue to travel through the region unharmed. [72]

66. F. NO CHANGE
G. region (like England)
H. region
J. England-like region

67. A. NO CHANGE
B. coast (but not rivers) and
C. coast, but not rivers, and
D. coast—but not rivers—and

68. F. NO CHANGE
G. We are those who wonder
H. Some wonder
J. Some of them are wondering

69. A. NO CHANGE
B. has been
C. is
D. have been

70. Is the mention of Juan de Bermudez appropriate?
F. No, because it connects two dissimilar things, exploration and the Bermuda Triangle.
G. Yes, because it provides background information while introducing the main subject of the passage.
H. Yes, because the passage suggests that exploration is more significant than the supernatural.
J. Yes, because Juan de Bermudez is the only person named in the passage.

71. A. NO CHANGE
B. which
C. how
D. OMIT the underlined portion.

72. Suppose that at this point the writer wanted to add more information. Which of the following additions would be most relevant?
F. A geographical description of the Bermuda Triangle
G. A brief allusion to other well-known supernatural phenomena
H. More evidence disputing the occurrence of supernatural forces
J. A discussion of Bermuda's tourist trade

GO ON TO NEXT PAGE

[4]

We may never be <u>certain in the way a judge is</u> of the
73
truth about the Bermuda Triangle. Yet people will
continue to be intrigued by the supernatural and the
strange. One thing we can be sure of is that this enigmatic
place will continue to fascinate the public and stir up
controversy for years to come.

73. **A.** NO CHANGE
B. absolutely certain
C. certain like a judge
D. certain as a judge is

Items 74–75 pose questions about the passage as a whole.

74. Suppose the editor of a travel magazine had
requested that the writer give an account of one
specific disappearance that has occurred in the
Bermuda region. Does this essay successfully
fulfill that request?
F. Yes, because the disappearances described
are actual events.
G. Yes, because the essay focuses on
mysterious disappearances in the Bermuda
Triangle.
H. No, because the writer has relied on
generalities in discussing the nature of
disappearances in the region.
J. No, because the essay lacks factual
information of any sort.

75. For the sake of unity and coherence, Paragraph
1 should be placed:
A. where it is now.
B. after Paragraph 2.
C. after Paragraph 3.
D. after Paragraph 4.

END OF TEST 1

STOP! DO NOT TURN THE PAGE UNTIL TOLD TO DO SO.

MATHEMATICS TEST

60 Minutes—60 Questions

DIRECTIONS: Solve each of the following problems, select the correct answer, and then fill in the corresponding space on your answer sheet.

Don't linger over problems that are too time-consuming. Do as many as you can, then come back to the others in the time you have remaining.

Note: Unless otherwise noted, all of the following should be assumed.

1. Illustrative figures are not necessarily drawn to scale.
2. All geometric figures lie in a plane.
3. The term line indicates a straight line.
4. The term average indicates arithmetic mean.

---

1. If $5x + 3 = -17$, then $x = ?$

   A. -25
   B. $-7\frac{1}{3}$
   C. -4
   D. 4
   E. $6\frac{1}{3}$

2. John wants to make fruit salad. He has a recipe that serves 6 people and uses 4 oranges, 5 pears, 10 apples, and 2 dozen strawberries. If he wants to serve 18 people, how many pears will John need?

   F. 5
   G. 10
   H. 15
   J. 20
   K. 25

3. What is the greatest integer that is a factor of both 8×10^9 and 6×10^3?

   A. 1×10^9
   B. 2×10^6
   C. 6×10^3
   D. 2×10^3
   E. 1×10^3

DO YOUR FIGURING HERE.

GO ON TO NEXT PAGE

4. What is the area of the rectangle in the standard (x, y) coordinate plane shown in the figure below?

DO YOUR FIGURING HERE.

F. 4
G. 7
H. 10
J. 12
K. 14

5. A costume designer wants to put a white silk band around a cylindrical top hat. If the radius of the cylindrical part of the top hat is 4 inches, how long, in inches, should the white silk band be to just fit around the top hat?

A. 8π
B. 25π
C. 50π
D. 100π
E. 200π

6. A large jar holds 48 olives while a small jar holds only 32 olives. Which of the following expressions represents the number of olives needed to fill x large jars and y small jars?

F. $48x + 32y$
G. $\frac{x}{48} + \frac{y}{32}$
H. $\frac{xy}{80}$
J. $80xy$
K. $\frac{1536}{xy}$

7. If $f(x) = 3x^2 + 4$, $f(x + 1) = ?$

A. $3x^2 + 5$
B. $3x^2 + x + 4$
C. $3x^2 + 4$
D. $3x^2 + 2x + 5$
E. $3x^2 + 6x + 7$

GO ON TO NEXT PAGE

KAPLAN

DO YOUR FIGURING HERE.

8. $5\frac{5}{6} + 3\frac{5}{8} + 1\frac{1}{3} = ?$

   F. $9\frac{11}{17}$

   G. $9\frac{19}{24}$

   H. $10\frac{9}{24}$

   J. $10\frac{4}{5}$

   K. $10\frac{19}{24}$

9. Jimmy's school is 10 miles from his house, on the same street. If he walks down his street directly from the school to his house he passes a candy store and a grocery store. The candy store is 2.35 miles from the school and the grocery store is 3.4 miles from the candy store. How many miles is it from the grocery store to Jimmy's house?

   A.   3.75
   B.   4.25
   C.   4.75
   D.   5.25
   E.   5.75

10. Harry is a piano student who can learn 2 new pieces in a week. If his piano teacher gives him 3 new pieces every week for 4 weeks, how many weeks will it take Harry to learn all these pieces?

   F.   6
   G.   7.5
   H.   8
   J.   12
   K.   15

11. In $\triangle DEF$ below, the measure of $\angle EDF$ is 35° and the measure of $\angle DFE$ is 65°. What is the measure of $\angle DEF$?

   A.   35°
   B.   45°
   C.   75°
   D.   80°
   E.   100°

GO ON TO NEXT PAGE

12. Randy scored 150, 195, and 160 in 3 bowling games. What should she score on her next bowling game if she wants to have an average score of exactly 175 for the 4 games?

    F. 205
    G. 195
    H. 185
    J. 175
    K. 165

13. Which of the following best describes a triangle in the standard (x, y) coordinate plane with vertices having coordinates $(0, 0)$, $(3, 5)$, and $(0, 2)$?

    A. All three angles measure less than 90°.
    B. All three sides are the same length.
    C. Exactly two sides are the same length.
    D. One angle measures 90°.
    E. One angle measures more than 90°.

14. What is the sum of the solutions of the equation $2y^2 - 4y - 6 = 0$?

    F. −4
    G. −2
    H. −1
    J. 2
    K. 4

15. Which of the following is the decimal equivalent of $\frac{7}{8}$?

    A. 1.125
    B. 1.120
    C. 0.875
    D. 0.870
    E. 0.625

16. June, Maria, and Billy each have a collection of marbles. June has 20 more marbles than Billy, and Maria has 3 times as many marbles as Billy. If altogether they have 100 marbles, how many marbles does Billy have?

    F. 16
    G. 20
    H. 25
    J. 30
    K. 32

DO YOUR FIGURING HERE.

GO ON TO NEXT PAGE

KAPLAN

17. The equation $3x - 2y = 4$ can be graphed in the standard (x, y) coordinate plane. What is the y-coordinate of a point on the graph whose x-coordinate is 6?

   A. 11
   B. 7
   C. 5
   D. 3
   E. −11

18. In the figure below, parallel lines r and s are cut by transversal t. The measure of $\angle p$ is 20° less than three times the measure of $\angle q$. What is the value of $p - q$?

   F. 80°
   G. 90°
   H. 100°
   J. 130°
   K. 160°

19. Which of the following systems of equations does NOT have a solution?

   A. $x + 3y = 19$
       $3x + y = 6$

   B. $x + 3y = 19$
       $x - 3y = 13$

   C. $x - 3y = 6$
       $3x - y = 7$

   D. $x - 3y = 19$
       $3x + y = 6$

   E. $x + 3y = 6$
       $3x + 9y = 7$

GO ON TO NEXT PAGE

20. In the figure below, L, M, R, and S are collinear. $\overline{LS}$ is 50 units long; $\overline{MS}$ is 38 units long; and $\overline{MR}$ is 13 units long. How many units long is $\overline{LR}$?

F. 13
G. 20
H. 23
J. 25
K. 37

DO YOUR FIGURING HERE.

21. If $33\frac{1}{3}$ % of t is 9, what is $133\frac{1}{3}$ % of t?

A. 12
B. 18
C. 27
D. 36
E. 42

22. In $\triangle DEF$ below, $\overline{DE} = 1$ and $\overline{DF} = \sqrt{2}$. What is the value of tan x?

F. $\frac{\sqrt{2}}{2}$
G. 1
H. $\sqrt{2}$
J. $\sqrt{3}$
K. 2

23. A circle with center at the origin and radius 7 is graphed in the standard (x, y) coordinate plane. Which of the following is NOT a point on the circumference of the circle?

A. $(7, 0)$
B. $(-3, 2\sqrt{10})$
C. $(\sqrt{7}, 3)$
D. $(0, -7)$
E. $(-\sqrt{26}, -\sqrt{23})$

GO ON TO NEXT PAGE

KAPLAN

24. Points A and B have integral coordinates in the standard (x, y) coordinate plane below. What is the product of the y-coordinates of A and B?

F. 12
G. 6
H. −2
J. −6
K. −12

25. In the figure below, line m is parallel to line n, point A lies on line m, and points B and C lie on line n. If $\angle BAC$ is a right angle, what is the measure of $\angle y$?

A. 54°
B. 90°
C. 124°
D. 136°
E. 154°

26. If $s = -3$, then $s^3 + 2s^2 + 2s = ?$

F. −15
G. −10
H. −5
J. −5
K. 33

GO ON TO NEXT PAGE

27. For all r, s, t, and u, $r(t + u) - s(t + u) = $?
   A. $(r + s)(t + u)$
   B. $(r - s)(t - u)$
   C. $(r + s)(t - u)$
   D. $(r - s)(t + u)$
   E. 0

DO YOUR FIGURING HERE.

28. In the figure below, $\angle ABC$ is a right angle and $\overline{DF}$ is parallel to AC. If $\overline{AE}$ is 8 units long, $\overline{BC}$ is 6 units long and $\overline{DB}$ is 4 units long, what is the area in square units of $\triangle DBF$?

   F. 6
   G. 12
   H. 16
   J. 24
   K. 48

29. What is the value of cos 225°?

   A. $-\frac{\sqrt{2}}{2}$

   B. $-\frac{\sqrt{3}}{3}$

   C. $-\frac{1}{2}$

   D. $\frac{1}{2}$

   E. $\frac{\sqrt{2}}{2}$

30. In triangle $\triangle XYZ$ below, $\overline{XS}$ and $\overline{SZ}$ are 3 and 12 units long, respectively. If the area of $\triangle XYZ$ is 45 square units, how many units long is altitude $\overline{YS}$?

   F. 3
   G. 6
   H. 9
   J. 12
   K. 15

GO ON TO NEXT PAGE

DO YOUR FIGURING HERE.

31. In the figure below, O is the center of the circle, C and D are points on the circle, and C, O, and D are collinear. If the length of $\overline{CD}$ is 10 units, what is the circumference, in units, of the circle?

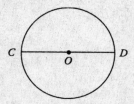

    A. 10π
    B. 20π
    C. 25π
    D. 40π
    E. 100π

32. The formula for the surface area of a right circular cone, including the base, is $A = \pi rs + \pi r^2$, where A is the surface area, r is the radius, and s is the length from the vertex to the edge of the cone. Which of the following represents an equivalent formula for A?

    F. $A = 2\pi rs$
    G. $A = 2\pi r^2 s$
    H. $A = \pi r(1 + s)$
    J. $A = \pi r^2(1 + s)$
    K. $A = \pi r(r + s)$

33. What is the slope of the line determined by the equation $5x + 3y = 13$?

    A. -15

    B. $-\frac{5}{3}$

    C. $-\frac{3}{5}$

    D. $\frac{3}{5}$

    E. $\frac{5}{3}$

34. Given any two real numbers a and b, which of the following is true about the quantity $|a - b| + \sqrt{b - a}$?

    F. It is always equal to an integer.
    G. It is positive if $b > a$.
    H. It is always positive.
    J. It is negative if $a = b$.
    K. It is always real.

GO ON TO NEXT PAGE

35. One of the solutions of the equation $x^2 - 7x + 8 = 0$ is $x = \dfrac{7 - \sqrt{17}}{2}$. What is the other solution?

    A. $-\dfrac{7}{2} - \sqrt{17}$

    B. $\dfrac{-7 - \sqrt{17}}{2}$

    C. $\dfrac{-7 + \sqrt{17}}{2}$

    D. $7 - \dfrac{\sqrt{17}}{2}$

    E. $\dfrac{7 + \sqrt{17}}{2}$

36. How many units long is one of the sides of a square that has diagonal 20 units long?

    F. 10
    G. $10\sqrt{2}$
    H. 15
    J. 20
    K. $15\sqrt{2}$

37. For all a, $(3a - 4)(a + 2) = ?$

    A. $3a^2 - 8$
    B. $3a^2 + 7a - 8$
    C. $3a^2 + 2a - 8$
    D. $3a^2 - 2a - 8$
    E. $3a^2 + 5a - 8$

38. The midpoint of line segment $\overline{AC}$ in the standard (x, y) coordinate plane has coordinates $(4, 8)$. The (x, y) coordinates of A and C are $(4, 2)$ and $(4, s)$, respectively. What is the value of s?

    F. 4
    G. 5
    H. 10
    J. 12
    K. 14

39. In a group of 3 numbers, the second number is 3 less than 4 times the first number, and the third number is 5 more than twice the first. If s represents the first number, which of the following expressions represents the sum of the three numbers in terms of s?

    A. $5s$
    B. $5s + 2$
    C. $6s + 8$
    D. $7s - 1$
    E. $7s + 2$

DO YOUR FIGURING HERE.

GO ON TO NEXT PAGE

40. In the figure below, line $\overline{PQ}$ intersects $\triangle ABC$ at points E and D. $\angle B$ measures 80°, $\angle SAB$ measures 130°, and $\angle CDQ$ measures 110°. What is the measure of $\angle DEC$?

F. 40°
G. 50°
H. 60°
J. 70°
K. 80°

41. Jack bought a painting for $200. A year later a friend bought it from him for $170. What percent of the original price did Jack lose in the overall transaction?

A. 10%
B. 12%
C. 15%
D. 22%
E. 25%

42. Which of the following is the set of all values of x such that $0 \leq x \leq 2\pi$ and $\cos x = -\frac{1}{2}$?

F. $\{\frac{\pi}{6}, \frac{5\pi}{6}\}$
G. $\{\frac{\pi}{3}, \frac{5\pi}{6}\}$
H. $\{\frac{\pi}{2}, \frac{3\pi}{2}\}$
J. $\{\frac{2\pi}{3}, \frac{4\pi}{3}\}$
K. $\{\frac{2\pi}{3}, \frac{5\pi}{3}\}$

43. The roots of the equation $5x^2 + 2x - 7 = 0$ are $x = 1$ and $x = ?$

A. -7
B. $-\frac{7}{5}$
C. -1
D. 0
E. $\frac{7}{5}$

GO ON TO NEXT PAGE

44. In the figure below, $\overline{PS}$ is parallel to $\overline{QR}$, and $\overline{PR}$ intersects $\overline{SQ}$ at T. If the measure of $\angle PST$ is 65° and the measure of $\angle QRT$ is 35°, then what is the measure of $\angle PTQ$?

F. 55°
G. 75°
H. 90°
J. 100°
K. 115°

45. Ms. Rodriguez leaves her office and drives east. At the same time, Ms. Green leaves the same office and drives west at a rate of speed that is 15 miles per hour faster than Ms. Rodriguez. At the end of 5 hours, the two cars are 475 miles apart. How many miles were traveled by the faster car?

A. 200
B. 250
C. 275
D. 300
E. 350

46. Line ℓ is graphed in the standard (x, y) coordinate plane as shown below. If the equation for line ℓ is written in the form $y = mx + b$, which of the following is true about m and b?

F. m and b are both positive.
G. m is negative and b is positive.
H. m is positive and b is negative.
J. Either m or b must equal 0.
K. m and b are both negative.

DO YOUR FIGURING HERE.

GO ON TO NEXT PAGE

KAPLAN

47. Which of the following must be true of the fraction $\frac{x^2}{y^2}$ if $|y| < |x|$, and $xy \neq 0$?

A. $\frac{x^2}{y^2}$ must be greater than or equal to 2.

B. $\frac{x^2}{y^2}$ must be greater than 1.

C. $\frac{x^2}{y^2}$ could equal 1.

D. $\frac{x^2}{y^2}$ must be less than 1.

E. $\frac{x^2}{y^2}$ cannot equal $\frac{3}{2}$.

48. What is the value of $a^2 - 2ab + b^2$ if $a - b = 12$?

F. 0
G. 24
H. 48
J. 144
K. 288

49. In $\triangle DEF$, x represents the measure of $\angle EDF$. The measure of $\angle DEF$ is 30° greater than the measure of $\angle EDF$, and the measure of $\angle EFD$ is 15° less than the sum of the measures of $\angle EDF$ and $\angle DEF$. Which of the following expressions represents the measure of $\angle EFD$?

A. $-2x + 15°$
B. $-x + 15°$
C. $x + 15°$
D. $2x - 15°$
E. $2x + 15°$

50. In the figure below, $\overline{CD}$ is parallel to $\overline{AB}$, and $\overline{PQ}$ intersects $\overline{CD}$ at R and $\overline{AB}$ at T. If the measure of $\angle CRP = 110°$, then what is the measure of $\angle ATQ$?

DO YOUR FIGURING HERE.

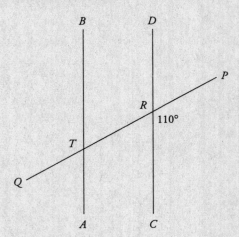

- **F.** 30°
- **G.** 50°
- **H.** 70°
- **J.** 90°
- **K.** 110°

51. If $x = \sin\theta$, $y = \cos\theta$, and $z = \tan\theta$, then $x^2 + y^2 = ?$

- **A.** z^2
- **B.** $(x + y)^2$
- **C.** $2y$
- **D.** 0
- **E.** 1

52. Line T in the standard (x, y) coordinate plane has y-intercept -3 and is parallel to the line determined by the equation $3x - 5y = 4$. Which of the following is an equation for line T?

- **F.** $y = -\frac{3}{5}x + 3$
- **G.** $y = -\frac{5}{3}x - 3$
- **H.** $y = \frac{3}{5}x + 3$
- **J.** $y = \frac{5}{3}x + 3$
- **K.** $y = \frac{3}{5}x - 3$

GO ON TO NEXT PAGE

KAPLAN

DO YOUR FIGURING HERE.

53. On the number line below, what is the distance from A to B?

A. 1
B. 4
C. 5
D. 9
E. 18

54. In the standard (x, y) coordinate plane shown in the figure below, points A and B lie on line m, and point C lies below it. The coordinates of points A, B, and C are $(0, 5)$, $(5, 5)$, and $(3, 3)$, respectively. What is the shortest distance from point C to line m?

F. 2
G. $2\sqrt{2}$
H. 3
J. $\sqrt{13}$
K. 5

55. Which of the following inequalities is equivalent to $-2 - 4x \leq -6x$?

A. $x \geq -2$
B. $x \geq 1$
C. $x \geq 2$
D. $x \leq -1$
E. $x \leq 1$

GO ON TO NEXT PAGE

56. In the figure below, each corner of the polygon is a right angle. What is the area of the polygon?

F. 50
G. 56
H. 62
J. 72
K. 80

57. In the standard (x, y) coordinate plane shown below, two circles of the same radius r are enclosed by rectangle $ABCD$. Which of the following expressions is equal to $a - b$?

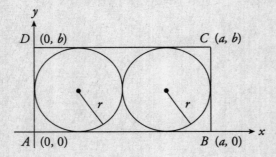

A. $-r$
B. 0
C. r
D. $2r$
E. $4r$

58. Each one of the 60 teenagers in an after-school club is 14, 15, 16, 17 or 18 years old. 20 teenagers are 15 years old, 8 are 18 years old, and 20% are 14 years old. There are twice as many 16-year-olds as there are 18-year-olds. What percent of the teenagers are either 17 or 18 years old?

F. 10%
G. 15%
H. 20%
J. 25%
K. 30%

GO ON TO NEXT PAGE

59. Darryl has 5 blue T-shirts and 7 orange T-shirts. If he picks one T-shirt at random, what is the probability that it will NOT be blue?

A. 1

B. $\frac{7}{12}$

C. $\frac{1}{2}$

D. $\frac{5}{12}$

E. $\frac{1}{6}$

60. What is the equation of the ellipse graphed in the standard (x, y) coordinate plane below?

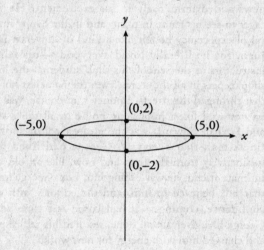

F. $\frac{x^2}{25} + \frac{y^2}{4} = 1$

G. $\frac{x^2}{25} - \frac{y^2}{9} = 1$

H. $\frac{x^2}{25} - \frac{y^2}{4} = 1$

J. $\frac{x^2}{25} + \frac{y^2}{9} = 1$

K. $\frac{x^2}{20} + \frac{y^2}{4} = 1$

DO YOUR FIGURING HERE.

END OF TEST 2

STOP! DO NOT TURN THE PAGE UNTIL TOLD TO DO SO.

READING TEST

35 Minutes—40 Questions

DIRECTIONS: This test contains four passages, each followed by several questions. After reading a passage, select the best answer to each question and fill in the corresponding oval on your answer sheet. You are allowed to refer to the passages while answering the questions.

Passage I

It was late afternoon and the shadows were slanting swiftly eastward when George Webber came to his senses somewhere in the wilds of the upper Bronx. How he got there he never knew. All he could remember
[5] was that suddenly he felt hungry and stopped and looked about him and realized where he was. His dazed look gave way to one of amazement and incredulity, and his mouth began to stretch into a broad grin. In his hand he still held the rectangular
[10] slip of crisp yellow paper, and slowly he smoothed out the wrinkles and examined it carefully.

It was a check for five hundred dollars. His book had been accepted, and this was an advance against his royalties.

[15] So he was happier than he had ever been in all his life. Fame, at last, was knocking at his door and wooing him with her sweet blandishments, and he lived in a kind of glorious delirium. The next weeks and months were filled with the excitement of the impend-
[20] ing event. The book would not be published till the fall, but meanwhile there was much work to do. Foxhall Edwards had made some suggestions for cutting and revising the manuscript, and, although George at first objected, he surprised himself in the
[25] end by agreeing with Edwards, and he undertook to do what Edwards wanted.

George had called his novel *Home to Our Mountains,* and in it he had packed everything he knew about his home town in Old Catawba and the
[30] people there. He had distilled every line of it out of his own experience of life. And, now that the issue was decided, he sometimes trembled when he thought that it would only be a matter of months before the whole world knew what he had written. He loathed the
[35] thought of giving pain to anyone, and that he might do so had never occurred to him until now. But now it was out of his hands, and he began to feel uneasy. Of course it was fiction, but it was made as all honest fiction must be, from the stuff of human life. Some
[40] people might recognize themselves and be offended,

and then what would he do? Would he have to go around in smoked glasses and false whiskers? He comforted himself with the hope that his characterizations were not so true as, in another mood, he liked to think
[45] they were, and he thought that perhaps no one would notice anything.

Rodney's Magazine, too, had become interested in the young author and was going to publish a story, a chapter from the book, in their next number. This
[50] news added immensely to his excitement. He was eager to see his name in print, and in the happy interval of expectancy he felt like a kind of universal Don Juan, for he literally loved everybody—his fellow instructors at the school, his drab students, the little
[55] shopkeepers in all the stores, even the nameless hordes that thronged the streets. Rodney's, of course, was the greatest and finest publishing house in all the world, and Foxhall Edwards was the greatest editor and the finest man that ever was. George had liked him
[60] instinctively from the first, and now, like an old and intimate friend, he was calling him Fox. George knew that Fox believed in him, and the editor's faith and confidence, coming as it had come at a time when George had given up all hope, restored his self-respect
[65] and charged him with energy for new work.

Already his next novel was begun and was beginning to take shape within him. He would soon have to get it out of him. He dreaded the prospect of buckling down in earnest to write it, for he knew the agony of
[70] it. It was like a demoniacal possession, driving him with alien force much greater than his own. While the fury of creation was upon him, it meant sixty cigarettes a day, twenty cups of coffee, meals snatched anyhow and anywhere and at whatever time of day or
[75] night he happened to remember he was hungry. It meant sleeplessness, and miles of walking to bring on the physical fatigue without which he could not sleep, then nightmares, nerves, and exhaustion in the morning. As he said to Fox:

[80] "There are better ways to write a book, but this, God help me, is mine, and you'll have to learn to put up with it."

KAPLAN

When *Rodney's Magazine* came out with the story, George fully expected convulsions of the earth, falling
85 meteors, suspension of traffic in the streets, and a general strike. But nothing happened. A few of his friends mentioned it, but that was all. For several days he felt let down, but then his common sense reassured him that people couldn't really tell much about a new author
90 from a short piece in a magazine. The book would show them who he was and what he could do. It would be different then. He could afford to wait a little longer for the fame which he was certain would soon be his.

1. Why does George think he would "have to go around in smoked glasses and false whiskers" (lines 41–42)?
   A. Famous authors have to protect their privacy from admiring strangers.
   B. A disguise would help him gather information for a new book.
   C. If he were going to be a famous writer he had better look the part.
   D. People he had offended might otherwise confront him.

2. According to George's description, the process of writing a novel:
   F. was similar to being overwhelmed by an alien spirit.
   G. was a time filled with unspoken rage.
   H. was best carried out during times when other people were asleep.
   J. could only be performed when he was physically exhausted.

3. By saying to Foxhall Edwards that "There are better ways to write a book, but this, God help me, is mine, and you'll have to learn to put up with it," (lines 80–82) George sought to:
   A. reassure Foxhall that the next book would, in fact, be completed.
   B. emphasize that the process, though difficult, could not be avoided.
   C. rebuke Foxhall for not having enough faith in his new project.
   D. suggest that his own approach to writing was really superior to other approaches.

4. Given George's expectations concerning the publication of his story in *Rodney's Magazine,* the public's response to the story can best be described as:
   F. sour.
   G. appropriate.
   H. ironic.
   J. enthusiastic.

5. According to the passage, Foxhall Edwards' belief in George's ability was important primarily because:
   A. George needed a friend he could confide in.
   B. *Home to Our Mountains* required extensive revision.
   C. George needed a friend he could look up to.
   D. Foxhall restored George's faith in his own work.

6. What was George's ultimate response to his story's publication in *Rodney's Magazine*?
   F. He refused to accept that the story had few readers.
   G. He expected that fame would come eventually anyway.
   H. He convinced himself that he had never wished for fame.
   J. He lost confidence in himself as a writer.

7. As it is used in the passage, the word *wooing* (line 16) means:
   A. courting.
   B. confusing.
   C. admiring.
   D. bothering.

8. The fact that George "sometimes trembled" (line 32) when he thought of his novel's publication indicates that he:
   F. secretly disliked Foxhall's suggestions.
   G. was eager to meet the people back in his home town.
   H. worried that some people would be hurt by his novel.
   J. feared that critics would denounce his novel.

9. George's estimation of his novel's achievement can best described as:
   A. vain but bitter.
   B. proud but concerned.
   C. modest but hopeful.
   D. angry but resigned.

10. The first paragraph suggests that, just prior to the moment at which this passage begins, George has most likely been:
    F. wandering in dazed excitement after learning that his book would be published.
    G. walking off nervous tension brought on by working on his second novel.
    H. trying to find his way home from his book publisher's office.
    J. in a joyous dream-state as a result of being relieved of his financial difficulties.

GO ON TO NEXT PAGE

SECTION V: PRACTICE TEST

Passage II

In the 500 years since Leonardo, two ideas about man have been especially important. The first is the emphasis on the full development of the human personality. The individual is prized for himself. His creative powers are seen as the core of his being. The unfettered development of individual personality is praised as the ideal, from the Renaissance artists through the Elizabethans, and through Locke and Voltaire and Rousseau. This vision of the freely developing man, happy in the unfolding of his own gifts, is shared by men as different in their conceptions as Thomas Jefferson and Edmund Burke. . . .

Thus the fulfillment of man has been one of the two most formative grand ideas. . . . Men have seen themselves entering the world with a potential of many gifts, and they have hoped to fulfill these gifts in the development of their own lives. This has come to be the unexpressed purpose of the life of individuals: fulfilling the special gifts with which a man is endowed.

The self-fulfillment of the individual has itself become part of a larger, more embracing idea, the self-fulfillment of man. We think of man as a species with special gifts, which are the human gifts. Some of these gifts, the physical and mental gifts, are elucidated for us explicitly by science; some of them, the aesthetic and ethical gifts, we feel and struggle to express in our own minds; and some of them, the cultural gifts, are unfolded for us by the study of history. The total of these gifts is man as a type or species, and the aspiration of man as a species has become the fulfillment of what is most human in these gifts.

This idea of human self-fulfillment has also inspired scientific and technical progress. We sometimes think that progress is illusory, and that the devices and gadgets which have become indispensable to civilized men in the last 500 years are only a self-propagating accumulation of idle luxuries. But this has not been the purpose in the minds of scientists and technicians, nor has it been the true effect of these inventions on human society. The purpose and the effect has been to liberate men from the exhausting drudgeries of earning their living, in order to give them the opportunity to live. From Leonardo to Franklin, the inventor has wanted to give, and has succeeded in giving, more and more people the ease and leisure to find the best in themselves which was once the monopoly of princes.

Only rarely has a thinker in the last 500 years gone back from the ideal of human potential and fulfillment. Calvin was perhaps such a thinker who went back, and believed as the Middle Ages did, that man comes into this world as a complete entity, incapable of any worthwhile development. And it is characteristic that the state which Calvin organized was, as a result, a totalitarian state. For if men cannot develop, and have nothing in them which is personal and creative, there is no point in giving them freedom.

The second of the two grand formative ideas is the idea of freedom. We see in fact that human fulfillment is unattainable without freedom, so that these two main ideas are linked together. There could be no development of the personality of individuals, no fulfillment of those gifts in which one man differs from another, without the freedom for each man to grow in his own direction.

What is true of individuals is true of human groups. A state or a society cannot change unless its members are given freedom to judge, to criticize, and to search for a new status for themselves. Therefore the pressure of ideas has been toward freedom as an expression of individuality. Sometimes men have tried to find freedom along quiet paths of change, as the humanists did on the eve of the Reformation, and as the dissenting manufacturers of the eighteenth century did. At other times, the drive for freedom has been explosive: intellectually explosive in the Elizabethan age and the Scientific Revolution, economically explosive in the Industrial Revolution, and politically explosive in the other great revolutions of our period, from Puritan times to the age of Napoleon.

. . .Freedom is a supple and elusive idea, whose advocates can at times delude themselves that obedience to tyranny is a form of freedom. Such a delusion ensnared men as diverse as Luther and Rousseau, and Hegel and Marx. Philosophically, there is indeed no unlimited freedom. But we have seen that there is one freedom which can be defined without contradiction, and which can therefore be an end in itself. This is freedom of thought and speech: the right to dissent.

Excerpt from *The Western Intellectual Tradition: From Leonardo to Hegel* by J. Bronowski and Bruce Mazlish. Copyright © 1960 by J. Bronowski and Bruce Mazlish; reprinted by permission of HarperCollins Publishers.

GO ON TO NEXT PAGE

11. The authors mention Calvin in the fifth paragraph (lines 48–57) in order to:

- **A.** introduce the topic of the Middle Ages.
- **B.** praise an unusual thinker.
- **C.** present a counterexample.
- **D.** illustrate a point made in the previous paragraph.

12. As it is used in line 24, the word "elucidated" means:

- **F.** decided.
- **G.** revealed.
- **H.** invented.
- **J.** judged.

13. The passage implies that, in the past 500 years, history has revealed two intellectual traditions that are:

- **A.** equally important, even though mutually exclusive.
- **B.** similarly important and closely tied together.
- **C.** only now being seen as particularly important.
- **D.** less important than freedom of thought and speech.

14. In the fourth paragraph (lines 32–47) the authors' point about "devices and gadgets" is that:

- **F.** all technological progress is an illusion.
- **G.** all inventors attain self-fulfillment.
- **H.** these inventions have allowed people to work less.
- **J.** these inventions are a necessary evil.

15. What do the authors suggest was "once the monopoly of princes" (lines 46–47)?

- **A.** Political power to create totalitarian states
- **B.** Vast amounts of wealth for personal use
- **C.** Leisure time for self-fulfillment
- **D.** Brilliant inventions to spur human progress

16. In the final paragraph, the authors indicate that the idea of freedom:

- **F.** always involves some element of political dissent.
- **G.** is actually a delusion.
- **H.** has, at times, been defined as obedience to tyranny.
- **J.** is sometimes seriously flawed.

17. Which of the following opinions concerning "the self-fulfillment of the individual" (line 20) would the authors most likely reject?

- **A.** Self-fulfillment requires a degree of leisure.
- **B.** Self-fulfillment is a praiseworthy but unreachable goal.
- **C.** Self-fulfillment is an ideal shared by diverse thinkers.
- **D.** Self-fulfillment means pursuing one's creative potential.

18. The authors clearly indicate that they believe freedom is:

- **F.** essential if societies are to progress.
- **G.** the product of stable societies only.
- **H.** a prerequisite for world peace.
- **J.** only attainable through revolution.

19. According to the passage, Luther, Rousseau, Hegel, and Marx have in common that they were:

- **A.** misled by a false idea of freedom.
- **B.** believers in unlimited freedom.
- **C.** supporters of the right to dissent.
- **D.** opponents of tyranny.

20. The authors' attitude toward intellectual, economic, and political revolutions is best characterized as:

- **F.** detached.
- **G.** concerned.
- **H.** suspicious.
- **J.** approving.

GO ON TO NEXT PAGE

Passage III

Italy emerged from World War I battered and humiliated. Although it was one of the victorious Allies, Italy's armies had made a poor showing, and Italy had realized few of the grandiose ambitions for
5 which it had entered the war. In the Paris peace settlements Italy had been awarded the adjacent Italian-speaking areas of Austria-Hungary but had been denied further acquisitions east of the Adriatic and in Asia and Africa, some of which it ardently desired.
10 These frustrations were severe blows to Italian national pride.

Italy's weak economy emerged from the war acutely maladjusted. The national debt was huge and the treasury empty. The inflated currency, together
15 with a shortage of goods, raised prices ruinously. Hundreds of thousands of demobilized veterans could find no jobs. In the summer of 1919, there was widespread disorder. Veterans began seizing and squatting on idle, and sometimes on cultivated, lands. Sit-down
20 strikes developed in the factories. During the winter of 1920–1921, several factories were seized by the workers, and Marxism seemed to be gaining strength. The Italian government, torn by factions, seemed too weak to prevent the disorder and protect private property.
25 Although the strife diminished and the Marxist threat waned before the end of 1921, the landlords and the factory owners were thoroughly frightened. Many of them, and indeed many small-business and professional people, longed for vigorous leadership and a strong
30 government. The vigorous leader who stepped forward was Benito Mussolini. The strong government was his Fascist dictatorship.

Mussolini was a dynamic organizer and leader. The son of a blacksmith, he became first a teacher and
35 later a radical journalist and agitator. Before World War I he was a pacifistic socialist, but during the war he became a violent nationalist. After the war he began organizing unemployed veterans into a political action group with a socialistic and extremely nationalistic
40 program. During the labor disturbances of 1919–1921, Mussolini stood aside until it became apparent that the radical workers' cause would lose; then he threw his support to the capitalists and the landlords. Crying that he was saving Italy from com-
45 munism and waving the flag of nationalism, Mussolini organized his veterans into terror squads of black-shirted "Fascisti," who beat up the leaderless radical workers and their liberal supporters. He thereby gained the support of the frightened capitalists and
50 landed aristocracy. By 1922 Mussolini's Fascist party was strong enough to "march on Rome" and seize control of the faction-paralyzed government. Appointed premier by the weak and distraught King Victor Emmanuel III, Mussolini acquired extraordi-
55 nary powers. Between 1924 and 1926 Mussolini

turned his premiership into a dictatorship. All opposition was silenced. Only the Fascist party could engage in organized political activity. The press and the schools were turned into propaganda agencies. The
60 secret police were everywhere. Eventually, the Chamber of Deputies itself was replaced by Mussolini's handpicked Fascist political and economic councils.

Italy's economic life was strictly regimented but
65 in such a way as to favor the capitalistic classes. Private property and profits were carefully protected. All labor unions were abolished except those controlled by the Fascist party. Strikes and lockouts were forbidden. Wages, working conditions, and labor-management
70 disputes were settled by compulsory arbitration under party direction. An elaborate system of planned economy was set up to modernize, coordinate, and increase Italy's production of both industrial and agricultural goods. The very complicated economic and political
75 machinery that Mussolini created for these purposes was called the corporate state. On the whole there was probably a small decline in per capita income under Italian fascism despite some superficial gains. The budget was balanced and the currency stabilized. But
80 Italy's taxes were the highest in the world, and labor's share of economic production was small.

Fascism, however, was primarily political in character, not economic. The essence of its ideology was nationalism run wild. Although Italy never became
85 such a full-blown, viciously anti-Semitic police state as Germany, Mussolini understood the dynamic, energizing quality of militant nationalism. His writings and speeches rang with such words as will, discipline, sacrifice, decision, and conquest. "The goal," he cried,
90 "is always—empire! To build a city, to found a colony, to establish an empire, these are the prodigies of the human spirit…We must resolutely abandon the whole liberal phraseology and way of thinking. …Discipline. Discipline at home in order that we may
95 present the granite block of a single national will. War alone brings up the highest tension, all human energy and puts the stamp of nobility upon the people who have the courage to meet it."

From *A Short History of Western Civilization*, by John B. Harrison, Richard E. Sullivan, Dennis Sherman. Copyright © 1990 by McGraw-Hill Inc.; reprinted by permission of McGraw-Hill, Inc.

21. According to information presented in the passage, "grandiose ambitions" (line 4) refers to Italy's desire for:

   A. territorial expansion.
   B. complete victory at the end of World War I.
   C. peace-time employment for all its veterans.
   D. a supremely powerful army.

GO ON TO NEXT PAGE

22. The passage suggests that Mussolini came to power in 1922 largely as a result of:

    I.   a desire for stability among property-owning middle classes.

    II. a lack of strong opposition from the government in Rome.

    III. his violent opposition to radical workers.

  F. I and II only

  G. I and III only

  H. II and III only

  J. I, II, and III

23. In which of the following ways does the passage support the theory that fascism arises after periods of diminished national pride?

  A. It attributes the fascists' seizure of power from the King to Mussolini's abilities as a leader.

  B. It demonstrates that Mussolini achieved national fame largely because of his eagerness to fight communism.

  C. It shows a connection between the growth of the corporate state and Mussolini's rise to power.

  D. It links Mussolini's ascendancy to the fact that Italy gained less than it hoped for after World War I.

24. The author suggests that, during the disturbances of 1919–1921, "Mussolini stood aside until it became apparent that the radical workers' cause would lose" (lines 41–42) because he was:

  F. secretly hoping the radical workers would win.

  G. an opportunist, waiting for his chance to seize power.

  H. unaware of the importance of the radicals' challenge.

  J. basically a pacifist at that time in his life.

25. A dictatorship is commonly defined as a form of government that has absolute authority over its citizens. Which of the following statements from the passage supports the view that Mussolini's government was a dictatorship?

  A. "Mussolini was a dynamic organizer and leader."

  B. "All labor unions were abolished except those controlled by the Fascist party."

  C. "Veterans began seizing and squatting on idle, and sometimes on cultivated, lands."

  D. "The budget was balanced and the currency stabilized."

26. It can be inferred from the passage that, to Mussolini, nationalism was a:

  F. way to protect Italy from German aggression.

  G. method to bring economic prosperity to war-ravaged Italy.

  H. powerful political tool.

  J. threat to his rise to power.

27. The passage suggests that if the rights of factory workers in 1920 were compared to their rights in 1926, one could accurately say that:

  A. while workers' per capita income rose, workers lost their rights to collectively bargain.

  B. labor's share of economic production grew.

  C. workers' collective action was increasingly disallowed.

  D. labor-management disputes were completely suppressed.

28. The passage suggests that under the Italian fascists, economic rebuilding was:

  F. undermined by labor disturbances.

  G. resisted by the corporate state.

  H. marred by excessively high taxation.

  J. slowed by a failure to balance the budget.

29. Based on information in the passage, the "corporate state" can best be defined as a:

  A. system of structuring government according to business practices.

  B. series of economic programs aimed at ending an inflated currency.

  C. negotiating team that arbitrated worker-management disputes.

  D. complex, planned economy designed to maximize the production of goods.

30. It can be inferred that the author quotes Mussolini's words in the last paragraph (lines 82–98) for the purpose of:

  F. illustrating the nationalistic element in his words.

  G. praising his abilities as a public speaker.

  H. condemning the ideas that Mussolini advances.

  J. demonstrating the difference between Italian and German fascism.

GO ON TO NEXT PAGE

SECTION V: PRACTICE TEST

Passage IV

Tornadoes have long been an enigma, striking sporadically and violently, generating the strongest of all surface winds, and causing more deaths annually in the United States than any other natural phenomenon other than lightning. It is estimated that tornadoes can generate a maximum wind speed of 300 miles per hour, based on analysis of motion pictures and damage to structures.

Tornadoes are formed in the updrafts of a thunderstorm or are associated with hurricanes when they pass over land. They are tightly wound vortexes of air, rarely more than several hundred feet across. They rotate in a counterclockwise direction in the Northern Hemisphere and a clockwise direction in the Southern Hemisphere. Drawn by the greatly reduced atmospheric pressure in the central core, air streams into the base of the vortex from all directions. The air then turns abruptly to spiral upward around the core, and finally merges with the airflow in the parent cloud at the upper end of the tornado. The pressure within the core might be as little as 10 percent lower than the surrounding atmosphere, which would be equivalent to a sudden drop in pressure from that at sea level to an altitude of 3000 feet.

The vortex frequently becomes visible as a wide, dark funnel cloud hanging partway or all the way to the ground. A funnel cloud can only form if the pressure drop in the core reaches a critical value, which depends on the temperature and humidity of the inflowing air. As air flows into the area of lower pressure, it expands and cools, causing water vapor to condense and form water droplets.

Sometimes, no condensation cloud forms, and the only way a tornado can reveal itself is by the dust and debris it carries aloft over land or water spray over the ocean. In that case, it becomes a waterspout, which often frequent the Florida coast and the Bahamas.

The funnel is usually cone shaped, but short, broad, cylindrical pillars up to a mile wide are formed by very strong tornadoes, and often, long, ropelike tubes dangle from the storm cloud. Over the tornado's brief lifetime, usually no more than a few hours, the size, shape, and color of the funnel might change markedly, depending on the intensity of the winds, the properties of the inflowing air, and the type of ground over which it hovers. The color varies from a dirty white to a blue gray when it consists mostly of water droplets, but if the core fills with dust, it takes on the color of the soil and other debris. Tornadoes are also noisy, often roaring, like a laboring freight train or a jet plane taking off. The sound results from the interaction of the concentrated high winds with the ground.

The world's tornado hot spot, with about 700 tornadoes yearly, is the United States, particularly the central and southeastern portions of the country, known as tornado alley. The states most frequently visited by tornadoes are Texas, Arkansas, Oklahoma, Kansas, Nebraska, and Missouri, with a high occurrence of tornadoes continuing on up into Canada.

Tornadoes develop in the spring and to a lesser extent in the fall, when conditions are ripe for the formation of tornado-generating thunderstorms. These conditions include a highly unstable distribution of temperature and humidity in the atmosphere, strong cold fronts that provide the lift needed to start convection, and winds in the upper atmosphere favorable for the formation of strong updrafts.

For a tornado to form, the air in the updraft must begin to rotate. This is accomplished by a wind shear where the wind speed increases with height and veers from southeast to west. Once rotation begins, the tornado builds down toward the ground, although not all tornadoes actually reach the ground. When on the ground, the tornado funnel sucks up air at its lower end, like the hose of a vacuum cleaner.

Tornadoes are steered by the jet stream, and generally travel in a northeasterly direction for about 5 to 15 miles. Their forward ground speed is normally slow enough (30 to 60 miles per hour) for them to be outrun by an automobile, although this is not always a recommended practice because of the unpredictable nature of tornadoes, which often hop about from place to place. Members of NOAA's National Severe Storms Laboratory at the University of Oklahoma actually chase tornadoes in vehicles carrying an instrument package known as TOTO which stands for Totable Tornado Observatory. This package is placed in the path of the tornado. TOTO is equipped to measure a tornado's behavior such as wind speed, wind direction, atmospheric temperature and pressure, and electric field strength.

Reprinted , with permission, from book #2942 *Violent Storms,* by Jon Erickson; Copyright © 1988 by TAB Books, a division of McGraw-Hill, Inc., Blue Ridge Summit, PA 17294-0850 (1-800-233-1128).

31. The author refers to tornadoes as "vortexes of air" (line 11) to emphasize the fact that the air is:

A. moving downward.
B. expanding.
C. dispersing.
D. whirling.

GO ON TO NEXT PAGE

KAPLAN

32. The inspection of films showing the action of tornadoes allowed researchers to determine that tornadoes:

    F. are often accompanied by lightning.

    G. gain maximum size when they pass over land.

    H. are caused by the updrafts of thunderstorms.

    J. reach wind speeds of up to 300 miles per hour.

33. The passage suggests that the direction of a tornado's rotation is influenced chiefly by:

    A. whether a hurricane or a thunderstorm has caused it to form.

    B. the difference in pressure between air in the core and air in the surrounding atmosphere.

    C. the direction of the airflow in its parent cloud.

    D. where the tornado is located on the earth's surface.

34. Researchers often have difficulty getting TOTO to record the information they need. Based on the information in the last paragraph, this is most likely true because:

    F. no scientific instruments can withstand a tornado's force.

    G. it is difficult to predict precisely the path a tornado will take.

    H. tornadoes' characteristics vary too much to accurately measure.

    J. the majority of tornadoes occur over water and are thus unapproachable.

35. If a tornado is to form, which of the following must occur first?

    A. Powerful updrafts and wind shear

    B. Movement of the funnel toward the ground

    C. Movement of air up the funnel from the ground

    D. Uniform distribution of temperature and humidity in the atmosphere

36. The expression "wind shear" (line 70) means that, while gaining altitude, wind:

    F. direction changes, while wind speed stays the same.

    G. speed changes, while wind direction stays the same.

    H. speed and wind direction both change.

    J. is sucked up the lower end of a funnel.

37. The passage suggests that it should be possible to predict when tornadoes are likely to form if:

    A. certain key atmospheric conditions are known.

    B. "tornado alley" can be accurately identified.

    C. the movement of warm fronts can be predicted.

    D. TOTO's readings are accurate.

38. According to the passage, a condensation cloud is created when:

    F. water vapor entering the funnel is affected by changes in air pressure.

    G. the funnel passes over a body of water.

    H. cool air rushes into the funnel and immediately forms droplets.

    J. dust and debris are sucked into the funnel.

39. The main purpose of the third and fourth paragraphs (lines 25–38) is to describe:

    A. how funnels are formed.

    B. how a condensation cloud is formed.

    C. the main factors that make tornadoes visible.

    D. how funnel clouds can vary in color, shape, and size.

40. Based on information presented in the passage, it is a fact that all tornadoes:

    F. are colored by the dust and debris they carry.

    G. touch the earth's surface.

    H. occur in the spring.

    J. are steered by the jet stream.

END OF TEST 3

STOP! DO NOT TURN THE PAGE UNTIL TOLD TO DO SO.

SCIENCE REASONING TEST

35 Minutes—40 Questions

DIRECTIONS: Each of the following seven passages is followed by several questions. After reading each passage, decide on the best answer to each question and fill in the corresponding oval on your answer sheet. You are allowed to refer to the passages while answering the questions.

Passage I

Medical researchers and technicians can track the characteristic radiation patterns emitted by certain inherently unstable isotopes as they spontaneously decay into other elements. The half-life of a radioactive isotope is the amount of time necessary for one-half of the initial amount of its nuclei to decay. The decay curves of isotopes $_{39}Y^{90}$ and $_{39}Y^{91}$ are graphed below as functions of the ratio of N, the number of nuclei remaining after a given period, to N_0, the initial number of nuclei.

1. The half-life of $_{39}Y^{90}$ is approximately:
   A. 2.7 days.
   B. 5.4 days.
   C. 27 days.
   D. 58 days.

2. What will the approximate ratio of $_{39}Y^{90}$ to $_{39}Y^{91}$ be after 2.7 days if the initial samples of the two isotopes contain equal numbers of nuclei?
   F. 1:1
   G. 1:2
   H. 2:1
   J. 10:1

3. When inhaled by humans, $_{39}Y^{90}$ accumulates in the gastrointestinal tract, whereas $_{39}Y^{91}$ accumulates in the bones. If the total amount of each isotope inhaled goes to the specified area, which of the following situations will exist three days after a patient inhales these substances, assuming none of the isotopes leave the specified areas due to physiological factors?
   A. The amount of $_{39}Y^{91}$ in the gastrointestinal tract will be approximately equal to the total amount inhaled.
   B. The amount of $_{39}Y^{90}$ in the bones will be approximately one-half of the total amount inhaled.
   C. The amount of $_{39}Y^{90}$ in the gastrointestinal tract will be approximately one-half of the total amount inhaled.
   D. None of the $_{39}Y^{91}$ inhaled will be left in the bones.

GO ON TO NEXT PAGE

KAPLAN

4. Approximately how many $_{39}Y^{91}$ nuclei will exist after three half-lives have passed, if there are 1,000 nuclei to begin with?

F. 50
G. 125
H. 250
J. 500

5. Which of the following conclusions is/are supported by the information given in the passage?

   I. $_{39}Y^{90}$ is less stable than $_{39}Y^{91}$
   II. Only one-quarter of the original amount of $_{39}Y^{90}$ will remain after 116 days.
   III. $_{39}Y^{90}$ and $_{39}Y^{91}$ are both radioactive.

A. I only
B. III only
C. I and II only
D. I and III only

GO ON TO NEXT PAGE

Passage II

Recently, college teams from all over the country sent tennis players to participate in a series of experiments conducted by the Physical Education Department of a major university. A variety of coaching methods was used to improve the players' serves, as described below.

Experiment 1

Two groups of 50 tennis players worked on the speed of their basic serves for two weeks. One group consisted solely of right-handed players; the other consisted solely of left-handed players. Half of each group watched videos of a right-handed tennis coach, while the other half watched videos of a left-handed coach. Each player was told to pattern his or her serve on that of the coach in the video. The players received no verbal or physical guidance. The average speed of each player's serve was measured at the beginning and end of the two-week period, and changes were recorded in Table 1.

Table 1

Players' handedness	Coach's handedness	Average change in speed (mph)
Right	Right	+5
Right	Left	+2
Left	Right	−1
Left	Left	+8

Experiment 2

For two weeks, a second group of 100 right-handed tennis players watched the same videos of the right-handed tennis coach. The coach also physically guided 50 of those players through the motions of the serve. Again, no verbal instruction was given during the experiment. The average speed and accuracy of each player's serves were recorded at the beginning and end of this two-week period. The results are recorded in Table 2.

Table 2

Guided	Average Change in Speed (mph)	Average Change in Accuracy
No	+5	+15%
Yes	+9	+25%

Experiment 3

For two weeks, a third group of 100 right-handed tennis players worked on their basic serves. 50 players received no verbal instruction; they watched the same video of the right-handed tennis coach, who also physically guided them through the motions of the serve. The other 50 players did not observe the video but received verbal instruction from the coach, who then physically guided them through the motions of the serve. The results are shown in Table 3.

Table 3

Guided Plus	Average Change in Speed (mph)
Video	+7
Verbal Coaching	+10

6. Which of the following results would be expected if Experiment 3 were repeated using left-handed tennis players and a left-handed coach?

   F. The average service accuracy of all the players would increase by at least 30%.

   G. The average service speed of all the players would decrease slightly.

   H. Verbal coaching would improve average service speed less than would watching the video.

   J. The average service speed of the players who watched the video would increase by at least 8 mph.

GO ON TO NEXT PAGE

7. Which of the following conclusions could NOT be supported by the results of Experiment 1?

   A. Imitating someone whose handedness is the opposite of one's own will cause one's skills to deteriorate.

   B. Left-handed people are better than right-handed people at imitating the movement of someone with similar handedness.

   C. People learn more easily by observing someone with similar handedness than by observing someone with handedness opposite their own.

   D. Right-handed people are better than left-handed people at imitating the movement of someone whose handedness is opposite their own.

8. Which of the following hypotheses is best supported by the results of Experiment 2?

   F. Instructional videos are more helpful for right-handed tennis players than is verbal instruction.

   G. Instructional videos are more helpful for left-handed tennis players than for right-handed tennis players.

   H. Physical guidance by a coach improves both speed and accuracy of service for right-handed tennis players.

9. Suppose 50 left-handed tennis players watch a video of a left-handed coach and are also physically guided by that coach. The results of the experiments suggest that the players' average change in service speed will most closely approximate:

   A. −1 mph.
   B. +5 mph.
   C. +8 mph.
   D. +12 mph.

10. Which of the following hypotheses is best supported by the results of Experiment 1 alone?

    F. Tennis players improve less by observing coaches whose handedness is the opposite of their own than by observing those with similar handedness.

    G. Right-handed tennis players are coached by left-handed coaches more frequently than left-handed players are coached by right-handed coaches.

    H. Right-handed coaches are better models for all tennis players than are left-handed coaches.

    J. People learn much better from physical contact plus a visual stimulus than from the visual stimulus alone.

11. What change in procedure would allow a researcher to best determine the effects of verbal instruction on the average service speed of tennis players?

    A. Repeating Experiment 3 with left-handed players

    B. Repeating Experiment 2 with an instructional audio tape instead of a video

    C. Measuring the service speed of 100 tennis players before and after they listened to an instructional audio tape

    D. Verbally coaching 50 left-handed and 50 right-handed tennis players and then measuring their service speed

GO ON TO NEXT PAGE

Passage III

The temperature of any stellar body causes it to emit a characteristic spectrum of radiation. The apparent color of the star corresponds to the wavelength at which most of its radiation is emitted. Stars are assigned to spectral classes according to these characteristic wavelengths, with O as the bluest/warmest and M as the reddest/coolest. The Hertzsprung-Russell (H-R) diagram below plots each known star within 5 parsecs of the Sun by spectral class and absolute magnitude. Absolute magnitude is a measure of luminosity as viewed from a distance of 10 parsecs. An absolute magnitude of +1.0 indicates maximum brightness. (1 parsec = 3.23 light years.)

12. According to the data shown, most stars within 5 parsecs of the Sun have:
    F. a spectral class of M.
    G. an absolute magnitude of +11.0.
    H. a mass similar to that of the Sun.
    J. a bluish color.

13. According to the information given, which of the following stars—Sirius, Altair, α-Centauri—are likely to be hotter than the Sun?
    A. Sirius, Altair, and α-Centauri
    B. Sirius and Altair
    C. Sirius
    D. α-Centauri

14. The faintest stars that are visible to the naked eye are of the 6th magnitude. On the basis of this information and the data given, which of the following conclusions is most likely to be valid?
    F. The majority of stars within 5 parsecs of the Sun are visible from a distance of 10 parsecs.
    G. The majority of stars within 5 parsecs of the Sun are not visible from a distance of 10 parsecs.
    H. Stars in spectral classes K and M are visible from a distance of 10 parsecs.
    J. Stars in spectral class B are visible from a distance of 10 parsecs.

15. The data given in the passage support which of the following conclusions?
    I.   α-Centauri is redder in color than Sirius.
    II. The Sun has a higher surface temperature than does Altair.
    III. If both the Sun and Procyon were viewed at a distance of 10 parsecs, the Sun would appear brighter.
    A. I only
    B. III only
    C. I and II only
    D. II and III only

16. In which of the following ways would a Hertzsprung-Russell diagram that included all of the known stars within 10 parsecs of the Sun differ from the one shown here?
    F. The number of points on the graph would approximately double, while the shape would remain the same.
    G. Most of the additional stars would fall in the portion of the graph between Sirius and α-Centauri.
    H. Most of the additional stars would be in spectral class M with an absolute magnitude of less than +16.0
    J. It cannot be determined from the information given.

GO ON TO NEXT PAGE

Passage IV

The reaction of a certain cobalt complex with sodium nitrite ($NaNO_2$) can yield two different products. Product A is a light orange solid with a melting point measured at approximately 90.5° C; Product B is a dark pink solid with a melting point of 68° C. A series of experiments was performed to determine the reaction conditions that favor each product.

Experiment 1

Two separate solutions of the cobalt complex were prepared as follows. Solution 1 was acidified to pH 5.5; Solution 2 was made basic to pH 8.5. All other conditions were identical for the two solutions. When $NaNO_2$ was added to Solution 1, a dark pink solid with a melting point of 68° C was formed. Adding $NaNO_2$ to Solution 2 produced a white solid with a melting point of 81° C.

Experiment 2

Two separate solutions of the cobalt complex were prepared as above. After addition of $NaNO_2$, the solutions were heated to 110° C for 20 minutes. Solution 1 produced a dark pink solid with a melting point of 68° C. Solution 2 produced a light orange solid which melted at 91° C.

Experiment 3

Two separate solutions were prepared as in the previous experiments. After the addition of $NaNO_2$, each solution was treated with a small amount of citrate ion and then heated as in Experiment 2. Solution 1 remained a clear purple liquid. Solution 2 produced a light orange solid which melted at 90° C.

17. The experimental results indicate that Product B is most likely to form when one heats:
    A. a basic solution with added citrate ion.
    B. an acidic solution with added citrate ion.
    C. an acidic solution with no added citrate ion.
    D. a basic solution with no added citrate ion.

18. Which of the following conclusions is NOT supported by the experimental results?
    F. The formation of Product B is not affected by the presence of citrate ion.
    G. The formation of Product B is not affected by the heating of the solution.
    H. Products A and B form under different conditions.
    J. The formation of Product A is affected by the heating of the solution.

19. Which of the following additional experiments would yield the most useful data concerning the reaction conditions that favor each product?
    A. Varying the concentration of the solutions
    B. Testing with pH levels of 7.0
    C. Heating the solutions to 175° C
    D. Freezing the solutions

20. Which of the following hypotheses is supported by the results of Experiment 2 only?
    F. Products A and B can both be formed in solutions heated to 110° C.
    G. Solution 1 must be heated to yield any product.
    H. Citrate ion prevents the formation of Product A.
    J. Product B forms more readily at lower temperatures.

21. Which of the following conditions remain(s) constant in all three experiments?
    A. The temperature of the solutions during the experiments
    B. The initial amount of cobalt complex present
    C. The amount of citrate ion present
    D. The amount of cobalt complex and the amount of citrate ion present

22. It is suggested that Product B may react to form other, more readily dissolved compounds in the presence of certain ions. Such a hypothesis is best supported by the fact that:
    F. Product A forms at a different pH than Product B.
    G. Solution 2 yields a different color solid when heated.
    H. Product B is unstable in the presence of Product A.
    J. no solid forms in Solution 1 when citrate ion is added prior to heating.

GO ON TO NEXT PAGE

Passage V

Two scientists present various grounds for classifying the giant panda (*Ailuropoda melanoleuca*) as a raccoon or as a bear.

Scientist 1

Although the giant panda superficially resembles a bear (*Ursidae*), many of its anatomical, behavioral, and genetic characteristics are closer to those of raccoons (*Procyonidae*). The bones and teeth of *Ailuropoda melanoleuca*, for example, are very similar in structure to those of the raccoon. While male bears can be up to 100% larger than females of the same species, male giant pandas and raccoons differ very little in size from females of their species. Like the raccoon, the giant panda has a friendly greeting which consists of bleating and barking. When intimidated, both animals cover their eyes with their front paws. Most bears do not exhibit these behaviors. Finally, *Ailuropoda melanoleuca* and the *Procyonidae* have 21 and 19 pairs of chromosomes, respectively, while the *Ursidae* have 36 pairs.

Scientist 2

Giant pandas should be classified as *Ursidae*. Research studies have shown that the ancestors of *Ailuropoda melanoleuca* had about 40 chromosomal pairs, and geneticists theorize that the reduction occurred when the chromosomes underwent head-to-head fusion. Other research has shown that the DNA of the giant panda is far more similar to that of the *Ursidae* than to that of any other family. Furthermore, giant pandas and other bears are not only of similar size, but also have very similar body proportions and walk with the same pigeon-toed gait. Giant pandas display aggressive behavior in the same manner as do other bears, by swatting and trying to grab adversaries with their forepaws.

23. Which of the following, if true, would provide additional support for the hypothesis of Scientist 2?

    A. The blood proteins of giant pandas are very similar to those of several bear species.

    B. Giant pandas and raccoons have similar markings, including dark rings around their eyes.

    C. Giant pandas have 21 pairs of chromosomes while raccoons have only 19 pairs.

    D. There is little difference in size between male and female giant pandas.

24. Scientist 1 and Scientist 2 would agree on which of the following points?

    F. Giant pandas should be classified in a separate family.

    G. The giant panda should not be classified as a raccoon.

    H. Raccoons and bears are physically and behaviorally very similar.

    J. Animals should be classified into families based on their physical, behavioral, and genetic characteristics.

25. Which of the following characteristics would support the classification of a mammal as a member of the *Ursidae*?

    I. 36 pairs of chromosomes and DNA similar to that of many bear species

    II. Raccoonlike markings and 19 pairs of chromosomes

    III. 62% greater average size among males than among females

    A. I only

    B. II only

    C. I and III only

    D. II and III only

GO ON TO NEXT PAGE

26. According to Scientist 1, which of the following is the giant panda most likely to do when frightened?

    F. Bleat and bark

    G. Cover its eyes with its paws

    H. Swat and grab with its forepaws

    J. Walk away pigeon-toed

27. According to Scientist 2, the giant panda should be classified as a bear because:

    A. there is little disparity in the size of male and female giant pandas.

    B. the greeting rituals of the giant panda resemble those of bears.

    C. both bears and giant pandas are herbivorous.

    D. the DNA of giant pandas is similar to that of bears.

28. Suppose that giant pandas have glandular scent areas. This fact could be used to support the viewpoint of:

    F. Scientist 1, if it were also shown that raccoons also have glandular scent areas.

    G. Scientist 2, if it were also shown that bears do not have glandular scent areas.

    H. Scientist 1, if it were also shown that raccoons have a very poor sense of smell.

    J. Scientist 2, if it were also shown that bears urinate to lay down their scent.

29. Which of the following arguments could Scientist 1 use to counter Scientist 2's claim about the behavior of giant pandas and bears?

    A. The giant panda walks with a pigeon-toed gait.

    B. Unlike most bears, but like raccoons, an aggressive giant panda bobs its head up and down.

    C. The giant panda swats and grabs at its adversaries.

    D. Unlike most bears, the giant panda has only 19 pairs of chromosomes.

GO ON TO NEXT PAGE

SECTION V: PRACTICE TEST

Passage VI

The graph below shows different primary energy sources as percentages of energy consumption in the United States during selected years from 1850 to 1985.

Energy sources over the last 150 years

30. As the relative importance of petroleum as a primary energy source increased, the use of coal:

   F. also increased.

   G. decreased.

   H. remained constant.

   J. stopped completely.

31. The data shown support the hypothesis that the ability to utilize coal as an energy source:

   A. was developed during the 1900s.

   B. was dependent on the development of mechanized mining techniques.

   C. predated the ability to utilize natural gas.

   D. was predated by the ability to utilize natural gas.

GO ON TO NEXT PAGE

32. As the consumption of alternate energy sources increased, the use of farm animals:
    F. decreased to below 1% of the total.
    G. increased to over 30% of the total.
    H. increased, then decreased.
    J. remained the same.

33. Which of the following conclusions concerning energy consumption from 1900 to 1950 is supported by the information given in the graph?
    A. Energy sources became more diverse.
    B. Work animals became more important.
    C. Natural gas became the major energy source.
    D. Coal remained the largest single source of energy.

34. The data on the graph support which of the following conclusions?
    I. Energy consumption in 1985 relied in part on technologies that did not exist in 1850.
    II. The largest source of energy in the United States has always been coal.
    III. The short supply of available petroleum will lead to a decrease in its use.
    F. I only
    G. III only
    H. I and II only
    J. II and III only

GO ON TO NEXT PAGE

Passage VII

The regenerative powers of *Asterias rubens*, a common starfish, were investigated in the following experiments.

Experiment 1

Randomly selected starfish were divided into five groups of 25 each. The individuals in one group were left intact. Members of the other four groups were subjected to selective amputation, as indicated in the table below. The starfish were kept in laboratory tanks simulating the natural environment of *Asterias rubens* for nine months. The results of periodic observations are recorded in Table 1.

Table 1

	# fully regenerated after[†]:			
Removed Portion	3 mos.	6 mos.	9 mos.	# of starfish dead after 9 mos.
None	—	—	—	3
Outer arm	20	23	23	2
Whole arm	15	22	22	3
Arm & 1/5 body	6	21	23	2
2 arms & 1/3 body	5	12	24	1

[†]cumulative total

Experiment 2

The regenerative powers of portions of Asterias rubens were investigated next. Five groups of pieces of Asterias rubens were selected at random, placed in separate laboratory tanks under the same conditions as in Experiment 1, and observed for one year. The combined results from all five tanks are presented in Table 2.

Table 2

	# of starfish fully regenerated after[†]:				
Remaining Body Portion	3 mos.	6 mos.	9 mos.	1 yr.	# dead after 1 yr.
Lower arm	0	0	0	0	3
Arm & 1/5 body	0	0	8	20	2
2 arms & 1/3 body	0	2	13	22	2

[†]cumulative total

35. According to the experimental results, approximately what percentage of *Asterias rubens* specimens can regenerate two entire arms and part of the central body within six months?

    A. 25%
    B. 50%
    C. 75%
    D. 100%

36. Which of the following conclusions is supported by the results of Experiment 2 only?

    F. Starfish are only capable of regenerating arms.
    G. Starfish with larger portions removed regenerate at faster rates.
    H. Some starfish die as a result of confinement in laboratory tanks.
    J. Regeneration is dependent upon the existence of a portion of the central body.

GO ON TO NEXT PAGE

37. The information given supports which of the following conclusions?

    I. *Asterias rubens* are often found in very deep water.

    II. *Asterias rubens* can regenerate limbs lost due to attack by other marine animals.

    III. The population of *Asterias rubens* would probably increase if body parts were broken off.

A. I only

B. III only

C. II and III only

D. I, II, and III

38. The first group of starfish was used in Experiment 1:

F. as a control to see how many starfish were likely to die under the conditions of the experiment.

G. as a control for the second experiment.

H. to test the natural recuperative powers of *Asterias rubens*.

J. to determine the effect of a fresh water environment on *Asterias rubens*.

39. In Experiment 2, the sum of fully regrown and dead starfish after one year did not always equal 25. The hypothesis which best explains this is that:

A. some of the starfish were lost during the experiment.

B. the researchers miscalculated somewhere during the course of the experiment.

C. some body parts fused together to form single starfish.

D. some of the starfish were alive but not fully regenerated.

40. Starfish prey on abalone. At one time it was common practice for abalone fishermen to chop starfish into pieces and throw them back into the ocean. What was the most probable result of this practice?

F. The starfish population immediately skyrocketed.

G. The starfish population increased over a period of time as some pieces underwent regeneration.

H. The starfish population decreased drastically.

J. Every piece that was returned to the ocean eventually became a complete starfish again.

END OF TEST 4

STOP! DO NOT TURN TO ANY OTHER TEST.

COMPUTE YOUR SCORE

1 **Figure out your score in each section.** Refer to the answer keys to figure out the number right in each test section. Enter the results below:

RAW SCORES

English: [　　　] Reading: [　　　]

Math: [　　　] Science Reasoning: [　　　]

2 **Find your practice test score.** Find your raw score on each section in the table below. The score in the far left column indicates your estimated scaled score if this were an actual ACT.

SCALED SCORE	RAW SCORES			
	TEST 1 ENGLISH	TEST 2 MATHEMATICS	TEST 3 READING	TEST 4 SCIENCE REASONING
36	75	60	40	40
35	74	60	40	40
34	73	59	39	39
33	72	58	39	39
32	71	57	38	38
31	70	55–56	37	37
30	69	53–54	36	36
29	68	50–52	35	35
28	67	48–49	34	34
27	65–66	45–47	33	33
26	63–64	43–44	32	32
25	61–62	40–42	31	30–31
24	58–60	38–39	30	28–29
23	56–57	35–37	29	26–27
22	53–55	33–34	28	24–25
21	49–52	31–32	27	21–23
20	46–48	28–30	25–26	19–20
19	44–45	26–27	23–24	17–18
18	41–43	23–25	21–22	16
17	39–40	20–22	19–20	15
16	36–38	17–19	17–18	14
15	34–35	15–16	15–16	13
14	30–33	13–14	13–14	12
13	28–29	11–12	12–13	11
12	25–27	9–10	10–11	10
11	23–24	8	9	9
10	20–22	7	8	8
9	17–19	6	7	7
8	14–16	5	6	6
7	12–13	4	5	5
6	9–11	3	4	4
5	7–8	2	3	3
4	4–6	1	2	2
3	3	1	1	1
2	2	0	0	0
1	1	0	0	0

To calculate your estimated composite score, simply add together your scaled scores on each subsection and divide by four.

COMPOSITE SCORE: [　　　]

ANSWERS AND EXPLANATIONS

English Answer Key

1. B	21. B	41. C	61. C
2. H	22. H	42. J	62. G
3. D	23. D	43. A	63. D
4. H	24. J	44. J	64. J
5. A	25. C	45. B	65. A
6. J	26. H	46. G	66. H
7. A	27. B	47. C	67. A
8. G	28. J	48. H	68. H
9. D	29. B	49. B	69. D
10. J	30. J	50. H	70. G
11. D	31. D	51. D	71. C
12. F	32. H	52. J	72. H
13. B	33. B	53. A	73. B
14. H	34. J	54. G	74. H
15. B	35. A	55. D	75. B
16. F	36. G	56. G	
17. B	37. C	57. D	
18. F	38. J	58. H	
19. C	39. B	59. C	
20. F	40. H	60. F	

The questions fall into the following categories, according to the skills they test. If you notice that you're having trouble with particular categories, review the following:

1. REDUNDANCY—English Workout 1

2. RELEVANCE—English Workout 1

3. VERBOSITY—English Workout 1

PASSAGE I

1. (B)—Pronouns

A plural pronoun must logically refer to the closest plural noun that came before it. Choice A is incorrect because the word *they* can't logically stand for *people* here. It must mean *fish*, but *fish* hasn't been used yet in the sentence. Choices C and D make the same error but use *these* and *them*. This sentence fragment, you might have noticed, also suffers from wordiness.

2. (H)—Pronouns

Trust your ear. In original version F, you wouldn't say "origins who." *Who* can refer only to people. Choice G correctly uses *which*, but its singular verb, *begins*, can't go with the plural *origins*. Along with the faulty pronoun *who*, J contains the unidiomatic *beginning at*.

3. (D)—Redundancy

The words *keep(ing)*, *possess(ing)*, *having* and *have* all essentially mean the same thing. Using two of them together (choices A, B, and C) adds redundancy, not meaning, to the sentence.

4. (H)—Verb Usage

Trust your ear. The infinitive form of the verb is *to breed*, so the correct choice is H. The other options produce the incorrect verb forms *to breeds* (choice F), *to breeded* (choice G), and *to bred* (choice J).

5. (A)—Logic

Trust your ear, and make it make sense. Choices B, C, and D don't add anything to the sentence that isn't already expressed in correct choice A. In fact, the sentence makes no sense when B or C is plugged into it. The "nevertheless" in choice D suggests some sort of contrast, but there is none; the Romans are just another example of fish keepers.

6. (J)—Verb Usage

What happened in seventeenth-century England? Goldfish "were kept" in glass containers. The verb tense is wrong in choices F, G, and H.

7. (A)—Verb Usage

Ask yourself how the underlined verb is being used. It's the main verb for the subject *relationship*. A is the only choice that works. In choice B, the sentence won't make sense if we insert *which*. C is wrong because a main verb can never have an *-ing* form unless there is some form of the verb *to be* in front of it. You can say "I am running," but not "I running."

8. (G)—Reading-Type Question

The preceding sentence tells you how the need for small aquariums was met. It does not indicate that the container was inappropriate (choice F), contradict a statement about English containers (choice H), or talk about goldfish life spans (choice J).

9. (D)—Sentence Structure

The full sentence from which this question is taken is actually two short but complete sentences: "The first display aquariums opened . . . in London" and "aquariums soon appeared in Naples, Berlin, and Paris." When two short sentences are joined into one, and linked by a comma, the comma must be followed by a conjunction—a word like *and, but,* or *or*. In this case, the word is *and*.

10. (J)—Pronouns

Choices F and G are incorrect because they use *it* or *its* to refer to *the growth in aquariums* without having first used the longer phrase. Choice H is incorrect because it does not say what has been slowed.

11. (D)—Relevance

It is irrelevant to mention a television show about dolphins (choices A, B, and C) in a passage that discusses aquariums, even though dolphins are sometimes found in aquariums.

12. (F)—Logic

The two ideas here are *causally* related: You would share fish trivia *because* fish keeping has an interesting history. "For" (choice F) illustrates this connection. Choice G illogically sets "fish trivia" apart from the rest of the sentence. Choice J uses one set of quotation marks, but quotation marks always come in pairs.

13. (B)—Verb Usage

Trust your ear. *Have playing* sounds weird, and it doesn't mean anything. Choices C and D also sound odd. Whenever a sentence has more than one verb, there must be a conjunction between them. ("Fish keeping is [verb] . . . but [conjunction] . . . it also has [verb] . . . ") There is no conjunction before the underlined phrase, so it cannot be a verb [choices C and D]. It's really a descriptive phrase [choice B].

14. (H)—Reading-Type Question

This passage is about the history of aquariums. It doesn't discuss the study of history in general (choice F) or the responsibility involved in maintaining an aquarium (choice J). It mentions that an aquarist might enjoy "fish trivia," but doesn't state that such trivia must be learned (choice G).

15. (B)—Structure and Purpose

Look at the first and last paragraphs. The first paragraph of the passage leads into, or introduces, the discussion of the history of aquariums. It's not an example (choice A) or a historical survey (choice C). The last paragraph is a wrap-up for the passage, not a personal account (choice D).

PASSAGE II

16. (F)—Punctuation

The sentence is correct as it stands. There is clearly a pause between *mobility* and *horizontal*, so we need some form of punctuation between the two words. Choice H uses a semicolon, but semicolons connect two phrases that could be sentences by themselves. The phrase *horizontal and vertical* could not be a sentence. F and J correctly use a colon, which introduces a list or definition. However, J unnecessarily inserts the word *being*. Don't add what you don't need.

17. (B)—Redundancy

The words *pay* and *salary* have approximately the same meaning. It is redundant to use both (choices A and C). Choice D produces the phrase *firms that are comparable pay in terms of salary and prestige*, which makes no sense.

18. (F)—Pronouns

Think about what the sentence is saying. G, H, and J add unnecessary pronouns to the sentence. The subject, *change*, is right there, so it's wrong to throw in the pronoun *they* or *it*.

19. (C)—Logic

The mention of the Russian Revolution illustrates the point made in the preceding sentence, that social mobility "may change the entire social system." *For instance* (choice C) correctly indicates this. A, B, and D are wrong because this sentence does not offer a conclusion based on the preceding sentence.

20. (F)—Completeness

We hope your ear told you that G and J sound funny. Since choices G and J are complete sentences in themselves, you can't connect them to another complete sentence, "social mobility occurs at a variety of rates," with a comma. We also hope you steered clear of choice H, with its incorrect and confusing phrase *change's differing degrees*.

21. (B)—Completeness

The underlined word occurs in an incomplete sentence that lacks a verb. Choices A, C, and D are incorrect because they do not create complete sentences. C adds the verb *is*, but doesn't tell us *what* the athlete is. Choice B, however, adds a verb and completes the meaning.

22. (H)—Structure and Purpose

Sentence 6 says that gradual changes can accomplish social mobility, so it makes most sense before sentence 5, which gives an example of a gradual change. Choice H is correct.

23. (D)—Completeness

The phrase *in that* (choice A) sounds funny and makes the sentence incomplete. Changing the phrase to *in* (choice B) or *on* (choice C) still doesn't complete the sentence. Omitting the phrase, however, leaves a complete sentence.

24. (J)—Logic

The preceding sentence stated that some people view large-scale mobility negatively. This sentence offers a contrasting opinion. The words *accordingly* (choice F), *similarly* (choice G), and *likewise* (choice H) are incorrect because they imply agreement. The phrase *on the other hand* (choice J) correctly introduces a differing thought.

25. (C)—Pronouns

Your ear can help on this one. You might say *they attempt*, but not *they attempting* (choice B). In choice A, *they are attempting* sounds okay until you keep reading. Ask yourself what *they are attempting to rise validate* means.

26. (H)—Relevance

The main theme of the passage is social mobility. The American educational system (choice F), salary ranges (choice G), or a rock video (choice J) have nothing to do with this. The correct choice is H, since it talks about some benefits of social mobility.

27. (B)—Verb Usage

The sentence compares two verbs: *destroy* and *reinforce*. Things that are compared need to be in the same form. *Destroying* ends in -*ing*, so we need the -*ing* form of *reinforce*. Only choice B uses this form.

28. (J)—Logic

OMIT the underlined portion (choice J). It's not clear how a flat tire benefits anyone. G and H don't help.

29. (B)—Verb Usage

The subject of the sentence is *crowd*, not *yuppies*. A crowd is singular, no matter how many yuppies are in it, so we need the singular *shows* instead of *show*.

30. (J)—Verbosity

The point of the sentence is that vertical mobility is not a passing phenomenon. The underlined portion is not necessary and only distracts from this point.

PASSAGE III

31. (D)—Sentence Structure

D is the simplest version, and it's right. Use your ear, or ask yourself what the subject of *is* or *being* is, in choices A, B, and C. It can't be *that* because *that* isn't a pronoun here; so *is* or *being* doesn't refer to anything here. Rather, *that* is a conjunction, a word which combines one phrase, "The critic George Moore once said of this artist," with another, *her pictures are the only pictures.* . . .

32. (H)—Verb Usage

Use your ear: *statement are* sounds funny. That's because a singular noun must have a singular verb. *Statement* is singular, but *are* is plural. Choice H corrects the problem by making the verb singular. Choice J corrects it by making the noun plural, but *statement* also has to agree with *shows*, so we need the singular form in choice H.

33. (B)—Pronouns

A pronoun must refer to something. In A and D, we can guess that *it* refers to politics, but this isn't made clear in the sentence. Choice C adds the word *politics*, but the construction is clumsy. Correct choice B is simplest and clearest.

34. (J)—Logic

Trust your ear. *Being her earliest childhood* (choice F) sounds odd, and it is. It means that she *was* her earliest childhood. Choice G starts with the word *from* set off with a comma. The only time this construction is used is when someone is signing a letter.

35. (A)—Relevance

The passage is talking about the painters Morisot studied with, not about their nationalities. Manet's heritage, no matter how it is phrased, is not relevant. Choice A is correct.

36. (G)—Idiom

Make it all match. *Either* goes with *or*. *Neither* goes with *nor*. The two *n* words go together. Choices G and J use a correct pair, but J leaves out the verb. Choice G correctly uses a singular verb form.

KAPLAN

(Although *either/or* and *neither/nor* compare two things, they treat each thing separately, as a singular subject.)

37. (C)—Pronouns
Who is doing the facing? Morisot's male colleagues are, so they should be referred to by the pronoun *who*. The passage is talking about Morisot's lifetime, which was in the *past*. So we use the past tense, *faced*.

38. (J)—Logic
The previous sentence talks about Morisot's setbacks. This sentence talks about the way she overcame them. We are looking for a connecting word that implies *contrast:* Morisot did well *in spite of* her hardships. *However* (choice J) provides the contrast we are looking for.

39. (B)—Completeness
In choice A, *Portraying women performing domestic and social activities* is not a complete sentence. It has no subject. Choice C uses the word *insofar* incorrectly. Choice D says "her sphere *were*." Since *sphere* is singular, we would have to say "her sphere *was*." Correct choice B makes the fragment into a sentence by giving it the subject *she* and using an appropriate form of the verb (began to portray).

40. (H)—Structure and Purpose
We're looking for a statement that will present Morisot in a more positive light. Choice H suggests that while her subject matter may *appear* limited, it could *actually* be considered quite meaningful, given the social context in which it was produced. Choices F, G, and J, in contrast, are all somewhat negative in tone.

41. (C)—Punctuation
We can introduce a list of examples with a colon or with the words *such as,* but not with both, so choice A is wrong. Double dashes do not introduce a list of examples, so choice B is wrong. Choice D is wrong because it uses a comma after the phrase *such as.* If you read the sentence with a pause after *such as,* it sounds awkward.

42. (J)—Redundancy
Choices F, G, and H are redundant. By definition, successors are the people who follow in order or sequence someone else.

43. (A)—Structure and Purpose/Relevance
Ask yourself: What is the main point of the passage? The passage is about Morisot's experience as a female artist. Only choice A is relevant to that topic. Choice C refers to George Moore, who is mentioned in the passage in relation to Morisot. To devote a section of the passage to him, however, would change its focus. Likewise, a discussion of Impressionism would divert the focus of the passage away from Morisot.

44. (J)—Judging the Passage/Relevance

Does the inclusion of dates seem appropriate? Well, the passage is a biography, and dates are generally appropriate in a biography, so the correct answer is J. The story of Morisot isn't unbelievable, so the author would have no reason to introduce something just to make us believe it (choice H).

45. (B)—Structure and Purpose

First, try to find an appropriate beginning. Paragraph 1 is especially easy to eliminate, since it refers to "this artist" without ever telling us her name. Paragraph 3 is less obvious, but it talks about Morisot's subject matter and style without telling us who she is. The passage can't start with paragraph 4, because none of the answer choices do. Paragraph 2 provides general background information on Morisot, so it should be first. That leaves choices B and C. Paragraph 3 introduces Morisot's subject matter, which paragraph 4 talks about in greater detail. So it makes sense to put paragraph 3 immediately before 4.

PASSAGE IV

46. (G)—Verb Usage

Make sure everything matches. Ask, *what is the subject?* Even though *exception* occurs right before the verb, the subject is *movies. Movies* is plural, so we need a plural verb. *Were being replaced* (choice H) is plural, but it illogically changes the tense. We're talking about a change in movies right now, not in the distant past. Use your ear. You should be able to tell that choice H sounds funny.

47. (C)—Punctuation

"The slasher movie" is the "new breed of horror film." We need something to connect a thing and its definition: either punctuation or a connecting phrase. Choice D inserts an unnecessary comma, and both B and D are wordy. A colon, in choice C, works just fine.

48. (H)—Completeness

The subject of the sentence is *the first commercially successful low-budget chiller.* Choices F, G, and J separate *first* from *commercially successful low-budget chiller.* The sentence doesn't make sense this way. *The first* tells us *which* "commercially successfully low budget film" we are talking about, so it must be connected to that phrase.

49. (B)—Verb Usage

Plug the choices in. Choices A, C, and D don't make sense. That's because the verb is *have glutted,* and the whole verb has to go in one place.

50. (H)—Verbosity

Choices F and J sound funny. That's because they use complicated expressions. Not only does G use an awkward construction, it also eliminates the subject (popularity). Simpler is better. Choice H is the right answer.

51. (D)—Redundancy
The word *filmmakers* is all that's needed.

52. (J)—Verbosity
Trust your ear. *Increasing gory* sounds a bit off. Choice J adds an *ly* which makes it correct. Notice that *increasingly* describes *gory*. Gory is an adjective, and if you want to describe anything that's not a noun, you need an adverb. Most adverbs (like *increasingly*) are formed by adding *ly* to an adjective (like *increasing*).

53. (A)—Punctuation
Ask yourself what job the punctuation is doing. In this sentence, the punctuation indicates a slight pause. Since commas do that, the comma (choice A) is correct.

54. (G)—Redundancy
When in doubt, take it out. *Periphery* means *fringe,* so using both words is unnecessary.

55. (D)—Verb Usage
They're may sound like *there are* but it means *they are,* which doesn't make sense here. Also, *they're* is the same as *they are,* in choice B. There can't be two correct answers, so whenever two answers mean the same thing they must both be wrong.

56. (G)—Tone
Try to decide on appropriateness first. "That's a big wad of cash!" sounds out of place because it is very informal, while the passage is relatively formal. So we can decide that the statement is not appropriate, and look for an answer that gives us this reason. The correct choice G refers to the passage's tone.

57. (D)—Sentence Structure
Conjunctions are words that combine one phrase with another. Using two conjunctions, like *although* and *however* in choice A, is redundant, illogical, and wrong. Choices B and C make this same mistake. You should be able to hear these errors, but be careful! You have to read the entire sentence in order to notice the *although*.

58. (H)—Redundancy
Increasingly, evermore, and *more, and more, and more* all mean the same thing, just as *violent* and *full of anger, blood and shooting* mean the same thing. Say each once.

59. (C)—Redundancy
The public is, by definition, made up of human beings, so choices A and B are redundant. In choice D, *human's* refers to one specific being, but the passage is talking about the general taste.

60. (F)—Tone
Answer one part of the question first. Look at the tone. People who make sarcastic remarks are being harsh, derisive, and often ironic—that is, they mean the opposite of what they say. The passage does not do this, nor is it light-hearted, so we can eliminate choices G and H. The author is serious, and does discuss a change in entertainment, so F is correct.

PASSAGE V

61. (C)—Redundancy
"Unexplained" things *are* things that haven't been explained yet. When in doubt, take it out.

62. (G)—Redundancy
Abandoned means "deserted," so don't say both.

63. (D)—Verb Usage
Listen to the sentence as it stands. It sounds odd, because *having* can't be the main verb of a sentence. You can say "I am going," or "I go," but not, "I going." Choice D is simple and it has a subject (*some ships*) and an acceptable verb (*have vanished*).

64. (J)—Idiom
Trust your ear. English speakers use certain idioms or expressions, just because that's the way we say things. Something ranges "from the interference of UFOs to the existence of powerful fields," *not* "to or toward the interference of UFOs to the existence of powerful fields," as in choices F and G.

65. (A)—Redundancy
So far means the same *as yet,* so choices B, C, and D are all redundant. Also, if you read choice D back into the sentence, you'll hear that it leaves out the verb (*have been*). Choice A is correct.

66. (H)—Relevance
It's not important to the passage that England is also triangular. When in doubt, take it out.

67. (A)—Logic
Think about it: If a country's coast is a boundary, why bring rivers into the discussion?

68. (H)—Verbosity
Say it simply. Choices F, G, and J are all wordy and awkward. Those qualities are not admired by the ACT test makers.

69. (D)—Verb Usage
The first problem here is verb tense. The meaning of the sentence as it stands is that strange events were reported in the *past,* but people are wondering about the region *now.* If the events "had" been

reported (choice A) the author would be talking about a *past* conception of the Bermuda Triangle. The second problem is number. *Events* is plural. *Is* (choice C) and *has* (choice B) are singular.

70. (G)—Relevance
Inappropriate statements usually stick out. You stop reading and wonder why you were told something. That doesn't happen here, so the mention of Juan de Bermudez is probably appropriate. Now consider why it is appropriate. Choice H is incorrect and choice J has nothing to do with *why* the mention of Bermudez is appropriate. Choice G is correct. (If you're not sure the statement is relevant, look at the reason given for saying it's not: Exploration and the Bermuda Triangle are not dissimilar, since we are talking about the exploration of Bermuda.)

71. (C)—Sentence Structure
Trust your ear. What are they questioning?

72. (H)—Relevance
What new information would be a continuation of the topic? The passage at this point isn't talking about geography (choice F), the tourist trade (choice J), or other supernatural phenomena (choice G). It is discussing doubts about whether there have been supernatural occurrences in the Bermuda Triangle.

73. (B)—Redundancy
We know what *certain* means. Adding a definition is redundant.

74. (H)—Structure and Purpose
Answer the question first. The passage talks about many events, not just one, so the answer to the question is "no." Now look at the reasons. The passage does contain factual information, so choice J is wrong. Choice H is correct because the writer does not focus on one specific disappearance.

75. (B)—Structure and Purpose
Paragraph 1 is a discussion of the *types* of strange events that have been reported. It should logically come after the introduction of the fact that strange events have been reported. Choice B is correct since paragraph 2 introduces the fact that strange events have been reported.

Math Answer Key

1. C	16. F	31. A	46. G
2. H	17. B	32. K	47. B
3. D	18. F	33. B	48. J
4. J	19. E	34. G	49. E
5. A	20. J	35. E	50. H
6. F	21. D	36. G	51. E
7. E	22. G	37. C	52. K
8. K	23. C	38. K	53. D
9. B	24. K	39. E	54. F
10. F	25. D	40. H	55. E
11. D	26. F	41. C	56. H
12. G	27. D	42. J	57. D
13. E	28. F	43. B	58. H
14. J	29. A	44. J	59. B
15. C	30. G	45. C	60. F

1. (C)—Math Appendix, #63: Solving a Linear Equation

Find x by getting it by itself on one side of the equation:

$$5x + 3 = -17$$

Subtract 3 from both sides $\quad 5x = -20$

Divide both sides by 5 $\quad x = \frac{-20}{5}$

Simplify $\quad x = -4$

Alternatively, use backsolving. $5x + 3 = -17$ will be true for the correct value of x only. Since the answer choices are in numerical order, try C first.

$$x = -4, \text{ then } 5(-4) + 3 = -17$$
$$-20 + 3 = -17$$
$$-17 = -17$$

This is true, so C must be correct.

2. (H)—Math Appendix, #38: Solving a Proportion

Six people are served by 4 oranges, 5 pears, 10 apples, and 24 strawberries. Eighteen people—that is, 3×6 people—will need 3 times as much, that is, 3 times as many of each ingredient. So John needs $3 \times 5 = 15$ pears.

3. (D)—Math Appendix, #15: Greatest Common Factor

Factor both numbers:

$8 \times 10^9 = 2 \times 2 \times 2 \times 10 \times 10 \times 10 \times 10 \times 10 \times 10 \times 10 \times 10 \times 10$

$6 \times 10^3 = 2 \times 3 \times 10 \times 10 \times 10$

Since both numbers have a factor of 2 and three factors of 10, the greatest integer that is a factor of both will be $2 \times 10 \times 10 \times 10 = 2 \times 10^3$.

4. (J)—Math Appendix, #87: Areas of Special Quadrilaterals

Area of a rectangle = length × width

From the diagram, length = 4 and width = 3. Therefore area = 4 × 3 = 12.

5. (A)—Math Appendix, #89: Circumference of a Circle

Draw a diagram to help visualize the situation:

As can be seen from the diagram, the length of the band is the same as the circumference of the cylinder. The circumference of a cylinder and the circumference of a circle are determined in the same way:

Circumference = $2\pi r = 2 \times \pi \times 4 = 8\pi$.

6. (F)—Math Appendix, #65: Translating from English into Algebra

For every large jar there are 48 olives, so x large jars hold $48x$ olives.

For every small jar there are 32 olives, so y small jars hold $32y$ olives.

The total number of olives needed is $48x + 32y$.

This problem could also be attacked by picking numbers. Let $x = 1$ and $y = 2$. Then there is one large jar needing 48 olives, and two small jars needing $2 \times 32 = 64$ olives, for a total of $48 + 64 = 112$ olives. Any answer choice which does not result in 112 when $x = 1$ and $y = 2$ may be eliminated.

(F) $48x + 32y = 48 \times 1 + 32 \times 2 = 112$ —This may be correct.

(G) $\frac{x}{48} + \frac{y}{32} = \frac{1}{48} + \frac{2}{32} \neq 112$ —Discard.

(H) $\frac{xy}{80} = \frac{1 \times 2}{80} = \frac{2}{80} \neq 112$ —Discard.

(J) $80xy = 80 \times 1 \times 2 \neq 112$ —Discard.

(K) $\frac{1536}{xy} = \frac{1536}{1 \times 2} = 768 \neq 112$ —Discard.

Since answer choice (A) was the only one to give the appropriate number, it is correct.

7. (E)—Math Appendix, #52: Evaluating an Algebraic Expression

Substitute $x + 1$ for x in the expression $3x^2 + 4$:

$$3(x + 1)^2 + 4$$

Expand $(x + 1)^2$. $= 3(x^2 + 2x + 1) + 4$

Multiply out parentheses. $= 3x^2 + 6x + 3 + 4$

Gather like terms. $= 3x^2 + 6x + 7$

8. (K)—Math Appendix, #25: Converting a Mixed Number to an Improper Fraction, and Math Appendix, #22: Adding/Subtracting Fractions

$$5\frac{5}{6} + 3\frac{5}{8} + 1\frac{1}{3} = 5 + 3 + 1 + \frac{5}{6} + \frac{5}{8} + \frac{1}{3}$$

$$= 9 + \frac{5}{6} + \frac{5}{8} + \frac{1}{3}$$

$$= 9 + \frac{20}{24} + \frac{15}{24} + \frac{8}{24}$$

$$= 9 + \frac{43}{24}$$

$$= 9 + 1\frac{19}{24}$$

$$= 10\frac{19}{24}$$

9. (B)—(Miscellaneous Line Segments)

Draw a diagram:

It is $2.35 + 3.4 = 5.75$ miles from the school to the grocery store. The distance from the grocery store to home is the remaining portion of the 10 miles between school and home. That is, (10 miles) − (5.75 miles) = 4.25 miles.

10. (F)—Math Appendix, #39: Rate

The teacher gives him 3 pieces every week for 4 weeks, for a total of $3 \times 4 = 12$ pieces.

He can learn 2 new pieces per week. To learn 12 pieces will take him $12 \div 2 = 6$ weeks.

11. (D)—Math Appendix, #80: Interior Angles of a Triangle

The sum of the interior angles of any triangle is 180°. So:

$$\angle EDF + \angle DFE + \angle DEF = 180°$$
$$35° + 65° + \angle DEF = 180°$$
$$\angle DEF = 180° - 35° - 65°$$
$$\angle DEF = 80°$$

12. (G)—Math Appendix, #44: Averages—Finding the Missing Number

$$\text{Average} = \frac{\text{Sum of Terms}}{\text{Number of Terms}}$$

In this case she needs an average of 175. Let the score on the next game be x.

$$\text{Then } 175 = \frac{150 + 195 + 160 + x}{4}$$
$$175 \times 4 = 150 + 195 + 160 + x$$
$$700 = 505 + x$$
$$700 - 505 = x$$
$$195 = x$$

So she must score 195 on the next game for an average of 175.

13. (E)—(Miscellaneous Coordinate Geometry and Triangles)

Draw a diagram:

Note: Points have been labeled for clarity.

Run through the answer choices to see which one works.

(A) $\angle ABC$ is *greater* than 90°—Discard.
(B)   All three sides are *not* the same length—Discard.
(C)   *No* sides are the same length—Discard.
(D)   *No* angle measures 90°—Discard.
(E)   One angle, $\angle ABC$, is greater than 90°—This is correct.

14. (J)—Math Appendix, #66: Solving a Quadratic Equation

$2y^2 - 4y - 6 = 0$ is of the form $ax^2 + bx + c = 0$, and so its roots can be found by the quadratic formula.

$$x = \frac{-b \pm \sqrt{b^2 - 4ac}}{2a}$$

$$= \frac{-(-4) \pm \sqrt{(-4)^2 - 4 \times 2 \times (-6)}}{4}$$

$$= \frac{4 \pm \sqrt{16 + 48}}{4} = 1 \pm 2,$$ which is 3 or −1. The sum of 3 and −1 is 2.

15. (C)—Math Appendix, #29: Converting Fractions and Decimals

Eliminate answer choices (A) and (B) straight off, since the numerator is less than the denominator, $\frac{7}{8}$ must be less than 1.

$$\frac{1}{8} = 0.125, \text{ so } \frac{7}{8} = 7 \times 0.125 = 0.875$$

16. (F)—Math Appendix, #65: Translating from English into Algebra; and Math Appendix, #67: Solving a System of Equations

Translate:

"June has 20 marbles more than Billy." $J = B + 20$

"Maria has 3 times as many marbles as Billy." $M = 3B$

"Altogether they have 100 marbles." $J + M + B = 100$

We need B, the number of marbles Billy has.

Substitute the expressions in terms of B for J and M.

$$B + 20 + 3B + B = 100$$

Gather like terms. $5B + 20 = 100$

Subtract 20. $5B = 80$

Divide by 5. $B = 16$

So Billy has 16 marbles.

17. (B)—Math Appendix, #63: Solving a Linear Equation

Rather than graphing the equation, the quickest way to solve this is to substitute 6 for x in the equation, and to solve for y.

$$3x - 2y = 4$$

Substitute $x = 6$. $3(6) - 2y = 4$

Multiply out parentheses. $18 - 2y = 4$

Subtract 18 from both sides. $-2y = -14$

Divide both sides by −2. $y = \frac{-14}{-2}$

Simplify. $y = 7$

KAPLAN

18. (F)—Math Appendix, #79: Parallel Lines and Transversals

When a transversal cuts parallel lines, all acute angles formed are equal and all obtuse angles formed are equal. So here all obtuse angles have measure p and all acute angles measure q. The question says that "the measure of $\angle p$ is 20° less than three times the measure of $\angle q$." That is, $p = 3q - 20$. Also $p + q = 180$, since p and q are supplementary angles; that is, they form a straight line.
   Solve for q:

$$p + q = 180$$

Substitute $3q - 20$ for p. $3q - 20 + q = 180$
Gather like terms. $4q - 20 = 180$
Add 20 to both sides. $4q = 200$
Divide both sides by 4. $q = 50$
So $p = 3q - 20 = 3(50) - 20 = 150 - 20 = 130$
$$p - q = 130 - 50 = 80$$

(*Note*: By eyeballing you could have eliminated answer choices J and K as too large.)

19. (E)—Math Appendix, #67: Solving a System of Equations

Do not solve all the systems of equations—this would be too time consuming. Think about the problem first. The solution of a system of equations is the point these equations intersect—if the lines are parallel, they will not intersect, and there will be no solution. The lines that are parallel will have the same slope. The answer choices are all in the form $Ax + By = C$. You could find the slopes if the equations were in the slope-intercept form. This can be done by subtracting Ax from both sides, and dividing by B to get $y = -\frac{A}{B}x + \frac{C}{B}$, so here slope $= -\frac{\text{coefficient of } x}{\text{coefficient of } y} = -\frac{A}{B}$.

(A)   Slope of 1st equation $= -\frac{1}{3}$
Slope of 2nd equation $= -\frac{3}{-1} = -3$
The slopes are different—Discard.

(B)   Slope of 1st equation $= -\frac{1}{3}$
Slope of 2nd equation $= \frac{1}{3}$
The slopes are different—Discard.

(C)   Slope of 1st equation $= -\frac{1}{-3} = \frac{1}{3}$
Slope of 2nd equation $= -\frac{3}{-1} = 3$
The slopes are different—Discard.

(D)   Slope of 1st equation $= -\frac{1}{-3} = \frac{1}{3}$
Slope of 2nd equation $= -\frac{3}{1} = -3$
The slopes are different—Discard.

(E) Slope of 1st equation = $-\frac{1}{3}$
Slope of 2nd equation = $-\frac{3}{9} = -\frac{1}{3}$

Since these slopes are the same, there is no solution to this system of equations.

20. (J)—(Miscellaneous Line Segments)
Mark in the lengths:

The distance *LR* is the distance *LM* plus the distance *MR*.
The distance *MR* is 13.
The distance *LM* is the distance *LS* minus the distance *MS*. That is $50 - 38 = 12$.
Therefore $LR = 12 + 13 = 25$.
(*Note:* You could have discarded answer choice F straight away—*LR* must be longer than *MR*.)

21. (D)—Math Appendix, #32: Percent Formula

$133\frac{1}{3}\%$ is 4 times $33\frac{1}{3}\%$.

So, if $33\frac{1}{3}\% = 9$, then $133\frac{1}{3}\% = 4 \times 9 = 36$.

22. (G)—Math Appendix, #96: Sine, Cosine, and Tangent of Acute Angles—SOHCAHTOA

Since tan = $\frac{\text{opposite}}{\text{adjacent}}$, you need to know the lengths of the side opposite *x*, $\overline{DE}$, and the side adjacent to *x*, $\overline{FE}$.
Since $DE = 1$ and $DF = \sqrt{2}$, this must be an isosceles right triangle with sides in the ratio 1 : 1 : $\sqrt{2}$. (You could also show this by using the Pythagorean theorem.) So $DE = FE = 1$.

$$\tan x = \frac{\text{opposite}}{\text{adjacent}} = \frac{DE}{FE} = \frac{1}{1} = 1$$

23. (C)—Math Appendix, #75: Equation For a Circle
Draw a diagram:

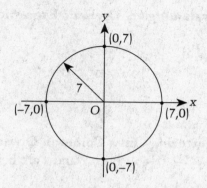

Obviously A and D lie on the circle—Eliminate these answer choices.

The formula for a circle is $(x - a)^2 + (y - b)^2 = r^2$, where a and b are the x- and y-coordinates of the center, and r is the radius. In this case the center is $(0, 0)$ and r is 7. Therefore the equation of this circle is $x^2 + y^2 = 49$, and any point that is not on the circle will not satisfy this equation.

(B) $(-3, 2\sqrt{10})$: $(-3)^2 + (2\sqrt{10})^2 = 9 + 40 = 49$—Discard.

(C) $(\sqrt{7}, 3)$: $(\sqrt{7})^2 + 3^2 = 7 + 9 = 16 \neq 49$—This point is not on the circle, and so C is correct.

24. (K)—(Miscellaneous Coordinate Geometry)

Point A is 4 units above the x-axis, so its y-coordinate is 4.

Point B is 3 units below the x-axis, so its y-coordinate is -3.

The product of the y-coordinates is $4 \times (-3) = -12$.

25. (D)—Math Appendix, #78: Intersecting Lines; and Math Appendix, #79: Parallel Lines and Transversals

Since y is greater than 90°, answer choices A and B can be eliminated by eyeballing.

Since the angle marked 46°, the right angle, and angle s make up a straight line, they sum to 180°. So $46 + 90 + s = 180$, or $s = 44$. Both s and t are acute angles formed by the same transversal, $\overline{AC}$, so t also has a measure of 44°.

Since y and t are supplementary, $y + t = 180$. That is $y = 180 - 44 = 136$.

26. (F)—Math Appendix, #52: Evaluating an Algebraic Expression

Plug in (-3) for s:

$$s^3 + 2s^2 + 2s = (-3)^3 + 2(-3)^2 + 2(-3)$$
$$= -27 + 2(9) + (-6)$$
$$= -27 + 18 - 6$$
$$= -15$$

27. (D)—Math Appendix, #58: Factoring Out a Common Divisor

Notice that in the expression $r(t + u) - s(t + u)$ both r and s are being multiplied by $t + u$. Factor this out to get $(r - s)(t + u)$.

If you didn't see this, you could have tried picking numbers. Let $r = 2$, $s = 3$, $t = 4$, and $u = 5$.

Then $r(t + u) - s(t + u) = 2(4 + 5) - 3(4 + 5) = 18 - 27 = -9$.

Any of the answer choices that does not give a value of -9 for these values of r, s, t, and u may be discarded.

(A) $(r + s)(t + u) = (2 + 3)(4 + 5) = (5)(9) = 45$—Discard.
(B) $(r - s)(t - u) = (2 - 3)(4 - 5) = (-1)(-1) = 1$—Discard.
(C) $(r + s)(t - u) = (2 + 3)(4 - 5) = (5)(-1) = -5$—Discard.
(D) $(r - s)(t + u) = (2 - 3)(4 + 5) = (-1)(9) = -9$—This may be correct.
(E) 0 —Discard.

So answer choice D is the only one that gives a value of -9 for the chosen values, and so it must be correct.

28. (F)—Math Appendix, #82: Similar Triangles; and Math Appendix, #83: Area of a Triangle

$\triangle ABC$ and $\triangle DBF$ are similar, since corresponding angles are of the same measure. Therefore their sides are proportional.

That is $\frac{AB}{BC} = \frac{DB}{BF}$, or $\frac{8}{6} = \frac{4}{BF}$, so $BF = 3$.

The area of a triangle is $\frac{1}{2}(\text{base} \times \text{height}) = \frac{1}{2}(3 \times 4) = 6$.

Note: You could have discarded answer choices J and K by logic—the area of the smaller triangle must be less than the area of the larger triangle, which is $\frac{1}{2}(6 \times 8) = 24$.

29. (A)—Math Appendix, #98: Trigonometric Functions of Other Angles
Consider the unit circle:

The cosine of any value is the *x*-coordinate when plotted on the unit circle, so cos 225° is the *x*-coordinate of *A*. Note that this point is below the *x*-axis, so the *x*-coordinate must be negative—eliminate answer choices D and E. Also notice that *x* is the length of the leg of the right triangle formed by dropping a line perpendicular to the *x*-axis from *A*. This is an isosceles right triangle, since it has interior angles of 45° and 90°. The ratio of side lengths in such a triangle is 1: 1:$\sqrt{2}$. Since the hypotenuse has a length of 1, the legs must have lengths of $\frac{1}{\sqrt{2}} = \frac{1}{\sqrt{2}} \times \frac{\sqrt{2}}{\sqrt{2}} = \frac{\sqrt{2}}{2}$. So cos 225° = $-\frac{\sqrt{2}}{2}$.

30. (G)—Math Appendix, #83: Area of a Triangle
The area of a triangle is $\frac{1}{2}$ (base $\times$ height). In this case the area is 45 square units, and the base is *XZ*, which is 3 + 12 = 15. The height is *YS*.

$$\text{So } 45 = \tfrac{1}{2}(15 \times YS)$$
$$45 \times 2 = 15 \times YS$$
$$90 \div 15 = YS$$
$$6 = YS$$

Since this diagram looks to be drawn to scale, you could also have eliminated answer choices J and K as too large, and answer choice F as too small.

31. (A)—Math Appendix, #89: Circumference of a Circle
The circumference of a circle is πd, where *d* is the diameter. Here the diameter is 10, so the circumference is 10π.

32. (K)—Math Appendix, #58: Factoring Out a Common Divisor

Rearrange the formula:

$$A = \pi rs + \pi r^2$$

Factor out π.
$$A = \pi(rs + r^2)$$
$$A = \pi(rs + rr)$$

Factor out an r.
$$A = \pi r(s + r)$$

Alternatively, pick numbers. Let $r = 2$ and $s = 3$. Then $A = \pi rs + \pi r^2 = \pi(2)(3) + \pi(2)^2 = 10\pi$

Any answer choice which does not give a result of 10π can be eliminated.

(F) $\quad A = 2\pi rs = 2\pi(2)(3) = 12\pi$—Discard.
(G) $\quad A = 2\pi r^2 s = 2\pi(2)^2(3) = 24\pi$—Discard.
(H) $\quad A = \pi r(1 + s) = \pi(2)(1+ 3) = 8\pi$—Discard.
(J) $\quad A = \pi r^2(1 + s) = \pi(2)^2(1 + 3) = 16\pi$—Discard.
(K) $\quad A = \pi r(r + s) = \pi(2)(2 + 3) = 10\pi$—This must be correct.

33. (B)—Math Appendix, #73: Using an Equation to Find the Slope

Get $5x + 3y = 13$ into the slope-intercept form, $y = mx + b$. Then m will be the slope.

$$5x + 3y = 13$$

Subtract $5x$. $\qquad 3y = -5x + 13$

Divide by 3. $\qquad y = -\frac{5}{3}x + \frac{13}{3}$

So $\qquad m = \text{slope} = -\frac{5}{3}$.

34. (G)—(Miscellaneous Number Properties)

Try to disprove the statements by picking numbers. Let $a = b = 1$. Then:

$$|a - b| + \sqrt{b - a} = |1 - 1| + \sqrt{1 - 1} = 0 + 0 = 0.$$ So if $a = b$, the answer is not always negative, so

discard answer choice J. Since 0 is neither positive nor negative, also discard H.

Try fractions. Let $a = \frac{1}{2}$ and $b = \frac{3}{4}$. Then $|a - b| + \sqrt{b - a} = |\frac{1}{2} - \frac{3}{4}| + \sqrt{\frac{3}{4} - \frac{1}{2}} = |-\frac{1}{4}| + \sqrt{\frac{1}{4}} = \frac{1}{4} +$

$\frac{1}{2} = \frac{3}{4}$. Now this is not equal to an integer, so discard answer choice F.

What if $a = -1$ and $b = -2$? Then $|a - b| + \sqrt{b - a} =$

$$|(-1) - (-2)| + \sqrt{(-2) - (-1)} = |1| + \sqrt{-1}$$

Now the square root of -1 is not real, so discard answer choice K. That leaves only answer choice G, which must then be correct.

35. (E)—Math Appendix, #66: Solving a Quadratic Equation

The quadratic formula states that the roots of an equation in the form $ax^2 + bx + c = 0$ are $\dfrac{-b \pm \sqrt{b^2 - 4ac}}{2a}$.

In this case $a = 1$, $b = -7$ and $c = 8$, so the roots are:

$$\frac{-(-7) \pm \sqrt{(-7)^2 - 4 \times 1 \times 8}}{2 \times 1} = \frac{7 \pm \sqrt{17}}{2} = \frac{7 + \sqrt{17}}{2} \text{ or } \frac{7 - \sqrt{17}}{2}$$

That is, answer choice E.

36. (G) Math Appendix, #85: Special Right Triangles
Draw a diagram:

The sides of the square are the legs of a right triangle. By the Pythagorean theorem:

$$\text{leg}_1{}^2 + \text{leg}_2{}^2 = \text{hypotenuse}^2$$
$$x^2 + x^2 = 20^2$$
$$2x^2 = 400$$
$$x^2 = 200$$
$$x = \sqrt{200}$$

Get the radical into the form of the answer choices:
$$x = \sqrt{200} = \sqrt{100} \times \sqrt{2} = 10\sqrt{2}$$

37. (C)—Math Appendix, #56: Multiplying Binomials—FOIL
$(3a - 4)(a + 2)$:

First	$3a \times a = 3a^2$
Outer	$3a \times 2 = 6a$
Inner	$-4 \times a = -4a$
Last	$-4 \times 2 = -8$

Combine: $3a^2 + 6a - 4a - 8 = 3a^2 + 2a - 8$

38. (K)—Math Appendix, #71: Finding the Distance Between Two Points
Draw a diagram:

The midpoint must be the same distance from A as from C. Since it is 6 units above point A it must be 6 units below point C; i.e., C must have a y-coordinate of 14.

39. (E)—Math Appendix, #65: Translating from English into Algebra
Translate into math.
The question says s represents the first number.
"The second number is 3 less than 4 times the first number," i.e., $4s - 3$
"The third number is 5 more than twice the first," i.e., $2s + 5$
The sum of all three numbers is then

$$s + 4s - 3 + 2s + 5 = 7s + 2$$

40. (H)—Math Appendix, #78: Intersecting Lines; Math Appendix, #80: Interior Angles of a Triangle; and Math Appendix, #81: Exterior Angles of a Triangle
Since $\angle SAB$ and $\angle BAC$ are supplementary, $\angle SAB + \angle BAC = 180°$. Since $\angle SAB = 130°$, $\angle BAC = 50°$. We now have two of the interior angles of $\triangle ABC$. Since the sum of the interior angles in a triangle is $180°$, $\angle BAC + \angle ABC + \angle ACB = 180°$. That is $50° + 80° + \angle ACB = 180°$. Therefore $\angle ACB = 50°$.

$\angle EDC$ is supplementary to $\angle QDC$. Since $\angle QDC = 110°$, $\angle EDC = 70°$. We now have two interior angles of $\triangle DEC$. The third is $\angle DEC$. Since the sum of the interior angles in a triangle is $180°$, $\angle DEC + \angle DCE + \angle EDC = 180°$. That is $\angle DEC + 50° + 70° = 180°$. Therefore $\angle DEC = 60°$.

41. (C)—Math Appendix, #33: Percent Increase and Decrease
Jack lost $200 - $170 = $30.

$$\text{Percent} = \frac{\text{Part}}{\text{Whole}} \times 100\%$$
$$= \frac{\$30}{\$200} \times 100\% = 15\%$$

42.—(J) Math Appendix, #98: Trigonometric Functions of Other Angles

Consider the unit circle:

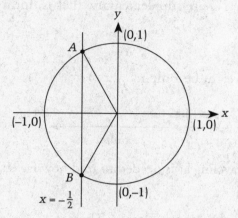

Cosine $x = -\frac{1}{2}$ for those values where $x = -\frac{1}{2}$ on the unit circle, in this case A and B. From the diagram, it can be seen that this occurs at $\frac{2\pi}{3}$ and $\frac{4\pi}{3}$.

43. (B)—Math Appendix, #66: Solving a Quadratic Equation

The fastest way to solve is by backsolving. Plug the answer choices into $5x^2 + 2x - 7$ and see which one equals 0:

(A) $5(-7)^2 + 2(-7) - 7 = 245 - 14 - 7 = 224$—Discard.

(B) $5(-\frac{7}{5})^2 + 2(-\frac{7}{5}) - 7 = 5(\frac{49}{25}) - \frac{14}{5} - 7$

$$= \frac{49}{5} - \frac{14}{5} - 7$$

$$= \frac{35}{5} - 7$$

$$= 0$$

This is the correct answer.

44. (J)—Math Appendix, #78: Intersecting Lines; Math Appendix, #79: Parallel Lines and Transversals; Math Appendix, #80: Interior Angles of a Triangle; and Math Appendix, #81: Exterior Angle of a Triangle

It might help to redraw the diagram, extending lines:

What you have is two parallel lines and two transversals. Since all acute angles formed by a transversal are the same size, $\angle PST = \angle TQR$. So ΔQRT has an interior angle of $65°(\angle TQR)$, and another of $35°(\angle QRT)$. Since the sum of interior angles in a triangle is $180°$, $\angle QTR = 180° - 65° - 35° = 80°$. Since $\angle QTR$ and $\angle PTQ$ are supplementary, that is, form a straight line, $\angle PTQ = 180° - \angle QTR = 180° - 80° = 100°$.

45. (C)—Math Appendix, #39: Rate
Let the rate that Ms. Rodriguez travels at be x mph.

The speed at which the cars were traveling at is needed to find how far either car traveled. Use the distance formula to find x :

$$\text{Distance} = \text{Rate} \times \text{Time}$$

In this case:

Distance = (Ms. Rodriguez's speed $\times$ 5 hours) + (Ms. Green's speed $\times$ 5 hours)
475 miles = (x mph $\times$ 5 hours) + [$(x + 15)$mph $\times$ 5 hours]
475 miles = $5x$ miles + $5x$ miles + 75 miles
400 miles = $10x$ miles
40 = x

So Ms. Rodriguez drives at 40 mph, and Ms. Green at 55 mph.
In 5 hours the faster car will travel 55 mph $\times$ 5 hours = 275 miles.

46. (G)—Math Appendix, #73: Using an Equation to Find the Slope; and Math Appendix, #74: Using an Equation to Find an Intercept
If the equation of a line is expressed in the form $y = mx + b$, then m is the slope and b is the y-intercept. From the graph it can be seen that the slope is negative, since y decreases as x increases (any line that rises as you move right has a positive slope; any that falls off as you go right has a negative slope). So m is negative. Also from the graph, it can be seen that the line crosses the y-axis above the x-axis—that is, the y-intercept is positive—so b, the y-intercept, is positive. The only answer choice that agrees with this is answer choice G.

47. (B)—Math Appendix, #68: Solving an Equation that Includes Absolute Value Signs
If $xy \neq 0$ then $x \neq 0$ and $y \neq 0$.

The square of any nonzero number is positive, so x^2 and y^2 are positive.
The larger the magnitude of any number, the larger the square of that number.

So if $|y| < |x|$, that means $y^2 < x^2$.
Since x^2 and y^2 are also both positive, and $x^2 > y^2$, the numerator of the fraction $\frac{x^2}{y^2}$ will be greater than the denominator; i.e., the entire fraction must be greater than 1.

KAPLAN

48. (J)—Math Appendix, #52: Evaluating an Algebraic Expression; and Math Appendix, #60: Factoring the Square of a Binomial

If you did not recognize the common quadratic $a^2 - 2ab + b^2 = (a - b)^2$, you could factor the expression $a^2 - 2ab + b^2$ using FOIL in reverse.

$a^2 - 2ab + b^2 = (a - b)(a - b) = (12)(12) = 144$

49. (E)—Math Appendix, #65: Translating From English Into Algebra; and Math Appendix, #80: Interior Angles of a Triangle

$\angle EDF = x$.

"$\angle DEF$ has a measure of 30° more than $\angle EDF$" means that $\angle DEF = x + 30$.

"$\angle EFD$ is 15° less than the sum of the measures of $\angle EDF$ and $\angle DEF$" means that

$\angle EFD = (x + x + 30) - 15 = 2x + 15$.

50. (H)—Math Appendix, #79: Parallel Lines and Transversals

When a transversal cuts parallel lines, all acute angles formed are equal and all obtuse angles formed are equal.

So $\angle ATR = \angle CRP = 110°$

Since $\angle ATQ$ and $\angle ATR$ form a straight line, their sum is 180°.

So $\angle ATQ + 110° = 180°$

$\angle ATQ = 70°$

51. (E)—Math Appendix, #99: Simplifying Trigonometric Expressions

Since $\sin^2\theta + \cos^2\theta = 1$, for all values of θ, and $x = \sin\theta$ and $y = \cos\theta$, then $x^2 + y^2 = 1$.

52. (K)—Math Appendix, #73: Using an Equation to Find the Slope; and Math Appendix, #74: Using an Equation to Find an Intercept

All answer choices are in the slope-intercept form, $y = mx + b$, where m is the slope and b is the y-intercept.

Line T has a y-intercept of –3, so in this case $b = -3$. Discard answer choices F, H, and J.

Since T is parallel to $3x - 5y = 4$, they have the same slope. Find the slope of $3x - 5y = 4$:

$$3x - 5y = 4$$
$$-5y = -3x + 4$$
$$y = \frac{3}{5}x - \frac{4}{5}$$

So the slope is $\frac{3}{5}$ and line T has equation $y = \frac{3}{5}x - 3$.

53. (D)—Math Appendix, #5: Adding/Subtracting Signed Numbers

Simply count the number of spaces between A and B on the number line. If the distance is too great to count, in general the distance between any two points, A and B, is $|A - B|$.

54. (F)—Math Appendix, #71: Finding the Distance Between Two Points

As can be seen from the diagram above, the shortest distance between C and line m is segment $\overline{CD}$. Since $\overline{CD}$ is parallel to the y-axis, the length of $\overline{CD}$ is the difference between the y-coordinates of D and C. Since line m is parallel to the x-axis, and passes through point $(0, 5)$, all points on line m have a y-coordinate of 5. Since C has a y-coordinate of 3, the distance CD is $5 - 3$, or 2.

55. (E)—Math Appendix, #69: Solving an Inequality
Rearrange the inequality:

$$-2 - 4x \leq -6x$$

Add 2 to both sides.	$-4x \leq -6x + 2$
Add $6x$ to both sides.	$2x \leq 2$
Divide both sides by 2.	$x \leq 1$

56. (H)—Math Appendix, #87: Areas of Special Quadrilaterals
The figure is a rectangle with two smaller rectangles cut out of it. The total area is the area of the large rectangle minus the area of the cutouts.

The area of any rectangle is length $\times$ width.
The area of the large rectangle = $8 \times 10 = 80$.
The area of the top cutout rectangle = $3 \times 4 = 12$.
The area of the bottom cutout rectangle = $3 \times 2 = 6$.
Total area = $80 - 12 - 6 = 62$.

57. (D)—(Miscellaneous Quadrilaterals and Circles)

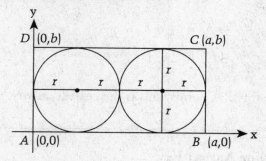

As can be seen from the above diagram, a is the distance between A and B, that is, the length of the rectangle $ABCD$. This is equal to $4r$.

Similarly, b is the distance between A and D, that is, $2r$.

So $a - b = 4r - 2r = 2r$.

58. (H)—Math Appendix, #32: Percent Formula

Find the number of teenagers in each age group:

"20 teenagers are 15 years old"—20, 15-year-olds

"8 teenagers are 18 years old"—8, 18-year-olds

"20% are 14 years old"—20% of 60 = $\frac{1}{5} \times 60 = 12$—12, 14-year-olds

"There are twice as many 16-year-olds as 18-year-olds"—There are 8, 18-year-olds, so there are 2 $\times$ 8 = 16, 16-year-olds

Since there are 60 teenagers total, the remainder are 17 years old.

$60 - 20 - 8 - 12 - 16 = 4$, 17-year-olds.

There is a total of $4 + 8 = 12$, 17- and 18-year-olds.

Since Percent = $\frac{\text{Part}}{\text{Whole}} \times 100\%$, in this case Percent = $\frac{12}{60} \times 100\% = 20\%$.

59. (B)—Math Appendix, #46: Probability

Probability of an event occurring = $\frac{\text{Number of favorable outcomes}}{\text{Number of possible outcomes}}$

In this case, a favorable outcome is not picking a blue T-shirt. Since 7 T-shirts are not blue, the number of favorable outcomes is 7.

The number of outcomes is the total number of t-shirts that could be picked, that is, 5 + 7, or 12.

So the probability of not picking a blue T-shirt = $\frac{7}{12}$.

60. (F)—Math Appendix, #77: Equation for an Ellipse

The correct equation will be true for all the points on the ellipse. Four points are given in the diagram. Run them through the equations in the answer choices; if the equation is not true for any one of these points, it may be discarded.

(F) Try $(0, 2)$; $\frac{x^2}{25} + \frac{y^2}{4} = \frac{0^2}{25} + \frac{2^2}{4} = \frac{4}{4} = 1$

Now try (5, 0); $\frac{x^2}{25} + \frac{y^2}{4} = \frac{5^2}{25} + \frac{0^2}{4} = \frac{25}{25} = 1$

Now try (–5, 0); $\frac{x^2}{25} + \frac{y^2}{4} = \frac{(-5)^2}{25} + \frac{0^2}{4} = \frac{25}{25} = 1$

Now try (0, –2); $\frac{x^2}{25} + \frac{y^2}{4} = \frac{0^2}{25} + \frac{(-2)^2}{4} = \frac{4}{4} = 1$

Since the equation is true for all 4 points, this is the correct answer.

Reading Answer Key

1. D	11. C	21. A	31. D
2. F	12. G	22. J	32. J
3. B	13. B	23. D	33. D
4. H	14. H	24. G	34. G
5. D	15. C	25. B	35. A
6. G	16. H	26. H	36. H
7. A	17. B	27. D	37. A
8. H	18. F	28. H	38. F
9. B	19. A	29. D	39. C
10. F	20. J	30. F	40. J

PASSAGE I

Prose Fiction

This is a Prose Fiction passage, so remember to ask yourself the three important questions:

- *Who are these people?*

  George Webber is a young writer who has just heard that his novel has been accepted for publication.

- *What is their state of mind?*

  George is feeling many things at once: happiness about having a novel accepted for publication; fear that parts of the novel might offend some people; eagerness to see a chapter of his novel published in a magazine; dread at the prospect of writing a second novel; and disappointment when people did not react to his writing in the way he had expected.

- *What's going on?*

  George is going through some very mixed feelings. Although he is extremely excited about realizing his dream of becoming a writer, at the same time he's realizing that what is so momentous to him—the publication of his novel—is not really all that important to the rest of the world.

1. (D)—Inference Question

Remember to check back to the passage to make sure that your answer works in context. Lines 38–41 explain that George was concerned that "some people might recognize themselves and be offended." This is what made him think he might have "to go around in smoked glasses and false whiskers."

2. (F)—Detail Question

The sixth paragraph (lines 63–75) discusses George's feelings about writing his next novel. Lines 67–68 state that writing for him is "like a demoniacal possession, driving him with alien force much greater than his own." This idea is paraphrased by choice F.

3. (B)—Inference Question

The paragraph (lines 63–75) preceding the quote by George Webber to Foxhall Edwards explains the difficult, tortuous process that George goes through in writing. George probably sensed that his agony and fatigue would be obvious to Fox and others, but he knew that without this agony he would not be able to do good work. Line 65 especially shows that George knew that the act of writing would be painful—he would "get it out of him." Therefore, choice B best describes George's reason for offering the quote in question.

4. (H)—Inference Question

George "expected convulsions of the earth" (line 80) when his story was published. He had worried that "people might recognize themselves and be offended" (lines 38–39). Instead, "nothing happened. A few of his friends mentioned it, but that was all" (lines 82–83). No one was offended. For all the worrying and wondering that George did, the contrast between this calm public response and the anticipated response could be best characterized as "ironic."

5. (D)—Detail Question

Lines 59–62 discuss the very positive impact that Fox had on George. The text says that "the editor's faith and confidence, coming as it had come at a time when George had given up all hope, restored his self-respect and charged him with energy for new work." This idea is best summarized by choice D.

6. (G)—Detail Question

The last paragraph (lines 79–89) describes what happened when *Rodney's Magazine* came out with George's story. After an initial letdown (lines 83–84), George decided that "people couldn't really tell much about a new author from a short piece in a magazine. . . . He could afford to wait a little longer for the fame which he was certain would soon be his" (lines 85–89). Therefore, choice G best answers the question.

7. (A)—Detail Question

"Fame, at last, was knocking at his door and wooing him with her sweet blandishments" (lines 16–17). Typically, a suitor *woos* the object of his desire with gifts. In the previous paragraph we learned that George had just received a check for $500 as "an advance against his royalties" (lines 13–14) on a book he had written. This money could be considered fame's gift. The word *courting* in choice A best captures this concept of *wooing*.

8. (H)—Inference Question

The source of George's trembling (line 31) is explained in subsequent sentences. "He loathed the thought of giving pain to anyone. . . . But...some people might recognize themselves and be offended" (lines 33–39).

9. (B)—Inference Question

To select the correct choice for this difficult question, you must analyze George's behavior. George is very proud of his work. This can be inferred from several parts of the passage. Lines 29–30 are worded to convey his pride of authorship when they say, "He had distilled every line of it out of his own experiences of life." His extremely high (and unrealistic) expectations about the effect of having his story published in *Rodney's Magazine* (lines 79–82) also convey George's belief that his work was very important. George did have concerns, though. The fourth paragraph (lines 26–44) discusses his worry that his fictional characterizations might offend the real people on which they were based. This pride mixed with concern is expressed in choice B.

10. (F)—Inference Question

When George is described early in this passage, the word *dazed* is used (in line 6). In lines 2–3 the reader learns that George has come "to his senses somewhere in the wilds of the Upper Bronx." In lines 12–14 the reader learns that the paper George was happily looking at earlier is a $500 royalty check. Therefore, you can infer that George has been wandering around dazed after learning that his book has been accepted for publication—choice F. Choice J might have been tempting, but it's the fact that his book will be published, not the money he'll earn from it, that makes George dazed and happy.

PASSAGE II

Humanities

This rather confusing passage deals with the connection between two "grand ideas": human self-fulfillment and freedom. Here's a road map to the passage:

- The **first and second paragraphs** provide some historical perspective about the ideal of human self-fulfillment.

- The **third paragraph** explains what the authors have in mind when they speak of human self-fulfillment.

- The **fourth paragraph** mentions that self-fulfillment has led to scientific and technical progress, which, in turn, has made individual self-fulfillment easier.

- The **fifth paragraph** discusses one thinker, Calvin, who did not believe in human self-fulfillment, and the consequences of this attitude.

- The **sixth and seventh paragraphs** tie together the ideals of human self-fulfillment and freedom, saying that the former is not possible without the latter, and introduces some historical examples to support this thesis.

- Finally, the **eighth paragraph** mentions some thinkers who distorted the idea of freedom, and the importance of freedom of thought and speech.

11. (C)—Big Picture Question
The passage talks about self-fulfillment and freedom and what these great ideas have inspired. Paragraph five (lines 47–56) begins with the sentence: "Only rarely has a thinker...gone back from the ideal of human potential and fulfillment." The next sentence, which introduces Calvin, says "Calvin was perhaps such a thinker who went back and believed. . . . that man [is]. . . . incapable of any worthwhile development" (lines 49–52). Calvin, therefore, is a counterexample offered to show that not everyone over the past five hundred years has believed in the ideals of self-fulfillment and human potential.

12. (G)—Detail Question
Reread the lines surrounding the word *elucidated* in line 24 to get its meaning. Lines 25–27 say "aesthetic and ethical gifts, we feel and struggle to express in our own minds." Lines 27–28 say "cultural gifts, are unfolded for us by the study of history." Considering this, "revealed," choice G, best captures this idea of unfolding and struggling to express gifts.

13. (B)—Big Picture Question
Lines 58–60 explain that "human fulfillment is unattainable without freedom, so that these two main ideas are linked together." The sixth paragraph begins talking about freedom by describing it as "the second of the two grand formative ideas." This follows the first five paragraphs which discuss fulfillment. This information supports B as the correct answer.

14. (H)—Detail Question
Lines 40–42 explain that, "The purpose and the effect [of devices and gadgets] has been to liberate men from the exhausting drudgeries of earning their living." Choice H best paraphrases these ideas.

15. (C)—Inference Question
Lines 45–46 indicate that, before the development of all sorts of work-saving devices and gadgets, princes alone had the "leisure to find the best in themselves."

16. (H)—Inference Question

In lines 79–82 Bronowski and Mazlish explain that "freedom . . . advocates can at times delude themselves that obedience to tyranny is a form of freedom." Therefore, the author's ideas are best expressed by choice H.

17. (B)—Big Picture Question

You can find the answer to this question by a process of elimination (remember, you're looking for the choice that the authors would *reject*). Choice A is supported by the discussion in paragraph four (lines 32–46): People are able to find the best in themselves when they have more leisure time. Choice C is supported by paragraph one (lines 1–12): The authors mention various people in diverse professions in various eras who have all praised the development of the individual. Choice D is supported in lines 54–55, where the authors contend that men develop by having something in them "which is personal and creative." This leaves choice B—nowhere in the text do the authors say or imply that "self-fulfillment is a praiseworthy but unreachable goal." Indeed the authors seem to believe that self-fulfillment is possible.

18. (F)—Big Picture Question

Lines 58–59 say that freedom is necessary for human fulfillment. Lines 32–33 talk about self-fulfillment inspiring progress. The final paragraph talks about the importance of freedom of thought and speech. Thus, the authors would undoubtedly contend that freedom is necessary for a society to make progress.

19. (A)—Detail Question

Lines 79–83 talk about the delusion that "ensnared" Luther, Rousseau, Hegel, and Marx. According to the authors, all of them confused freedom with obedience to tyranny. Choice A, therefore, is the answer.

20. (J)—Big Picture Question

The authors make it clear throughout the passage that they feel freedom is a valuable ideal. In the seventh paragraph, they suggest that revolutions have often made societies more free. Considering this, choice J is the best answer.

PASSAGE III

Social Studies

This well-organized passage is about Mussolini's rise to power in postwar Italy. A road map:

- The **first two paragraphs** discuss the territorial and economic problems that set the stage for Mussolini's rise to power.

- The **third paragraph** outlines the events that resulted in Mussolini's dictatorship.

- The **fourth and fifth paragraphs** explore Mussolini's economic and political philosophy.

21. (A)—Detail Question
Lines 5–9 talk about the lands that Italy obtained and hoped to obtain as it emerged from World War I. The author explains that in spite of being given land in Austria-Hungary, the Italians were disappointed not to be awarded "further acquisitions east of the Adriatic and in Asia and Africa." "Grandiose ambitions," therefore, refers to the desire for more land.

22. (J)—Big Picture Question
There is evidence in this passage to support all three of the statements. Lines 25–28 explain the reaction of landlords, factory owners, small businesses and professional people to the economic unrest in Italy following the war—they "longed for vigorous leadership and a strong government." In other words, they desired the stability that Mussolini's regime seemed to offer, as statement I suggests. Statement II also contributed to Mussolini's rise to power. Line 50 explains that he seized "control of the faction-paralyzed government" in Rome. Statement III also was important. Lines 44–46 explain that Mussolini's veterans terrorized "the leaderless radical workers and their liberal supporters." The answer is choice J which states that Statements I, II, and III were all important factors in Mussolini's rise to power.

23. (D)—Big Picture Question
The authors describe the rise of fascism in paragraphs 1 through 3. Paragraph 1 explains how the peace settlements following World War I resulted in "severe blows to Italian national pride" because Italy was awarded less land than it hoped for. This is discussed as the first of many problems that laid the groundwork for a new nationalistic, fascist leader like Mussolini to rise to power. So the way that the passage supports the theory (that fascism arises after periods of diminished national pride) is best stated by choice D.

24. (G)—Inference Question
From the text it seems that Mussolini had organized unemployed veterans into a political action group (lines 36–39) before the end of the labor disturbances in 1921. Mussolini eventually sent his veterans to beat up the radical workers and their supporters (lines 42–46) in an effort to get the support of the capitalists and the landlords (lines 41–42). However, he waited to do so until it became clear that the workers would lose (lines 39–41). The reason he waited to commit his group of veterans was that he wanted to join up with the side that would ultimately be victorious. This certainly sounds opportunistic to us.

25. (B)—Inference Question
The correct answer should convey the idea that Mussolini had absolute power over the citizens of Italy. Choice B—abolishing all non-Fascist unions—is the only choice that conveys Mussolini's control over the lives of individuals.

26. (H)—Inference Question
Lines 79–84 describe the role of nationalism in Mussolini's Italy. The authors explain that Mussolini used the "energizing quality" of militant nationalism for political purposes—to attract support for his new regime. Choice H paraphrases this idea best.

27. (D)—Inference Question
One aspect of Mussolini's rise that comes across in paragraphs 2 through 4 is his hard-line policy towards labor. Lines 18–19 indicate that Italian workers were conducting sit-down factory strikes in 1920. By 1926 these workers were forbidden to strike and were subject to compulsory arbitration (lines 65–68). Choice D best states this crackdown on workers' rights.

28. (H)—Inference Question
The fourth paragraph (lines 61–78) talks about Italy's economic life under Mussolini's corporate state. Lines 75–78 describe the economic effects of Mussolini's policies—even though he balanced Italy's budget and stabilized its currency, taxes reached record levels, leading to a decline in per capita income. Choice H is the correct answer here—excessively high taxation disrupted economic rebuilding.

29. (D)—Detail Question
Lines 68–70 describe the corporate state as a "planned economy [that] was set up to modernize, coordinate, and increase Italy's production of both industrial and agricultural goods." Choice D best paraphrases this information.

30. (F)—Inference Question
In the final paragraph in lines 80–81 the authors contend that fascism was nationalism "run wild." The subsequent quotes are intended to provide an illustration of those nationalistic ideas.

PASSAGE IV

Natural Sciences
The title of this wide-ranging passage could be: "Everything You Ever Wanted to Know About Tornadoes." Or perhaps "Everything You Never Wanted to Know About Tornadoes." In any case, it's all here:

- The **first paragraph** mentions the destructive power of tornado winds.

- The **second, third, fourth, and fifth paragraphs** talk about the formation, structure, and physical appearance of tornadoes.

- The **sixth paragraph** discusses where tornadoes are most likely to form, in a place called (appropriately enough) "tornado alley."

- The **seventh and eighth paragraphs** explain when and under what conditions tornadoes are likely to emerge.

- The **ninth paragraph** talks about the unpredictable movements of tornadoes and why this makes them difficult to track and study.

31. (D)—Detail Question
The term *vortexes of air* appears in line 10. The text immediately following the use of this term dis-

cusses the rotation of tornadoes, mentioning that air streams into the base and then spirals upward (lines 11–18).

32. (J)—Detail Question
Lines 5–7 explain that the wind speeds of tornadoes have been determined "based [in part] on analysis of motion pictures."

33. (D)—Inference Question
Tornado rotation is discussed in lines 11–13. The direction of rotation is based on the hemisphere in which the tornado occurs.

34. (G)—Inference Question
Lines 79–81 in the last paragraph describe "the unpredictable nature of tornadoes, which often hop about from place to place." Since scientists operate the TOTO device by placing it "in the path of the tornado," you can infer that the unpredictable movements of tornadoes might make TOTO hard to use.

35. (A)—Detail Question
Paragraphs seven and eight (lines 58–73) discuss the conditions required for tornadoes to form. Lines 64–65 explain the need for strong updrafts. Lines 66–69 explain the effect of wind shear on the initiation of tornado rotation. These two factors are listed in choice A.

36. (H)—Detail Question
Lines 67–69 explain what happens during wind shear—"wind speed increases with height and veers from southeast to west." Choice H accurately rewords this information.

37. (A)—Inference Question
Paragraphs seven and eight (lines 58–73) discuss the factors that determine the formation of tornadoes. These factors are based on weather conditions in the sky. You can infer from this information that it would be possible to predict the formation of tornadoes if these atmospheric conditions were known.

38. (F)—Detail Question
This question requires a careful reading of the text. At the end of paragraph three, the author describes the formation of funnel clouds—we're told that a pressure drop in the core of the cloud causes air to flow in, where it hits an area of lower pressure, and causes water vapor to condense into droplets. The term *condensation cloud* is never used to describe a funnel cloud in paragraph three. However, the terms are synonymous. This becomes clear when you read the beginning of paragraph four: "Sometimes, no condensation cloud forms" (line 31). So correct choice F accurately describes the formation of condensation clouds.

39. (C)—Big Picture Question
Paragraph three (lines 23–30) begins "The vortex frequently becomes visible" (line 23). Paragraph

four begins "Sometimes . . . the only way a tornado can reveal itself" (lines 31–32). So both paragraphs address what makes a tornado visible. The answer is Choice C.

40. (J)—Big Picture Question
Line 74 states that tornadoes "are steered by the jet stream." Choice J is the answer. Based on information in the passage choices F, G, and H are not true of *all* tornadoes.

Science Reasoning Answer Key

1. A	11. C	21. B	31. C
2. G	12. F	22. J	32. F
3. C	13. B	23. A	33. D
4. G	14. G	24. J	34. F
5. D	15. A	25. C	35. B
6. J	16. J	26. G	36. J
7. A	17. C	27. D	37. C
8. H	18. F	28. F	38. F
9. D	19. B	29. B	39. D
10. F	20. F	30. G	40. G

PASSAGE I

The first passage mostly requires an ability to read the two given graphs, each of which traces the rate of decay in a different radioactive isotope. The y-axis of each graph represents the proportion of remaining (undecayed) nuclei to original nuclei, while the x-axis of each represents time. Notice, though, that the first graph runs from 0 days to just 6 days, while the second graph runs from 0 days to 180 days. That's a big difference, indicating that the second isotope—$_{39}Y^{91}$—decays at a much slower rate.

1. (A)
In the introduction to the passage, the "half-life" of an isotope is defined as the amount of time needed for one-half of the initial number of nuclei to decay. To figure out the half-life of $_{39}Y^{90}$, look at the first graph. When half of the nuclei have decayed, the N/N_0 ratio would be .5 (since there'd be half as many nuclei after the half-life as there were originally). Draw a horizontal line across the graph at the level of .5. The horizontal line will intersect the curve at a specific point; from this point, draw a vertical line down to the x-axis. The vertical line intersects the x-axis somewhere between 2.5 and 3 days, which means that the amount of time it takes for half of the nuclei to decay is between 2.5 and 3 days. Choice A is the only answer that falls in this range.

2. (G)

Since N_0 is the same for both samples, you can use the two graphs to figure out the ratio of $_{39}Y^{90}$ to $_{39}Y^{91}$ after 2.7 days. You know from having done the previous question that after 2.7 days about .5 of $_{39}Y^{90}$ still remains. Take a look at the graph for $_{39}Y^{91}$: After 2.7 days, hardly any will have decayed at all. Therefore, the ratio of $_{39}Y^{90}$ to $_{39}Y^{91}$ will be .5 to 1, or 1 to 2 (G).

3. (C)

This is a rather strange, convoluted question, but what it means is that one isotope ($_{39}Y^{90}$) will accumulate in the gastrointestinal tract while the other ($_{39}Y^{91}$) will accumulate in the bones. Since none of the isotopes leave the bones or the gastrointestinal tract as a result of processes that normally occur in the human body, you can use the values for the half-lives given in the graphs. So after three days, a little over half of the original $_{39}Y^{90}$ will be left (in the gastrointestinal tract), but just about all of the $_{39}Y^{91}$ will be left (in the bones). With this information in hand, you just have to examine the choices. Choice A is incorrect because $_{39}Y^{91}$ accumulates in the bones, not the gastrointestinal tract. Choice B is incorrect since $_{39}Y^{90}$ accumulates in the gastrointestinal tract, not in the bones. Choice C is correct because, as we said, about half of the nuclei of $_{39}Y^{90}$ decay after 3 days, so about half of the inhaled amount will be in the gastrointestinal tract after 3 days. Choice D is out because after 3 days, almost all of the $_{39}Y^{91}$ will be left in the bones.

4. (G)

After one half-life has passed, half of the original 1,000 nuclei will have decayed, leaving 500. After the second half-life has passed, half of the 500 will be gone, leaving 250. When the third half-life has passed, half of the 250 will have decayed, leaving 125, choice G.

5. (D)

Statement I is true: $_{39}Y^{90}$ is less stable than $_{39}Y^{91}$ because $_{39}Y^{90}$ decays more rapidly (remember that the x-axes are scaled differently). This rules out choice B. Statement II is wrong because a very small fraction (much less than a quarter) of $_{39}Y^{90}$ would remain after 116 days. Choice C can thus also be eliminated. Statement III is obviously true, given the fact that they decay in this manner, making D the correct answer.

PASSAGE II

This passage involves three tennis-training experiments, the results of each being summarized in a table. Remember to look for patterns in the data. Notice, for instance, that in Table 1 the greatest increases in serving speed were obtained when right-handed players watched a right-handed coach and when left-handed players watched a left-handed coach. Similarly, in Table 2, coach guidance caused higher increases in *both* serving speed and serving accuracy. This kind of observation about the data should help you to formulate theories (e.g., that training is more effective when the coach uses the same hand as the player).

6. (J)
In Experiment 1, left-handed video watchers watching a left-handed coach improved their service speed by 8 mph. Since right-handed players in Experiment 3 (the one asked about here) improved even more with a combination of videos and physical instruction than with videos alone, lefties will probably improve at least as much in Experiment 3 as they did in Experiment 1, making choice J the right answer.

7. (A)
Choice A is the only conclusion that cannot be supported by the data of Experiment 1. Imitating someone with opposite handedness does not always cause a deterioration of skills: Right-handed players actually improved somewhat when they watched videos of left-handed coaches.

8. (H)
Experiment 2 was designed to determine whether right-handed players improve more with videos alone or with videos and physical guidance combined. The players given a combination of videos and guidance clearly showed greater improvement in both service speed and service accuracy as compared to those who just used videos. This supports the hypothesis (choice H) that physical guidance by a coach improves both speed and accuracy of service for right-handed players. (Note: There is nothing in Experiment 2 to support any conclusion whatsoever about left-handed players, since none were involved in the experiment.)

9. (D)
In Experiments 1 and 2, right-handed players who watched a right-handed coach on video improved 5 mph in speed. According to Experiment 2, right-handed players who watched videos and received physical guidance improved by 9 mph (4 mph more than with videos alone). Guidance appears to further improve service speed. Since left-handers improve by 8 mph with videos alone (Experiment 1), adding physical guidance to their training should make their overall improvement in service speed greater than 8 mph. The only choice greater than 8 mph is D.

10. (F)
Experiment 1 investigated the effect of watching videos of left- or right-handed coaches on the service speed of left- or right-handed players. The results support the conclusion in choice F. Players watching videos of coaches with the same handedness improved their speeds by 5 mph (righties) and 8 mph (lefties), whereas players watching videos of coaches with the opposite handedness improved their speed only a little (2 mph for righties) or not at all (for lefties). Tennis players seem to improve less when observing coaches whose handedness is opposite to their own.

11. (C)
Choice C is the best procedure to determine the effects of verbal instruction on average service speed because it measures he amount of improvement that is due solely to verbal instruction. In

addition, all of the players receive the exact same verbal instruction, since the instructions have been recorded (personal verbal instruction may vary considerably). Choice A's procedure is not optimal because Experiment 3 involves the factors of videos and physical guidance as well as verbal instruction. Choice B's procedure involves physical guidance so it is also not ideal. Choice D's procedure does not measure the players' service speed before instruction, so there is no way to gauge improvement.

PASSAGE III

This passage hinges on the Hertzsprung-Russell diagram, which plots individual stars in terms of their absolute magnitude (brightness, in other words) on the y-axis, and their spectral class (which is a measure of color/temperature) on the x-axis. What does this mean? It means that stars that are high on the chart are brighter than those that are low on the chart (because the greater the number for absolute magnitude, the dimmer the star). It also means that stars that are on the right side of the chart (which most of them are) are M class (i.e., the reddest and coolest), while those toward the left side of the chart are the bluest and warmest.

12. (F)
Nearly all of the stars on the diagram fall in the spectral class M, so choice F is correct.

13. (B)
The text explains that the spectral classes of stars on the diagram go from warmest on the left (O) to coolest on the right (M). Therefore, any stars in a spectral class to the left of G, the Sun's spectral class, are warmer than the Sun. Of the three named stars, only two are in a spectral class to the left of G: Sirius and Altair.

14. (G)
Most of the stars on the diagram fall below the absolute magnitude of 6; that is, they would not be visible to the naked eye from a distance of 10 parsecs. (Remember that 1.0 is the maximum brightness and that stars with absolute magnitudes of 15.0 to 17. 0 are very dim.)

15. (A)
A quick review: Moving across the spectral classes from left to right, the stars go from warm to cool and from blue to red. Statement I is correct because α-Centauri is in a spectral class to the right of Sirius' spectral class. This means that you can eliminate choices B and D, which do not contain Statement I. Statement II is incorrect because the Sun is to the right of Altair on the diagram, indicating that the Sun is cooler. This eliminates choice C. Choice A is the correct answer, and you don't even have to look at Statement III (though if you do, you'll find that it's incorrect, since the Sun is lower on the diagram than is Procyon.)

16. (J)
It's impossible to know what the diagram of stars within 10 parsecs of the Sun would look like, even though you have the graph of the stars within 5 parsecs of the sun in front of you. It may be

tempting to assume that by doubling the distance the number of stars would be doubled as well (F). However, when you double the distance from the Sun, you more than double the volume of space; there may be, for all you know, many more than double the original number of stars on the new diagram. There is similarly no basis on which to judge the absolute magnitude or the spectral class of the additional stars (G and H).

PASSAGE IV

This passage is based around three different experiments, all designed to determine what conditions favor Product A and what conditions favor Product B when a particular cobalt complex reacts with sodium nitrite. Remember to note the differences in the procedures of the three experiments. Experiment 2 differs from Experiment 1 in that the solutions were heated after $NaNO_2$ was added. Experiment 3 differs from Experiment 1 in that after $NaNO_2$ was added, citrate ion was added and the solutions were heated.

17. (C)

To answer this question, look at the conditions in which Product B was formed. Solution 1 in Experiment 1 and Solution 1 in Experiment 2 both yielded Product B. These solutions were both acidic, so the correct answer must be either choice B or choice C. The next step is to determine whether Product B was formed when citrate ion was added. The results of Experiment 3 show that there is no yield of Product B with added citrate ion, so choice C is the correct answer.

18. (F)

Choice F is the conclusion that is not supported by the experimental results. As you know from the previous question, Product B is not formed when citrate ion is added to the solution. Since it does form in the same solution if no citrate ion is added (Experiment 2), the presence of citrate ion does indeed affect the formation of Product B. All of the other choices are legitimate conclusions based on the experimental data.

19. (B)

Varying the pH (choice B) may well show that different degrees of acidity or basicity will have a marked impact on product formation. Heating the solutions has been tried already, and freezing the solutions should stop the reactions altogether. Varying the concentration, meanwhile, won't alter the ability of the known compound to react.

20. (F)

When you're answering a question that's based on only part of the data, make sure that the answer you choose is based only on the relevant data. In Experiment 2, it was found that when the solutions were heated to 110°C, both Product A and Product B were formed. Therefore, choice F is supported by the results of Experiment 2. All of the other choices are hypotheses that could only be supported or refuted using the results of Experiments 1 and 3 along with the results of Experiment 2.

21. (B)

This question asks you to identify the condition or conditions that are held constant through all three experiments. The temperature was varied, ruling out choice A, and the amount of citrate ion was not the same in all three experiments, so you can eliminate choices C and D. Only choice B remains. You are never told the specific quantity of cobalt complex used, but you can assume it was the same in all three experiments since the solutions of Experiments 2 and 3 were prepared just as they were in Experiment 1.

22. (J)

The fact that Product B is formed in Solution 1 when heated but is not formed when citrate ion is added prior to heating (J) is evidence to support the hypothesis that Product B may react to form other more readily dissolved compounds in the presence of certain ions. None of the other choices involves the presence of any type of ion.

PASSAGE V

This is the conflicting viewpoints passage; the viewpoints that are in question are different suggested classifications for the giant panda—as a raccoon or as a bear. Examine the scientists' positions carefully. Scientist 1 votes for a raccoon classification, citing as evidence anatomical similarities, comparable size among males and females, similar noises and eye-covering behavior, and certain chromosomal similarities. Scientist 2 votes for a bear classification, citing evidence such as DNA similarities, similar body proportions, and aggressive behavior.

23. (A)

In this question you are asked to determine which of the four choices would provide additional support for the viewpoint expressed by Scientist 2. Similarities between the blood proteins of giant pandas and several bear species (A) would certainly indicate that pandas should be classified as bears, which is Scientist 2's viewpoint. Watch out for choices that support the other position in questions like this: Choices B and D, for instance, are wrong because they support Scientist 1's argument that pandas should be classified as raccoons, not bears. Choice C, meanwhile, is inconclusive.

24. (J)

Both scientists make their arguments by comparing the physical, behavioral, and genetic characteristics of the giant panda to the characteristics of either the bear or the raccoon family. They would definitely agree that animals should be classified into families based on these criteria.

25. (C)

Let's take a look at the statements. You know from Scientist 1's statement that Ursidae (bears) have 36 pairs of chromosomes, so Statement I would support the classification of the mammal as a bear. This narrows the possible choices down to A and C. You also know from Scientist 1 that male bears can be twice the size of female bears, whereas male and female raccoons are the same size. Statement III, therefore, also supports the classification of the mammal as a bear. Choice C is the right choice, and you don't even have to look at Statement II (which would would argue *against* a classification as a bear).

26. (G)

Scientist 1 explains that both raccoons and pandas cover their eyes with their front paws whenever intimidated.

27. (D)

Scientist 2 mentions that research has shown that the giant panda's DNA is far more similar to a bear's DNA than to that of any other family. Choice D paraphrases this idea.

28. (F)

If giant pandas and raccoons both had glandular scent areas, this would be evidence to support the viewpoint of Scientist 1, who thinks that giant pandas should be classified as raccoons.

29. (B)

Scientist 2 contends that giant pandas display the same aggressive behavior as bears do: They swat and try to grab adversaries with their forepaws. The only choice that is a counter argument to this claim is B: An aggressive panda's behavior is like a raccoon's behavior, not a bear's, in that the panda bobs its head up and down like a raccoon.

PASSAGE VI

This passage consists almost exclusively of a complex bar graph recording primary energy sources at various times in history—namely, 1850, 1900, 1950, and 1985. Notice the changing proportions. Fuel wood, which was an extremely important source of energy in 1850, virtually disappeared by 1950 and 1985. Petroleum, on the other hand, which barely registers on the 1900 graph (and not at all on the 1850 graph) has by 1985 become the dominant source of energy. One reasonable conclusion to be drawn from these data trends? As technology changes over time, the fuels of choice seem to change as well.

30. (G)

Petroleum first appears on the graph as an energy source in 1900 and accounts for an increasingly greater percentage of total energy consumption in 1950 and 1985, judging by the increasing size of the petroleum portion of the bar. The portion of the bar representing coal, on the other hand, decreases from 1900 to 1950 and again from 1950 to 1985.

31. (C)

Focus on the coal portion of each bar. Coal was an energy source in 1850, so the ability to utilize it was developed well before the 1900s—choice A is wrong. The graph tells you nothing about mechanized mining techniques, so choice B is out, too. To choose between choices C and D you have to determine if the use of coal predated natural gas or vice versa. The first time coal appears on the graph is 1850, while the first time natural gas appears on the graph is 1900. Therefore, the use of coal must have predated the use of natural gas, making C the correct choice.

32. (F)

The portion of the bar that includes farm animals as an energy source is over 30 percent of the total in 1850, but it gets smaller in 1900 and 1950 until it disappears altogether by 1985. Choice F is the correct answer.

33. (D)

Compare the bars for 1900 and 1950. Choice A is wrong because the number of major energy sources was the same (six) in 1900 as in 1950. Choice B is out for reasons discussed in the previous question. Since coal, not natural gas, has the largest portion of the bar for 1950 (as it did for 1900), choice D is the correct answer.

34. (F)

Statement I is supported by the graph because nuclear power, natural gas, and petroleum were all energy sources in 1985 that did not exist in 1850. The graph does not support Statements II or III, however. Coal was not the largest source of energy in 1850 or 1985, which rules out II, and there is no way to know from the graph whether there is indeed a short supply of petroleum, so III is out. This makes choice F the correct answer.

PASSAGE VII

The scientists conducting the two experiments in this last passage might have a little trouble with animal-rights advocates if they're not careful. They apparently spend their days chopping body parts off of starfish and watching what happens. The results are recorded in two tables. Basically, the data in Table 1 seem to indicate that the bigger the chunk of a starfish you cut off, the longer it takes for the remaining starfish to regenerate the missing part (nothing surprising there). But starfish are strange creatures, and sometimes their missing parts themselves can regenerate into full starfish. That's what Table 2 records. Here, the data indicate that the smaller the chopped-off body part, the less likely it is to regenerate into a full starfish (and the more likely it is to be dead after a year). The general lesson to be learned here is that the bigger the chunk of starfish you have left, the more likely it is that it will eventually regenerate into a whole, live starfish. Now aren't you glad to know that?

35. (B)

According to the bottom row of Table 1, 12 of the starfish that had 2 arms and 1/3 of their body removed were fully regenerated after 6 months. Since each group started out with 25 starfish, 12 out of 25 starfish, or roughly 50 percent, regenerated 2 entire arms and part of the central body after 6 months. Choice B is correct.

36. (J)

In Experiment 2 certain body portions of *Asterias rubens* were allowed to regenerate. The number of whole starfish was recorded at 3-month intervals over the course of a year. According to the table of the results, no starfish was regenerated when only the lower arm was present. This would support the conclusion in choice J—that regeneration is dependent upon the existence of a portion of the central body. The results of Experiment 1 are not relevant to this conclusion, so choice J is the correct answer. The conclusion in choice H, that some starfish die from confinement in lab tanks, is not supported by the results of Experiment 2, since no healthy starfish were studied. In order to conclude that starfish die from confinement in lab tanks and not as a result of amputating portions of their bodies, the scientists would have to study starfish with intact bodies as they did in Experiment 1. You are only supposed to consider the results of Experiment 2 here, so choice H is not correct.

37. (C)

There is no mention of water depth in the passage, the experiments, or the results, so Statement I is out. This means that you can eliminate choices A and D since both of them include Statement I. Statement II is supported by the experimental results that show starfish can regenerate limbs they have lost (how they lose them doesn't matter). Since Statement II is true, choice C must be the answer. Although it would not be necessary at this point to verify that Statement III is true, the data indicate that if a body part that includes some of the central body is broken off from a starfish, the part will regenerate to become an entirely new, separate starfish. This would increase the population of starfish, so Statement III is correct.

38. (F)

Look back quickly at Table 1. The starfish in the first group were whole throughout the experiment—nothing was chopped off, in other words. The group acted as a control for the experiment in that the effect of the artificial environment could be measured apart from the effect of amputation. Three intact starfish in Group 1 died solely from being kept in lab tanks. If this group had not been included in the experiment, the deaths of starfish in other groups would have been attributed solely to the effect of amputation. Choice F is the correct answer.

39. (D)

As the question indicates, the sum of fully regenerated starfish plus dead starfish does not equal 25 for the last two rows of Table 2. Partially regenerated, living starfish would be omitted from this count, which makes choice D the correct explanation.

40. (G)

You know from Experiment 2 that starfish body parts can regenerate into whole starfish over time as long as there is a portion of the central body present. Immediate skyrocketing of the population (F) is not possible due to the amount of time it takes for starfish to regenerate. Choice J is wrong because some pieces will not contain portions of the central body and therefore will not regenerate. Choice G takes the time factor into account as well as the evidence from Experiment 2 that some pieces do not undergo regeneration, so choice G is the correct answer.

SECTION VI
APPENDICES

ENGLISH APPENDIX

PUNCTUATION REVIEW

COMMAS

1. Use commas to separate items in a series

If more than two items are listed in a series, they should be separated by commas. The final comma—the one that precedes the word "and"—may be omitted. An omitted final comma would not be considered an error on the ACT.

> Example: My recipe for buttermilk biscuits includes flour, baking soda, salt, shortening, and buttermilk.
>
> ALSO RIGHT: My recipe for buttermilk biscuits includes flour, baking soda, salt, shortening and buttermilk.

Be watchful for commas placed **before** the first element of a series or **after** the last element.

> WRONG: My recipe for chocolate cake includes, flour, baking soda, sugar, eggs, milk and chocolate.
>
> WRONG: Flour, baking soda, sugar, eggs, milk and chocolate, are the ingredients in my chocolate cake.

2. Use commas to separate two or more adjectives before a noun

> Example: I can't believe you sat through that long, dull movie three times in a row.

It is **incorrect** to place a comma **after** the last adjective in a series.

> WRONG: The manatee is a blubbery, bewhiskered, creature.

3. Use commas to set off parenthetical clauses and phrases

If a phrase or clause is not necessary to the main idea expressed by a sentence, it should be set off by commas.

> Example: Phillip, who never had any formal chef's training, bakes excellent cheesecake.

The main idea here is that Phillip bakes an excellent cheesecake. The intervening clause merely serves to further identify Phillip; it should therefore be enclosed in commas.

4. Use commas after introductory phrases

> Example: Having watered his petunias every day during the drought, Harold was disappointed when his garden was destroyed by aphids.
>
> Example: After the banquet, Harold and Melissa went dancing.

5. Use commas to separate independent clauses

Use a comma before a conjunction (and, but, nor, yet, etcetera.) that connects two independent clauses.

> Example: Marta is good at basketball, but she's better at soccer.

SEMICOLONS

Like commas, semicolons can be used to separate independent clauses. As we saw above, two related independent clauses that are connected by a conjunction such as and, but, nor, or yet should be punctuated by a comma. If the words and, but, nor, or yet aren't used, the clauses should be separated by a semicolon.

Example: Whooping cranes are an endangered species; there are only fifty of them alive today.

Example: Whooping cranes are an endangered species, and they are unlikely to survive if we continue to pollute their habitat.

Semicolons may also be used between independent clauses connected by words like therefore, nevertheless, and moreover. For more on this topic, see the section on "Sentence Structure" in this Appendix.

COLONS

In Standard Written English, the colon is used only as a means of signaling that what follows is a list, definition, explanation, or restatement of what has gone before. A word or phrase such as like the following, as follows, namely, or this is often used along with the colon to make it clear that a list, summary, or explanation is coming up.

Example: This is what I found in her refrigerator: a moldy lime and a jar of peanut butter.

Example: Your instructions are as follows: read the passage carefully, answer the questions, and turn over your answer sheet.

THE DASH

The dash has two uses. One is to indicate an abrupt break in thought.

Example: The alligator, unlike the crocodile, will usually not attack humans—unless, that is, she feels that her young are in danger.

The dash can also be used to set off a parenthetical expression from the rest of the sentence.

Example: At 32° Fahrenheit—which is zero on the Celsius scale—water will freeze.

THE APOSTROPHE

The apostrophe has two distinct functions. It is used with contracted verb forms to indicate that one or more letters have been eliminated:

Example: The **boy's** an expert at chess. (The boy is an expert at chess.)

Example: The **boy's** left for the day. (The boy has left for the day.)

The apostrophe is also used to indicate the possessive form of a noun.

Example: The **boy's** face was covered with mosquito bites after a day in the swamp.

GRAMMAR REVIEW

SUBJECT-VERB AGREEMENT

The form of a verb must match, or agree with, its subject in two ways: person and number.

1. Agreement of Person

When we talk about person, we're talking about whether the subject and verb of a sentence show that the author is making a statement about himself (first person), about the person he is speaking to (second person), or about some other person, place, or thing (third person).

> • *First Person Subjects: I, we.*
> Example: **I am** going to Paris. **We are** going to Rome.
> • *Second Person Subject: you.*
> Example: **Are you** sure you weren't imagining that flying saucer?
> • *Third Person Subjects: he, she, they, it, and names of people, places and things.*
> Example: **He is driving** me crazy.

2. Agreement of Number

When we talk about number, we're talking about whether the subject and verb show that one thing is being discussed (singular) or that more than one thing is being discussed (plural).

> *HINT: Subjects and verbs must agree in number. Subjects and verbs that don't agree in number appear very frequently on the ACT.*

WRONG: The **children catches** the school bus every morning.

RIGHT: The **children catch** the school bus every morning.

Be especially careful of subject-verb agreement when the subject and verb are separated by a long string of words.

WRONG: **Wild animals** in jungles all over the world **is** endangered.

RIGHT: **Wild animals** in jungles all over the world **are** endangered.

PRONOUNS

A pronoun is a word that is used in place of a noun. The antecedent of a pronoun is the word to which the pronoun refers.

> Example: <u>Mary</u> was late for work because <u>she</u> forgot
>   ANTECEDENT   PRONOUN
> to set the alarm.

Occasionally, an antecedent will appear in a sentence *after* the pronoun.

> Example: Because <u>he</u> sneezes so often, <u>Arthur</u> always
>   PRONOUN   ANTECEDENT
> thinks <u>he</u> might have the flu.
>   PRONOUN

1. Pronouns and Agreement

In clear, grammatical writing, a pronoun must clearly refer to and agree with its antecedent.

Number agreement of pronouns is more frequently tested on the ACT than person agreement, although you may see a question that tests person agreement.

Number and Person

	Singular	Plural
First Person	I, me my, mine	we, us our, ours
Second Person	you your, yours	you your, yours
Third Person	he, him she, her it one	they, them
	his her, hers its one's	their, theirs

Number Agreement

Pronouns must agree in number with their antecedents. A singular pronoun should stand in for a singular antecedent. A plural pronoun should stand in for a plural antecedent. Here's a typical ACT pronoun error.

> WRONG: The bank turned Harry down when he applied for a loan because **their** credit department discovered that he didn't have a job.

What does the plural possessive *their* refer to? The singular noun *bank*. The singular possessive *its* is what we need here.

> RIGHT: The bank turned Harry down for a loan because **its** credit department discovered that he didn't have a job.

Person Agreement

Pronouns must agree with their antecedents in person too. A first-person pronoun should stand in for a first-person antecedent, and so on.

One more thing to remember about which pronoun to use with which antecedent: Never use the relative pronoun *which* to refer to a human being. Use *who* or *whom* or *that*.

> WRONG: The woman **which** is standing at the piano is my sister.

> RIGHT: The woman **who** is standing at the piano is my sister.

2. Pronouns and Case

A more subtle type of pronoun problem is one in which the pronoun is in the wrong case. Look at the following chart:

Case

	Subjective	Objective
First Person	I we	me us
Second Person	you	you
Third Person	he she it they one	him her it them one
Relative Pronouns	who that which	whom that which

When to Use Subjective Case Pronouns

• Use the subjective case for the subject of a sentence.

> Example: **She** is falling asleep.

> WRONG: Nancy, Claire, and **me** are going to the ballet.

> RIGHT: Nancy, Claire, and **I** are going to the ballet.

• Use the subjective case after a linking verb like *to be*.

> Example: It is **I**.

• Use the subjective case in comparisons between the subject of verbs that are not stated, but understood.

> Example: Gary is taller than **they** (are).

When to Use Objective Case Pronouns

• Use the objective case for the object of a verb.

> Example: I called **her.**

• Use the objective case for the object of a preposition.

> Example: I laughed at **him.**

• Use the objective case after infinitives and gerunds.

> Example: Asking **him** to go was a big mistake.
>
> Example: To give **him** the scare of his life, we all jumped out of his closet.

• Use the objective case in comparisons between objects of verbs that are not stated but understood.

> Example: She calls you more than (she calls) **me.**

3. Who and Whom

Another thing you'll need to know is when to use the relative pronoun *who* (subjective case) and when to use the relative pronoun *whom* (objective case: *whom* goes with *him* and *them*). The following method is very helpful when you're deciding which one to use.

> Example: Sylvester, (*who* or *whom?*) is afraid of the dark, sleeps with a Donald Duck night-light on.

• Look only at the relative pronoun in its clause. Ignore the rest of the sentence.

> (Who or Whom?) is afraid of the dark. . . .

• Turn the clause into a question. Ask yourself:

> Who or Whom is afraid of the dark?

• Answer the question with an ordinary personal pronoun.

> He is.

• If you've answered the question with a subjective case pronoun (as you have here), you need the subjective case *who* in the relative clause.

> Sylvester, **who** is afraid of the dark, sleeps with a Donald Duck night-light on.

If you answer the question with an objective case pronoun, you need the objective case *whom* in the relative clause.

> *Try answering the question with*
> he *or* him. Who *goes with* he
> *(subjective case) and* whom *goes*
> *with* him *(objective case).*

SENTENCE STRUCTURE

A sentence is a group of words that can stand alone because it expresses a complete thought. To express a complete thought, it must contain a subject, about which something is said, and a verb, which says something about the subject.

> Example: Dogs bark.
>
> Example: The explorers slept in yak-hide tents.
>
> Example: Looking out of the window, John saw a flying saucer.

Every sentence consists of at least one clause. Many sentences contain more than one clause (and phrases, too).

A **clause** is a group of words that contains a subject and a verb. "Dogs bark," "The explorers slept in a yak-hide tent," and "John saw a flying saucer" are all clauses.

A **phrase** is a group of words that does not have both a subject and a verb.

> *Looking out of the window* is a phrase.

1. Sentence Fragments

On the ACT, some of those innocent-looking groups of words beginning with capital letters and ending with periods are only masquerading as sentences. In reality, they're sentence fragments.

A sentence fragment is a group of words that seems to be a sentence but which is *grammatically* incomplete because it lacks a subject or a verb, **or** which is *logically* incomplete because other elements necessary for it to express a complete thought are missing.

> WRONG: Eggs and fresh vegetables on sale at the farmers' market.

This is not a complete sentence because there's no verb to say something about the subject, *eggs and fresh vegetables*.

> WRONG: Because Richard likes hippopotamuses.

Even though this contains a subject (Richard) and a verb (likes), it's not a complete sentence because it doesn't express a complete thought. We don't know what's true "*because* Richard likes hippopotamuses."

> WRONG: Martha dreams about dinosaurs although.

This isn't a complete sentence because it doesn't express a complete thought. What makes Martha's dreaming about dinosaurs in need of qualification or explanation?

2. Run-On Sentences

Just as unacceptable as an incomplete sentence is a "too-complete" sentence, a run-on sentence.

A run-on sentence is actually two complete sentences stuck together either with just a comma or with no punctuation at all.

> WRONG: The children had been playing in the park, they were covered with mud.
>
> WRONG: The children had been playing in the park they were covered with mud.

There are a number of ways to fix this kind of problem. They all involve a punctuation mark or a connecting word that can properly connect two clauses.

• Join the clauses with a semicolon.

> RIGHT: The children had been playing in the park; they were covered with mud.

• Join the clauses with a coordinating conjunction and a comma.

> RIGHT: The children had been playing in the park, and they were covered with mud.
>
> (Coordinating Conjunctions: *and, but, for, nor, or, so, yet*)

• Join the clauses with a subordinating conjunction.

> RIGHT: Because the children had been playing in the park, they were covered with mud.
>
> OR
>
> RIGHT: The children were covered with mud because they had been playing in the park.
>
> (Subordinating Conjunctions: *after, although, if, since, while.*)

• And, of course, the two halves of a run-on sentence can be written as two separate, complete sentences.

> RIGHT: The children had been playing in the park. They were covered with mud.

VERBS

On the ACT you'll find items that are wrong because a verb is in the wrong tense. To spot this kind of problem, you need to be familiar both with the way each tense is used **and** with the ways the tenses are used together. English has six tenses, and each has a simple form and a progressive form.

	Simple	**Progressive**
PRESENT	I work	I am working
PAST	I worked	I was working
FUTURE	I will work	I will be working
PRESENT PERFECT	I have worked	I have been working
PAST PERFECT	I had worked	I had been working
FUTURE PERFECT	I will have worked	I will have been working

1. Using the Present Tense

Use the present tense to describe a state or action occurring in the present time.

> Example: I **am** a student.
> Example: They **are studying** the Holy Roman Empire.

Use the present tense to describe habitual action.
> Example: They **eat** at Joe's Diner every night.
> Example: My father never **drinks** coffee.

Use the present tense to describe things that are always true.

> Example: The earth **is** round.
> Example: Grass **is** green.

2. Using the Past Tense

Use the simple past tense to describe an event or state that took place at a specific time in the past and is now over and done with.

> Example: Norman **broke** his toe when he tripped over his son's tricycle.

3. Using the Future Tense

Use the future tense for actions expected in the future.

> Example: I **will call** you on Wednesday.

We often express future actions with the expression *to be going to*:

> Example: I **am going to move** to another apartment soon.

4. Using the Present Perfect Tense

Use the present perfect tense for actions and states that started in the past and continue up to and into the present time.

> Example: I **have been living** here for the last two years.

Use the present perfect for actions and states that happened a number of times in the past and may happen again in the future.

> Example: I **have heard** that song several times on the radio.

Use the present perfect for something that happened at an unspecified time in the past.

> Example: Anna **has seen** that movie already.

5. Using the Past Perfect Tense

The past perfect tense is used to represent past actions or states that were completed before other past actions or states. The more recent past event is expressed in the simple past, and the earlier past event is expressed in the past perfect.

> Example: When I turned my computer on this morning, I realized that I **had exited** the program yesterday without saving my work.

6. Using the Future Perfect Tense

Use the future perfect tense for a future state or event that will take place before another future event.

> Example: By the end of the week, I **will have worked** four hours of overtime.

ADJECTIVES AND ADVERBS

On the ACT, you may find an occasional item that's wrong because it uses an adjective where an adverb is called for, or vice versa.

An adjective modifies, or describes, a noun or pronoun.

> Example: A woman in a **white** dress stood next to the **old** tree.

> Example: The boat, **leaky and dirty**, hadn't been used in years.

An adverb modifies a verb, an adjective, or another adverb. Most, but not all, adverbs end in *-ly*. (Don't forget that some **adjectives**—*friendly, lovely*—also end in *-ly*.)

> Example: The interviewer looked **approvingly** at the **neatly** dressed applicant.

STYLE REVIEW

PRONOUNS AND REFERENCE

When we talk about pronouns and their antecedents, we say pronouns refer to or refer back to their antecedents. We talked earlier about pronouns that didn't agree in person or number with their antecedents. But a different kind of pronoun reference problem exists when a pronoun either doesn't refer to any antecedent at all or doesn't refer clearly to one, and only one, antecedent.

Sometimes an incorrectly used pronoun has no antecedent.

> POOR: Joe doesn't like what **they play** on this radio station.

Who are they? We can't tell, because there is no antecedent for they. On the ACT, this sort of usage is an error.

> RIGHT: Joe doesn't like what **the disc jockeys play** on this radio station.

Don't use pronouns without antecedents when doing so makes a sentence unclear. Sometimes a pronoun seems to have an antecedent until you look closely and see that the word that appears to be the antecedent is not a noun, but an adjective, a possessive form, or a verb. The antecedent of a pronoun must be a noun.

> WRONG: When you are painting, make sure you don't get **it** on the floor.

> RIGHT: When you are painting, make sure you don't get **paint** on the floor.

Other examples of pronoun reference problems:

WRONG: I've always been interested in astronomy and finally have decided to become **one**.

RIGHT: I've always been interested in astronomy and finally have decided to become **an astronomer**.

Don't use pronouns with remote references. A pronoun that is too far away from what it refers to is said to have a remote antecedent.

WRONG: Jane quit smoking and, as a result, temporarily put on a lot of weight. **It** was very bad for her health.

RIGHT: Jane quit smoking because **it** was very bad for her health, and, as a result, she temporarily gained a lot of weight.

Don't use pronouns with faulty broad reference. A pronoun with broad reference is one that refers to a whole idea instead of to a single noun.

WRONG: He built a fence to stop people from looking into his backyard. **That**'s not easy.

RIGHT: He built a fence to stop people from looking into his backyard. **The fence** was not easy **to build**.

REDUNDANCY

This type of style error is frequently tested on the ACT. Words or phrases are redundant when they have basically the same meaning as something already stated in the sentence. Don't use two phrases when one is sufficient.

WRONG: The school was **established and founded** in 1906.

RIGHT: The school was **established** in 1906.

RELEVANCE

Irrelevant asides, even when set off in parentheses, are to be avoided on the ACT. Everything in the sentence should serve to get across the point in question. Something unrelated to that point should be cut.

POOR: No one can say for sure just how successful the new law will be in the fight against crime (just as no one can be sure whether he or she will ever be a victim of a crime).

BETTER: No one can say for sure just how successful the new law will be in the fight against crime.

VERBOSITY

Sometimes having extra words in a sentence results in a style problem. Conciseness is something that is valued on the ACT.

WORDY: The supply of **musical instruments that are antique** is limited, so they become more valuable each year.

BETTER: The supply of **antique musical instruments** is limited, so they become more valuable each year.

WORDY: We **were in agreement with each other** that Max was an unsuspecting old fool.

BETTER: We **agreed** that Max was an unsuspecting old fool.

REVIEW OF COMMONLY MISUSED WORDS

AMONG/BETWEEN

In most cases, you should use *between* for two items and *among* for more than two.

Example: The competition **between** Anne and Michael has grown more intense.

Example: He is always at his best **among** strangers.

But use common sense. Sometimes *among* is not appropriate.

> Example: Plant the trees in the area **between** the road, the wall, and the fence.

AMOUNT/NUMBER

Amount should be used to refer to a uncountable quantity. *Number* should refer to a countable quantity.

> Example: The **amount** of food he threw away would feed a substantial **number** of people.

ANOTHER/THE OTHER

Another refers to any other. *The other* is more specific; it refers to one particular other.

> Example: Put **another** log on the fire (any one).
>
> Example: Put **the other** log on the fire (the last one).
>
> Example: The men were passing the pipe from one to **the other** (two men—back and forth).
>
> Example: They passed the pipe from one to **another** (three or more).

AS/LIKE

Like is a preposition; it takes a noun object. *As,* when functioning as a conjunction, introduces a subordinate clause. Remember, a clause is a part of a sentence containing a subject and verb.

> Example: He sings **like** an angel.
>
> Example: He sings **as** an angel sings.

AS . . . AS . . .

The idiom is *as . . . as . . .* , **not** *as . . . than . . .*

> WRONG: That suit is **as** expensive **than** this one.
>
> RIGHT: That suit is **as** expensive **as** this one.

FEWER/LESS

Use *fewer* before a plural noun; use *less* before a singular one.

> Example: There are **fewer** apples on this tree than there were last year.
>
> Example: He makes **less** money than she does.

NEITHER . . . NOR . . .

The correlative conjunction is *neither . . . nor . . .* , **not** *neither . . . or . . .*

> Example: He is **neither** strong **nor** flexible.

Avoid the redundancy caused by using *nor* following a negative.

> WRONG: Alice's departure was **not** noticed by Debby **nor** Sue.
>
> RIGHT: Alice's departure was **not** noticed by Debby **or** Sue.

ITS/IT'S

Many people confuse *its* and *it's*. *Its* is possessive; *It's* is a contraction of *it is*:

> Example: The cat licked **its** paws.
>
> Example: **It's** raining cats and dogs.

THEIR/THEY'RE/THERE

Many people confuse *their*, *there*, and *they're*. *Their* is possessive; *they're* is a contraction of *they are*:

> Example: The girls rode **their** bikes home.
>
> Example: **They're** training for the big race.

There has two uses: It can indicate place and it can be used as an expletive—a word that doesn't do anything in a sentence except delay the subject.

> Example: Put the book over **there**.
>
> Example: **There** will be fifteen runners competing for the prize.

MATH GLOSSARY

ABSOLUTE VALUE—the magnitude of a number, irrespective of its sign. Written as a number inside vertical lines: $|3| = 3$ *and* $|-3| = 3$.

ACUTE ANGLE—an angle measuring less than 90°. *A triangle with three acute angles is called an acute triangle.*

ADJACENT ANGLES—two angles having a common side and a common vertex.

In the figure above, angles x and y are adjacent. (They are also supplementary.)

ALGEBRAIC EXPRESSION—one or more algebraic terms connected with plus and minus signs. *An algebraic expression is not an equation because it has no equal sign.*

ALTITUDE—a perpendicular segment whose length can be used in calculating the area of a triangle or other polygon.

In the figure above, $\overline{BD}$ is an altitude of $\triangle ABC$, and $\overline{GJ}$ is an altitude of parallelogram EFGH.

ANGLE—two line segments coming together at a point called the vertex.

The angle pictured above could be called $\angle ABC$, $\angle B$, or $\angle x$.

ARC—a portion of the circumference of a circle.

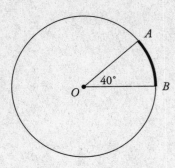

Because the central angle is $\frac{1}{9}$ of a full circle's

360°, the length of minor arc AB is $\frac{1}{9}$ the circumference.

AREA—a measure, in square units, of the size of a region in a plane. *Finding the area of a figure invariably involves multiplying two dimensions, such as length and width, or base and height.*

AVERAGE—the sum of a group of numbers divided by the number of numbers in the group. *To find the average of 2, 7, and 15, divide the sum (2 + 7 + 15 = 24) by the number of numbers (3): 24 ÷ 3 = 8.*

AVERAGE RATE— Average A per $B = \dfrac{\text{Total } A}{\text{Total } B}$

. Average speed $= \dfrac{\text{Total distance}}{\text{Total time}}$. *To get the average speed, don't just average the speeds.*

AXES—the perpendicular "number lines" in the coordinate plane.

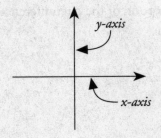

BASE—a side of a polygon that will be used with an altitude in calculating the area; a face of a solid, the area of which will be used with an altitude in calculating the volume.

In the figure above, $\overline{AC}$ *is the base of the triangle, and circle O is the base of the cone.*

BINOMIAL—an algebraic expression with two terms. *The FOIL method of multiplying works only for a pair of binomials.*

BISECTOR—a line or line segment that divides an angle in half. *The bisector of a 90° angle divides it into two 45° angles.*

CENTRAL ANGLE—an angle formed by two radii of a circle.

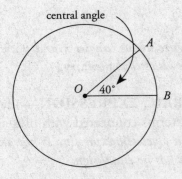

In the figure above, $\angle AOB$ *is a central angle.*

CHORD—a line segment connecting two points on a circle.

KAPLAN

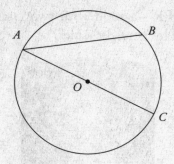

In the figure above, $\overline{AB}$ and $\overline{AC}$ are chords of circle O. Because it passes through the center, $\overline{AC}$ is also a diameter.

CIRCLE—the set of points in a plane at a particular distance from a central point. *A circle is not a polygon because it is not made up of straight sides.*

CIRCUMFERENCE—the distance around a circle. *The circumference of a circle is analogous to the perimeter of a polygon.*

CIRCUMSCRIBED—drawn outside another figure with as many points touching as possible.

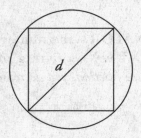

In the figure above, the circle is circumscribed about the square; d is both a diagonal of the square and a diameter of the circle.

COEFFICIENT—the numerical or "constant" part of an algebraic term. *In the monomial $-4x^2y$, the coefficient is -4. In the expression ax^2+bx+c, a, b, and c are the coefficients.*

COMMON DENOMINATOR—a number that can be used as the denominator for two or more fractions so that they can be added or subtracted. *Before you can add the fractions $\frac{5}{6}$ and $\frac{5}{8}$, you must first re-express the fractions with a common denominator, such as 24: $\frac{5}{6}=\frac{20}{24}$ and $\frac{5}{8}=\frac{15}{24}$.*

COMMON FACTOR—a factor shared by two integers. *Any two integers will have at least 1 for a common factor.*

COMMON MULTIPLE—a multiple shared by two integers. *You can always get a common multiple for two integers by multiplying them, though that will not necessarily be the least common multiple.*

COMPLEMENTARY ANGLES—two angles whose measures add up to 90°. *A 30° angle and a 60° angle are complementary.*

CONE—a solid with a circle at one end and a single point at the other.

CONGRUENT—identical; of the same size and shape. *Congruent polygons have the same angles and side lengths.*

CONSECUTIVE—one after another, in order, without skipping any. *The numbers 6, 9, 12, 15, 18, and 21 are consecutive multiples of 3.*

COORDINATES—the pair of numbers, written inside parentheses, that specifies the location of a point in the coordinate plane. *The first number is the x-coordinate and the second number is the y-coordinate.*

COSECANT—the ratio of the hypotenuse to the opposite leg. *The cosecant of $\angle A$ in the figure below is $\frac{hypotenuse}{opposite} = \frac{13}{5}$.*

COSINE—the ratio of the adjacent leg to the hypotenuse. *The cosine of $\angle A$ in the figure above is $\frac{adjacent}{hypotenuse} = \frac{12}{13}$.*

COTANGENT—the ratio of the adjacent leg to the opposite leg. *The cotangent of $\angle A$ in the figure above is $\frac{adjacent}{opposite} = \frac{12}{5}$.*

CUBE—a rectangular solid whose faces are all squares.

CUBE (of a number)—the third power. *The cube of a negative number is negative.*

CYLINDER—a solid with two circular ends connected by "straight" sides.

DECIMAL—a noninteger written with digits and a decimal point. *A decimal is equivalent to a common fraction whose denominator is 10, 100, or 1,000, etc.*

DEGREE OF AN EQUATION—the greatest exponent in a single-variable equation. *The equation $x^3 - 9x = 0$ is a third-degree equation because the biggest exponent is 3.*

DEGREE—one 360th of a full rotation. *A right angle measures 90 degrees—often written 90°.*

DENOMINATOR—the number below the fraction bar. *When you increase the denominator of a positive fraction, you decrease the value of the fraction: $\frac{7}{11}$ is less than $\frac{7}{10}$.*

DIAGONAL—a line segment connecting two nonadjacent vertices of a polygon. *A diagonal divides a rectangle into two right triangles.*

DIAMETER—(the length of) a line segment connecting two points on a circle and passing through the center. *A diameter is a chord of maximum length.*

DIFFERENCE—the result of subtraction. *The positive difference between 3 and 7 is 4.*

DIGIT—one of the numbers from 0 through 9. *In the 3-digit number 355, the hundreds' digit is 3, the tens' digit is 5, and the ones' digit is 5.*

DISTINCT—different, distinguishable. *The number 355 has 2 distinct digits: 3 and 5.*

EDGE—a line segment formed by the intersection of two faces.

A rectangular solid has 12 edges.

ELLIPSE—a set of points in a plane for which the sum of the distances from two points (called *foci*) is constant.

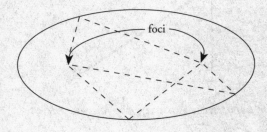

EQUATION—a statement of equality between two quantities. *It's an equation if it includes an equal sign.*

EQUATION OF A LINE—an equation that describes the relationship between the *x*- and *y*-coordinates of every point on the line in the coordinate plane. *The equation of the x-axis is y = 0, and the equation of the y-axis is x = 0.*

EQUILATERAL TRIANGLE—a triangle with three equal sides.

All equilateral triangles are similar—they all have three 60° angles,

EVEN NUMBER—a multiple of 2. *The set of even numbers includes not only 2, 4, 6, etc., but also 0, –2, –4, –6, etc.*

EXPONENT—the small, raised number written to the right of a variable or number, indicating the number of times that variable or number is to be used as a factor. *In the expression $-4x^3$, the exponent is 3, so $-4x^3 = -4 \cdot x \cdot x \cdot x$.*

EXTERIOR ANGLE—the angle created outside a polygon when one side is extended. *The exterior angles of any polygon add up to 360°*

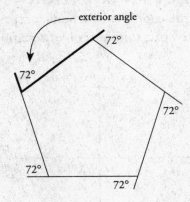

The exterior angles of a regular pentagon each measure 72°.

FACE—a polygon formed by edges of a solid.

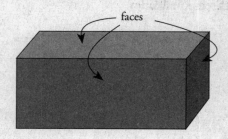
faces

A rectangular solid has 6 faces.

FACTOR (of *n*)—a positive integer that divides into *n* with no remainder. *The complete list of factors of 18 is: 1, 2, 3, 6, 9, and 18.*

FACTORING (a polynomial)—re-expressing a polynomial as the product of simpler expressions. *The complete factorization of* $2x^2 + 7x + 3$ *is (2x + 1)(x + 3).*

FRACTION—a number expressed as a ratio. *In everyday speech, the word* fraction *implies something less than 1, but to a mathematician, any number written in the form* $\frac{A}{B}$ *is a fraction.*

GRAPH OF AN EQUATION—a line or curve in the coordinate plane that represents all the ordered pair solutions of an equation.

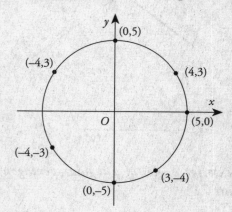

The figure above shows the graph of the equation $x^2 + y^2 = 25$

GREATEST COMMON FACTOR—the greatest integer than is a factor of both numbers under consideration. *The greatest common factor (GCF) of relative primes is 1.*

HEXAGON—a six-sided polygon.

Regular hexagon

The six angles of a regular hexagon each measure 120°.

HYPOTENUSE—the side of a right triangle opposite the right angle.

hypotenuse

The hypotenuse is always the longest side.

IMAGINARY—not real, usually because of the square root of a negative number. *The square root of –4 is an imaginary number.*

IMPROPER FRACTION—a fraction with a numerator that's greater than the denominator. $\frac{35}{8}$ *is an improper fraction and is therefore greater than 1.*

INEQUALITY—a statement that compares the size of two quantities. *There are four inequality symbols:* < *("less than"),* ≤ *"(less than or equal to"),* > *("greater than"), and* ≥ *("greater than or equal to").*

INSCRIBED—drawn inside another figure with as many points touching as possible.

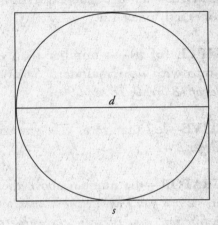

When a circle is inscribed within a square, the diameter d of the circle is the same as a length of a side s of the square.

INTEGER—a whole number; *325, 0, and –29 are integers.*

INTERCEPT—the point where a given line crosses the *x*-axis or *y*-axis.

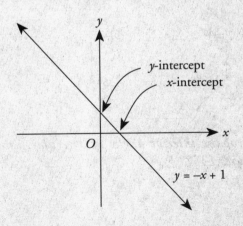

The y-intercept is the b in the slope-intercept form $y = mx + b$.

INTERIOR ANGLE—an angle inside a polygon formed by two adjacent sides. *Every polygon has the same number of interior angles as sides.*

The interior angles of a regular pentagon each measure 108°.

IRRATIONAL—real, but not capable of being expressed as a ratio of integers. $\sqrt{2}$, $\sqrt{3}$, *and* π *are irrational numbers.*

ISOSCELES TRIANGLE—a triangle with two sides of equal length.

The angles opposite the equal sides of an isosceles triangle are also equal.

LEAST COMMON MULTIPLE—the smallest number that is a multiple of both given numbers. *The least common multiple of relative primes is their product.*

LEGS (of a right triangle)—the sides that make up the right angle.

You can use the legs as the base and altitude to find the area of a right triangle.

LIKE TERMS—algebraic terms in which the elements other than the coefficients are alike. *2ab and 3ab are like terms, and so they can be added: 2ab + 3ab = 5ab.*

LINE—a straight row of points extending infinitely in both directions. *A line has only one dimension.*

LINE SEGMENT—a straight row of points connecting two endpoints. *Each side of a polygon is a line segment.*

LINEAR EQUATION—a single-variable equation with no exponent greater than 1. *A linear equation is also called a first-degree equation.*

MIDPOINT—the point that divides a line segment in half.

In the figure above, B is the midpoint of $\overline{AC}$, so AB = BC.

MIXED NUMBER—a noninteger greater than 1 written with a whole number part and a fractional part. *The mixed number $4\frac{2}{3}$ can also be expressed as the improper fraction $\frac{14}{3}$.*

MONOMIAL—an algebraic expression consisting of exactly one term.

MULTIPLE (of n)—a number than *n* will divide into with no remainder. *Some of the multiples of 18 are: 0, 18, and 90.*

NEGATIVE—less than zero. *The greatest negative integer is −1.*

NUMERATOR—the number above the fraction bar. *When you increase the numerator of a positive fraction, you increase the value of the fraction: $\frac{12}{17}$ is greater than $\frac{12}{17}$.*

OBTUSE ANGLE—an angle measuring more than 90° and less than 180°. *An obtuse triangle is one that has one obtuse angle.*

OCTAGON—an eight-sided polygon.

Each of the interior angles of a regular octagon measures 135°.

KAPLAN

ODD NUMBER—an integer that is *not* a multiple of 2. *Any integer that's not even is odd.*

ORIGIN—the point where the *x*- and *y*-axes intersect. *The origin represents the point (0,0).*

PARABOLA—the set of points in a plane that are the same distance from a point called the *focus* and a line called the *directrix.*

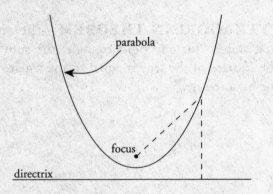

PARALLEL LINES—coplanar lines that never intersect. *Parallel lines are the same distance apart at all points.*

PARALLELOGRAM—a quadrilateral with two pairs of parallel sides.

Parallelograms
Parallelograms

Opposite sides of a parallelogram are equal; opposite angles of a parallelogram are also equal.

PENTAGON—a five-sided polygon.

Regular pentagon

The interior angles of any pentagon add up to 540°. Each of the interior angles of a regular pentagon measures 108°.

PERCENT—one hundredth. *20% means 20 hundredths, or $\frac{20}{100} = \frac{1}{5}$.*

PERCENT INCREASE/DECREASE—amount of increase or decrease expressed as a percent of the original amount. *A decrease from 100 to 83 is a 17% decrease.*

PERIMETER—the sum of the lengths of the sides of a polygon. *Two polygons with the same area do not necessarily have the same perimeter.*

PERPENDICULAR—intersecting at a right angle. *The altitude and base of a triangle are perpendicular.*

PI—an irrational number, approximately 3.14, which is equal to the ratio of the circumference of any circle to its diameter. The symbol for pi is π. *Pi appears in the formulas for the circumference and area of a circle, as well for the volumes of a sphere, a cylinder, and a cone.*

POINT—a precise position in space. *A point has no length, breadth, or thickness.*

POLYGON—a closed figure composed of any number of straight sides.

Polygons

Triangles, squares, trapezoids, and pentagons are all polygons, but circles and ellipses are not.

POLYNOMIAL—an algebraic expression that is the sum of two or more terms. *Binomials and trinomials are just two types of polynomials.*

POSITIVE—greater than zero. *Zero is not a positive number.*

POWER—a product obtained by multiplying a quantity by itself one or more times. *The fifth power of 2 is 32.*

PRIME FACTORIZATION—an integer expressed as the product of prime numbers. *The prime factorization of 60 is $2 \times 2 \times 3 \times 5$.*

PRIME NUMBER—an integer greater than 1 that has no factors other than 1 and itself. *The first 10 prime numbers are: 2, 3, 5, 7, 11, 13, 17, 23, 29, and 31. Notice that 2 is the only even prime number.*

PROBABILITY—the likelihood of a particular event, expressed as the ratio of the number of "favorable" occurrences to the total number of possible occurrences. *Probability is a part-to-*

whole ratio and can therefore never be greater than 1.

PRODUCT—the result of multiplication. *The product of 3 and 4 is 12.*

PROPORTION—an expression of the equality of ratios. *Corresponding sides of similar figures are proportional.*

PYTHAGOREAN THEOREM—the rule that states, "for any right triangle, the sum of the squares of the legs is equal to the square of the hypotenuse."

If you call the lengths of the legs a and b and the length of the hypotenuse c, you can write "$a^2 + b^2 = c^2$."

QUADRANT—one of the four regions into which the axes divide the coordinate plane.

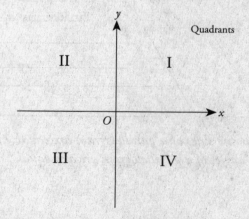

Quadrants

When you know the signs of the coordinates, you know which quadrant contains that point. For any point in Quadrant IV, for example, the x-coordinate is positive and the y-coordinate is negative.

QUADRATIC EQUATION—a second-degree equation. *Quadratic equations with one unknown often have two solutions.*

QUADRILATERAL—a four-sided polygon.

Quadrilaterals

Squares, rectangles, parallelograms, and trapezoids are all quadrilaterals.

QUOTIENT—the result of division. *When 12 is divided by 3, the quotient is 4.*

RADIAN—a unit for expressing the measure of an angle.

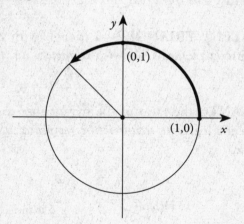

The angle shown in the figure above measures $\frac{3\pi}{4}$ radians, which is the same as 135°. It's no coincidence that $\frac{3\pi}{4}$ is also the length of the arc shown.

RADICAL—the symbol $\sqrt{}$, which by itself represents the positive square root, and with a little number written in—as in $\sqrt[5]{32}$ —represents a higher root. *By convention, $\sqrt{}$ represents the positive square root only.*

RADIUS—(the length of) a line segment connecting the center and a point on a circle. *The radius is half the diameter.*

RATE—a ratio of quantities measured in different units. *The most familiar rates have units of time after the word "per," such as: meters per second, pages per hour, inches per year.*

RATIO—a fraction that expresses the relative sizes of two quantities. *A ratio is generally expressed with the words "of" and "to": as in "the ratio of girls to boys."*

RATIONAL—capable of being expressed as a ratio of integers. *The repeating decimal .074074074074 . . . is a rational number because it can be written as $\frac{2}{27}$.*

REAL—having a place on the number line. π *is a real number because it has a location—somewhere just to the right of 3.14—on the number line.*

RECIPROCALS—a pair of numbers whose product is 1. *To get the reciprocal of a fraction, switch the numerator and denominator: the reciprocal of $\frac{2}{7}$ is $\frac{7}{2}$.*

RECTANGLE—a quadrilateral with four right angles. *All rectangles are parallelograms, but not all parallelograms are rectangles.*

RECTANGULAR SOLID—a solid whose faces are all rectangles.

Rectangular Solids

REDUCING A FRACTION—expressing a fraction in lowest terms by factoring out and canceling common factors. $\frac{6}{8}$ reduces to $\frac{3}{4}$.

REGULAR POLYGON—a polygon with all equal sides and all equal angles. *Equilateral triangles and squares are regular polygons.*

Regular polygons

RELATIVE PRIMES—positive integers that have no factors in common. *Thirty-five and 54 are relative primes because their prime factorizations (35 = 5 × 7, and 54 = 2 × 3 × 3 × 3) have nothing in common.*

REPEATING DECIMAL—a decimal with a digit or cluster of digits that repeats indefinitely. *The fraction $\frac{1}{7}$ is equivalent to the repeating decimal .142857142857142857. . . , which can be written as $.\overline{142857}$.*

RHOMBUS—a quadrilateral with four equal sides.

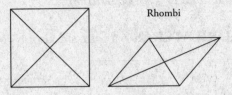

Rhombi

The diagonals of a rhombus are perpendicular.

RIGHT ANGLE—an angle measuring 90°. *A rectangle is a polygon with four right angles.*

RIGHT TRIANGLE—a triangle with a right angle. *Every right triangle has exactly two acute angles.*

ROOT—a number that multiplied by itself a certain number of times will yield the given quantity. *The third root of 8 is 2.*

SCALENE TRIANGLE—a triangle with sides of different lengths. *A 3-4-5 triangle is a scalene triangle.*

SECANT—the ratio of the hypotenuse to the adjacent leg. *The secant is the reciprocal of the cosine.*

In the figure above, the secant of $\angle A$ is $\frac{13}{12}$.

KAPLAN

SECTOR—a region bounded by two radii and an arc.

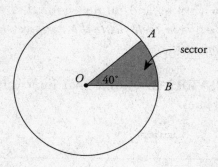

Because the central angle of 40° is $\frac{1}{9}$ of the full circle's 360°, the area of the shaded sector is $\frac{1}{9}$ of the area of the whole circle.

SIMILAR—proportional; of the same shape. *Similar polygons have the same angles.*

Similar triangles

SINE—the ratio of the opposite leg to the hypotenuse.

In the figure above, the sine of $\angle A$ is $\frac{5}{13}$.

SLOPE—a description of the "steepness" of a line in the coordinate plane, defined as $\frac{\text{Change in } y}{\text{Change in } x}$. *Lines that go "uphill" (left to right) have positive slopes, and lines that go "downhill" have negative slopes. A horizontal line—that is, a line parallel to the x-axis—is "flat" and has a slope of 0.*

SLOPE-INTERCEPT FORM—an equation in the form $y=mx+b$. *In this form, m is the slope and b is the y-intercept. Line 1 in the figure above has a slope of 1 and a y-intercept of 4, so its equation is $y = x+4$. Line 2's equation is $y = 4$. Line 3's equation is $y = -x - 3$.*

SOLID—a three-dimensional figure.

Cubes, cylinders, cones, and spheres are all solids.

SOLVING—isolating the given variable.

SPHERE—the set of all points in space a particular distance from a central point. *Visualize a sphere as a ball.*

SQUARE—a quadrilateral with four equal sides and four right angles. *A square can be thought of as a rectangular rhombus.*

SQUARE ROOT—a number that when squared yields the given quantity. *Positive numbers each have two square roots, but negative numbers have no real square roots.*

SUM—the result of addition. *The sum of 3 and 4 is 7.*

SUPPLEMENTARY ANGLES—two angles whose measures add up to 180°.

SURFACE AREA—the sum of the areas of the surfaces of a solid. *Surface area is measured in square units.*

SYSTEM OF EQUATIONS—two or more equations in which each variable represents the same quantity in one equation as in another.

TANGENT (of a circle)—a line that intersects a circle at exactly one point. *Visualize a tangent as a line that just barely "touches" the circle.*

tangent

TANGENT—the ratio of the opposite leg to the adjacent leg.

TERM—a part of an algebraic expression that either stands by itself or is connected to other terms with plus and minus signs. *A term has three parts: the coefficient, the variable(s), and the exponent(s).*

TRANSVERSAL—a line that intersects two parallel lines.

transversal

A transversal across parallel lines creates two sets of four equal angles.

TRAPEZOID—a quadrilateral with one pair of parallel sides.

Trapezoids

TRIANGLE—a three-sided polygon. *The three angles of a triangle add up to 180°.*

UNDEFINED—not covered by the rules. *Division by 0 is undefined.*

VARIABLE—a letter representing an unknown or unspecified quantity. *The letter most commonly used for a variable is x.*

VERTEX—a point of intersection, such as a corner of a rectangular solid or a polygon.

vertices

VERTICAL ANGLES—angles across the vertex of intersecting lines. *Vertical angles are equal.*

In the figure above, –q and –s are vertical angles, as are –p and –r.

VOLUME—a measure of the amount of "space" contained within a solid. *Computing volume invariably involves multiplying three dimensions, such as length, width, and height.*

MATH APPENDIX: 100 THINGS TO KNOW FOR THE ACT

NUMBER PROPERTIES

1. UNDEFINED
On the ACT, *undefined* almost always means **division by zero**. The expression $\dfrac{a}{bc}$ is undefined if either b or c equals 0.

2. REAL/IMAGINARY
A real number is a number that has a **location on the number line**. On the ACT, imaginary numbers are numbers that involve the square root of a negative number. $\sqrt{-4}$ is an imaginary number.

3. INTEGER/NONINTEGER
Integers are **whole numbers**; they include negative whole numbers and zero.

4. RATIONAL/IRRATIONAL
A **rational number** is a number that can be expressed as a **ratio of two integers**. **Irrational numbers** are real numbers—they have locations on the number line—they just **can't be expressed precisely as a fraction or decimal**. For the purposes of the ACT, the most important **irrational numbers** are $\sqrt{2}$, $\sqrt{3}$, and π.

5. ADDING AND SUBTRACTING SIGNED NUMBERS
To **add a positive and a negative**, first ignore the signs and find the positive difference between the number parts. Then attach the sign of the original number with the larger number part. For example, to add 23 and −34, first we ignore the minus sign and find the positive difference between 23 and 34—that's 11. Then we attach the sign of the number with the larger number

part—in this case it's the minus sign from the −34. So, 23 + (−34) = −11.

Make **subtraction** situations simpler by turning them into addition. For example, think of −17 − (−21) as −17 + (+21).

To **add or subtract a string of positives and negatives**, first turn everything into addition. Then collect the positives and negatives and reduce the string to the sum of a positive and a negative.

6. MULTIPLYING and DIVIDING SIGNED NUMBERS
To multiply and/or divide positives and negatives, treat the number parts as usual and **attach a minus sign if there were originally an odd number of negatives**. For example, to multiply −2, −3, and −5, first multiply the number parts: $2 \times 3 \times 5 = 30$. Then go back and note that there were *three*—an *odd* number—negatives, so the product is negative: $(-2) \times (-3) \times (-5) = -30$.

7. PEMDAS
When performing multiple operations, remember **PEMDAS**, which means **Parentheses** first, then **Exponents**, then **Multiplication/Division** (left to right), and lastly **Addition/Subtraction** (left to right).

In the expression $9 - 2 \times (5-3)^2 + 6 \div 3$, begin with the parentheses: $(5 - 3) = 2$. Then do the exponent: $2^2 = 4$. Now the expression is: $9 - 2 \times 4 + 6 \div 3$. Next do the multiplication and division to get $9 - 8 + 2$, which equals 3.

KAPLAN 385

8. ABSOLUTE VALUE

Treat absolute value signs a lot like **parentheses**. Do what's inside them first and then take the absolute value of the result. Don't try to take the absolute value of each piece between the bars before calculating. For example, in order to calculate $|(-12) + 5 - (-4)| - |5 + (-10)|$, first do what's inside the bars to get: $|-3| - |-5|$, which is $3 - 5$, or -2.

9. COUNTING CONSECUTIVE INTEGERS

To count consecutive integers, **subtract the smallest from the largest and add 1**. To count the integers from 13 through 31, subtract: $31 - 13 = 18$. Then add 1: $18 + 1 = 19$.

DIVISIBILITY

10. FACTOR/MULTIPLE

The **factors** of integer n are the positive integers that divide into n with no remainder. The **multiples** of n are the integers that n divides into with no remainder. For example, 6 is a factor of 12, and 24 is a multiple of 12. 12 is both a factor and a multiple of itself.

11. PRIME FACTORIZATION

To find the prime factorization of an integer, just keep breaking it up into factors until **all the factors are prime**. To find the prime factorization of 36, for example, you could begin by breaking it into 4×9:

$$36 = 4 \times 9 = 2 \times 2 \times 3 \times 3$$

12. RELATIVE PRIMES

To determine whether two integers are relative primes, break them both down to their prime factorizations. For example: $35 = 5 \times 7$, and $54 = 2 \times 3 \times 3 \times 3$. They have **no prime factors in common**, so 35 and 54 are relative primes.

13. COMMON MULTIPLE

You can always get a common multiple of two numbers by **multiplying** them, but, unless the two numbers are relative primes, the product will not be the *least* common multiple. For example, to find a common multiple for 12 and 15, you could just multiply: $12 \times 15 = 180$.

14. LEAST COMMON MULTIPLE

To find the least common multiple, check out the **multiples of the larger number** until you find one that's **also a multiple of the smaller.** To find the LCM of 12 and 15, begin by taking the multiples of 15: 15 is not divisible by 12; 30's not; nor is 45. But the next multiple of 15, 60, *is* divisible by 12, so it's the LCM.

15. GREATEST COMMON FACTOR

To find the greatest common factor, break down both numbers into their prime factorizations and take **all the prime factors they have in common**. $36 = 2 \times 2 \times 3 \times 3$, and $48 = 2 \times 2 \times 2 \times 2 \times 3$. What they have in common is two 2s and one 3, so the GCF is $= 2 \times 2 \times 3 = 12$.

16. EVEN/ODD

To predict whether a sum, difference, or product will be even or odd, just **take simple numbers like 1 and 2 and see what happens**. There are rules—"odd times even is even," for example—but there's no need to memorize them. What happens with one set of numbers generally happens with all similar sets.

17. MULTIPLES OF 2 AND 4

An integer is divisible by 2 (even) if the **last digit is even**. An integer is divisible by 4 if the **last two digits make a multiple of 4**. The last digit of 562 is 2, which is even, so 562 is a multiple of 2. The last two digits make 62, which is *not* divisible by 4, so 562 is not a multiple of 4.

18. MULTIPLES OF 3 AND 9

An integer is divisible by 3 if the **sum of its digits is divisible by 3**. An integer is divisible by 9 if the **sum of its digits is divisible by 9**. The sum of the digits in 957 is 21, which is divisible by 3 but not by 9, so 957 is divisible by 3 but not 9.

19. MULTIPLES OF 5 AND 10

An integer is divisible by 5 if the **last digit is 5 or 0**. An integer is divisible by 10 if the **last digit is 0**. The last digit of 665 is 5, so 665 is a multiple 5 but *not* a multiple of 10.

20. REMAINDERS

The remainder is the **whole number left over after division**. 487 is 2 more than 485, which is a multiple of 5, so when 487 is divided by 5, the remainder will be 2.

FRACTIONS AND DECIMALS

21. REDUCING FRACTIONS

To reduce a fraction to lowest terms, **factor out and cancel** all factors the numerator and denominator have in common.

$$\frac{28}{36} = \frac{4 \times 7}{4 \times 9} = \frac{7}{9}$$

22. ADDING/SUBTRACTING FRACTIONS

To add or subtract fractions, first find a **common denominator**, and then add or subtract the numerators.

$$\frac{2}{15} + \frac{3}{10} = \frac{4}{30} + \frac{9}{30} = \frac{4+9}{30} = \frac{13}{30}$$

23. MULTIPLYING FRACTIONS

To multiply fractions, **multiply** the numerators and **multiply** the denominators.

$$\frac{5}{7} \cdot \frac{3}{4} = \frac{5 \cdot 3}{7 \cdot 4} = \frac{15}{28}$$

24. DIVIDING FRACTIONS

To divide fractions, **invert** the second one and **multiply**.

$$\frac{1}{2} \div \frac{3}{5} = \frac{1}{2} \cdot \frac{5}{3} = \frac{1 \cdot 5}{2 \cdot 3} = \frac{5}{6}$$

25. CONVERTING A MIXED NUMBER TO AN IMPROPER FRACTION

To convert a mixed number to an improper fraction, **multiply** the whole number part by the denominator, then **add** the numerator. The result is the new numerator (over the same denominator). To convert $7\frac{1}{3}$, first multiply 7 by 3, then add 1, to get the new numerator of 22. Put that over the same denominator, 3, to get $\frac{22}{3}$.

26. CONVERTING AN IMPROPER FRACTION TO A MIXED NUMBER

To convert an improper fraction to a mixed number, **divide** the denominator into the numerator to get a **whole number quotient with a remainder**. The quotient becomes the whole number part of the mixed number, and the remainder becomes the new numerator—with the same denominator. For example, to convert $\frac{108}{5}$, first divide 5 into 108, which yields 21 with a remainder of 3. Therefore, $\frac{108}{5} = 21\frac{3}{5}$.

27. RECIPROCAL

To find the reciprocal of a fraction, **switch** the numerator and the denominator. The reciprocal of $\frac{3}{7}$ is $\frac{7}{3}$. The reciprocal of 5 is $\frac{1}{5}$. The product of reciprocals is 1.

28. COMPARING FRACTIONS

One way to compare fractions is to re-express them with a **common denominator**. $\frac{3}{4} = \frac{21}{28}$ and $\frac{5}{7} = \frac{20}{28}$. $\frac{21}{28}$ is greater than $\frac{20}{28}$, so $\frac{3}{4}$ is greater than $\frac{5}{7}$.

Another way to compare fractions is to convert them both to **decimals**. $\frac{3}{4}$ converts to .75, and $\frac{5}{7}$ converts to approximately .714.

29. CONVERTING FRACTIONS AND DECIMALS

To convert a fraction to a decimal, **divide the bottom into the top**. To convert $\frac{5}{8}$, divide 8 into 5, yielding .625.

30. REPEATING DECIMAL

To find a particular digit in a repeating decimal, note the **number of digits in the cluster that repeats**. If there are 2 digits in that cluster, then every 2nd digit is the same. If there are 3 digits in that cluster, then every 3rd digit is the same. And so on. For example, the decimal equivalent of $\frac{1}{27}$ is .037037037..., which is best written $.\overline{037}$.

There are 3 digits in the repeating cluster, so every 3rd digit is the same: 7. To find the 50th digit, look for the multiple of 3 just less than 50—that's 48. The 48th digit is 7, and with the 49th digit the pattern repeats with 0. The 50th digit is 3.

31. IDENTIFYING THE PARTS AND THE WHOLE

The key to solving most fractions and percents story problems is to identify the part and the whole. Usually you'll find the **part** associated with the verb *is/are* and the **whole** associated with the word *of*. In the sentence, "Half of the boys are blonds," the whole is the boys ("*of* the boys), and the part is the blonds ("*are* blonds").

PERCENTS

32. PERCENT FORMULA

Whether you need to find the part, the whole, or the percent, use the same formula:

Part = Percent × Whole

| Example: | What is 12% of 25? |
| Setup: | Part = .12 × 25 |

| Example: | 15 is 3% of what number? |
| Setup: | 15 = .03 × Whole |

| Example: | 45 is what percent of 9? |
| Setup: | 45 = Percent × 9 |

33. PERCENT INCREASE AND DECREASE

To increase a number by a percent, **add the percent to 100%**, convert to a decimal, and multiply. To increase 40 by 25%, add 25% to 100%, convert 125% to 1.25, and multiply by 40. 1.25 × 40 = 50.

34. FINDING THE ORIGINAL WHOLE

To find the **original whole before a percent increase or decrease**, set up an equation. Think of a 15% increase over x as $1.15x$.

Example: After a 5% increase, the population was 59,346. What was the population *before* the increase?
Setup: $1.05x = 59{,}346$

35. COMBINED PERCENT INCREASE AND DECREASE

To determine the combined effect of multiple percents increase and/or decrease, **start with 100 and see what happens**.

Example: A price went up 10% one year, and the new price went up 20% the next year. What was the combined percent increase?
Set-up: First year: 100 + (10% of 100) = 110. Second year: 110 + (20% of 110) = 132. That's a combined 32% increase.

RATIOS, PROPORTIONS, AND RATES

36. SETTING UP A RATIO

To find a ratio, put the number associated with the word *of* on top and the quantity associated with the word *to* on the bottom and reduce. The ratio of 20 oranges to 12 apples is $\frac{20}{12}$, which reduces to $\frac{5}{3}$.

37. PART-TO-PART RATIOS AND PART-TO-WHOLE RATIOS

If the parts add up to the whole, a part-to-part ratio can be turned into 2 part-to-whole ratios by putting **each number in the original ratio over the sum of the numbers**. If the ratio of males to females is 1 to 2, then the males-to-people ratio is

$\dfrac{1}{1+2}=\dfrac{1}{3}$ and the females-to-people ratio is

$\dfrac{2}{1+2}=\dfrac{2}{3}$. Or, $\dfrac{2}{3}$ of all the people are female.

38. SOLVING A PROPORTION

To solve a proportion, **cross multiply:**

$$\frac{x}{5}=\frac{3}{4}$$

$$4x=5\cdot3$$

$$x=\frac{15}{4}=3.75$$

39. RATE

To solve a rates problem, **use the units** to keep things straight.

Example: If snow is falling at the rate of 1 foot every 4 hours, how many inches of snow will fall in 7 hours?
Setup:

$$\frac{1\text{ foot}}{4\text{ hours}}=\frac{x\text{ inches}}{7\text{ hours}}$$

$$\frac{12\text{ inches}}{4\text{ hours}}=\frac{x\text{ inches}}{7\text{ hours}}$$

$$4x=12\cdot7$$

$$x=21$$

40. AVERAGE RATE

$$\text{Average }A\text{ per }B=\frac{\text{Total }A}{\text{Total }B}$$

$$\text{Average Speed}=\frac{\text{Total distance}}{\text{Total time}}$$

To find the average speed for 120 miles at 40 mph and 120 miles at 60 mph, **don't just average the two speeds.** First figure out the total distance and the total time. The total distance is 120 + 120 = 240 miles. The times are 3 hours for the first leg and 2 hours for the second leg, or 5 hours

total. The average speed, then, is $\dfrac{240}{5}=48$ miles per hour.

AVERAGES

41. AVERAGE FORMULA

To find the average of a set of numbers, **add them up and divide by the number of numbers.**

$$\text{Average}=\frac{\text{Sum of the terms}}{\text{Number of terms}}$$

To find the average of the 5 numbers 12, 15, 23, 40, and 40, first add them up: 12 + 15 + 23 + 40 + 40 = 130. Then divide the sum by 5: 130 ÷ 5 = 26.

42. AVERAGE OF EVENLY SPACED NUMBERS

To find the average of evenly spaced numbers, just **average the smallest and the largest.** The average of all the integers from 13 through 77 is the same as the average of 13 and 77.

$$\frac{13+77}{2}=\frac{90}{2}=45$$

43. USING THE AVERAGE TO FIND THE SUM

$$\text{Sum}=(\text{Average})\times(\text{Number of terms})$$

If the average of 10 numbers is 50, then they add up to 10 × 50, or 500.

44. FINDING THE MISSING NUMBER

To find a missing number when you're given the average, **use the sum.** If the average of 4 numbers is 7, then the sum of those 4 numbers is 4 × 7, or 28. Suppose that 3 of the numbers are 3, 5, and 8. These 3 numbers add up to 16 of that 28, which leaves 12 for the fourth number.

POSSIBILITIES AND PROBABILITY

45. COUNTING THE POSSIBILITIES

The fundamental counting principle: if there are

m **ways** one event can happen and *n* **ways** a second event can happen, then there are *m* × *n* **ways** for the two events to happen. For example, with 5 shirts and 7 pairs of pants to choose from, you can put together 5 × 7 = 35 different outfits.

46. PROBABILITY

$$\text{Probability} = \frac{\text{Favorable outcomes}}{\text{Total possible outcomes}}$$

For example, if you have 12 shirts in a drawer and 9 of them are white, the probability of picking a white shirt at random is $\frac{9}{12} = \frac{3}{4}$. This probability can also be expressed as .75 or 75%.

POWERS AND ROOTS

47. MULTIPLYING AND DIVIDING POWERS
To multiply powers, **add the exponents:** $x^3 \cdot x^4 = x^{3+4} = x^7$. To divide powers, **subtract the exponents:** $y^{13} \div y^8 = y^{13-8} = y^5$.

48. RAISING POWERS TO POWERS
To raise a power to a power, **multiply the exponents.** $(x^3)^4 = x^{3 \times 4} = x^{12}$.

49. SIMPLIFYING SQUARE ROOTS
To simplify a square root, **factor out the perfect squares** under the radical, unsquare them and put the result in front. $\sqrt{12} = \sqrt{4 \times 3} = \sqrt{4} \times \sqrt{3} = 2\sqrt{3}$.

50. ADDING AND SUBTRACTING ROOTS
You can add or subtract radical expressions **only if the part under the radicals is the same.**

51. MULTIPLYING AND DIVIDING ROOTS
The product of square roots is equal to the **square root of the product:** $\sqrt{3} \times \sqrt{5} = \sqrt{3 \times 5} = \sqrt{15}$. The quotient of square roots is equal to the **square root of the quotient:** $\frac{\sqrt{6}}{\sqrt{3}} = \sqrt{\frac{6}{3}} = \sqrt{2}$.

ALGEBRAIC EXPRESSIONS

52. EVALUATING AN ALGEBRAIC EXPRESSION
To evaluate an algebraic expression, **plug in** the given values for the unknowns and calculate according to PEMDAS. To find the value of $x^2 + 5x - 6$ when $x = -2$, plug in -2 for x: $(-2)^2 + 5(-2) - 6 = 4 - 10 - 6 = -12$.

53. ADDING AND SUBTRACTING MONOMIALS
To combine like terms, **keep the variable part unchanged while adding or subtracting the coefficients.** $2a + 3a = (2a + 3)a = 5a$

54. ADDING AND SUBTRACTING POLYNOMIALS
To add or subtract polynomials, **combine like terms.** $(3x^2 + 5x - 7) - (x^2 + 12) =$ $(3x^2 - x^2) + 5x + (-7 - 12) = + 2x^2 + 5x - 19$

55. MULTIPLYING MONOMIALS
To multiply monomials, **multiply the coefficients and the variables separately.** $2a \cdot 3a = (2 \cdot 3)(a \cdot a) = 6a^2$.

56. MULTIPLYING BINOMIALS—FOIL
To multiply binomials, use **FOIL.** To multiply $(x + 3)$ by $(x + 4)$, first multiply the **F**irst terms: $x \cdot x = x^2$. Next the **O**uter terms: $x \cdot 4 = 4x$. Then the **I**nner terms: $3 \cdot x = 3x$. And finally the **L**ast terms: $3 \cdot 4 = 12$. Then add and combine like terms: $x^2 + 4x + 3x + 12 = x^2 + 7x + 12$.

57. MULTIPLYING OTHER POLYNOMIALS
FOIL works only when you want to multiply two binomials. If you want to multiply polynomials with more than two terms, make sure you **multiply each term in the first polynomial by each term in the second.**

$$(x^2 + 3x + 4)(x + 5) =$$
$$x^2(x + 5) + 3x(x + 5) + 4(x + 5) =$$
$$x^3 + 5x^2 + 3x^2 + 15x + 4x + 20 =$$
$$x^3 + 8x^2 + 19x + 20$$

FACTORING ALGEBRAIC EXPRESSIONS

58. FACTORING OUT A COMMON DIVISOR

A factor common to all terms of a polynomial can be **factored out**. All three terms in the polynomial $3x^3 + 12x^2 - 6x$ contain a factor of $3x$. Pulling out the common factor yields $3x(x^2 + 4x - 2)$.

59. FACTORING THE DIFFERENCE OF SQUARES

One of the test maker's favorite factorables is the **difference of squares**.

$$a^2 - b^2 = (a - b)(a + b)$$

$x^2 - 9$, for example, factors to $(x - 3)(x + 3)$.

60. FACTORING THE SQUARE OF A BINOMIAL

Learn to recognize polynomials that are squares of binomials:

$$a^2 + 2ab + b^2 = (a+b)^2$$

$$a^2 - 2ab + b^2 = (a-b)^2$$

For example, $4x^2 + 12x + 9$ factors to $(2x+3)^2$, and $n^2 - 10n + 25$ factors to $(n-5)^2$.

61. FACTORING OTHER POLYNOMIALS— FOIL IN REVERSE

To factor a quadratic expression, **think about what binomials you could use FOIL on to get that quadratic expression**. To factor $x^2 - 5x + 6$, think about what **F**irst terms will produce x^2, what **L**ast terms will produce $+6$, and what **O**uter and **I**nner terms will produce $-5x$. Some common sense—and a little trial and error—lead you to $(x - 2)(x - 3)$.

62. SIMPLIFYING AN ALGEBRAIC FRACTION

Simplifying an algebraic fraction is a lot like simplifying a numerical fraction. The general idea is to **find factors common to the numerator and denominator and cancel them**. Thus, simplifying an algebraic fraction begins with factoring. For example, to simplify $\dfrac{x^2 - x - 12}{x^2 - 9}$, first factor the numerator and denominator:

$$\frac{x^2 - x - 12}{x^2 - 9} = \frac{(x-4)(x+3)}{(x-3)(x+3)}$$

Canceling $x + 3$ from the numerator and denominator leaves you with $\dfrac{x-4}{x-3}$.

SOLVING EQUATIONS

63. SOLVING A LINEAR EQUATION

To solve an equation, do whatever necessary to both sides to **isolate the variable**. To solve the equation $5x - 12 = -2x + 9$, first get all the x's on one side by adding $2x$ to both sides: $7x - 12 = 9$. Then add 12 to both sides: $7x = 21$. Then divide both sides by 7 to get: $x = 3$.

64. SOLVING "IN TERMS OF"

To solve an equation for one variable in terms of another means to **isolate the one variable on one side of the equation**, leaving an expression containing the other variable on the other side of the equation. To solve the equation $3x - 10y = -5x + 6y$ for x in terms of y, isolate x:

$$3x - 10y = -5x + 6y$$
$$3x + 5x = 6y + 10y$$
$$8x = 16y$$
$$x = 2y$$

65. TRANSLATING FROM ENGLISH INTO ALGEBRA

To translate from English into algebra, look for the **key words** and systematically turn **phrases into algebraic expressions** and **sentences into equations**. Be careful about order, especially when subtraction is called for.

Example: The charge for a phone call is r cents for the first 3 minutes and s cents for each minute thereafter. What is the cost, in cents, of a phone call lasting exactly t minutes? ($t > 3$)

Setup: The charge begins with r, and then something more is added, depending on the length of the call. The amount added is s times the number of minutes past 3 minutes. If the total number of minutes is t, then the number of minutes past 3 is $t - 3$. So the charge is $r + s(t - 3)$.

INTERMEDIATE ALGEBRA

66. SOLVING A QUADRATIC EQUATION

To solve a quadratic equation, put it in the "$ax^2 + bx + c = 0$" form, **factor** the left side (if you can), and set each factor equal to 0 separately to get the two solutions. To solve $x^2 + 12 = 7x$, first rewrite it as $x^2 - 7x + 12 = 0$. Then factor the left side:

$$(x-3)(x-4)=0$$
$$x-3=0 \text{ or } x-4=0$$
$$x=3 \text{ or } 4$$

Sometimes the left side might not be obviously factorable. You can always use the **quadratic formula**. Just plug in the coefficients a, b, and c from $ax^2 + bx + c = 0$ into the formula:

$$x = \frac{-b \pm \sqrt{b^2 - 4ac}}{2a}$$

To solve $x^2 + 4x + 2 = 0$, plug $a = 1$, $b = 4$, and $c = 2$ into the formula:

$$x = \frac{-4 \pm \sqrt{4^2 - 4 \cdot 1 \cdot 2}}{2 \cdot 1}$$
$$= \frac{-4 \pm \sqrt{8}}{2} = -2 \pm \sqrt{2}$$

67. SOLVING A SYSTEM OF EQUATIONS

You can solve for 2 variables only if you have 2 distinct equations. **Combine the equations** in such a way that **one of the variables cancels out.**

To solve the 2 equations $4x + 3y = 8$ and $x + y = 3$, multiply both sides of the second equation by -3 to get: $-3x - 3y = -9$. Now add the 2 equations; the $3y$ and the $-3y$ cancel out, leaving: $x = -1$. Plug that back into either one of the original equations and you'll find that $y = 4$.

68. SOLVING AN EQUATION THAT INCLUDES ABSOLUTE VALUE SIGNS

To solve an equation that includes absolute value signs, **think about the two different cases**. For example, to solve the equation $|x-12|=3$, think of it as two equations:

$$x - 12 = 3 \text{ or } x - 12 = -3$$
$$x = 15 \text{ or } 9$$

69. SOLVING AN INEQUALITY

To solve an inequality, do whatever is necessary to both sides to **isolate the variable**. Just remember that when you **multiply or divide both sides by a negative number**, you must **reverse the sign**. To solve $-5x + 7 < -3$, subtract 7 from both sides to get: $-5x < -10$. Now divide both sides by -5, remembering to reverse the sign: $x > 2$.

70. GRAPHING INEQUALITIES

To graph a range of values, use a thick, black line over the number line, and at the end(s) of the range, use a **solid circle** if the point *is included* or an **open circle** if the point is *not included*. The figure below shows the graph of $-3 < x \le 5$.

COORDINATE GEOMETRY

71. FINDING THE DISTANCE BETWEEN TWO POINTS

To find the distance between points, **use the Pythagorean Theorem or special right triangles.** The difference between the x's is one leg and the difference between the y's is the other leg.

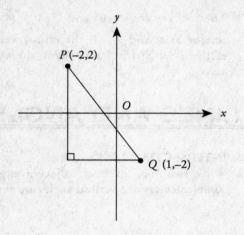

In the figure above, $\overline{PQ}$ is the hypotenuse of a 3-4-5 triangle, so $PQ = 5$.

You can also use the **distance formula**:

$$d = \sqrt{(x_1 - x_2)^2 + (y_1 - y_2)^2}$$

To find the distance between $R(3,6)$ and $S(5,-2)$:

$$d = \sqrt{(3-5)^2 + [6-(-2)]^2}$$
$$= \sqrt{(-2)^2 + (8)^2}$$
$$= \sqrt{68} = 2\sqrt{17}$$

72. USING TWO POINTS TO FIND THE SLOPE

$$\text{Slope} = \frac{\text{Change in } y}{\text{Change in } x} = \frac{\text{Rise}}{\text{Run}}$$

The slope of the line that contains the points $A(2,3)$ and $B(0,-1)$ is:

$$\frac{y_A - y_B}{x_A - x_B} = \frac{3-(-1)}{2-0} = \frac{4}{2} = 2$$

73. USING AN EQUATION TO FIND THE SLOPE

To find the slope of a line from an equation, put the equation into the **slope-intercept** form:

$$y = mx + b$$

The **slope is m**. To find the slope of the equation $3x + 2y = 4$, re-express it:

$$3x + 2y = 4$$
$$2y = -3x + 4$$
$$y = -\frac{3}{2}x + 2$$

The slope is $-\frac{3}{2}$.

74. USING AN EQUATION TO FIND AN INTERCEPT

To find the y-intercept, you can either put the equation into $y = mx + b$ (**slope-intercept**) form—in which case b **is the y-intercept**—or you can just **plug $x = 0$** into the equation and **solve for y**. To find the x-intercept, **plug $y = 0$** into the equation and **solve for x**.

75. EQUATION FOR A CIRCLE

The equation for a circle of radius r and centered at (h, k) is

$$(x - h)^2 + (y - k)^2 = r^2$$

The figure below shows the graph of the equation $(x-2)^2 + (y+1)^2 = 25$:

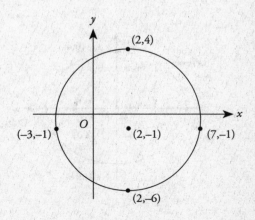

76. EQUATION FOR A PARABOLA

The graph of an equation in the form $y = ax^2 + bx + c$ is a parabola. The figure below shows the graph of seven pairs of numbers that satisfy the equation $y = x^2 - 4x + 3$:

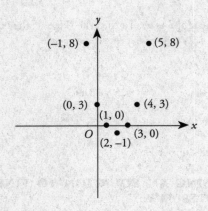

:

77. EQUATION FOR AN ELLIPSE

The graph of an equation in the form

$$\frac{x^2}{a^2} + \frac{y^2}{b^2} = 1$$

is an ellipse with $2a$ as the sum of the focal radii and with foci on the x-axis at $(0, -c)$ and $(0, c)$, where $c = \sqrt{a^2 - b^2}$. The figure below shows the graph of $\frac{x^2}{25} + \frac{y^2}{16} = 1$:

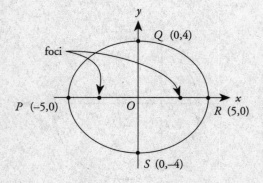

The foci are at $(-3, 0)$ and $(3, 0)$. $\overline{PR}$ is the **major axis**, and $\overline{QS}$ is the **minor axis**. This ellipse is symmetrical about both the x- and y-axes.

LINES AND ANGLES

78. INTERSECTING LINES

When two lines intersect, **adjacent angles are supplementary** and **vertical angles are equal**.

In the figure above, the angles marked $a°$ and $b°$ are adjacent and supplementary, so $a + b = 180$. Furthermore, the angles marked $a°$ and 60° are vertical and equal, so $a = 60$.

79. PARALLEL LINES AND TRANSVERSALS

A transversal across parallel lines forms **four equal acute angles and four equal obtuse angles**.

In the figure above, line 1 is parallel to line 2. Angles a, c, e, and g are obtuse, so they are all equal. Angles b, d, f, and h are acute, so they are all equal

Furthermore, **any of the acute angles is supplementary to any of the obtuse angles**. Angles *a* and *h* are supplementary, as are *b* and *e*, *c* and *f*, and so on.

TRIANGLES

80. INTERIOR ANGLES OF A TRIANGLE

The three angles of any triangle **add up to 180°**.

In the figure above, *x* + 50 + 100 = 180, so *x* = 30.

81. EXTERIOR ANGLES OF A TRIANGLE

An exterior angle of a triangle is equal to the **sum of the remote interior angles**.

In the figure above, the exterior angle labeled *x*° is equal to the sum of the remote interior angles: *x* = 50 + 100 = 150.

The three exterior angles of any triangle add up to 360°.

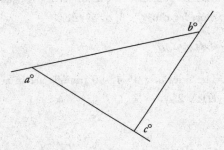

In the figure above, *a* + *b* + *c* = 360.

82. SIMILAR TRIANGLES

Similar triangles have the same shape: **corresponding angles are equal and corresponding sides are proportional**.

The triangles on the previous page are similar because they have the same angles. The 3 corresponds to the 4 and the 6 corresponds to the *s*.

$$\frac{3}{4} = \frac{6}{s}$$
$$3s = 24$$
$$s = 8$$

83. AREA OF A TRIANGLE

$$\text{Area of Triangle } = \frac{1}{2}(\text{base})(\text{height})$$

The height is the perpendicular distance between the side that's chosen as the base and the opposite vertex.

In the triangle above, 4 is the height when the 7 is chosen as the base.

$$\text{Area } = \frac{1}{2}bh = \frac{1}{2}(7)(4) = 14$$

RIGHT TRIANGLES

84. PYTHAGOREAN THEOREM

For all right triangles:

$$(\text{leg}_1)^2 + (\text{leg}_2)^2 = (\text{hypotenuse})^2$$

If one leg is 2 and the other leg is 3, then:

$$2^2 + 3^2 = c^2$$
$$c^2 = 4 + 9$$
$$c = \sqrt{13}$$

85. SPECIAL RIGHT TRIANGLES

• 3-4-5

If a right triangle's leg-to-leg ratio is 3:4, or if the leg-to-hypotenuse ratio is 3:5 or 4:5, then it's a 3-4-5 triangle and you don't need to use the Pythagorean theorem to find the third side. Just figure out what multiple of 3-4-5 it is.

In the right triangle above, one leg is 30 and the hypotenuse is 50. This is 10 times 3-4-5. The other leg is 40.

• 5-12-13

If a right triangle's leg-to-leg ratio is 5:12, or if the leg-to-hypotenuse ratio is 5:13 or 12:13, then it's a 5-12-13 triangle and you don't need to use the Pythagorean theorem to find the third side. Just figure out what multiple of 5-12-13 it is.

Here one leg is 36 and the hypotenuse is 39. This is 3 times 5-12-13. The other leg is 15.

• 30-60-90

The sides of a 30-60-90 triangle are in a ratio of $1:\sqrt{3}:2$. You don't need to use the Pythagorean theorem.

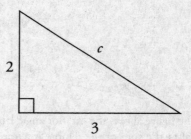

If the hypotenuse is 6, then the shorter leg is half that, or 3; and then the longer leg is equal to the short leg times $\sqrt{3}$, or $3\sqrt{3}$.

• 45-45-90

The sides of a 45-45-90 triangle are in a ratio of $1:1:\sqrt{2}$.

If one leg is 3, then the other leg is also 3, and the hypotenuse is equal to a leg times $\sqrt{2}$, or $3\sqrt{2}$.

OTHER POLYGONS

86. CHARACTERISTICS OF SPECIAL QUADRILATERALS

• *Rectangle*

A rectangle is a **4-sided figure with 4 right angles**. Opposite sides are equal. Diagonals are equal.

Quadrilateral *ABCD* above is shown to have three right angles. The fourth angle therefore also measures 90°, and *ABCD* is a rectangle.

• *Parallelogram*

A parallelogram has **two pairs of parallel sides.** Opposite sides are equal. Opposite angles are equal. Consecutive angles add up to 180°.

In the figure above, *s* is the length of the side opposite the 3, so *s* = 3.

• *Square*

A square is a **rectangle with 4 equal sides**.

If *PQRS* is a square, all sides are the same length as $\overline{QR}$.

• *Trapezoid*

A **trapezoid** is a quadrilateral with one pair of parallel sides and one pair of nonparallel sides.

In the quadrilateral above, sides $\overline{EF}$ and $\overline{GH}$ are parallel, while sides $\overline{EF}$ and $\overline{GH}$ are not parallel. *EFGH* is therefore a trapezoid.

87. AREAS OF SPECIAL QUADRILATERALS

Area of Rectangle = Length × Width

The area of a 7-by-3 rectangle is $7 \times 3 = 21$.

Area of Parallelogram = Base × Height

In parallelogram *KLMN* above, 4 is the height when *LM* or *KN* is used as the base. Base × Height = $6 \times 4 = 24$.

Area of Square = (Side)²

The square above, with sides of length 5, has an area of $5^2 = 25$.

$$\text{Area of Trapezoid} = \left(\frac{\text{base}_1 + \text{base}_2}{2}\right) \times \text{height}$$

Think of it as the average of the bases (the two parallel sides) times the height (the length of the perpendicular altitude).

In the trapezoid *ABCD* above, you can use side $\overline{AD}$ for the height. The average of the bases is $\frac{2+14}{2} = 8$, so the area is 5×8, or 40.

88. INTERIOR ANGLES OF A POLYGON

The **sum of the measures of the interior angles of a polygon is $(n - 2) \times 180$**, where *n* is the number of sides.

Sum of the angles = $(n - 2) \times 180$

The eight angles of an octagon, for example, add up to $(8 - 2) \times 180 = 1,080$.

To find **one angle of a regular polygon**, divide the sum of the angles by the number of angles (which is the same as the number of sides). The formula, therefore, is:

$$\text{Interior angle} = \frac{(n-2) \times 180}{n}$$

KAPLAN

Angle A of regular octagon $ABCDEFGH$ above measures $\dfrac{1{,}080}{8} = 135$ degrees.

CIRCLES

89. CIRCUMFERENCE OF A CIRCLE

$$\text{Circumference of a circle} = 2\pi r$$

In the circle above, the radius is 3, and so the circumference is $2\pi(3) = 6\pi$.

90. LENGTH OF AN ARC

An **arc** is a piece of the circumference. If n is the measure of the arc's central angle, then the formula is:

$$\text{Length of an Arc} = \left(\dfrac{n}{360}\right)(2\pi r)$$

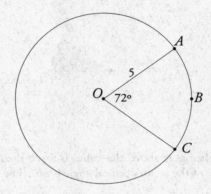

In the figure above, the radius is 5 and the measure of the central angle is 72°. The arc length is $\dfrac{72}{360}$ or $\dfrac{1}{5}$ of the circumference:

$$\left(\dfrac{72}{360}\right)(2\pi)(5) = \left(\dfrac{1}{5}\right)(10\pi) = 2\pi$$

91. AREA OF A CIRCLE

$$\text{Area of a circle} = \pi r^2$$

The area of the circle above is $\pi(4)^2 = 16\pi$.

92. AREA OF A SECTOR

A **sector** is a piece of the area of a circle. If n is the measure of the sector's central angle, then the formula is:

$$\text{Area of a Sector } = \left(\frac{n}{360}\right)\left(\pi r^2\right)$$

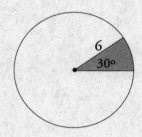

In the figure above, the radius is 6 and the measure of the sector's central angle is 30°. The sector has $\frac{30}{360}$ or $\frac{1}{12}$ of the area of the circle:

$$\left(\frac{30}{360}\right)\left(\pi\right)\left(6^2\right) = \left(\frac{1}{12}\right)\left(36\pi\right) = 3\pi$$

SOLIDS

93. SURFACE AREA OF A RECTANGULAR SOLID

The surface of a rectangular solid consists of 3 pairs of identical faces. To find the surface area, find the area of each face and add them up. If the length is l, the width is w, and the height is h, the formula is:

$$\text{Surface Area} = 2lw + 2wh + 2lh$$

The surface area of the box above is:

$$2 \cdot 7 \cdot 3 + 2 \cdot 3 \cdot 4 + 2 \cdot 7 \cdot 4 = 42 + 24 + 56 = 122$$

94. VOLUME OF A RECTANGULAR SOLID

$$\text{Volume of a Rectangular Solid} = lwh$$

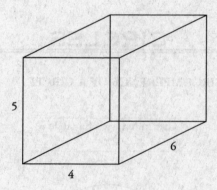

The volume of a 4-by-5-by-6 box is

$$4 \times 5 \times 6 = 120$$

A cube is a rectangular solid with length, width, and height all equal. If e is the length of an edge of a cube, the volume formula is:

$$\text{Volume of a Cube} = e^3$$

The volume of the cube above is $2^3 = 8$.

95. VOLUME OF OTHER SOLIDS

Volume of a Cylinder = $\pi r^2 h$

In the cylinder above, $r = 2$, and $h = 5$, so:

Volume = $\pi(2^2)(5) = 20\pi$

Volume of a Cone = $\frac{1}{3}\pi r^2 h$

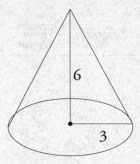

In the cone above, $r = 3$, and $h = 6$. So the volume of the cone is:

Volume = $\frac{1}{3}\pi(3^2)(6) = 18$

Volume of a Sphere = $\frac{4}{3}\pi r^3$

If the radius of a sphere is 3, then:

Volume = $\frac{4}{3}\pi(3^3) = 36\pi$

TRIGONOMETRY

96. SINE, COSINE, AND TANGENT OF ACUTE ANGLES

To find the sine, cosine, or tangent of an acute angle, use **SOHCAHTOA**, which is an abbreviation for the following definitions:

$Sine = \dfrac{\text{Opposite}}{\text{Hypotenuse}}$

$Cosine = \dfrac{\text{Adjacent}}{\text{Hypotenuse}}$

$$Tangent = \frac{\text{Opposite}}{\text{Adjacent}}$$

In the figure above:

$$\sin A = \frac{8}{17}$$

$$\cos A = \frac{15}{17}$$

$$\tan A = \frac{8}{15}$$

97. COTANGENT, SECANT, AND COSECANT OF ACUTE ANGLES

Think of the cotangent, secant, and cosecant as the reciprocals of the SOHCAHTOA functions:

$$Cotangent = \frac{1}{\text{Tangent}} = \frac{\text{Adjacent}}{\text{Opposite}}$$

$$Secant = \frac{1}{\text{Cosine}} = \frac{\text{Hypotenuse}}{\text{Adjacent}}$$

$$Cosecant = \frac{1}{\text{Sine}} = \frac{\text{Hypotenuse}}{\text{Opposite}}$$

In the figure above:

$$\cot D = \frac{2}{3}$$

$$\sec D = \frac{\sqrt{13}}{2}$$

$$\csc D = \frac{\sqrt{13}}{3}$$

98. TRIGONOMETRIC FUNCTIONS OF OTHER ANGLES

To find a trigonometric function of an angle greater than 90°, sketch a circle of radius 1 and centered at the origin of the coordinate grid. Start from the point (1, 0) and rotate the appropriate number of degrees counterclockwise.

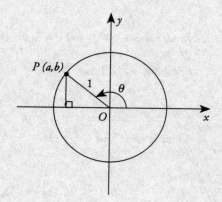

In the "unit circle" setup on the previous page, the basic trigonometric functions are defined in terms of the coordinates a and b:

$$\sin \theta = b$$

$$\cos \theta = a$$

$$\tan \theta = \frac{a}{b}$$

Example: sin 210° = ?

Setup: Sketch a 210° angle in the coordinate plane:

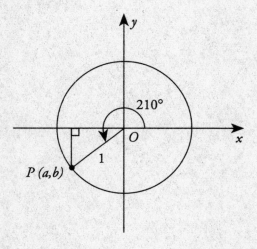

Because the triangle shown in the figure above is a 30-60-90 right triangle, we can determine that the coordinates of point P are $\left(-\frac{\sqrt{3}}{2}, -\frac{1}{2}\right)$. The sine is therefore $-\frac{1}{2}$.

99. SIMPLIFYING TRIGONOMETRIC EXPRESSIONS

To simplify trigonometric expressions, use the inverse function definitions along with the fundamental trigonometric identity:

$$\sin^2 x + \cos^2 x = 1$$

Example: $\dfrac{\sin^2 \theta + \cos^2 \theta}{\cos \theta} = ?$

Setup: The numerator equals 1, so:

$$\frac{\sin^2 \theta + \cos^2 \theta}{\cos \theta} = \frac{1}{\cos \theta} = \sec \theta$$

100. GRAPHING TRIGONOMETRIC FUNCTIONS

To graph trigonometric functions, use the x-axis for the angle and the y-axis for the value of the trigonometric function. Use special angles—0°, 30°, 45°, 60°, 90°, 120°, 135°, 150°, 180°, etc.—to plot key points.

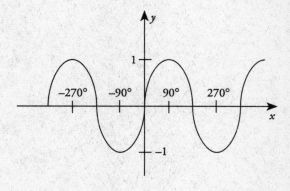

The figure above shows a portion of the graph of $y = \sin x$.

NOTES

NOTES

NOTES

NOTES

About

Educational Centers

Kaplan Educational Centers is one of the nation's premier education companies, providing individuals with a full range of resources to achieve their educational and career goals. Kaplan, celebrating its 60th anniversary, is a wholly-owned subsidiary of The Washington Post Company.

TEST PREPARATION & ADMISSIONS

Kaplan's nationally-recognized test prep courses cover more than 20 standardized tests, including entrance exams for secondary school, college, and graduate school as well as foreign language and professional licensing exams. In addition, Kaplan offers private tutoring and comprehensive, one-to-one admissions and application advice for students applying to graduate school.

SCORE! EDUCATIONAL CENTERS

SCORE! after-school learning centers help students in grades K-8 build academic skills, confidence, and goal-setting skills in a motivating, sports-oriented environment. Kids use a cutting-edge, interactive curriculum that continually assesses and adapts to their academic needs and learning style. Enthusiastic Academic Coaches serve as positive role models, creating a high-energy atmosphere where learning is exciting and fun for kids. With nearly 40 centers today, SCORE! continues to open new centers nationwide.

KAPLAN LEARNING SERVICES

Kaplan Learning Services provides customized assessment, education, and training programs to K-12 schools, universities, and businesses to help students and employees reach their educational and career goals.

KAPLAN INTERNATIONAL

Kaplan serves international students and professionals in the U.S. through Access America, a series of intensive English language programs, and LCP International Institute, a leading provider of intensive English language programs at on-campus centers in California, Washington, and New York. Kaplan and LCP offer specialized services to sponsors including placement at top American universities, fellowship management, academic monitoring and reporting, and financial administration.

KAPLOAN

Students can get key information and advice about educational loans for college and graduate school through **KapLoan** (Kaplan Student Loan Information Program). Through an affiliation with one of the nation's largest student loan providers, **KapLoan** helps direct students and their families through the often bewildering financial aid process.

KAPLAN PUBLISHING

Kaplan Books, a joint imprint with Simon & Schuster, publishes books in test preparation, admissions, education, career development and life skills; Kaplan and *Newsweek* jointly publish the highly successful guides, **How to Get Into College** and **How to Choose a Career & Graduate School**. *SCORE!* and *Newsweek* have teamed up to publish **How to Help Your Child Suceed in School**.

Kaplan InterActive delivers award-winning, high quality educational products and services including Kaplan's best-selling **Higher Score** test-prep software and sites on the internet (**http://www.kaplan.com**) and America Online. Kaplan and Cendant Software are jointly developing, marketing and distributing educational software for the kindergarten through twelfth grade retail and school markets.

KAPLAN CAREER SERVICES

Kaplan helps students and graduates find jobs through Kaplan Career Services, the leading provider of career fairs in North America. The division includes **Crimson & Brown Associates**, the nation's leading diversity recruiting and publishing firm, and **The Lendman Group and Career Expo**, both of which help clients identify highly sought-after technical personnel and sales and marketing professionals.

COMMUNITY OUTREACH

Kaplan provides educational resources to thousands of financially disadvantaged students annually, working closely with educational institutions, not-for-profit groups, government agencies and other grass roots organizations on a variety of national and local support programs. Also, Kaplan centers enrich local communities by employing high school, college and graduate students, creating valuable work experiences for vast numbers of young people each year.

Want more information about our services, products, or the nearest Kaplan center?

 Call our nationwide toll-free numbers:

 1-800-KAP-TEST for information on our live courses, private tutoring and admissions consulting
1-800-KAP-ITEM for information on our products
1-888-KAP-LOAN* for information on student loans

 Connect with us in cyberspace:

 On AOL, keyword:"Kaplan"
On the World Wide Web, go to: http://www.kaplan.com
Via e-mail: info@kaplan.com

3 Write to:

Kaplan Educational Centers
888 Seventh Avenue
New York, NY 10106

Paying for college just got easier...

KapLoan*, the Kaplan Student Loan Information Program, is a free service designed to guide you through the financial aid process.

KapLoan will send you a FREE booklet with valuable financial aid information and connect you with one of the nation's largest student loan providers. With KapLoan, you'll receive personalized guidance through the financial aid process and access to some of the least expensive educational loans available.

- **The Federal Stafford Loan**—Eligible students can borrow various amounts depending on their year in college. Loan amounts range from $2,625-$5,500 for dependent students and $6,625-$10,500 for independent students.

- **The Federal Parent Loan for Undergraduate Students (PLUS)**—Eligible parents may borrow up to the total cost of education, less other financial aid received.

Make the most of your financial aid opportunities.

The Kaplan Student Loan Information Program

Plan Ahead!

When you return this form to Kaplan, you and your family will receive a copy of KapLoan's free Financial Aid Handbook. Then, we'll send you your federal Stafford and federal PLUS loan applications.

It's Easy!

Yes! Please send us our free Financial Aid Handbook, as well as our educational loan kit with applications for the Federal Stafford (student) and Federal PLUS (parent) loans.

Last Name _____ First Name _____

Parent Last Name _____ Parent First Name _____

Permanent Address _____

City _____ State _____ Zip _____

Phone (Daytime) _____ Phone (Evening) _____ E-mail Address _____

Top School Choice(s) _____ Current GPA _____

_____ Earliest Start Date (month/year) _____

Please return this form to Kaplan at:

Kaplan Educational Centers
888 Seventh Avenue
22nd Floor, attn: KapLoan
New York, NY 10106

You may also return it by faxing toll free any time to 1-800-844-7458

The Kaplan Student Loan Information Program

BACT

Please return this form to:

Kaplan Educational Centers
Attn: KapLoan—22nd Floor
888 Seventh Avenue
New York, NY 10106

Life is a series of tests.

Some of them just count more.

Kaplan can help you score higher on the tests that matter. With Kaplan's private tutoring and live classes, you'll receive the expert instruction and personal attention you need to score your best. Find out why 3 million students have chosen Kaplan.

Call 1-800-KAP-TEST to enroll today.

1-800-KAP-TEST

the leader in test prep

www.kaplan.com

*SAT is a registered trademark of the College Entrance Examination Board; ACT is a registered trademark of ACT, Inc.